Step by Step
A Complete Movement Education Curriculum

Second Edition

Sheila Kogan

Human Kinetics

Library of Congress Cataloging-in-Publication Data

Kogan, Sheila.
    Step by step : a complete movement education curriculum / Sheila
Kogan.--2nd ed.
        p. cm.
    ISBN 0-7360-4409-4 (softcover)
    1.   Physical education for children. 2.   Movement education.   I.
Title.

    GV443.K56 2004

    372.86'8--dc22   2003017924

ISBN: 0-7360-4409-4

This book is a revised edition of *Step by Step: A Complete Movement Education Curriculum From Preschool to 6th Grade,* published in 1982 by Front Row Experience.

Acquisitions Editor: Judy Patterson Wright, PhD; **Developmental Editor:** Myles Schrag; **Assistant Editor:** Ragen E. Sanner; **Copyeditor:** Joyce H. Sexton; **Proofreader:** Joanna Hatzopoulos Portman; **Permission Manager:** Dalene Reeder; **Graphic Designer:** Fred Starbird; **Graphic Artist:** Yvonne Griffith; **Photo Manager:** Kareema McClendon; **Cover Designer:** Andrea Souflée; **Photographer (cover and interior):** Photography by Don Crowe; **Art Manager:** Kelly Hendren; **Illustrator:** Valerie Winemiller; **Printer:** United Graphics

Where The Wild Things Are, *Where The Wild Things Are* by M. Sendak, New York: HarperCollins; Jig Along Home, *Jig Along Home* by Woody Gruthie, RTO Publishers; Corner Grocery Store, *Corner Grocery Store* by Raffi, Troubadour Record, Ltd.; Bears in the Night, *Bears in the Night* by Stan and Jan Berenstain, Random House.

We thank Downer Elementary School in San Pablo, California, for assistance in providing the location for the photo shoot for this book.

Printed in the United States of America   10 9 8 7 6 5 4 3 2 1

Human Kinetics
Web site: www.HumanKinetics.com

United States: Human Kinetics, P.O. Box 5076, Champaign, IL 61825-5076
800-747-4457
e-mail: humank@hkusa.com

Canada: Human Kinetics, 475 Devonshire Road Unit 100, Windsor, ON N8Y 2L5
800-465-7301 (in Canada only)
e-mail: orders@hkcanada.com

Europe: Human Kinetics, 107 Bradford Road, Stanningley, Leeds LS28 6AT, United Kingdom
+44 (0) 113 255 5665
e-mail: hk@hkeurope.com

Australia: Human Kinetics, 57A Price Avenue, Lower Mitcham, South Australia 5062
08 8277 1555
e-mail: liaw@hkaustralia.com

New Zealand: Human Kinetics, Division of Sports Distributors NZ Ltd.
P.O. Box 300 226 Albany, North Shore City, Auckland
0064 9 448 1207
e-mail: blairc@hknewz.com

To B.

Contents

Preface

Improving education is the current political Holy Grail. The result is that teachers are under increased pressure to focus on standards and improve test scores. More and more teachers are discouraged, if not downright prevented, from teaching "fun" activities. We are admonished to get busy diagnosing and remediating reading inadequacies, practicing test-taking techniques, and drilling computation skills because these activities can raise test scores the most quickly. We are no longer encouraged to teach our passions, and we are no longer encouraged to consider what would be most beneficial to a child's long-range development. The sad result is that teaching is not as much fun as it used to be.

In the midst of this I want you to consider teaching movement education to your class. I understand completely that you do not have the time. You cannot fit in the required curriculum as it is. I understand that you do not have the energy. Teaching, which used to nourish you and which felt so rewarding, is simply becoming exhausting. I understand that you are wary about the prospect of reading another book on teaching since you have not yet read the manuals assigned to you.

Despite knowing all this, I am asking you to teach movement for two reasons. First, the children will absolutely love it and as a result you will have a great time with them. Second, you will be able to teach—really teach and not just drill—an amazing number of concepts that will help them throughout their lives as well as on the next standardized test. Let me immediately address those of you who are saying, "Great, but I don't think I can do it" and "Great, but you don't know the class I have this year":

1. This curriculum is for all teachers—teachers of all ages, physical conditions, experience levels, and varieties of background knowledge. You do not have to do the movements to teach an excellent program. I have taught while being nine months pregnant and I have taught sitting with my sprained knee hoisted on a chair.

2. This curriculum is for all children—children of all ages, every socioeconomic status, all experience levels; and children who may be disabled or gifted; and children in any school regardless of the quality of its facilities. The results may not look the same, but all children enjoy the program and benefit from it.

Step by Step: A Complete Movement Education Curriculum started well over 30 years ago. I was teaching movement in the public schools under a funding grant that allowed me to work with a class for a year if the classroom teacher continued the program independently the following year. I typed and mimeographed a three-page handout to help the teachers remember what we had covered. But even then it was clear to me that if the teachers did not know why they were doing an activity it would not be as effective. Presenting a lesson without understanding the principles underpinning its construction is much like decoding words without comprehension. Also, my experience is that this does not work in the long run. Teaching movement is difficult; and if the reasons for the activities are not clear, it is too tempting to cut corners that could actually be the essence of the lesson. Let me give you an example: A great majority of the lessons start with locomotor movements done in the Free Traveling Structure, which you will discover in chapter 2. Children move freely about the room with only an aural cue for starting and stopping. A first grade teacher had seen a couple of my classes but had never taken a workshop. She decided to try movement with her rambunctious class (for which I give her a standing ovation) but was nervous about this "free" warm-up. She had the children start with locomotor movements but had them stepping on the basketball lines marked on the gym floor. This gave her more control—which was a desirable goal—but lost the essence of the warm-up. The children were not able to fully release their energy because they were limited to the traffic of the line patterns. They also were not required to practice much self-discipline, they were not given the opportunity to practice movements at their own pace, and they were not very exuberant or excited. To be honest, they were quite happy, which reinforces my belief that any movement is better than none; but my point is that students benefit much more when you understand what you are teaching.

About This Book

Step by Step: A complete movement education curriculum went from three mimeographed pages to a three-part book: part I, "Basic Movement Concepts"; part II, "Building on the Basics"; and part III, "Lesson Plans." Part I gives you grounding in the basic concepts of movement. After encouraging you with the benefits of movement education in chapter 1, chapter 2 provides an overview of the three organizational techniques—Free Traveling Structure, Perfect Spots, and Diagonal Structure—that allow movement classes to be *controlled* and *orderly*.

These structures are crucial because so many (even veteran) teachers get scared by the exuberance that comes from a good movement class. As I will repeat later, this is probably the most important part of this book; and teachers have reported that the management techniques started in movement class have transferred to the classroom and playground, creating an overall atmosphere of control. Chapters 3 through 6 offer the fundamentals that underlie all movement activities, dance, gymnastics, sport, and so on. For many people, movement, especially dance, seems like a mysterious, perhaps even esoteric activity. This is not so. Movement is made up of recognizable components: locomotor (movements that "go," chapter 3) and nonlocomotor (movements that "stay," chapter 4), levels (varying heights, chapter 5), and directions and floor patterns (designs on the floor, chapter 6). Every action, from the simplest to the most complex, encompasses these fundamental components. In addition, though the combinations are limitless, there are actually a limited number of actual steps or moves. This movement vocabulary is cataloged in the chapters on locomotor and nonlocomotor

movements, and these catalogs will be valuable reference sources for you later. To understand basic movement concepts, to realize that movement vocabulary can be grasped, is not to devalue the beauty or mystery of an exquisite dance. This understanding will increase your appreciation for all movement activities and will give you a solid foundation from which to teach any movement skill.

Part II builds on these basic concepts by introducing partner activities (chapter 7), obstacle courses and stations (chapter 8), props (chapter 9), miscellaneous tricks of the trade (chapter 10), activities that reinforce classroom work (chapter 11), and advanced skills (chapter 12). These secondary concepts are walls built on the foundation that is part I, and these are what distinguishes this book from most others. The activities in part II are not a random collection; rather, they grow out of the physical, cognitive, and social concepts introduced in part I. As an example, chapter 9 includes a partner ball activity in which children roll the ball back and forth, working on *near* and *far*, and then pass the ball in a variety of ways. On the surface this activity looks almost simplistic. But if we look more deeply, partner ball pass is developing numerous concepts:

1. The class is in control—the children know how to freeze to an aural cue, and that discipline frees them and the teacher to have safe fun. The class might be a bit noisy, but the tone is calm and the teacher is relaxed because the class management is firmly in place. It might be possible to simply jump into this activity without teaching the Free Traveling Structure, but I do not think this would work very well with most classes. Even more importantly, the children will not grasp the underlying discipline. If you do not establish an underlying class management organization, whatever discipline you use to control an activity will have to be retaught every time.

2. Working on *near, nearer, far,* and *farther* is excellent language work in itself and also is practice for the second class management organization—Perfect Spots. Free Traveling Structure and Perfect Spots are powerful management tools. Classes that have established these structures are primed for learning. (And this attitude will carry over into the classroom and play yard.)

3. This ball activity includes work on the concepts locomotor, nonlocomotor, and level. Children roll the ball in a stationary position, trying out different levels, and then pass it while traveling in different ways. The value of knowing concepts is demonstrated when the students create their own ball studies incorporating movement concepts.

4. The children are working cooperatively with partners. Partner ball roll is one in a long line of activities geared to actually teach social skills. Children come to school with varying degrees of social acuity. We cannot transform them, but we can give them tools as we would in any other subject. For most of them the choice of not *acting* on their feelings will be a brand-new idea.

5. Ball handling is excellent eye-hand coordination work. We have in mind physical conditioning that will make children's lives healthier and happier. We also draw in sensory integration work—like stimulating the vestibular system and crossing the midline—that will help the children become receptive to learning in general. Sure, you could just start with partner ball rolls (there are plenty of books that will give you an array of terrific movement activities), but it would be a shot in the dark. The children would be missing out on a true developmental, holistic curriculum. And you would be missing out on the control and clarity of direction that come with a conceptual approach.

Because we cannot teach everything at once, we learn to juggle. We use what we need and teach it when we can. For example, the partner ball roll is introduced several lessons before a formal presentation of nonlocomotor movements. We use nonlocomotor movements, but we do not use the term or assume that the concept has been taught.

Preceding the lessons in part III is an overview of the organization, setup, and format of the plans (chapter 13). This part of the book then divides into three age-appropriate curriculums:

- Preschool through first grade (chapter 14)
- Second and third grades (chapter 15)
- Fourth through sixth grades (chapter 16)

Each curriculum starts with an introduction of its own, including an easy-to-use chart that lists the 15 lesson plans for the given grade level, as well as a brief explanation of the goals of each plan and the way the plan fits into the curriculum as a whole.

That brings us to the lesson plans. Here is what you will find in each one:

1. Teacher to Teacher: Your personalized coach starts off with a few tips.
2. Student Objectives: What the children will accomplish.
3. Materials Needed: Equipment and supplies you will need.
4. Teaching Instructions: The exact progression of the lesson.
5. Adaptations: How to make the lesson easier, harder, or adapt it to English language learners.
6. Assessment: Assessment possibilities for individual children and the class as a whole.

The lesson plans are in a specific developmental sequence. Occasionally between lessons I stop for a moment and offer "Reflections and Options," explaining *why* I decided to follow a certain progression. My hope is that the chapter 13 overview, the lessons themselves, and the reflections and options offer you plans that you can follow as well as a curriculum that you can make your own. Because of the many adaptation and developmental possibilities, these lesson plans will extend well beyond 15 class times.

Step by Step: A Complete Movement Education Curriculum is based 100% on experience. All activities have been tested for at least 10 years, and most for more than 20 years. All activities have succeeded in different classroom situations: lower-economic-level schools, middle income schools, private schools, and dance studios. Whenever possible, I have asked other teachers to implement these activities so that I am sure they are successful with different personalities. Because the program comes from direct experience, it is reality based. *No previous training is necessary.* Classroom teachers, special education teachers, dance teachers, movement teachers, physical education teachers, occupational and movement therapists, private school teachers, and children's center and day care teachers will find the program useful and extremely adaptable.

I hope that this book will encourage you to start or expand a program of movement education. I hope that the teaching techniques and concepts learned here will benefit your entire curriculum. Most importantly, it is my hope that you and your students will experience the joy and power that come from moving.

How to Use This Book

You know the old line—"Call me anything you want, just call me for dinner"? Well, use this book any way you want, just use it. This sounds simplistic, but I am not completely joking; you have your own learning style, and that is fine. The way I envision readers using this book is as follows. Start at the beginning and do a relaxed read of part I—suspend all concerns about how in the world you would actually *do* any of it and just skim the specific examples, exercises, and studies. My intention, at the end of this first part, is for you to have a grasp of the three class management techniques and the five foundational concepts of movement education—to start talking movement. Then, I hope you will look over part II and say, "Wow, these activities look like great fun. I want to try them." Once you reach the lesson plans in part III, you will have a background of movement concepts and activities that allows you to teach this program with confidence and success.

The lesson plans provide a model of how the curriculum can actually work. They also provide a progression of how lessons build on one another. The order is very important, and you can see that order at a glance in the charts that open chapters 14 through 16. At first you might want to follow the lesson plans fairly closely; but as you gain experience and confidence, the curriculum will reflect your individual style. If you run across an activity in the lessons that seems to require further explanation, check the "Activity Finder" at the front of the book to locate where the activity is introduced in parts I or II and whether it appears in any other of the 45 lessons. It also is helpful to realize that you can use the "Activity Finder" to pursue a specific subject such as partner or parachute activities. At a glance, you can find out where in the book you can get the essential details to put activities to use with your students.

Throughout the chapters I offer choreographed dances and studies that exemplify the concept work presented. Generally, dance moves are grouped into phrases using beats. Beats are the underlying pulse within all music and dance. Beats have a downward accent called "downbeats" and are signified by numbers. Between each beat is an upward pull called an "upbeat" signified be an "and" count. Therefore a measure (grouping) of four beats would be counted 1-and, 2-and, 3-and, 4-and. Whenever possible, I include the words to the dance to clarify the beat and phrase structure.

The book also includes side boxes with specific safety and troubleshooting tips that you can put to use, plus some real-life anecdotes to remind you that others have dealt with your frustrations before and might be able to offer some help.

My goal is for this book to be useful and that movement becomes a real and vibrant language for you. I look forward to you experiencing the intense joy that I have felt when sharing movement with children.

Acknowledgments

I thank God with all my heart.

I thank Gertrude Blanchard, who took a chance on me and taught me most of what I know.

I thank master teacher Ruth Bossieux for unwavering help and support.

I thank my friends and family for putting up with me.

I thank all my students for teaching me.

Activity Finder

Activity	Good for	Page and chapter number(s)	Lesson plan grades and plan number(s)
Are you alive?	Calming a young child Class tone	p. 147, Chapter 10	
Bag a partner	Partner cooperation Coordination	p. 107, Chapter 7	
Balance beam	Balance Control Coordination Perceptual awareness	p. 122, Chapter 8	**Pre-1:** 7 **2-3:** 4, 12 **4-6:** 1, 12
Balloons	Eye-hand coordination Language Sport skills	p. 135, Chapter 9	**Pre-1:** 7 **2-3:** 4, 12, 15 **4-6:** 1, 12
Balls	Eye-hand coordination Eye-foot coordination Sequencing	p. 128, Chapter 9	**Pre-1:** 1, 2, 3, 4, 7 **2-3:** 1, 2, 4, 12 **4-6:** 1, 2, 3, 12
Beanbags	Eye-hand coordination Balance	p. 143, Chapter 9	**Pre-1:** 7 **2-3:** 4, 8, 12 **4-6:** 1, 7, 14, 15
Bears in the night dance	Prepositions Beginning sequence	p. 172, Chapter 11	**Pre-1:** 12
Blastoff	Warm-up Balance Bridge Shoulder stand	p. 24, Chapter 2	**Pre-1:** 3, 4, 5 **2-3:** 2, 3
Body wave warm-up	Nonlocomotor swing Warm-up	p. 69, Chapter 4 p. 183, Chapter 12	
Brain catcher	Mental and physical warm-up	p. 152, Chapter 10	**2-3:** 9 **4-6:** 11
Broken leg	Rope exploration	p. 132, Chapter 9	**Pre-1:** 13, 14 **2-3:** 10, 11
Camptown races dance	Advanced sequence Precise footwork	p. 46, Chapter 3	
Cancan	Group locomotor movement	p. 41, Chapter 3 p. 111, Chapter 7	
Cat dance	Advanced sequence Falls Strength Flexibility	p. 190, Chapter 12	
Chase	Preliminary ball skill	p. 128, Chapter 9	**Pre-1:** 1, 2, 3

(continued)

Activity	Good for	Page and chapter number(s)	Lesson plan grades and plan number(s)
Chinese ropes	Flexibility Freedom of expression Geometry Partner cooperation	p. 133, Chapter 9	
Circus	Showmanship End of obstacle course	p. 118, Chapter 8	
Cops and robbers	Laterality Side-slide	p. 79, Chapter 6	**Pre-1:**8
Crazy walk	Integrating the two sides of the brain Freedom of expression Rope exploration	p. 132, Chapter 9	**Pre-1:**12 **2-3:**10
Eensy weensy spider	Beginning sequence	p. 46, Chapter 3	**Pre-1:**5, 6
Eight plus eight dance	Intermediate sequence Differentiating locomotor and nonlocomotor movements	p. 69, Chapter 4	**2-3:**3, 5 **4-6:**3, 4
Fall dance	Advanced sequence	p. 190, Chapter 12	
Firecracker	Reinforcing perfect spots	p. 21, Chapter 2	**Pre-1:**3, 4 **2-3:**2
Fishturn	Advanced spin	p. 57, Chapter 4	**4-6:**9
Floor patterns	Spatial awareness Map reading Locomotor movements Sequencing Geometry Symmetry Language	p. 86, Chapter 6	**Pre-1:** 8, 9, 10, 11, 14, 15 **2-3:**7, 8, 9, 10, 11, 13 **4-6:**4, 5, 6, 8, 9, 10, 11
Flying	Locomotor movement with parachute Freedom of expression	p. 140, Chapter 9	**Pre-1:**2, 12.5 **2-3:**14
Foam jump	Hurdle move Math computations	p. 142, Chapter 9	**Pre-1:**11, 12 **2-3:**10, 12 **4-6:**5, 6, 12
Freeway	Reinforcing diagonal structure Motor planning	p. 29, Chapter 2	**2-3:**5, 14 **4-6:**13
Frog balance	Preliminary gymnastics Balance	p. 68, Chapter 4	**2-3:**4, 12 **4-6:**1, 8, 12, 13
Grocery store dance	Beginning sequence Language	p. 44, Chapter 3	**Pre-1:**14, 15 **2-3:**11
Gymnastics	Conditioning Strength Flexibility Balance Sequencing	p. 38, Chapter 3 p. 99, Chapter 6 p. 116, Chapter 8 p. 185, Chapter 12	**Pre-1:**3, 4, 5, 7 **2-3:**3, 4, 12 **4-6:**1, 3, 12, 13, 14

Activity	Good for	Page and chapter number(s)	Lesson plan grades and plan number(s)
Hamburgers and french fries	Motor planning with parachute	p. 139, Chapter 9	**Pre-1:** 13, 14 **4-6:** 10
Hello and good-bye	Warm-up Coordination	p. 21, Chapter 2	**Pre-1:** 1, 2, 3 **2-3:** 1, 2, 5
Horse in a corral	Group cooperation Coordination	p. 111, Chapter 7	
Horsie	Partner cooperation	p. 108, Chapter 7	**Pre-1:** 5 **2-3:** 6, 7 **4-6:** 5
Horsie with ropes	Partner cooperation	p. 132, Chapter 9	**Pre-1:** 12, 13, 14, 15 **2-3:** 10, 11
In and out game	Prepositions Geometry Problem solving Sportspersonship	p. 161, Chapter 11	**Pre-1:** 11 **2-3:** 8 **4-6:** 7, 15
Incline mat activities	Tumbling skills Coordination	p. 142, Chapter 9	**Pre-1:** 2, 3, 4, 5, 7 **2-3:** 3, 8, 9 **4-6:** 1, 3, 4, 7, 12, 15
Jazzy rope	Freedom of expression	p. 132, Chapter 9	**Pre-1:** 13, 14 **2-3:** 10, 11
Jig along dance	Intermediate sequence Partner cooperation Language	p. 44, Chapter 3	**2-3:** 6, 7, 11
Jump pattern	Intermediate sequence Precise footwork	p. 69, Chapter 4	**2-3:** 1, 2, 10
Jump your name	Introductions Motor planning	p. 148, Chapter 10	
Leaping logs	Partner skills Motor planning	p. 108, Chapter 7	
Lifting	Conditioning Flexibility Partner skills	p. 109, Chapter 7	
Machine	Group cooperation Freedom of expression	p. 96, Chapter 6	
Magic scarf	Conditioning Freedom of expression	p. 130, Chapter 9	**Pre-1:** 9 **2-3:** 5, 6 **4-6:** 7
Magician with scarf	Freedom of expression	p. 130, Chapter 9	**4-6:** 7
Massage	Partner consideration	p. 120, Chapter 8	**4-6:** 12
Maybe I don't; maybe I do	Isolation of shoulders	p. 26, Chapter 2	**Pre-1:** 4
Merry-go-round	Group cooperation Balance	p. 139, Chapter 9	**4-6:** 11

(continued)

Activity	Good for	Page and chapter number(s)	Lesson plan grades and plan number(s)
Microphone	Language development Freedom of expression	p. 132, Chapter 9	**Pre-1:** 12, 13, 14 **2-3:** 10
Mirror and shadow	Partner cooperation Proprioceptive sense Symmetry	p. 109, Chapter 7	**4-6:** 8
Monster rises	Movement sequence on diagonal	p. 69, Chapter 4	
Ms. Monster	Group cooperation with parachute	p. 140, Chapter 9	
Mushroom	Group cooperation with parachute Motor planning	p. 141, Chapter 9	**Pre-1:** 14, 15 **2-3:** 13, 14 **4-6:** 10, 11
Obstacle course	Conditioning Sequencing Gymnastics Balance Testing	p. 113, Chapter 8	**Pre-1:** 7 **2-3:** 4, 12 **4-6:** 1, 12
Ocean	Energy release with parachute	p. 138, Chapter 9	**Pre-1:** 13, 14 **4-6:** 10, 11
Opposite game	Language	p. 170, Chapter 11	**2-3:** 15 **4-6:** 14, 15
Orchestra and dancers	Movement sequence Memory Attention	p. 151, Chapter 10	
Pachelbel canon dance	Advanced sequence	p. 194, Chapter 12	**4-6:** 9
Parachute activities	Sensory work Motor planning Group cooperation Language	p. 138, Chapter 9	**Pre-1:** 13, 14, 15 **2-3:** 13, 14 **4-6:** 10, 11
Partner activities	Cooperation and friendship Motor planning Warm-up	p. 105, Chapter 7	**Pre-1:** 4, 5, 6, 9, 10, 12, 13, 14 **2-3:** 6, 7, 10, 11, 12, 13, 15 **4-6:** 4, 5, 6, 8, 9, 12, 13
Partner ball pass	Eye-hand coordination Partner skills	p. 129, Chapter 9	
Partner carry	Group cooperation Motor planning	p. 111, Chapter 7	
Partner carry with balls	Partner skills Coordination	p. 130, Chapter 9	
Partner dance	Advanced sequence Focus of attention Partner cooperation	p. 193, Chapters 12	**4-6:** 5, 6
Partner opposites	Language development Partner skills Coordination	p. 170, Chapters 11	

Activity	Good for	Page and chapter number(s)	Lesson plan grades and plan number(s)
Partner shake	Preliminary partner skill	p. 105, Chapter 7	**Pre-1:** 4
Plastic hoops	Coordination Sequencing and memory skills	p. 134, Chapter 9	**2-3:** 4, 12, 14, 15 **4-6:** 7, 12, 15
Prop activities	Warm-up Conditioning Sports skills Sequencing Partner and group cooperation Problem solving Motor planning	p. 126, Chapter 9	**Pre-1:** 1, 2, 3, 4, 5, 7, 8, 9, 10, 11, 12, 13, 14, 15 **2-3:** 1, 2, 3, 4, 5, 6, 8, 9, 10, 11, 12, 13, 14, 15 **4-6:** 1, 2, 3, 4, 5, 6, 7, 8, 10, 11, 12, 13, 14, 15
Pyramids	Group cooperation Balance Problem solving Symmetry	p. 192, Chapter 12	**4-6:** 8, 13
Right and left bug	Laterality Warm-up	p. 79, Chapter 6	**Pre-1:** 4, 5 **2-3:** 13
Rock and wave	Motor planning with parachute Levels Focus of attention	p. 140, Chapter 9	
Rocking as a relaxer	Calming energy	p. 153, Chapter 10	
Rocking song	Beginning movement experience Stopping on an aural cue Language	p. 17, Chapter 2	**Pre-1:** 1, 2
Ropes	Coordination Conditioning Line shapes Fantasy Cooperation	p. 92, Chapter 6 p. 132, Chapter 9	**Pre-1:** 7, 12, 13 **2-3:** 4, 10, 11, 12 **4-6:** 1, 12
Row, row, row your boat dance	Intermediate sequence Directions Problem solving	p. 83, Chapter 6	**2-3:** 13, 14
Scarves	Coordination English language developement Line shapes Fantasy Sequencing	p. 130, Chapter 9	**Pre-1:** 7, 8, 9, 10, 15 **2-3:** 4, 5, 6, 12 **4-6:** 1, 7, 8, 12
Scooter line	Visual perceptual work Conditioning Coordination Partner cooperation	p. 123, Chapter 8 p. 137, Chapter 9	**Pre-1:** 7 **2-3:** 4 **4-6:** 1
Shark	Group cooperation with parachute	p. 140, Chapter 9	**Pre-1:** 13, 14 **2-3:** 13, 14 **4-6:** 11
Spaghetti	Group cooperation Sensory work	p. 154, Chapter 10	**2-3:** 7

(continued)

Activity Finder *(continued)*

Activity	Good for	Page and chapter number(s)	Lesson plan grades and plan number(s)
Swordfish	Beginning conditioning Balance	p. 23, Chapter 2	**Pre-1:** 1, 2, 3 **2-3:** 1, 2
Stations	Conditioning Coordination Balance	p. 121, Chapter 8	
Tackle	Motor planning with incline mat	p. 142, Chapter 9	**2-3:** 8, 9 **4-6:** 4, 12
Telephone	Language development Partner skills	p. 132, Chapter 9	**Pre-1:** 12, 13, 14 **2-3:** 10
Temper tantrum	Self-control	p. 73, Chapter 5	**Pre-1:** 8, 9 **2-3:** 5, 6
Trap	Motor planning with parachute	p. 139, Chapter 9	**2-3:** 14 **4-6:** 11
Trust walk	Partner consideration	p. 120, Chapter 8 p. 131, Chapter 9	**4-6:** 12
Tumbling	Improve strength Agility Coordination Control Self-worth	p. 99, Chapter 6 p. 122, Chapters 8	
Voice box	Language development	p. 99, Chapter 6	
Walk down your front	Directionality Flexibility	p. 76, Chapter 6	**Pre-1:** 4, 5 **2-3:** 13
Wheelbarrow	Partner skills Conditioning	p. 108, Chapter 7	**Pre-1:** 5 **2-3:** 6, 7 **4-6:** 5
Where the wild things are dance	Intermediate sequence Language	p. 173, Chapter 11	**2-3:** 14, 15
Whoosh	Motor planning with parachute	p. 138, Chapter 9	**Pre-1:** 13, 14 **2-3:** 13, 14 **4-6:** 10, 11
Wring out the dishrag	Partner skills Coordination	p. 107, Chapter 7	**2-3:** 6, 7 **4-6:** 5, 8
Yankee doodle dance	Intermediate sequence Precise footwork	p. 46, Chapter 3	**4-6:** 15

Part I

Basic Movement Concepts

Wait! I know how tempting it is to skip this introductory text in search of the "real" meat-and-potatoes activities that you can use next Monday. I know how many memos, manuals, texts, journals, and instructions you are asked to read. I know how the paperwork part of teaching seems to be taking over the whole job. What I ask—despite all the demands on your time—is that you simply read part I. Would you clear just one hour to read this beginning text in a relaxed, non-goal-oriented, manner? If you could just read part I without the anxiety of organizing all this information into a plausible lesson, I guarantee I will walk you through the lesson formation process in part III.

Part I presents two conceptual foundations. The first is class management—how to control the class so that we are actually able to teach the curriculum. The second is an overview of the broadest strokes that underlie all movement activities—dance, sport, gymnastics, games, exercise, and so on. A catalog of locomotor movements and a catalog of nonlocomotor movements can be found at the end of chapter 3 and chapter 4, respectively. These two catalogs provide an easy reference source when you begin putting these movements into practice. You could run a movement program without understanding the foundations, but you would stand on shifting sands rather than solid rock.

Part I might seem like an overload of information. But if you focus on the concepts, skim the examples, and do not worry about lessons yet, it will be less daunting and well worth the effort. Whether you are looking for a curriculum to implement in a professional dance studio or are considering venturing into a weekly half-hour movement class, I congratulate you and welcome you to the joyous world of movement.

Chapter 1

What Is Movement Education?

"This is my day!" a little boy shouts. Children start ripping off their shoes and socks even before reaching the gym door. They rush in, stash their belongings, and begin energetically skipping around the room. This is the start of a typical movement class.

During the class, children move strenuously, touching on elements of strength, flexibility, agility, and endurance. They work on coordination, balance, and spatial awareness. They develop their social skills and reinforce academic concepts. They feel good about themselves and have fun. No small feat!

Scope of a Movement Program

Movement works with the whole child, physically, socially, academically; these areas are integrated together and are of equal importance. A complete movement curriculum offers class management organizations that allow all future activities to be orderly and fun for both students and teachers. This type of program builds sequentially, one skill becoming the foundation for more complex skills (hence the title *Step by Step: A Complete Movement Education Curriculum*). It is quite different from a collection of activities, however enticing, in which one lesson randomly follows another.

Assessment

We have gone assessment crazy. As a classroom teacher, I sometimes feel I have to squeeze in teaching among all the assessments. But assessment itself is not bad. The pendulum needed to shift some; it was tempting to blithely teach what we wanted and assume that the children were getting what they needed. Movement education allows us to make assessments without taking away enjoyment or valuable education time. Here are five reasons why movement education is an excellent context for assessments:

1. We are able to identify difficulties with motor skills, especially the preacademic skills that undergird school success, even if those difficulties are masked by athleticism.

2. Problems with attention deficit and hyperactivity are seen in another context. Sometimes a child appears hyperactive in the classroom and not in movement class, or the other way around; this is a valuable piece of information when we are attempting an accurate diagnosis.

3. Difficulties with spatial awareness, visual perception, midline, and directionality can be pinpointed. Sometimes perceptual problems look like inattentiveness, and sometimes they manifest themselves as generalized academic trouble. Reading requires good tracking skills, and math

requires visual organization to understand place value. If these perceptual skills are lacking, the child will appear unmotivated.

4. Social skills (or a lack of them) stand out in a movement program. Activities like partner and group work obviously necessitate social interaction. But other movement lessons will point out potential social difficulties that might otherwise be overlooked. For example, the self-discipline needed to stop on cue is part of an overall ability to control oneself; without control, a child will tend to be too rough and insensitive to social clues. The self-assertion necessary to perform a dance is part of the overall ability required to reach out to others and form friendships.

5. Movement class will point out individual learning styles and "life skills." A child's ability to lead as well as follow, his ability to concentrate and remember, his sense of responsibility and perseverance, his acceptance of himself and capacity for enjoyment—all are characteristics that will come out during the course of a movement program.

Recently all academic curriculums have been broken down into standards of achievement that teachers are required to cover. District assessments and national standardized tests evaluate children according to this framework. Physical education too has been organized into standards. For example, according to the Physical Education Framework adopted by the State Board of Education, there are three main goals of physical education: movement skills and knowledge, self-image and personal development, and social development. Like other states' goals, these correspond with nationally accepted standards for the subject of physical education. These national standards were considered in the development of the lessons included in this book. The following grade level expectations, adopted by the state of California, where I teach, are an example of the goals states ask physical education teachers to satisfy:

Kindergarten

1. Travel in different ways in a large group without bumping into others or falling.

2. Balance while bending, twisting, or stretching.

3. Strike a stationary ball with any part of the body.

4. Identify various parts of the body and their location—for example, arms, legs, and hands.

5. Recognize changes in heart rate.

6. Follow adult-delivered rules.

First Grade

1. Travel and change direction quickly in response to a signal.

2. Travel in relationship to objects: over, under, behind, and through.

3. Place the body and limbs in different positions, demonstrating high, middle, and low levels.

4. Toss and catch a ball alone or with a partner.

5. Learn to use equipment safely and responsibly.

6. Begin to recognize changes in one's body, such as changes in height and weight.

7. Develop responsibility for expected behaviors on the playground and in the classroom.

Second Grade

1. Move backward and change direction quickly and safely without falling.

2. Jump and land, using a combination of one- and two-foot takeoffs and landings.

3. Throw a ball hard, demonstrating an overhand technique, a side orientation, and opposition.

4. Jump a self-turned rope repeatedly.

5. Skip, hop, gallop, and slide.

Third Grade

1. Combine locomotor and nonlocomotor movements, such as combining various travel patterns in relation to music.

2. Dribble a ball continuously, using the hands or feet to control it.

3. Maintain flexibility by combining shapes, levels, and pathways into simple sequences.

4. Recognize similar movement concepts in a variety of skills. For example, an underhand movement can be used in a variety of ways.

5. Accept the feelings resulting from challenge, success, and failure in physical activity.

6. Play and assist others in activities in groups of three to five.

Fourth Grade

1. Leap, leading with either foot.
2. Hand-dribble and foot-dribble a ball while moving within a group.
3. Jump and land for height and distance.
4. Maintain continuous aerobic activity for a specified time.
5. Describe healthful benefits that result from regular participation in physical activity.
6. Recognize the fundamental strategies in simple games.

Fifth Grade

1. Manipulate objects with accuracy and speed.
2. Be involved in gamelike activities, with emphasis on more than two skills.
3. Distinguish between compliance and noncompliance with game rules.
4. Use fundamental strategies (i.e., offensive and defensive strategies) in simple games.
5. Recognize that different body types are more effective in certain movement skills and activities.
6. Begin to appreciate individual differences within small-group competition and cooperation.
7. View the practice and perfection of performance in line and folk dances positively.

Sixth Grade

1. Throw a variety of objects, demonstrating both accuracy and distance (e.g., disc-like objects, deck tennis rings, footballs).

2. Design and play small-group games that involve cooperating with others to keep an object away from opponents (basic offensive and defensive strategy—for example, by throwing kicking, or dribbling a ball).

3. Design and refine a routine, combining various jump rope movements to music, so that it can be repeated without error.

4. Demonstrate correctly activities designed to improve and maintain muscular strength and endurance, flexibility, and cardiorespiratory functioning.

5. Participate in games, sports, dance, and outdoor pursuits, both in and outside of school, according to individual interests and capabilities.

6. Recognize the role of games, sports, and dance in getting to know and understand people of diverse cultures.

The lessons presented in *Step by Step: A Complete Movement Education Curriculum* thoroughly cover 95% of these standards. What is not covered are factors inherent in competitive games. There is virtually no competition in this movement program; the closest we come is the possibility of "winning" in the In and Out Game. Therefore standards like "Accept and respect the decisions made by game officials" and the one relating to offensive and defensive strategies are not tested. I believe that most of the competitive standards will be taught in sport activities both in and out of school. The thrust of this movement program is a strenuous but safe arena for exploring a full range of movement experiences.

Each lesson plan contains a section on assessment. The lessons presenting obstacle courses include grids to help assess individual motor development (pp. 225, 256, and 288). This evaluation could be used several times during the year for a formal charting of progress. In addition, more informal assessments of social and cooperative skills, concentration and memory, and spatial awareness and visual perception are suggested throughout the program.

Benefits of Movement

When I wrote the first edition of this book, having taught approximately 12 years, I listed three benefits of movement. Now, after almost 30 years of teaching movement, I find the benefits innumerable. Here is a partial list:

1. The number-one benefit of movement education is that it makes kids happy. This is not insignificant. A relaxed, happy child is more excited about learning in general, is more willing to take risks, and is more cooperative. Once a child realizes that you genuinely promote her happiness, she will be loyally on your side. What makes movement so much fun is the inherent excitement and challenge.

2. Movement aids physical well-being. So many children today are out of shape! There has been a 70% increase in the number of overweight youngsters within the last 12 years. An October 26, 1999, report from the Centers for Disease Control and Prevention in the Journal of the American Medical Association noted that "specialists are practically begging for a national obesity prevention strategy" and suggested cutting back on television for children and increasing physical education in schools. These statistics are, unfortunately, repeatedly confirmed in the mainstream media. On January 29, 2003, KRON San Francisco reported that California schoolchildren across the board failed a state physical fitness test—scores ranged from 2% to 60% depending on the socioeconomic level of the community. According to an article titled "Our Super Sized Children" in the February 2003 issue of Ladies' Home Journal, the number of overweight children in the United States has tripled in the last 35 years.

Even children who are not overweight often do not have the agility, strength, flexibility, and endurance they could have. Most children have weak abdominal muscles, bad posture, and a tendency to stop any activity when they feel the least bit tired. I have, at four months pregnant, challenged entire classes to sit-up contests and won. This is disheartening. A once-a-week movement class will not in itself get children into shape, but the joy of moving and the knowledge of movement vocabulary will encourage children to move

in other settings. I remember a little girl who started the year so shy and physically withdrawn she could hardly participate. At the end of the year she did a rollicking solo dance for the whole class. The more we enjoy moving, the more we want to move.

Further, a strenuous movement class allows children to let off steam. Today's children are under a lot of pressure. Inner city kids are often burdened by enormous problems and fears, and more affluent children often feel pressured to produce and succeed. All children need the stress release that exercise can provide.

3. Movement teaches and promotes social skills. There are countless opportunities for partner and group activities. These are a perfect vehicle for actively teaching cooperation, compromise, and kindness. In addition, it is possible to establish a supportive, noncompetitive tone for the whole class. "We are on this earth to help one another," I tell students. The more a child accepts himself, the more he is willing to extend himself to others; completing the circle. The more a child extends himself to others, the happier he is with himself. In a directed, safe, noncompetitive environment, children learn how to make friends and be a friend.

4. Movement provides preacademic skills. There is mounting documentation that motor development is a major force in a child's academic, social, and personal development. According to Jean Ayres, founder of sensory-integration therapy:

> The brain's mental and social functions are based on a foundation of sensory-motor processes. The sensory integration that occurs in moving, talking, and playing is the groundwork for the more complex sensory integration that is necessary for reading, writing, and good behavior. (p. 7)

Sensory Integration and the Child, by A. Jean Ayres, PhD, Western Psychological Services, 12031 Wiltshire Boulevard, Los Angeles, CA 90025, 1979.

Ayres adds, "Motor activity is valuable in that it provides the sensory input that helps to organize the learning process" (p. 141). Teachers have known this for years. The child who has motor problems has many other troubles in the classroom. A child with motor problems might be withdrawn, aggressive, hyperactive, dull, awkward, or full of reversals. Her language or math skills, or both, might be below grade level, or she might do well academically but have trouble making friends. Not every child who has difficulties in the classroom has motor problems, but motor development should be one of the first areas checked.

How do you find the time to test motor development? If a specialist is not available, here are a few basics to check:

    a. Can the child, from first grade on up, walk easily on a balance beam?

    b. Can the child hop equally well on either foot? Can he skip?

    c. Can he catch a 6-inch ball?

    d. Can he follow a tape line that includes a loop?

If a child has a lot of difficulties with one of these tasks, this is a possible indication of motor problems; and further testing is in order. (Part III contains more extensive checklists: p. 200—checklist for preschool to first grade; p. 201—checklist for second and third grades; p. 202—checklist for fourth through sixth grades.)

Movement activities offer practice in balancing, crossing the midline, visual perception, and eye-hand and eye-foot coordination. In addition, classes provide vestibular stimulation, which affects how efficiently the brain processes information. This type of work is extremely worthwhile for all students; it is crucial for those with motor problems.

5. Movement is a fabulous medium for teaching academic skills. Educators are aware that there are different learning styles—visual, aural, and kinesthetic. Almost all teachers present material visually as well as aurally, but it is the kinesthetic sense that transfers information to the "gut level." For infants, the first mode of learning is the tactile-kinesthetic; and we know that even in adulthood, what is learned in the muscles is learned for keeps. Demonstrating a right angle with the legs and torso, devising a symmetrical shape with a partner, representing "beneath" by crawling under a table, showing "trudge" by walking reluctantly, remembering "circumference" by running around

the parachute—through these kinds of movement activities, many abstract and forgettable concepts become real and memorable.

On a deeper level, movement works with the underlying academic skills—concentration, memory, sequencing, patterning. Learning a long movement pattern is excellent practice in memory and focus of attention; drawing and executing a floor pattern (map) involve many visual and problem-solving skills; creating a group pattern showing six ways of moving with a scarf promotes divergent thinking, sequencing, and memory, as well as cooperation and teamwork.

6. Movement teaches life skills. On a still deeper level, a good movement program teaches life skills: perseverance, mastery, self-discipline, empathy. Despite the emphasis on high-stakes testing, I see these life skills as the core of education. Continuing to run leap beyond a little fatigue, practicing a dance until it is perfect, performing despite shyness, sitting with a ball in one's lap without touching it, helping a classmate—these are the skills that grow children into fulfilled human beings. On my wall is a beautifully framed piece of crumpled paper; in a second grade scrawl that reads, "In movement class I learned to turn fear into power."

Teaching Techniques

This program presents three general teaching techniques: teaching conceptually, precisely, and actively.

Conceptual Teaching

The conceptual approach means introducing an idea in its broadest scope and then exemplifying it with specifics. For example, *contract* is taught as any "energetic curling up"; it is not limited to the typical modern dance style contract of the torso. It can be done with a hand, an arm, a leg, the torso, the face, or the whole body in different positions. Contractions can be done on the floor, on mats, on chairs or tables. They can be demonstrated singly, in partners, or in groups. Only after the children understand and explore the full range of possible contractions do they learn a pattern that uses specific contractions.

This conceptual approach is like learning to read instead of memorizing lines. It opens up new worlds. First, knowing overall concepts allows children to understand movement patterns fully. A dance sequence is no longer an undifferentiated jumble of steps; it is an intelligible ordering of recognizable vocabulary. Because of this ordering, children learn startlingly long and complex patterns. Second, the conceptual approach promotes creativity. Since the children are not bound by set moves, they are free to use and expand their imaginations. Third, the teaching of concepts opens up new horizons for the teacher. Concepts can be combined or expanded in any number of ways—for example, children might be asked to "create a sequence of five different contract and stretches, use both locomotor and nonlocomotor movements and different levels, and include some with a partner and some done individually." New concepts are readily found in classroom work, and often the movement concepts reinforce academic work. For example, in my classroom, when studying contractions such as can't, the class physically contracts while saying "Can plus not, can't." Most importantly, the conceptual approach takes movement out of the realm of an esoteric art form and brings it into the realm of a comprehensible curriculum.

Precise Teaching

Teaching conceptually is an overall approach to curriculum; the goal within each lesson is clarity. In this world of general sloppiness we need to be bastions of precision. "Watch," I say, and I expect the children to be still and look, not to move with me. "Sit in your Perfect Spots" means that the children are to sit in their spots; they do not lie down, stand up, or twirl.

Why am I stating the obvious? Because it is easy to forget, and it is important. Clear thinking and clear talking are inseparable. It is hard to say which comes first, but it is easy to see that we cannot have one without the other. So, we can no longer say, "Get partner groups of four" when we mean "Get partners" or "Get into groups of four"; "Jump on one foot" when we mean "Hop"; "Do the movement backward" when we mean "Do the movement

in the reverse order"; "Can you?" when there is no question; "Do you want to?" when there is no option.

➡ TROUBLESHOOTING

A note on "want": I do not use the word "want" unless I am prepared to have the children make an actual choice. If I say, "Do you want to do this?" and they say "No," I do not do it. I have nothing against direct commands as long as they are honest commands: "We will do this"; "I expect you to do that"; "You are required to do this." To offer a choice and then take it away is not fair. To offer a choice and manipulate it away is completely foul play.

It is a waste of time to speak clearly and not demand results. At times I have stopped demonstrating and repeated "Watch!" seven times before everyone stopped moving and actually watched. Groups of three means groups of three even if the grouping breaks up a circle of friends. Certainly the line between precision and rigidity is a hair's breadth, but it is worthwhile walking the thin line.

Just as we must demand precision of ourselves, we must also demand it of our classes. I was recently asked whether my strict adherence to "perfection" did not stifle children's creative expression and lessen their feelings of self-worth. No. I do not believe in uniformity, but precision in movement structures, like finding Perfect Spots, is absolutely necessary for the functioning of the class. Precision in movement patterns—precise beginnings, moving energetically and without hesitation, and being on the beat—are elements that make the difference between a spectacular dance and a mediocre one. Precision in any subject is a measure of excellence toward which a child must strive. If everything is praised equally, why should a child strain to grow? As long as the standard of excellence is clear and within the child's reach (not easily attainable but within a strenuous reach), then the work on precision can only benefit a child's sense of accomplishment and true feeling of self-worth.

I believe not enough is asked of our children. Observers are sometimes shocked by what I expect physically and intellectually from my classes. I often introduce a concept by telling the class that it is probably too hard for them, but mostly the children come through. The pride that shows on their faces and in their bearings when they achieve what seemed unattainable convinces me that it is worth the work for them and for me.

Active Teaching

Children learn best in proportion to how active they are in the learning process. Information superimposed on a child slips away easily; information discovered by the child remains and grows. Active learning is increasingly accepted in teaching reading, language arts, and math. It is also important in teaching movement.

Traditionally, physical education and dance have been taught in an authoritarian, perhaps even sadistic, manner: "25 burpees . . . 50 sit-ups . . . 8 grande battements . . ." This is fine only for building muscles. My movement program has a broader scope. I want children to become physically stronger, and I want them to think.

This comes down to some basic teaching principles. Whenever I am able to pose a question instead of simply providing information (which is often), I do so. "Are you sure you are far from everything?" rather than "Albert, move over here." "Where do you guess a diagonal line is on the ceiling?" "How else can you move and stay in one place?" "How can you move a balloon without touching it?"

This questioning technique works well for teaching concepts but obviously does not work for teaching specific movement patterns. In teaching patterns I work as much as possible through imitation. Imitation is itself an important skill because the children have to transfer what is seen to what is felt. This strengthens their proprioceptive sense, which is the ability of muscles and joints to reproduce a physical position. The proprioceptive sense, in turn, is necessary for visual perception and sensory integration. As a last resort, when I am stuck or when I am teaching a very difficult movement, I physically help children rearrange arms and legs.

In short, when I can teach verbally rather than imitatively, I choose the verbal. If there is a choice between imitation and direct manipulation of bodies, I choose imitation. Only if the children are having difficulty with a particular movement will I help individual children with actual body placement.

➡ TROUBLESHOOTING

Even though this is a movement class, we need to be careful in the area of physically touching a child. Classroom teachers are told simply never to touch a child in any way. I grieve over this. I personally give each student a hug at the end of the day, but I emphasize two points: I hug them in open, public view, and—this is the most crucial factor—they can always refuse. A child should always have the option. Therefore, even in just helping correct placement during a movement exercise, I ask, "May I?"

Movement has for too long been removed from the mind. In the past, athletic people were viewed as mindless followers. But just as smart people are now becoming more aware of their bodies, the era of the "dumb dancer" is over.

What You Need to Start

If you are beginning a movement program, you are to be congratulated: You are brave! Teaching movement is different from teaching other subjects; using one's body often makes people feel vulnerable and exposed. Almost every teacher (even veteran educators) has felt this way. Remember that you do not need to be a certain size, be in shape, be graceful, or even be coordinated to teach an excellent movement program. Also remember that the work will be worth it because the children will grow immeasurably and they will love it.

Essentially all that is needed to start this movement program is a room. Ideally the room should be large, clear of most furniture, warm, and clean. But I have worked most of my life in conditions that were less than ideal. If a gym or multipurpose room is not available, consider the cafeteria first thing in the morning or, as a last resort, consider moving the furniture to the sides of a classroom once a week. I do not recommend working outside because of weather, glass, and other obstacles and because children have a much harder time concentrating in an open space. However, if it comes down to a choice of working outside or not doing any movement whatsoever, the answer is clear: Choose movement.

My ideal time framework is having class twice a week for 45 minutes. This rarely happens. Most teachers limit themselves to once a week.

I strongly urge 45-minute to 1-hour sessions so that the lessons can develop fully.

The children wear no special clothing. I ask them to wear play clothes so that their parents will not mind their getting on the floor. Girls wear pants or shorts under skirts. Since they work barefoot, it makes life easier if girls avoid wearing stockings. If you do not feel comfortable working barefoot, just wear shoes without any guilt. There are privileges to being the adult.

Because this movement program is based on concepts, equipment is not mandatory. With just a room, tambourine, paper, and crayons you can cover all the basic concepts: Free Traveling Structure, Perfect Spots, Diagonal Structure, locomotor and nonlocomotor movements, levels, directions, and floor patterns, plus partner activities and work on many academic skills.

However, props are a wonderful and useful addition to any movement program. Most school districts have all or most of the equipment mentioned in this book. If not, many schools have some funds set aside for new equipment. If not, many teachers have written and received mini-grants for starting a movement education program. If not, any money you spend is tax deductible. Table 1.1 lists, in order of importance, the equipment I would get with limited funds. The size and type of equipment are almost completely your preference; when these do matter, I have noted what is preferable.

Table 1.1 Movement Class Equipment Needs

Item	Number needed	Notes	Uses	Where to find
Balls	One per child (plus several extra)	I prefer 6-inch-diameter balls, but any ball that bounces will do.	Warm-up, partner work, eye-hand coordination, sequences, obstacle courses, and stations	Physical education catalogs, sporting goods stores, toy stores
Scarves	One per child (plus several extra)	Any size and type of washable material will do. I prefer the 2-foot-square sheer head scarves.	Warm-up, sequences, obstacle courses and stations, fantasy play and costumes, and juggling	Sport catalogs under juggling equipment
Jump ropes	One per child (plus several extra)	Any type will do, although I prefer the softer cloth kind instead of the plastic ones.	Warm-up, coordination work, partner work, obstacle courses and stations, work on line shapes, sequences, and games	Sport catalogs, sporting goods stores, toy stores
Foam rubber	One or more pieces; try to accumulate 10.	Pieces should be approximately 2 feet square, 4 inches thick. (Some nice parents sewed material over my foam squares, making them look like different-colored pillows; this was especially welcome since the foam by itself leaves some residue.)	Ending activities, games, obstacle courses and stations, and partner work	Craft stores, futon shops
Scooters	If you are planning to use the scooters within obstacle courses or in stations, you need only six; for partner work you will need half the number of children in a class.	Scooters look like square skateboards. Any type, with handles or not, wood or plastic, is fine.	Obstacle courses and stations, partner work, and visual perception assessment and reinforcement	Sport catalogs, educational supply stores

(continued)

Table 1.1   (continued)

Item	Number needed	Notes	Uses	Where to find
Parachute	One	24-foot diameter	Parachute activities	Sport catalogs, educational supply stores
Stegel or balance beam	One	A stegel is a wooden structure that has notches, allowing two or three balance beams to be placed at different heights. In addition, the structure usually includes a ladder and slide. This is a fabulous piece of equipment. It is expensive but well worth the investment; I have heard of kits to build a stegel. Balance beams are fairly easy to make: one sanded 4-inch by 8-foot plank, resting on two notched blocks, a couple of inches off the ground, will do just fine.	A balance beam in either form is an important element in obstacle courses and stations and in games such as the In and Out Game.	Sport catalogs, educational supply stores
Mats	Preferably 10 to 15	Any type of mat will do; I greatly prefer mats that are light enough for the children to carry and that have fasteners allowing them to be attached to one another. Soft mats are best for gymnastics work, but it is nice to have a few additional stiff mats for games.	Obstacle courses and stations, games, dances, and language and gymnastics work	Sport catalogs, sporting goods , educational supply stores
Incline mat	One	This is a special mat that is wedge shaped. Like a stegel, the incline mat is an expensive piece of equipment but well worth it. Get the largest size available.	Gymnastics, ending games, obstacle courses and stations, and partner work	Sport catalogs, educational supply stores
Tires, old	Approximately 10 bicycle and 5 car tires		Coordination and strength work, obstacle courses and stations, games, dances, and partner work	Scrap yards, friends and family, garages and mechanic shops

Item	Number needed	Notes	Uses	Where to find
Balloons	One per child (plus many extra)	I use only round balloons. Size is not as important as durability; the thicker, more expensive balloons will be cheaper in the long run (and you won't go crazy with all the popping). I have come to appreciate this prop more and more.	Warm-up, fantasy play, sequences, dances, eye-hand coordination, partner work, and obstacle courses and stations	Educational supply stores, drugstores, toy stores, discount stores, and the like
Plastic hoops	Enough for at least half your class; one per child would be best.	Plastic hoops are an excellent prop and would be a higher priority if they did not break so easily (they squish into a non-circle at the drop of a hat). Any type will do; I obviously recommend the best quality.	Sequencing, warm-up, partner work, patterning, coordination work, and obstacle courses and stations	Sport catalogs, sporting goods stores, educational supply stores, toy stores
Beanbags	Enough for one per child (plus several extra)	Just as with the plastic hoops, beanbags would be a higher priority if they did not rip so easily. Get the best available and have needle and thread ready.	Warm-up, partner work, balance and language work, games, eye-hand coordination, and obstacle courses and stations	Sport catalogs, educational supply stores
Hoppities	Four to six of the larger size	Hoppities are large air-filled rubber balls, with a handle, that children sit on and "ride."	Balance, strength, and coordination work, obstacle courses and stations	Sport catalogs, sporting goods stores
Foot stompers	Four to six	Foot stompers are rectangular pieces of wood, approximately 4 inches by 3 feet, with a piece of rounded molding glued in the middle underneath so that they look like small teeter-totters. A child places a beanbag at one end and stomps on the other end, sending the beanbag flying up ready to be caught.	Eye-hand coordination, obstacle courses and stations	Sport catalogs, sporting goods stores, or make your own

(continued)

Table 1.1 *(continued)*

Item	Number needed	Notes	Uses	Where to find
Balance boards	Two to four	Balance boards are like square teeter-totters. Children stand on them and balance.	Obviously great for balance work, used in—you guessed it—obstacle courses and stations	Sport catalogs, educational supply stores, or make your own
Scoopers	Enough for half the class	Scoopers are empty, clean bleach bottles cut so that they form a basketlike catcher. (You can also buy ready-made scoopers.) They are used with any small ball; soft tennis-size balls are perfect.	Eye-hand coordination work, obstacle courses and stations	Sport catalogs, sporting goods stores, or make your own
Foam shapes	One set	Sport and educational catalogs advertise sets of geometric shapes made out of colored foam.	Games, obstacles courses, and language work	Sport and educational catalogs
Bags, onion	Enough for half the class		Partner and coordination work	Can sometimes be found at old-fashioned produce stores or simply can be sewn up
Foam footballs	Four to six		Fun in obstacle courses and stations	Sport and educational catalogs, sporting goods stores, toy and drugstores.
Pogo balls and pogo sticks	Just a few		Wonderful for balance work, and, yes, obstacle courses and stations	Sport and educational catalogs, sporting goods stores, toy stores
Chinese jump ropes	One per child	These are circular elastic ropes.	Excellent for coordination and flexibility work, language, sequencing, and partner activities	Sport and educational catalogs, sporting goods stores
Ringtoss	One set		Any such eye-hand coordination games are great and can be included in obstacle courses.	Sport and educational catalogs, sporting goods stores, toy stores

Item	Number needed	Notes	Uses	Where to find
Be on the lookout for new and used items that can work in your class.		Virtually any piece of equipment that intrigues children can be used in movement class: a cloth tunnel, an exercise ball, pick-up sticks, jacks, a punching ball, or ankle bells.	If the piece of equipment is one item, consider putting it in an obstacle course (chapter 8). If you have enough individual props for at least half the class, use the formula for using props (chapter 9). Obstacle courses and stations are generally the easiest organizations for trying out more unusual items.	The best places for bargains are garage sales and flea markets. Wonderful items can be found in sports catalogs, educational supply stores, on the Internet, and in toy stores.

Closing Thoughts

We can make a difference. Movement classes can significantly change a child. I have a story of the amazing potential of movement. For many years I taught children's dance at a studio. A plump, passive, shy, awkward young girl joined my classes when she was 10 and continued until she was about 16. She left svelte, confident, and enthusiastic. Certainly movement was not the sole factor in her transformation, but it did make a difference. Her father said that I "had saved her life." What is ironic is that the father offered this gross exaggeration years later facing me as the head of the graduate department to which I was applying. He added that what he loved about the program, and what made it so powerful, was the total respect shown each child.

Our motivational bags are packed. We know that our children lack physical conditioning, and we have the assurance that this program fits within the required physical education standards. Our enthusiasm is pumped with the vast array of benefits children will derive from movement classes: preacademic and academic skills, social skills, and lifelong personal skills. We are inspired to try conceptual, precision, and active teaching, and we have a list of necessary equipment in our back pocket. We are ready to go, but the thought of all that moving energy is scary. What we need are class management techniques to keep everything under control—and these we consider in chapter 2.

Chapter 2

Three Class Management Structures

Every teacher has many good ideas. What is needed to implement these ideas is a foundation of class management techniques. Three structures are absolutely necessary for a sound movement program: Free Traveling Structure, Perfect Spots, and Diagonal Structure. These provide the boundaries essential for maintaining control. As all teachers know, control is crucial for any teaching to take place and for anyone to have fun.

1. Free Traveling Structure: The children travel anywhere in the room, moving to a sound, like a tambourine or piano, and freeze immediately when the sound stops.

2. Perfect Spots: The children situate themselves in the room with space all around. They are "far from everything, far from everybody, and facing front."

3. Diagonal Structure: Groups of children line up on one side of the room, move on the diagonal, and line up on the other side of the room. The process is repeated on the opposite diagonal so that the children return to their original places.

If you use nothing else from this book, teach these three structures. I cannot emphasize strongly enough how important these class management organizations are for your ongoing movement program. *Free Traveling Structure, Perfect Spots,* and *Diagonal Structure* are taught within the first four to six lessons. *All future activities use one of these structures as a foundation for control.* For exam-

ple, when one introduces balls, each child gets a ball and has some free time with it. This would be totally chaotic if the class were not trained in the Free Traveling Structure and therefore able to freeze immediately when the sound stopped. These class organizations will allow your year to flow smoothly and enjoyably, and they will also transfer ease of control to activities outside of movement class.

How quickly the structures are taught is up to you and your class. Sometimes two structures can be taught within the first lesson and the third taught next time. On the other hand, some young, immature classes need six months to understand all three structures. But during the time it takes to establish these three class management organizations, we are also teaching activities. For example, most of the first lesson for very young children is spent establishing the Free Traveling Structure; we then immediately use that organization to introduce balls. Even though we have not begun teaching Perfect Spots, we still do stationary exercises by gathering the class around us. Teaching is always juggling.

Once these three structures are taught, they are not taught again (except after a long break like winter vacation). The structures are not ends in themselves but rather a foundation for activities; their function is to facilitate future lessons. Therefore, after one establishes a structure, it is important to use that particular organization. This is somewhat like learning how to sew and then using that skill to make a garment. I have seen student teachers establish Perfect Spots and then immediately go on to an activity in Free Traveling Structure. It is more reasonable to teach Perfect Spots and then use that organization by working on exercises or a stationary movement study. It is also important to choose the correct structure for a planned activity. I have often seen student teachers establish Perfect Spots and then pass out balls. This is a contradiction. Balls cannot remain stationary; they need to be used in the Free Traveling Structure. A conflict in structures will blur the control.

Free Traveling Structure

The Free Traveling Structure teaches children to move to a sound (drum, tambourine, piano, tape, and so on) and stop immediately when the sound stops. It is possible to reverse the process—that is, move in virtual silence and stop at a given signal—but, except with obstacle courses, I use the former arrangement. The children move freely about the room without jostling or bumping into each other. For fast movements like skip, gallop, and run, they move in a tracklike circle; but for slower movements like hop, crawl, and roll, they move anywhere they want. Since everyone is moving at once, you can see if a class has a general idea but not specific footwork.

The Free Traveling Structure is good for

- warm-up activities,
- learning and practicing locomotor movements,
- partner work,
- stamina, and
- almost all work with props.

Teaching the Free Traveling Structure follows a precise sequence of steps. Go through each step, even if briefly. The older the class, the quicker the pace.

Step 1: The children gather on the floor around me (I do not use a circle arrangement); I have a tambourine nearby. "I want you to wiggle your fingers when I say 'start', and stop when I say 'stop.' OK? Start . . . Stop . . . Start . . . Stop . . . Start . . . Stop . . ." I vary the length of time between starts and stops to instill a sense of playfulness and unpredictability. "Now instead

of me saying start and stop, the tambourine will tell you. When you hear the tambourine, wiggle your fingers; when it stops, freeze." I shake the tambourine and slap it for distinct stops; again I play with the rhythm. Then I ask for the wiggle to be shown in the arms, legs, torso, and whole body. For the whole-body shake, I ask the children to go from sitting all the way up to a jump and back down again without stopping the shake. "Wow, that was great!"

If it is not great, do not go on. If your class is young (up to second grade) and not following directions, follow the guidelines for teaching the Free Traveling Structure to very young children as explained later in this section (p. 16). If your class is older (third grade on up) and not following directions, quicken the pace and get tougher. (See the section on discipline in chapter 13, p. 205.)

Step 2: With the idea of start and stop firmly established, we go on to different stationary movements to the tambourine sound: spin on seat; spin on knees; spin any way you want (remember to reverse the spin); bounce the head; stand and bounce shoulders, elbows, knees, bottoms, whole body. "What is it called when you bounce your whole body?" (Jump.) I am lax on the way these movements are executed but extremely strict that no one start before the sound and no one continue after it. I hold the freeze long enough to have it clearly established: "Are your fingers frozen? Are your eyes frozen? Your mouths? Your hair?" However, it is crucial to keep the pace fast and playful. See figure 2.1 for an example of stationary movement with bouncing elbows.

2.1

Step 3: Using jump, we transition from stationary to traveling movements. "You did a great job jumping in place. Now we'll make it harder. Instead of jumping right here, you can jump anywhere you like in our movement room. What do you do when the tambourine stops? . . . Right, freeze." (Be sure to include "in our movement room" for those literalists who are tempted to jump out the door.) From the jump, go on to several basic locomotor movements: hop, skip, gallop, jog.

Step 4: Pick one locomotor movement (I usually choose skip), and play with the length of sound. If you are going on to a different sound—the piano and taped music are optional choices—this is the time to switch. If you are sticking to the tambourine, that is fine. Let the sound last a long time (8 to 16 beats) and then have a series of shorter sound durations. Make it unpredictable. Children love this listening game.

Step 5: You are free to use any locomotor movements for any sound duration. Remember to include the lower-level movements, baby and crab crawl, roll, and slide on the floor. Then move back up to jazzy walk and conclude with an endurance-testing run and leap.

I strongly recommend strict starts and stops. Since the tambourine sound is the only structure here, the children's beginnings and endings need to be visible, clear, and precise. The structure needs to be completely under your control. Further, since Free Traveling Structure is one of the first foundations taught in movement class, the tone set here will carry into many other activities. My motto: Better strict and a bit petty than slack and later sorry.

Two common complaints about the Free Traveling Structure are children falling and children bumping into one another. It is an amazing thing about accidents—most need not happen. Falling and bumping are largely self-controlled. In my classes I place the responsibility fully on the child: "I want you on your feet. If you fall down again you will not be able to run with us." And it works. Of course it takes a snap decision to judge which falls or bumps are real and which are not, but most teachers have an excellent eye.

The key to avoiding accidents is follow-through. If the child is still falling after you warned him, sit him out. If a child continues to bump into others, put her out. Some children with learning disabilities have an almost impossible time with precise stops; decide if he is doing his best. If he is gradually coming to a stop and you believe he can do better, yes, put him out.

➡ TROUBLESHOOTING

We will talk about discipline in chapter 13, but I offer two notes for now. The first time a child sits out, it need be for only a few seconds. But if this is turning into a power struggle, you must win; sit her out for the rest of class. You do not need to be harsh—you can still smile—but the rules must prevail. Also, quicken the pace and make the class as challenging and as fun as possible so that sitting out is a true hardship.

Are you shaking your head in dismay because this work on the Free Traveling Structure seems simplistic? "All she has taught me so far is to get them to stop," you say? It's true. I ask you stay with me. Teaching your class the Free Traveling Structure before you attempt any other activities is the key to success. With just the Free Traveling Structure as a foundation, you can run almost an entire movement program. You will use this structure for most warm-ups, for all partner work, and for almost all work with props. That is well over half the program. Like any other foundation, this one is best if it is strong as steel and not visible. This means that the children need to accept the Free Traveling Structure as a given; you do not have to keep teaching it over and over, nor do you have to keep reminding them to freeze. This foundation allows you the freedom to implement any idea with confidence that the control is already there. It is invaluable.

For very young children (preschool through first grade), we need to approach the Free Traveling Structure in a slightly different way. Young children are often frightened of moving in space. Perhaps the space seems too big or unlimited. Perhaps they have a fear of something new. This fear manifests itself in different reactions: "I don't wanna," tears, or sometimes uncontrolled giggling. Therefore I introduce the Free Traveling Structure to very young children using the rocking lesson. As with the introduction explained previously, the progression is from smaller to bigger movements and from stationary to locomotor, but this lesson includes a security blanket. Because it

We are rocking, rocking, rocking. We are rocking, now we're still.

is safe and nonthreatening, the rocking lesson is an excellent first class for the very young.

The Rocking Song

We are rocking, rocking, rocking.

We are rocking,

Now we're still.

This is how the lesson came about: Many years ago I walked into a class of 15 preschool children who were coming to me for their first dance class. I had prepared what I thought was an excellent lesson: Jump Your Name, Hello and Good-Bye, and Swordfish, all done near me, and beginning locomotor movements done across the room with partners. It was a disaster. During that horrendous half-hour, 7 out of the 15 began to cry. It was definitely one of those "why-did-I-ever-go-into-this-profession" moments. Since then I developed the rocking lesson specifically for young children, and it has worked well.

The Rocking Song is an extremely valuable tool. In addition to being the crux of the following lesson, it can be used for leg and back stretches by varying the body position while rocking, it is useful to reinforce the concept level (chapter 5), and it is a good calming activity (chapter 10).

The rocking lesson has seven steps. If your class is more mature, pick up the pace rather than excluding any steps.

Step 1: Waste absolutely no time. As soon as most of the socks and shoes are put away, we sit on the floor cross-legged and sing the Rocking Song, rocking side to side. We do this once or twice.

Step 2: If the students look near tears I tell them, "Still means stop or freeze." If they look comfortable I take a minute and ask what they think *still* means. The children have already been freezing on the word *still* since they have been imitating me.

Step 3: We rock in several different ways:

a. Sitting with the legs straight ahead, we rock from side to side. The opposite leg lifts as the body leans sideways.

b. Sitting with legs wide, we rock forward and back. For the rock back, the legs lift and the seat rises high in the air (see figure 2.2).

2.2

c. "Let's make it harder," I say. We get on our knees and rock from side to side using hands to push the floor at either side.

d. "Even harder," I say as I pantomime evil intentions. We stand and rock from side to side. Hands do not touch the floor. The opposite leg lifts off the ground as the body leans sideways, and the freeze at the end is a one-foot balance.

Step 4: The Rocking Song is now completely familiar (we have sung it 6 to 10 times). The children and I sit down again. "Do you know what? We don't have to just rock to our song. We could, um, shake. When we shake we will sing, 'We are shaking, shaking, shaking, we are shaking, now we're still.'"

The tune and rhythm are exactly the same; just the one word is changed. We sing the song and shake while sitting. If the children look confident, I ask them to shake and jump in the air and then to shake while lying on the ground. We sing the song and shake, moving continuously from the air to the ground and back up.

Generally, step 4 is a process of changing the word *rocking* in the song to words for different stationary movements. The song is the same and the repetition seems to be quite soothing, but the movements change. Recommended beginning stationary movements are spinning on seats, kicking as in a tantrum, bouncing heads, wiggling, and jumping in place. Any of these words fit rhythmically into the song. Before doing a new movement I ask the children how the song will go. Nine out of 10 have it down pat by now.

Step 5: We are ready for the big step into locomotor movements. "You did jumping perfectly! We are going to jump again; but this time we will not stay right here, we'll jump anywhere we want in our movement room. Do you remember what to do for the word still? Right, freeze."

So we sing and jump around the room. This simple transition starts the children moving confidently in space. If they are with you here, you have them. We do the song using walking, hopping, skipping, galloping, crawling, rolling, running, whatever. By this time they are shouting suggestions to me.

Step 6: The next step introduces a more generalized start and stop structure. "This time when we skip to our song, don't sing out loud. Sing the song silently to yourself as I beat the rhythm on the drum. Remember to freeze on the word still even though we are not saying it out loud."

If you play the piano at all and can pick out the tune, that is better than the drum, but the drum rhythm works adequately. The children move and do not sing. They know rhythmically when to stop. We do this "silent tune" several times with different locomotor movements.

Step 7: Finally, we are ready for the last step. "You are starting and stopping when you hear the sound so well that I am going to make it harder. I am going to play anything I want on the piano [or drum]. As you did with the song, move when you hear the sound, and when the sound stops, freeze." The children have already been doing this but only to one predictable rhythmic length.

Now I play different-length tunes and expect precise starts and stops.

There it is, a simple, incredibly repetitious lesson that is conceptually chock-full. The tone of the class is set, the children have explored some nonlocomotor and locomotor movements, and they have begun the Free Traveling Structure. Most importantly, they have successfully survived their first movement class and so have you. The next lesson might repeat half of this first lesson. By then the children are ready to go on to other things.

Perfect Spots

A Perfect Spot is a stationary space of one's own. It is a place where everyone is "far from everybody, far from everything, facing front." A class should be able to get their Perfect Spots within 10 seconds. In their Perfect Spots, children can do nonlocomotor movements or exercises freely and safely; I can see them and they can see me. Perfect Spots is the most controlled of the three class management structures; just getting their own spots usually calms a class down. Further, the process of getting their own spots is good work in spatial awareness. Teachers love this structure, and many use it outside of movement class.

Perfect Spots are good for

- learning and practicing nonlocomotor movements,
- exercises,
- beginning work on levels,
- beginning work on directions, and
- quieting movements.

I have taught Perfect Spots in many ways. (I will later describe some early trials with spacing.) The most effective teaching method is through the concepts *near* and *far*. Before starting, have large cards with the words *near* and *far* printed on them.

"Why signs?" a kindergarten teacher asked me. Even if the children cannot read yet, the card focuses their attention and makes the lesson more formal, that is, more like a reading or math lesson. For those children who can read, the sign brings another sense into play. My basic teaching principle is simple: The more senses involved the better, and the more specific the concept the better. Therefore, I use the cards and very specific concepts, *near* and *far.*

Step 1: Hold up the card with *near* on it. Have the children come near you. Stop any jostling or pushing right away by praising those that came near quickly without bumping. Then have the children go near a wall, the chairs, the tables, the mats, the doors (if there are several doors in the room, accept children's being near any of them), the floor, the ceiling (by stretching upward), and finally near somebody. I play the tambourine and expect the children to stop when it stops, so that when they get near the designated object they do not keep running somewhere else. Ask them to come near you again in preparation for step 2.

Step 2: Hold the card with *far* on it and ask them to go far from you, far from the walls (all four walls), the doors, the piano, the stage, their shoes, the floor, the ceiling, and finally far from everybody. Far is definitely the harder of the two concepts. Very young children will go far from one wall by running across the room to the opposite wall. There is nothing to be done but run over there, slap the wall so it makes a noise, and ask, "Are you far from all the walls?" Very young children might need more than one lesson on far. "Are you really far from that door? . . . You are too near him; go far from everybody."

If you want, you can linger here and reinforce these two concepts by combining them. For example, I might have the children go near a wall and near a classmate; go near a chair but far from me; go far from the piano and near a door; go far from anybody and near a wall.

Step 3: Perfect Spots result from putting together two fars. "I am going to tell you two things to go far from, and this is going to be hard. Ready? Go far from everybody and far from everything. There you will have your Perfect Spot. When you have it, sit down."

The first few times the children find their Perfect Spots, if you (and your back) agree, walk around and shake hands—or feet—with them: "Congratulations! You found your Perfect Spot. How great!" I make sure everyone gets a correct spot and is included in the shake. Children like the shake, especially of their feet, and it reinforces the term Perfect Spots.

Step 4: After the children understand how to space themselves in a room (it might be in 15 minutes; it might be in a month), I add the final ingredient of a truly Perfect Spot: facing front. I designate one wall of the room as front and ask the children to align themselves so that they face it completely. "Face straight front, the way the floor boards go." If you have linoleum floors, you could refer to the lines created between the tiles. I physically help children who do not understand. It is important that they face the front wall and not the teacher, so that they do not end up angled in a semicircle. For the next few weeks I am extremely fussy that the children face absolutely straight front, and I will stop whatever I am doing to correct even a slightly angled child. It is important the class face straight front for several reasons:

a. Right and left are easily checked and later work on laterality is simplified.

b. It is safe to do large movements like kicks.

c. You are able to move around the classroom without the children constantly turning to face you.

Figure 2.3 shows a completed Perfect Spot structure.

What happens to children not in a Perfect Spot? If a child is next to something, like a chair, I bang on the object and say, "Are you far from everything?" The child usually realizes her mistake and finds a correct spot. Often children are oblivious of what is in back of them. They need to be reminded to look around and make sure they are far from everything. If a child is totally lost, for example under a table, I will gently drag him by the legs: "Let me give you a ride to your Perfect Spot. See, now you have room all round you." Usually totally lost children are just frightened, since Perfect Spots is one of the first lessons in movement class. They generally pick up the idea as soon as they relax a bit.

If more than three or four children are lost, start completely over. More likely than not this new start needs to be more formal, more academically oriented. Movement class is not physical education; it is education through the physical. To learn through movement the children need to follow your instructions precisely. Go slowly. If

2.3

the children go near a table when you have asked them to go near a chair, correct them. If they start to run wildly around the room, stop everything. Perhaps make a competitive game out of it: "Only the children who listen will be able to play; if you do not follow the instructions you will be out of the game." You probably will not need to do this; simply your attitude that this is a worthwhile subject will convey itself to the children and they will treat movement respectfully.

Let's pause for a brief testimonial. I asked a teacher friend to follow my instructions with her kindergarten class. After trying Perfect Spots the first time, she said the children went crazy: "I was scared and stopped, and we did something I was used to doing. But I was determined, so the second time I did exactly the same thing except I had a 'get tough' attitude. I insisted they do exactly as I wanted and I slowed down until they did. This movement doesn't mean move; it means move with a purpose. It worked and worked well."

I teach Perfect Spots this way to 5- and 12-year-olds. Despite the lesson's formality children find it fun. In addition, it works.

I cannot emphasize enough the importance of Perfect Spots. It is one of the basic structures necessary for future movement activities. Movement is a natural chaos producer. But chaos is

not freedom. I know you want your children to be uninhibited; however, they will not develop this freedom in an unstructured class. It is hard to be nice, to experiment, or to play with children if they are unruly. The class needs to be orderly and manageable, and you need to feel comfortable. You need to be able to say "Get your Perfect Spots" and know that within 10 seconds your entire class is there. Only then are you free to be spontaneous, and only then are the children free to experiment and create.

The method of teaching Perfect Spots conceptually through near and far works dramatically well. It was discovered after many years of trial and error, mostly error.

The first time I introduced Perfect Spots, I said to my class that their Perfect Spots were places where they could extend their arms, spin, and not touch anyone. I demonstrated spinning with extended arms, and the children started spinning with extended arms. The children would not stop spinning. They spun faster and faster, crashed into one another, fell down, and started fighting. That was the first dance class I ever taught!

I concluded that the children did not have an awareness of space around them. With a great deal of effort I made name cards for everyone and taped them down around the room in Perfect Spots. I did this for each class—and at that time

I taught six to eight classes a day! It was totally exhausting picking up and putting down all those name cards. (This brings me to a rather strange theory: If an activity takes too much work and is drudgery for you, it is probably irrelevant.) The children simply had to find their own name and they had a Perfect Spot. This was easy. We practiced several times and then removed the cards. What do you guess happened? The children remembered exactly who they were next to but had no idea of how far away from each other they had been; for example, Yolanda remembered she had been between Yvette and Robert, so she stood directly next to them and that was that.

In order to teach general spacing within a room, I decided we needed to scale it down so the children would understand the concept as a whole. I placed a large piece of paper on the floor and said, "This is our room." (This unfortunately was before I discovered room representations, which you will read about in chapter 6.) I gave each child a small rock and asked them to place the rocks in the "room" so there was plenty of paper showing around them. The result? There were a few rocks on the paper, some spaced and some not. However, most of the children became enamored of their rocks and would not give them up at all.

As they say in storybooks, that was when I sat down and thought for a long time. I came up with a basic question from my Montessori training: What preconcepts are the children lacking in order to understand the concept Perfect Spot? It became clear. They needed to know how near and how far they are from other people and things. That is how I came to a workable method of teaching Perfect Spots.

From this process, I have come up with several observations:

- To work, any teaching method must be right for you. What is right for you may not be right for another teacher.

- A workable teaching method must be comfortable and relatively easy.

- What did not work once may work later.

- What did not work once may have to be scrapped. (To discern what should be kept and what should be scrapped is the tricky part.)

- Teaching is hard work.

Firecracker

Once the children can find their own Perfect Spots, it is a good idea to play a game that speeds up the process. The end goal is for classes to find their spots within 10 seconds so that there is no interference in the flow to the Perfect Spots activity. Firecracker is played in the lesson or two after Perfect Spots is established; when Perfect Spots is first introduced, it is enough that the children find their spots once. Firecracker is appropriate for preschool to fourth grade; older children are simply admonished to get their Perfect Spots quickly.

Step 1: Gathering the children in one corner of the room, I say, "We are one big firecracker. I am going to light the fuse and when it pops, you run and find your Perfect Spot as fast as you can. Pssssssssss [I make the sound of a lighted fuse with my voice and the tambourine shaking] . . . POP!" The children run and find Perfect Spots. I discourage set spots, that is, always sitting in the same place. I quickly correct a child sitting near anything, and if more than two children need help, I consider reteaching Perfect Spots altogether.

Step 2: For the next round, I gather the children into a different corner of the room: "It took about 20 seconds to find your Perfect Spots. Do you think you could do a 10-second firecracker?" Then I try a 5-second firecracker, then possibly a 3-second one. In a typical game we play three or four rounds, getting faster and faster, until I pretend to faint because they are so terrific.

That's it. You can vary the game, if you need more control, so that the children are balloons: "You are all balloons floating around the room. When I touch you, pop to a Perfect Spot." This is a quieter version, but you will miss the exhilaration of the whole class rushing into their Perfect Spots.

Once Perfect Spots are established, I use the structure to introduce exercises. You can present any exercises with which you are familiar: calisthenics, yoga, and so forth. Following are a few beginning exercises that are actually loved.

Hello and Good-Bye

Hello and Good-Bye is an excellent first exercise that can range from preschool to sixth grade. It is good for

- foot and ankle warm-up,
- abdominal and back strength,
- coordination,
- understanding the concept word opposite, and
- focus of attention.

The children sit in Perfect Spots with their arms and legs straight in front of them. In the hello position, their feet and hands are flexed; that is, toes and fingers are pulled hard toward the ceiling (see figure 2.4).

2.4

In the good-bye position, hands and feet point down; that is, toes and fingers are pulled hard toward the floor, while arms and heels remain stationary (see figure 2.5).

2.5

Step 1: Stage 1 of this exercise simply alternates the hello and good-bye positions. Watch that the feet move distinctly and with energy. Stage 2 of Hello and Good-Bye uses opposites. First, both feet say hello while both hands say good-bye; they switch back and forth. Then, one hand and one foot say hello while the other hand and foot say good-bye (see figure 2.6).

2.6

Step 2: The hands and feet switch back and forth slowly and then in more complicated rhythms. Here is an example of a possible rhythm where each note is a switch position.

Finally, one foot says hello while the hand on the same side says good-bye; the other foot says good-bye while that hand says hello. In other words everything is in opposites. Switch everything!

Step 3: The last stage of Hello and Good-Bye includes the torso. (See the next section for an introduction to torso.) With the hands and feet saying hello the torso stretches tall, reaching for the ceiling (see figure 2.7).

2.7

With good-bye hands and feet, the torso lies back so that the body is fully extended on the ground (see figure 2.8). Allow the knees to bend a little so as not to strain the back. We go back and forth with full-body hellos and good-byes slowly to increase muscular control, and then more quickly. The children join me in calling out the hellos and good-byes, ending with a loud "Oh, good-bye!!" shouted as if in anger. This exercise is a fun way of doing sit-ups.

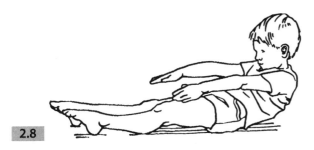

2.8

Torso

Teaching about the torso is appropriate for preschool to third grade and is good for

- learning this body part,
- isolation movement, and
- expanded movements.

Children start sitting in Perfect Spots. Teaching Torso works very well immediately following Hello and Good-Bye.

Step 1: I introduce torso by a process of elimination: "Shake your arm so hard [the children and I all shake an arm vigorously] that it flies away! [The arm circles back as if it had flown off and then returns to the side of the body.] Shake your other arm so hard [same movement] that it flies off! Shake your leg so hard . . . it flies away! Shake your other leg so hard . . . it flies away! Shake your head and neck [shake head gently; shaking too hard could cause strain or a headache] until it flies off!" (Head rolls back and returns to center.) "We have gotten rid of our arms, legs, heads, and necks. What is left?"

Children normally answer: "Stomach." "Our bodies." "Seat." "Waist."

"That's right. What is left is the middle part of our body, and that is called our torso."

Step 2: After we practice saying the word *torso*, extending the syllables, saying the word quickly, changing the syllable we accent, I ask the children to pat their own torsos all over and say the word as they do so. This is simply to associate the name with the place. Here we come to a policy decision. Whether you touch your breasts and lower abdominal area or you do not, the children will giggle. They giggle if you touch and they giggle if you avoid touching. I believe that too many people are alienated from their own bodies and that this distance usually stems from experiences in childhood. One movement teacher brazenly touching her own breasts will not sway this tide of alienation, but prim avoidance may reinforce it. I am not terribly uninhibited; I have a bit of trouble with this. But I very strongly want to impart to my children that the body, every part of it, is worthy of respect. So, without making a fuss or commotion about it we all gently pat our torsos, front, side, back, from shoulders to hip joints, while saying the word *torso*.

"Now that you know where you torso is, let's see how many different ways your torso can move." The children will come up with some ideas, for example, wiggling or shaking, twisting, bending and straightening. You might also suggest a curl-up or contract and stretch (even if this has not been officially taught), bouncing, circling, and swinging. It is best if just the torso initiates the movements. Arms and other parts of the body might follow, but we are finding ways the torso can essentially move on its own. After this lesson if you ask what *torso* means, most children will pat their middle and wiggle when they answer.

Swordfish

Swordfish is appropriate for preschool to third grade, but older children actually like it if they feel safe enough to pretend to be younger. The exercise is good for

- leg stretch and strength,
- abdominal control and strength, and
- balance.

The children sit in Perfect Spots with their legs straight in front of them.

Step 1: One leg lifts "straight as a swordfish," that is, very stretched with toes pointed, knees straight. (It is possible to ask specifically for right or left legs to reinforce those terms.) This "swordfish leg" proceeds to "swim"; that is, it moves about, crosses the body, and then stretches wide. The other leg remains on the floor.

Step 2: "Suddenly," you announce, "the mean old fisherman catches the swordfish." The children grab one of their legs with both hands behind the knee (see figure 2.9).

2.9

"The fish then says, 'Let me go! Let me go! Let me go! Free.'" For each "Let me go," the leg does tap-tap-stretch, touching the floor for each tap and lifting up for the stretch. For the word "free" the hands let go of the leg. The leg stays held rigid for a few seconds and then is lowered (see figure 2.10).

2.10

This process is repeated with the other leg. The children call out the words "Let me go! Let me go! Let me go! Freeeee" with me. I ask them to start sadly and then get louder and louder "like you're really mad." Children always seem so sur-

prised when I ask them to yell. (One first grader suggested that the fisherman would let go of the fish if we added a "please.")

Step 3: Next, both legs become "swordfish." I have the children lean on their elbows, rather than lie flat, to avoid back strain. The "swordfish legs" do the same thing as the single legs; they "swim" with knees straight and toes pointed. Sometimes the "swordfish become friends" (legs move parallel, close together); sometimes they "have a fight" (straight-leg scissors). "But they make up and are friends again" (parallel legs and kissing sounds), "and that is when the fisherman catches both of them!" The children sit up quickly and grab both legs behind the knees. "The swordfish say, 'Let us go! Let us go! Let us go! Free.'" As with the individual legs, both legs do tap-tap-stretch for the words "Let us go!" That means that the children must balance on their seats each time their legs stretch up; this is a good challenge (figure 2.11). Before they lower their legs on the word "free," see if the children can hold the ending balance on their seat with arms and legs outstretched.

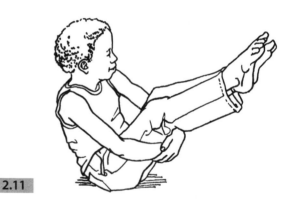

2.11

Blastoff

The movement sequence in this exercise is appropriate for preschool to sixth grade, but use the rocket ship image up to third grade only. It is good for

- total body conditioning and
- pre-gymnastics skills and challenges.

Children sit in Perfect Spots. There are three stages to Blastoff. Each stage proceeds through a countdown, "10, 9, 8, 7, 6, 5, 4, 3, 2, 1, 0," and

"Blastoff!" For each stage, the countdown is a downward stretch, and the "blastoff" is a held balanced position.

Step 1: The children sit on the floor with the soles of their feet "clapped" together. They grasp their ankles—not the toes—and straighten their backs "rocket ship straight" (see figure 2.12).

2.12

➡ *SAFETY*

When you tell the children to grasp their ankles, make sure that they aren't grabbing their toes instead. Grabbing the toes causes the feet to twist.

A note on how to help children pull torsos up: Put your knee against the middle of the child's back and gently but firmly pull back the shoulders. If you have an especially bony knee, use the side of the knee. (See "Alignment" in chapter 10 for overall posture correction.) The child is ready to count down and "blast off." For the count "10 . . . 0," slowly round the back toward the feet so that on "0" ideally the child's "nose is touching his toes" or is as near to the nose as possible (see figure 2.13).

2.13

For the "blastoff," the child puts her hand on the floor close to her seat, plants her feet on the floor, and stretches up with the other hand. This makes a high bridge stretching the pelvic area and torso in general. The child comes down, twirls on her seat, and does the same stretch on the other side. I then ask the class to lift one leg and balance on the remaining hand and foot—this is difficult. The trick is to stretch hard, lifting the weight up (see figure 2.14).

2.14

The children come down, ready for the next stage.

Step 2: The children sit with their legs straight in front of them. Legs are "railroad straight," with toes saying "good-bye" and torso "rocket ship straight." A body of mixed metaphors! Children slowly round their back down for the countdown, "10 . . . 0," ideally touching their nose to their knees by "0" (see figure 2.15).

2.15

"Blastoff" for stage 2 is a traditional bridge: Arms twist back, knees bend, and the child pushes up into a back bend. The trick is in the hands twisting back; once that is achieved the bridge

2.16

can get higher, with the arms straightening, and the head lifts off the floor (see figure 2.16).

It is important to insist on gently pushing up and, even more important, gently coming down. For coming down, I ask for one part of the body at a time: head, shoulder, waist, hips. In addition to preventing bruises, this slow round-down is good for strength and general control.

Step 3: The children sit with legs in wide stride. (After "turn out" is taught, as described in chapter 10, this is a good place to work on that technique. At this point just mention that the knees should not drop toward the center.) Again children work to sit "rocket ship straight," which is difficult in this position. They round down for the countdown "10 . . . 0" (see figure 2.17).

2.17

At this point, with the children working to round their backs while sitting in wide-stride position, you will probably have to deal with at least one child whining, "I can't do it." I do not have a set procedure for dealing with that awful sound. Sometimes I just ignore it. Sometimes I have long talks with the class about the futility of *can't*. Usually I say, "Go as far as you can. Let

it hurt a little to stretch you out but don't let it hurt too much."

"Blastoff" for stage 3 is a yoga plough position: The legs swing overhead, working to touch the ground behind the head with the knees straight (see figure 2.18). From the plough position, we carefully go up into a shoulder stand: The children hold their hips up with their hands, legs reaching for the ceiling.

2.18

Maybe I Don't; Maybe I Do

Maybe I Don't; Maybe I Do is appropriate for preschool to third grade. It is good for

- relaxed, lowered shoulders;
- isolation work; and
- coordination.

Children, as well as grown-ups, often confuse good posture with stiffness. This is especially noticeable in raised, tense shoulders. To unhitch this tension I use Maybe I Don't; Maybe I Do.

Step 1: The children sit with the soles of the feet clapped together, knees out, hands holding ankles. This is the stage 1 position of Blastoff, and I frequently do this exercise immediately before Blastoff. I ask the children to get "rocket ship straight" or simply ask them to pull up their torsos.

Step 2: Pulling my shoulders up to my ears, I say, "I don't know." (Children imitate gesture and words.) Usually I ham it up with exaggerated facial gestures of not knowing. Shoulders pulled way down go with the statement "Yes I do!" This alternation between "I don't know" and "Yes I do!" is repeated several times. From there, one shoulder goes up while the other stays down: "Maybe I do," "Maybe I don't," repeated. The children say the "maybes" as they alternate shoulders up and down. The "maybes" are repeated a few times; then one final "I don't know" (shoulders way up) is followed by an emphatic "Oh yes I do!!" (shoulders way down). After students learn Maybe I Don't; Maybe I Do, if somebody's upper back gets tense, ask for "Oh yes I do" shoulders.

Diagonal Structure

The Diagonal Structure moves children individually or in small groups across the diagonal, down the other side of the room, and across the opposite diagonal. It is the old dance studio form of moving across the floor. This structure allows the longest unencumbered space for locomotor movements (the diagonal of the room) and allows you to see each child clearly. In a perfectly functioning Diagonal Structure, the children quickly get their own groups (usually three to five in a group), remainders are identified and either form a smaller group or join others, and the groups start at a given time without you having to yell "Go."

The Diagonal Structure is good for

- working on difficult locomotor movements,
- locomotor movement patterns,
- some work on levels,
- some work on directions,
- some props,
- one game, and
- testing.

What the Diagonal Structure is not good for is introducing locomotor movement steps. When first trying a new movement or steps to a dance, people of all ages do not like to be watched. They want to minimize their risk by hiding in the group. So the Free Traveling Structure is preferable for introducing locomotor movements; the Diagonal Structure is better for showing them off. Also, because of the wait, the Diagonal Structure does not tire children out so it does not work for a warm-up. Do not get me wrong—the Diagonal Structure is very valuable, but it cannot replace the Free Traveling Structure.

Like the other two class organizations, the Diagonal Structure is taught in precise steps.

Step 1: I start by teaching the concept *diagonal*. Holding a piece of paper with a diagonal line drawn on it, I say, "This kind of line is a diagonal line." I point to another corner on the paper and ask, "Where would I have to go to make the same kind of line, a diagonal line, from this corner?" The second line is not visibly drawn but marked by a finger traversing the paper. We turn the paper over and find the diagonal lines on the back of the paper. This is done several times by individual children.

Most children 4 years old and up understand the idea of diagonal lines easily. If a majority of the class have it, I go on to the next step; the rest of the class will pick it up with repetition. If most of the children are having trouble finding the diagonal lines on the paper, I start over and visibly draw the lines. In this case I do not go on to the next step. I reintroduce diagonal lines another day, until the children can mark the diagonal lines on paper without a visual representation.

Step 2: The next step is to mark diagonal lines throughout the room. I find any clear rectangle or square, point to one corner, and ask, "Where do I have to go to make a diagonal line from this corner?" For example, we go to the chalkboard where I point to one corner and ask, "Where do I have to go from here on this chalkboard to make a diagonal line?" The line is traced in the air, landing in the appropriate corner. We do the same with windows, doors, piano backs, tabletops, mats, tissue boxes, whatever I find that can demonstrate clear diagonal lines. I move rather quickly from object to object, and the class runs with me. In tone, the lesson is like a game.

We then move on to the larger diagonals in the room. "If I were standing at this corner of the ceiling, where would I have to go to make a diagonal line?" The children find both diagonals on the ceiling and then find both diagonals on the floor. At this point the concept diagonal is firmly established.

Step 3: Before we can complete setting up the Diagonal Structure we have to detour into groups. It is extremely rare that I use the Diagonal Structure individually; it is not wise or workable to have 20 to 34 children waiting for one another to finish moving across the diagonal. Group work encompasses the children's ability to form their own groups and the group's ability to stay together. The most important technique in getting children to form their own groups is patience. "Get into groups of four" I say, and I wait. I have waited as long as 10 minutes! Asking children to get their own groups is a good responsibility and self-discipline exercise; once they understand that you will not do it for them, they will come through. At least one or two groups will form and I start them moving across the diagonal; the others will join. (If you have an unusually reluctant child, quickly stash him in a group yourself.) Recently, I have found that if I have used partners previously in the lesson, asking partners to remember who they were with, I can ask for the partners to combine into groups of four and this goes much faster. (Do not ask for remembered partners and then divide into groups of three.) The groups line up along one side of the room. In my movement room, I have the piano angled in the corner, forming a clear designation for the first corner—a cone or other marker would do just as well. The first group lines up behind the piano, and the other groups line up beside them.

If the division is uneven, I say, "You are all in groups of four and there is a remainder of one." In order to remove any stigma to the idea of remainder, I continue, "Congratulations, remainder [I shake her hand]—you get to join any group you want, and they will welcome you! That group will have five." A remainder of three becomes the last group. If you want, take a minute at this point and skip count your groups, "4, 8, 12 . . ." for an instant math reinforcement. Later in the year, for older classes, I quickly write the division problem that they have just executed; for example, 33 divided by 4 equals 8 with a remainder of 1.

What about meanness? If children state a preference in choosing their groups, "We want Howard," I think that is fine. If there is obvious exclusion, "We don't want Howard," I come down hard with full authority: "That is mean. You will not act like that. I do not care if you like Howard or not, but you absolutely cannot act in any way that makes him feel bad." I expect a genuine-sounding welcome, not reluctant compliance, or I will sit the offending children out. I do not use

heavy-handed authority much. I use it mostly when safety and meanness are at issue. In the long run the children appreciate this because if I will not let them be mean to Howard, I will not let Howard be mean to them.

In any case, everybody, including the youngest kindergarteners, gets his own group and lines up along one side of the room. Once the groups are formed, it is another story to keep them together—more on that later. Hopefully it will take you less time to set up the groups than it did to read this.

Step 4: Now we are ready to establish the Diagonal Structure. With the groups on one side of the room, the first group runs across the diagonal and then walks along the opposite side of the room. I do not specify how they should organize themselves as they move across the diagonal. Usually, they don't run single file or four across; they simply run in a bunch. As soon as the first group has started running, the second group gets ready in the beginning corner. When everyone has had a turn on the first diagonal, the process is repeated on the cross diagonal until each child is back at her starting place (see figure 2.19, a and b).

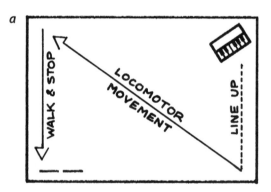

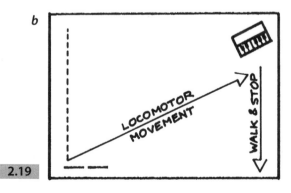

2.19

Two Important Refinements

We go on to practice many different locomotor movements on the diagonals: run and leap, run and leap turn, kicks, one-legged skips, jazzy walk, and so on. Two refinements make the Diagonal Structure easier to use: perfect corners and cause-and-effect starts. From the beginning I am fussy that the children use the corners fully. When a group finishes the diagonal they need to go all the way into the corner rather than rounding it out. These "perfect" corners are necessary to utilize the full length of the diagonal, and they make for a neater and more precise organization.

A cause-and-effect start refers to any system in which the children begin moving on the diagonal without your telling them. The easiest cause-and-effect start is this: "When the group ahead of you gets to the end of the diagonal, you start." Another basic start is having subsequent groups begin when the group ahead crosses the middle of the diagonal. I have the middle marked with a large tape "X" until the concept middle is taught later in the year (see chapter 6). Any clear mark can be used for the cause-and-effect start.

For young classes I stick with the end of the diagonal as the signal for the next group to go. For older classes I like to be able to switch: The end of the diagonal is used as the signal when the students are doing large, fast movements like leaps, and a shorter distance is used for slower movements. These different cause-and-effect starts are established in the course of the first five or six weeks of movement class.

Whatever the system, it is imperative that the children learn to watch and take responsibility for starting on their own. Easier said than done. "You're late! Come back, group 1, and let's see if group 2 can watch and start at the right time. No, you're too early! Wait until they are done with the diagonal. Where are you, group 3?"

The effort needed to establish this self-maintaining cause-and-effect start is worth it. It lets the Diagonal Structure move at a constant flow, releases you from a needless task, and imposes a good self-reliance problem on the children. The best thing about the Diagonal Structure is the exhilaration of moving unrestricted through a long, open space. Children today are very closed in; for many inner city kids it is not safe to move freely about the neighborhood. For a few seconds, flying down that diagonal, they are unfettered. The Diagonal Structure is also important for a sense of mastery, for polishing a movement and conquering a pattern. It is a useful assessment tool for you because you can stand back and clearly see who actually got it and who did not. As one of the three class management organizations, the Diagonal Structure serves as a foundation for a number of future activities.

Freeway

After the Diagonal Structure has been established for a while, it is time to try something that you will probably find scary. Have the children in groups of three or four on one side of the room: "Group 1, run on the diagonal . . . OK, group 2 . . . 3 . . . Now stop. Groups 4 through 6, stay on your side. Group 1, are you ready to go on your diagonal? Group 4, are you ready to go on your diagonal? [They will be crossing diagonals.] OK, both groups, you are going to run as fast as you can at the same time but with NO DISASTERS. Ready for Freeway? Go . . . Now groups 2 and 5 . . . Wow, that was a close call. Groups 3 and 6, are you ready?" I pick up the pace so that there is eventually no stop and the freeway just keeps going until the structure spontaneously falls apart into giggles.

In 30 years of doing Freeway I have not had one actual crash (plenty of near misses). If I even sensed real danger I would stop the activity at once. Children know how to avoid losing something they love.

Closing Thoughts

The three class management organizations—Free Traveling Structure, Perfect Spots, Diagonal Structure—are the most valuable tools I can impart. With this foundation in place you can proceed to teach any movement activity with ease and control. When children master these structures they understand that movement is a subject, not recess time. They also have a more complete awareness of themselves in space, and they have made great strides in self-discipline. Seems nothing short of a miracle.

With the control necessary to teach, we venture into what to present. Chapters 3 through 6 offer a foundation of basic movement concepts: locomotor and nonlocomotor movements, levels, directions, and floor patterns. These concepts organize our thinking about movement: which movements stay or go, what height they are, what plane of the body leads, and what spatial designs are made. These concepts are not fancy or flashy; they are the nuts and bolts groundwork of all physical activities, physical education, dance, gymnastics, and so on. We'll talk about flash in part II.

Chapter 3

Locomotor Movements

Locomotor movements are those that "go somewhere." Traveling through space—running, skipping, jumping, rolling, walking, leaping—is at the heart of most dance, at the heart of most children. In addition to being one of the most fun parts of movement class, locomotor movements are essential for muscular growth, endurance, and coordination. They are a central part of any movement program.

As natural as locomotor movements are to movement class, they are natural chaos producers. More than stationary movements, locomotor movements need to be ordered for safety and control. Therefore, once introduced, locomotor movements are executed in one of two class organizations described in the previous chapter: the Free Traveling Structure or the Diagonal Structure. The Free Traveling Structure is an efficient way to have everyone explore an activity without being watched too closely. It is best for warm-ups, introducing new moves, and working with props and partner activities. The Diagonal Structure allows small groups to freely access the longest line in the room. It is best for large locomotor movements and patterns, testing, and group work.

When we look at dance, it appears that there are an infinite number of locomotor movements, but essentially there are 12 movements and myriad variations on these basic steps. After introducing locomotor movements, this chapter presents a catalog of basic locomotor movements, their leading variations, and patterns and dances combining several movements.

Introducing Locomotor Movements

I formally introduce locomotor movements during the second or third class, although we have used these movements from the very start. We begin with the word. As with most definition work, I teach the sound of the word first and then its meaning. The children and I sit gathered on the floor. I say the word *locomotor* slowly and have the children say it after me. We play with the syllables, "loooooooooocomotor, locomoooooooooootor, lo-co-mo-tor, locomotor [very fast], loco-motor," until the word is familiar.

I point out that our word has a *motor* in it and ask the children for examples of things that have motors. This method of teaching the meaning of *locomotor* is effective but can be dangerous! Usually children will say "cars," "trucks," "motorcycles." This is great because all these things go somewhere. However, you might have one child who says "washing machine." If a child brings up an example of a stationary motor there is nothing to do but say that *locomotor* uses its motor to go somewhere. You can bypass the whole thing and simply tell the children the definition of *locomotor*; but you will also be bypassing some fun and a useful memory tool for this long word.

We then combine the word *locomotor* with locomotor movements so that the word is associated with the activity. I ask the children to stand on one side of the room.

"Locomotor means going somewhere," I say. "We are going to go somewhere, from this side of the room to the other. How can we go?"

"Run."

"Walk."

"Jump."

"I don't know."

"Skip."

"Run."

"Great," I say, "Let's start with walk. We will do the locomotor movement walk to the other side of the room. Walk and say the word 'lo-co-mo-tor' as you go. Do it as if you were angry so I can hear you." We stomp across the room, shouting lo-co-mo-tor—one syllable per step.

"What different locomotor movement can we do going back to the other side of the room?" (I use the entire phrase *locomotor movement* every time I refer to a movement in space, for example "Let's do the locomotor movement run" or "You did a wonderful locomotor movement skip," until the children are at ease with—perhaps tired of—the word.)

As the children think of possible locomotor movements, we do them across the room while sounding out the rhythm of the word *locomotor*. Jump (two feet), hop (one foot), and walk are done with the word broken into even syllables: lo-co-mo-tor. Skip and gallop bring an uneven rhythm into play:

skip

lo co mo tor

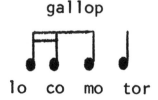

gallop

lo co mo tor

The movements roll, crawl, and slide on the floor are jumbled rhythmically.

I ask, "How else can we go from this side of the room to the other?" until the children come up with most of the basic locomotor movements: walk, run, jump, hop, skip, gallop, crawl, roll, and slide on the floor. If the children do not think of these movements, I gently prod: "How does a ball go downhill? How does a baby get somewhere? How does a snake move? How does a horse move?"

Run is the best, and I save it for last. If the children suggest it earlier I tell them we are saving it for the end. I ask the children to "run so fast that you go from this side of the room to the other just in the time it takes to shout 'locomotor' once." I demonstrate, running and shouting "loocoomootooooor," completing it at the moment I arrive. Each child tries it out. Hearing the word 20 times pretty well ingrains it! As a finale, we all charge and shout at once. This "charge" is a good example of exuberance resting on control. The class will of course be noisy, running and yelling in a loosely formed bunch, but there should be no wildness.

➜ SAFETY

The tone of the class should already be set by the three class management structures. It is one of unwavering self-discipline—fun is always within bounds. If you feel as though the class is verging out of control, stop and explain the need for restraint; no one can have fun if it is not safe. Do the charge over again until you achieve balance.

There is no doubt that at the end of this introduction the word *locomotor* and the idea of traveling in space will be firmly associated.

Most often I conclude a beginning lesson on locomotor movements with a simple study or pattern. For example, I might have the children do a different locomotor movement for each side of the room: skip along one side of the room, crawl backward along one side, roll on one side, and run on one side. I do a simple study like this even with older children, making the locomotor movements harder: skip backward on one side, jump and turn on one side, roll with your knees to your chin, and run the last side. Gentle classes can execute a study like this all together, but if you prefer, divide the class into halves or thirds. While one group performs, the rest of the class sits on one side of the room.

Here are a few more initial locomotor movement studies:

- Any visible mark can help establish a pattern. For example, I might say, "Start at the double doors; side-slide to the piano; hop to my desk; run to the stage; and slide on your back—pushing with just your legs—to the double doors, ready to start again."

- Have a long piece of tape marking the middle of the room. Children can start on one side; run to the middle, fall down, and roll to the other side; and jump back to the middle, fall down, and crawl to the original side.

- An initial study can use the diagonal lines in a room before you teach the concept *diagonal* if you signify corners of the room, for example: "Run to the corner where the piano is," or "Run to the corner near the side door." The diagonals afford children the longest unfettered space available, so this type of study can be very exciting. Have the children run one diagonal line, jump across the side of the room, skip the opposite diagonal line, and hop—changing feet every four beats—across the other side. The children move on the two diagonals at the same time, but "No disasters!"

Even at this early stage the children are asked to remember the study by themselves. I call it out or do it with them the first time, and then they practice until they can do it perfectly alone.

CATALOG OF LOCOMOTOR MOVEMENTS

Following is a catalog of locomotor movements and their leading variations. It is certainly not exhaustive, but my goal is twofold. I hope the realization that there are only 12 basic locomotor movements calms any fears that movement is esoteric or overwhelming. I also hope that the numerous variations open up vast possibilities, the limitless potential of movement.

This catalog covers a broad range of moves, from easy steps to professional dance vocabulary. Do not feel that you need to teach all movements. The variations are only possibilities. Start with the basic steps and expand as you and your class get more comfortable. Further, do not expect that all the movements will be done perfectly. The basic steps need to be clear and correct—jumps with solid two-foot landings, side-slides going straight to the side—but the execution of the more advanced steps is up to you. School classes would not be expected to polish the movements like studio classes.

❶ *Walk*

Walk is an alternation of weight within a momentum. (But you already knew how to walk.) A walk can have an uneven shift of weight (as in a limp),

the momentum can go in any direction, and the movement can use various body parts (such as hands as well as feet).

Variations

1. Directions: Forward, backward, sideways, turning.
2. Warming up the foot:
   a. Tiptoe.
   b. Walk on heels. (Do this only for a few seconds; otherwise it hurts.)
   c. Toe-toe-heel-heel, alternating two tiptoe walks with two heel walks.
   d. Toe-toe-heel-heel-in-in-out-out. This is two tiptoe steps, followed by two heel steps, followed by two inside arch steps, and finally two outside arch steps. Difficult!
   e. Roll from heel smoothly to toe and balance.
3. Emotions: Angry (stomp), joyous, scared (cowering), sneaky (creep), guilty, tired (trudge), and so on.
4. Silly.

5. Heavy; light.

6. High; low.

7. Twisted or crooked; straight.

8. Stiff, like a robot or soldier; limp, like a rag doll.

9. Noisily; quietly.

10. Age: Old, young, middle-aged, teenaged.

11. Leading part: Have one part of the body lead the walk—elbow, abdomen, chin, hip, foot, seat, and so on.

12. Focus on different body parts: Hand, knee, toe, elbow, and so on (see chapter 12).

13. Environments: Walk through glue (molasses, honey, etc.); on eggs and don't break them; through a jungle, feathers, stickers, whatever.

14. Jazzy walk. This is the all-time favorite. With jazzy music playing, ask for a walk that is jazzy, "cool," "bad," whatever is the current appropriate word. ("Groovy" is dead.)

→ TROUBLESHOOTING

Depending on the socioeconomic area of your school, you might see children pretending to smoke or act drunk for their jazzy walk. I believe we need to be a voice proclaiming, "You will not smoke. You will not get drunk." This type of action has the potential of bringing up some very personal issues. I remember a "macho" little boy who consistently pretended to smoke marijuana to look cool. Of course I denounced smoking in class, but later, privately and casually, I asked him about it. He shared concerns that were weighing heavily on him, and we were able to lance a very infected home situation. Movement can come close to therapy—we need to tread carefully.

15. Waltz walk: One low step followed by two high steps—low-high-high. This is a difficult movement, but it is basic dance vocabulary. What makes the waltz walk so hard is its "threeness"; that is, if the right foot steps low, followed by two high steps, then the left foot has to step low to start the new waltz walk. Because most mistakes are "fudges" so that the same foot can start each waltz walk, I start the introduction to this step by eliminating the alternation. We begin with four low steps and four high steps, then three low and three high, then two and two. Finally I ask for one low and two high steps, which is the waltz walk. For advanced students you can include waltz-walk turns. The turn occurs on the two high steps. If the right foot has stepped low, the turn moves to the right; if the left foot steps low, the turn moves to the left. The waltz-walk turn can be done to one side, that is, alternating one straightforward waltz walk and one turn waltz walk, or it can turn to each side.

16. Like your teacher.

17. Weird.

18. Grapevine: Step side, cross the other foot in front, step side, cross back.

19. Add nonlocomotor movements like swinging the arms, wiggling the hips, shaking the head, contracting and stretching the torso, opening and closing the mouth. It is perfectly fine to use these movements even though nonlocomotor has not yet been introduced; in fact it is a good foreshadowing of the forthcoming movements. Just name the action without using the term nonlocomotor. This same reasoning applies to adding the nonlocomotor movement variations in the 11 remaining locomotor movements in this catalog.

20. Walk like a stereotyped male; a stereotyped female. This is an excellent place to pause for a moment and talk about stereotyping, what it means, the images we carry with us, and how this form of prejudgment limits us.

21. Meander.

22. Amble; stroll.

23. Creep; slink.

24. March.

25. Trudge.

26. Plod.

27. Stride.

28. Stagger.

29. Strut; saunter.

❷ Run

A run is not really a fast walk because the movement lifts up into the air. Run is a series of small leaps.

Variations

1. Fast; slow motion.
2. Jog.
3. Run with knees up.
4. Run long steps.
5. Alternate four knees up with four long steps.
6. Tiny, mincing run.
7. Directions: Forward, backward, sideways, turning.
8. Lean the body forward; lean it back.
9. With a partner, hold both hands and turn twirling together; twirl in a group.
10. With a partner, hold one hand and run synchronized.
11. Add nonlocomotor movements: Shake the hands, wiggle the shoulders, strike the arms.
12. Prance: Legs move as if pushing a ball with the front of the foot.
13. Dodge: Run side to side as if avoiding something.
14. Race; sprint.
15. Scurry; bustle: "Running as if you are late."

❸ Jump

Jump is a lift into the air, landing evenly on two feet.

Variations

1. Directions: Forward, backward, sideways, turning.
2. Turning quarter-turns, half-turns, whole turns.
3. Big, high jumps.
4. Little, fast jumps.
5. Long jumps: "Can you make it to the end of the diagonal in just seven jumps?"
6. "Jump so high that your heels hit your seat. Ouch!"
7. Tuck jumps: Legs bend in the air, knees reach as close to the chest as possible.
8. Straddle jump: Legs stretch wide in the air.
9. Side-to-side jumps: Legs jump side to side while the torso remains relatively stationary—good to do over a jump rope laid straight on the floor.
10. Add nonlocomotor movements: Twist head, contract and stretch, wiggle shoulders, and so on.
11. Hop: Land on one foot. Do not forget to hop on the other foot.

➡ TROUBLESHOOTING

Please take note of how important it is to teach hop at this stage. Though hop is obviously a variation on the locomotor movement jump, it deserves special attention because it is the preparatory movement for all the more difficult locomotor movements. If a child can hop easily on either foot, he will be able to skip, gallop, side-slide, and leap with grace and confidence. Further, hop is excellent for general strength and coordination.

12. Hop holding the raised leg with a hand.
13. Hop adding nonlocomotor movements: Shake the raised leg, swing arms, twist head, and so on.
14. Hop changing feet every four beats.
15. With a partner, hop holding each other's raised legs.
16. Hopscotch: Alternate one jump with one hop—jump, hop on right foot, jump, hop on left foot.

❹ Skip

Skip alternates a step and a hop. It is the perfect locomotor movement with which to start a class because the ankles and knees warm up vigorously without strain. Skipping is not sacred. Teachers are sometimes overly concerned with teaching a child to skip. Since a skip is an alternating hop, a child must first be able to hop easily on either foot. If a child can do that, it is simple to nudge her into a skip: "Hop on one side . . . Hop on the other side . . . Change sides . . . Change sides . . . Change, change . . ." The "changes" get closer and closer together until they are one hop apart. In addition, I hold the child's hand and swing her arm in a strong upward rhythm as we skip together.

Variations

1. Directions: Forward, backward, sideways (cross leg in front and back), turning.
2. Add nonlocomotor movements: Swing arms, twist head, contract and stretch.
3. Skip for height; for distance.
4. Silly skip.
5. Jazzy skip.
6. Face a partner, link elbows ("elbow position"), and skip.
7. Skip with energy; skip tired.
8. One-legged skip: A skip on one side only, that is, step-step-hop (figure 3.1). The extra step creates a lopsided skip that mimics how very young children first attempt a skip. The one-legged skip is an extremely valuable element in the movement vocabulary: It is fun, it is easily varied, and it readily combines with many other movements. I teach this locomotor movement to third graders on up.

3.1

I teach the one-legged skip by demonstration: "I am going to skip but only one leg will come up." I hold my right pant leg above the knee and do a few one-legged skips. "See, I take an extra step so that this is the only leg that comes up." The children then grab their own pant legs (imaginary if they are wearing shorts) and imitate me by

having only that leg come up in the skip. Most children pick up the movement best this way. They get the idea and, because they are not entangled in specific footwork, they soon swing into a high, free, energetic motion. If a child is having a great deal of difficulty, I will privately go through "Step right, step left, hop left," and so on. When the one-legged skip is first taught, the "skipping" leg, that is, the leg that is high in the air during the hop, is bent in front of the body (as in an ordinary skip). After the children are at ease doing the one-legged skip, the skipping leg can be varied. It can be straightened in front of the body as in figure 3.2.

3.2

It can be bent to the side of the body, as in figure 3.3.

3.3

The leg can be extended back either bent or straight, as in figure 3.4.

3.4

These different leg positions can be mixed. For example, in three consecutive one-legged skips, the leg is straight front for the first skip, bent side for the second, and extended straight back for the third. The same leg is in the air for each position.

⑤ Gallop

A gallop is a step together of the legs going in the forward direction. The front foot steps forward, both legs come together briefly, and then the weight shifts to the back foot in order to repeat. Going sideways, the same motion is a side-slide.

Variations

1. Height: A gallop can be done very high if the back leg pushes hard off the floor.
2. Distance.
3. Alternate leading leg: Two gallops with the right leg leading, two with the left leg leading; one gallop with the right and one with the left (a polka).
4. Add nonlocomotor movements: Swing arms, shoulders up and down, bounce head, open and close mouth.
5. Alternate gallops and skips: One gallop, one skip. Difficult.
6. Alternate gallops and side-slides: The legs do essentially the same thing, but the body changes from facing front for the gallop to facing sideways for the side-slide.

⑥ Side-Slide

A side-slide is a sideways gallop. Side-slide is not under gallop as a variation because it is basic

dance vocabulary. In ballet, a side-slide is a chassé (pronounced "shah-say").

Variations

1. Changing sides: One side-slide with the right side leading, one with the left side leading; change sides while traveling in one line.
2. With a partner, hold both hands and side-slide.
3. With a partner, link elbows back-to-back and side-slide. If children are having trouble with this, it is probably because they are not going sideways. If they try to go forward, one child ends up dragging the other on her back.
4. Add nonlocomotor movements: Swing the arms, raise and lower shoulders, contract and stretch, turn head.

⑦ Roll

A roll is a rotation of the body on the floor. Sideways rolls can be done on the bare floor; forward and most back rolls need mats.

Variations

1. Log roll. The body is stretched straight while rolling ("Roll straight as a pencil"). The force for the log roll comes from an energized stretch of the torso. For the roll to stay on course, the arms and legs must stretch equally.
2. Add nonlocomotor movement contract and stretch to the log roll. The body curls into a contract while on the back and then stretches straight while rolling on the front—excellent conditioning and coordination work.
3. Cat or tuck roll. Knees are bent to chest. The knees stay together, close to the chest, throughout the roll (see figure 3.5, a and b).

3.5

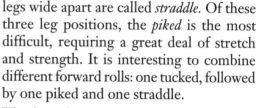

3.6 *a*   *b*   *c*   *d*

4. Alternate one log roll and one tuck roll.

5. Straddle roll. This is a log roll with legs stretching wide for an instant. Starting on the back, one leg crosses the body to fan around to the side; at that point the other leg lifts and stretches wide, effecting a wide-stride or straddle position. The legs close as the body rolls onto the tummy, and the process is repeated. Ideally the straddle roll should have a smooth, fluid opening and closing of the legs (figure 3.6, a-d).

6. Somersault or forward roll. The children stand on the mats, put their hands flat down near their feet, tuck their heads way under their feet, and roll. The knees bend, but the seat remains as high as possible (see figure 3.7).

   The crucial part of these instructions is placing the head back toward the feet; only the back of the head touches the mat. If a child tries to roll over the top of his head he will get "stuck" and perhaps hurt his neck.

   Once the form of a somersault is mastered, it can be executed with the legs in various positions. These are the basic gymnastics terms: Bent legs are called *tucked*; straight legs together are called *piked*; and straight

legs wide apart are called *straddle*. Of these three leg positions, the *piked* is the most difficult, requiring a great deal of stretch and strength. It is interesting to combine different forward rolls: one tucked, followed by one piked and one straddle.

The legs do not have to remain in these standard gymnastics molds; they can assume almost any position. For example, the legs can lunge (one leg bent and the other straight), the knees and feet can flex, or the legs can shake during the roll. Further, a somersault can be done at different speeds, from superfast to slow motion.

7. Backward roll. This is much harder than a forward roll. Two elements are necessary for a backward roll: (1) The hands must twist back, palms flat, fingers pointing toward the shoulders, in order to push the floor; and (2) there needs to be some rolling momentum. I ask the children to start in a standing squat position, rather than sitting. They sit back, throw their legs overhead, and push with their hands, all in one continuous flow.

   Once a backward roll is accomplished, it can be done with the legs in the same positions as the forward roll: tucked, piked (that means rolling over and pushing up onto straight legs; very hard!), and straddle. Or the legs can be varied in any way.

8. One-knee back roll. This is great! The one-knee back roll is easier than the standard backward roll. (Many children learn to do a standard back roll after mastering this roll.) It can be done on the floor without a mat and therefore can be used in dances as well as gymnastics routines; also, it is pretty.

3.7

3.8

➡ TROUBLESHOOTING

It is worth reiterating what I said at the start of this catalog of locomotor movements: If you are new to teaching movement, work with the easier movements and variations first, and progress toward the more difficult ones only at your own pace. This book includes information for beginning and experienced movement teachers, and this catalog provides a broad range of movement possibilities.

The one-knee back roll starts from a sitting position. The child rocks back and lifts into a shoulder stand, that is, hip held high with legs straight to the ceiling. The right knee bends, getting as close as possible to the right shoulder, while the other leg remains lifted high as in figure 3.8a.

This position, one knee bent and one leg straight, is the crucial point of success. Most children want to bend both legs, so I often hold the leg that is to remain straight, as in figure 3.8b. After the leg positions are clear,

gently push the torso to roll onto the bent knee, as in figure 3.8c. The roll is over the shoulder rather than over the back of the head. The ending position is on two hands and one knee with the other leg straight back, as in figure 3.8d.

⑧ Seat-Scoot

Seat-scoot is the fancy term for sliding the bottom on the floor. Babies sometimes meander into seat-scooting before starting an official crawl.

Variations

1. Directions: Forward, backward, sideways, turning. (For a turning seat-scoot, make sure the children actually get somewhere and do not just spin in one spot.)

2. Seat-scoot using only hands (feet are lifted); using only feet.

3. Walk on the seat. Legs are kept straight, hands are crossed on the chest. This is the old-fashioned hips and seat slimming

exercise found in women's magazines 20 years ago. (At one time a movement teacher I know used this seat walk as punishment: "If you fool around once more you'll have to seat walk all the way to the side of the room and back." It worked well enough except that the only way this movement is hard is if the legs are kept straight and the arms crossed, and that generally requires direct supervision.)

4. With a partner, sit facing each other, hold each other's ankles, and go somewhere.

5. With a partner, sit back-to-back, elbows linked, and go somewhere.

6. Add nonlocomotor movement: Twist head, contract and stretch, shake.

⑨ Sliding on the Floor

Sliding on the floor is just that: Sliding a plane of the body on the floor.

Variations

1. Slide on abdomen.

2. Slide on back.

3. Slide on side.

4. Slide on the back using only feet to push.

5. On the back, slide in different directions: Forward, backward, sideways, turning. If the children are unsure of directions while lying down, ask them to sit up for a minute to see how they would go sitting up. Then they do it lying down.

6. Slide ride. In partners, one child lies down on her back, hands behind head; the other child holds her ankles and gives her a ride. Of course, they switch. A note on this ride: Unless the lying-down child is obese, the other child can pull her. If I hear "She's too heavy," I insist, "But you are strong enough to pull her."

⇨ SAFETY

If the class is one in which the children tend to be rough with one another, I have them practice lifting and lowering ankles gently before they get the OK to give each other a slide ride.

⑩ Kicks

Kicks are shifts in weight that include a lift into the air with an extension of the other leg. They are easier to do than to define.

Variations

1. Little kicks. The body lifts with each kick so that as one leg returns, the other kicks out. These little kicks can be done to the front, side, or back of the body. An interesting study is four front kicks, four back kicks, and eight side kicks, then two front, two back, four side.

2. Directions. The little kicks can be done front, back, or side, and in addition, the body as a whole can move in each of the four directions: forward, backward, sideways, turning. You can have a directional field day. "Kick your legs to the front and move forward . . . Kick your legs to the front and move backward . . . Kick your legs to the back and move forward . . . Kick your legs to the back and move sideways . . . Kick your legs to the side and move turning."

3. "Kick the habit." Children take a running start and click heels in the air (see figure 3.9). This is hard. Once they get it, children beam with accomplishment.

3.9

4. Hitch kick. The legs kick high to the front, touching in the air, while remaining straight and pointed.

5. Cancan kicking. Just for fun, ask groups of 3 to 20 to link arms at the shoulders and cancan—alternate bending one leg up and then kicking it out like the old Rockettes. The key to a cancan is synchronizing the kicks.

6. Karate kick. Children do their versions of karate kicks. Ideally we work for that double kick in which both legs are high in the air at the same time. At this writing, the karate mania is just beginning to wane. For a while, structuring karate kicks into movement class was the only way I could reduce the karate eruptions all over the school.

⑪ *Leap*

A leap is a step in the air. Ideally the legs stretch straight as though one is "doing the splits in the air." It is a glorious movement. Beautiful leaps are often what bring ballet crowds to their feet shouting "Bravo!" I used to be fearful of teaching leaps outside of the dance studio. I have since realized my mistake. Now, if you were to ask the children I teach what their favorite locomotor movement is, 9 out of 10 would probably say "leap." The leap is not as hard to teach as it is cracked up to be. "A leap is a step in the air." I demonstrate. "The legs stay straight in the air. Take a few running steps to build up your speed so you can get very high." Most children pick up the leap that easily. If a child cannot get the idea from example, I go through this process: Take some little steps and then a big step, little-little-little-big. Make the big step get bigger and bigger until it is in the air. For young children I ask that they take a running start and *leap* to touch the ceiling. I demonstrate. However, I do not concern them or myself with the leg position; I just want the rush of speed and the burst of energy. Later they will get the leg position.

Variations

1. Directions: Forward, sideways, and turning. A turning leap is actually a ballet tour jeté,
but if you keep that to yourself the children will be able to do it. "Let's see run and leap. Now add a turn while you're in the air . . . Terrific."

2. Vary the number of steps preceding the leap: Three steps and a leap; two steps and a leap; one step and a leap; no steps, just leaps.

3. Stag leap. The front leg brushes straight to begin the leap, then bends sharply to touch the back knee for a second while the child is in the air.

4. Double bent leap. Both legs bend in the air. This is like a stag leap with the back leg also bent.

⑫ *Crawl*

A crawl is any four-body-part walk. A traditional baby crawl (two knees and two hands) is an extremely important developmental move. Entire movement therapies have been based on retraining the body to crawl. The key to a correct crawl is the opposition of hand and leg; that is, the right hand should land with the left knee.

Variations

1. Baby crawl.

2. Directions: Forward, backward, sideways, turning.

3. Backward stretch crawl. This is like a baby crawl, but the rear leg stretches completely straight while stepping backward (see figure 3.10).

3.10

4. Spider crawl: Hands and feet (not knees) touch the floor, seat remains high (see figure 3.11).

3.11

5. Crab crawl: Hands and feet on the floor, tummy facing the ceiling (see figure 3.12).

3.12

6. Inchworm crawl: Hands and feet move separately. Leaving the feet in place, the hands move forward as far as possible; the hands then remain in place and the feet catch up (see figure 3.13).

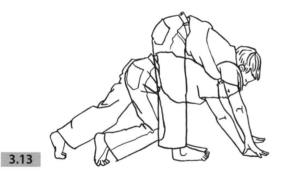

3.13

7. Add nonlocomotor movements: Wiggle the hips, shake the head, or contract and stretch. Contract and stretch are especially good to do in the baby crawl position. The contracted torso is like a "mad cat"; that is, the back is rounded with knees remaining on the floor. A straight back is like a "table," and a stretched or arched back is like an "old horse." I call out the descriptions as the children are crawling: "Mad cat . . . Old horse . . . Table."

8. Bridge crawl: Walking in a bridge (back bend) position (see figure 3.14).

3.14

This is a very difficult and strenuous crawl; attempt it only with children who have good, high bridges and only after they have thoroughly warmed up their backs.

Locomotor Movement Studies and Dances

Children love studies. Actually, children love to dance. When not handicapped with that word they love to learn set repeatable, patterns. "Hey, Mom, watch what I learned in movement class." "I've almost got that dance. I've just got to get that leap right." "I've been practicing this. Watch." "This study is ready for the stage." You know how children love productions, class plays, and projects that are completed. Studies and dances are microproductions; they are visual goals. Beyond that, they are excellent for memory work, for precision and control, for coordination, and often for group work and problem solving.

In order for studies to accomplish their goals, the children must be able to perform them by themselves. Generally, I do a study once with the class, call it out a few times, and then help them practice it until they are proficient by themselves. This section presents two types of culminating locomotor movement studies—teacher-taught combinations and group problems—followed by five choreographed dances to music.

Teacher-Taught Combinations

1. Kick front two, back two, side four, run four beats, and kick in the air ("Kick the habit").

2. Prance four times, jump-hop, jump-hop. Prance four times, jump-hop, jump-hop. Repeat going backward. One group starts going forward as the group ahead starts going backward. The backward group beckons the forward group with a "Come here" gesture.

3. This is one of my favorite locomotor studies: step-hop on right foot; step left and "kick the habit"; step right and turn in the air landing on both feet. Again step-hop on right foot; step left and "kick the habit"; end with three little runs and a leap. The rhythm goes step-hop, step kick, step turn; step-hop, step kick, run-run-run leap. The quality is small and light. This pattern fits Scott Joplin's "The Entertainer" from the album *The Sting*.

4. Waltz walk, one-legged skip, hitch kick, and step leap are all done in a three-beat rhythm. Therefore, they fit together nicely and are an almost unending source of pattern ideas:

   a. Waltz walk, one-legged skip, waltz walk (if possible, turn), step leap.
   b. Waltz walk, waltz walk, one-legged skip, step leap.
   c. One-legged skip, one-legged skip, run-run-run leap, hold in a balance.
   d. Hitch kick, one-legged skip, hitch kick, step leap.
   e. One-legged skip with the leg extended straight front, waltz walk, one-legged skip with the leg extended straight back, waltz walk backward.

Group Problems

1. The class is in groups of three to five children, ready to move on the diagonal. Have the children talk in their groups and decide on one locomotor movement to do to the middle of the diagonal and a different one to do from the middle to the end. (If the class knows "levels" and "directions"—chapters 5 and 6— have them include one or both of these concepts; e.g., "Each movement must be on a different level," or "Each movement must be on a different level and travel in a different direction.") Make sure the groups work together. They must make clear decisions, and all the group members must do the same two movements.

2. Groups ready to move on the diagonal pick four locomotor movements. They do one for the first diagonal, the second across the side of the room, the third on the crossing diagonal, and the fourth for the last side of the room. (If the class knows "levels" and "directions," include one or both of these concepts.) When the patterns are set, ask subsequent groups to start when the group ahead of them has gotten to the middle of the diagonal. This means that a number of groups will be going at the same time, crossing each other's diagonal. "No disasters!"

3. Tell the children to "somehow" fit in three different locomotor movements on one diagonal line. Older children might be asked to fit in five to seven different movements.

4. Select five different locomotor movements, on five different levels (if you want, including three different directions), and organize them in the room. For example, I might say, "Start at the door and skip to my desk, roll from the desk to the cabinets, leap from the cabinets to the piano," and so forth. "See what design you end up making in space." (This is an excellent foreshadowing of floor patterns, discussed in chapter 6.)

5. Tell the students you will give them 30 beats, that is, you will count from 1 to 30. Within that time they do four different locomotor movements. They need to make sure their group stays exactly together.

6. I have a large stack of small cards with different locomotor movements printed on each. The children are divided into groups, and each group receives a packet of cards (three to seven cards, depending on the children's ages). The groups arrange the cards in a sequence and do the appropriate movements to different points in the room. For example, they run to the corner, hop to the chair, and so on.

7. Give each group a packet of five cards, each naming a different locomotor movement. In addition, give each group five cards with numbers printed on them. A group might end up with "run," "jazzy walk," "roll," "skip," and "kick" and 9, 3, 3, 4, and 5. The children pair the movement cards with the number cards in any way they wish, then arrange the pairs of cards in any sequence they want. They perform the motion on each movement card for the number of steps indicated on the corresponding number card. For example, given the sequence just mentioned, the group has to run nine steps, take three jazzy walk steps, roll three times, skip four times, and kick five times. I ask for no stopping between movement changes. I do not attempt to keep a steady beat, but do ask the groups to stay together. This is difficult.

Dances

Two songs from Raffi's *The Corner Grocery Store* (MCA Records, Inc.) make a great introduction to dance: "The Corner Grocery Store" and "Jig Along Home."

The Grocery Store Dance

The Grocery Store Dance (figure 3.15, a-c) is appropriate for preschool to third grade but is dearly loved by older children. The class is divided in two, with the two halves lined up on opposite sides of the room. One side performs the verses and the other the refrain.

The verses are essentially pantomime: "cheese walking on knees," "plums twiddling thumbs," "corn blowing on horns," and "beans trying on jeans." When introducing the dance, it is best to bring in a piece of cheese (I prefer Swiss), a plum, an ear of corn, and a few string beans. This in itself is a good lesson for English learners and tends to expand the children's imagination for movement. Generally, they walk on their knees for the cheese; they walk turning, rounded like plums, while twiddling their thumbs (you will need to teach this); they silently pretend to blow on horns while marching like ears of corn; and as beans trying on jeans they pretend to struggle putting on too-tight jeans. Exhort them to be hammy.

The refrain has three phrases: Children skip forward for four beats; they side-slide sideways for four beats; and they run leap once, stretch as if they crashed into something, fall down, get up, and run back to their original places in eight beats. The half of the class that is dancing the refrain needs to be in two groups (see figure 3.15a).

Each group goes forward for the skips, then makes a right angle for the side-slides, like an "L." The run and leap, stretch, fall, and get up phrase returns them to the middle of the room, and they run back to their starting spot (see figure 3.15b).

The refrain is simplified if the two parts dancing the refrain are girls and boys. When teaching this dance I ask the boys to sit and watch the girls' part (because theirs will be similar). I practice with the girls a few times and then try the boys alone several times; only then are we ready to attempt the whole refrain.

When it is time to put the entire dance together, I ask all the girls and all the boys to line up on the refrain end of the room. I then take half of each gender group to the other side for the pantomime verses (figure 3.15c). It is paramount to switch the verse and refrain sides so everybody has a turn at each.

Jig Along Dance

On the same Raffi recording, *The Corner Grocery Store* (MCA Records, Inc.), is another terrific song, "Jig Along Home." The Jig Along Dance is a favorite of all ages. This dance requires partners and therefore might be better after partner activities have been introduced; I include it here because it is on the same tape or CD and it also relies on locomotor movements.

The refrain for the Jig Along Dance is essentially the same for all ages. Partners face one another in an elbow position, that is, elbows linked, and skip one way for four beats, switch elbows, and skip the other way for four beats. They then hold both hands and swing their arms a few times, lifting up to do Wring Out the Dishrag (see "Partner Activities," chapter 7). Younger children do not switch elbows during the skips, just continue for eight beats. Older children do switch elbows and "wring out the dishrag" several times.

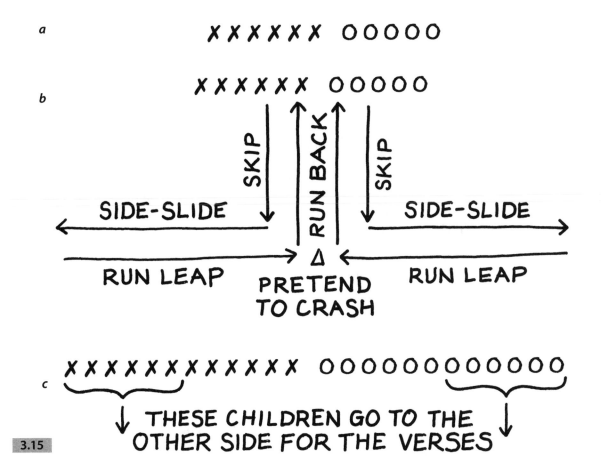

a

𝗫 𝗫 𝗫 𝗫 𝗫 𝗫   𝗢 𝗢 𝗢 𝗢 𝗢

b

𝗫 𝗫 𝗫 𝗫 𝗫 𝗫   𝗢 𝗢 𝗢 𝗢 𝗢

SKIP   RUN BACK   SKIP

SIDE-SLIDE   SIDE-SLIDE

RUN LEAP   PRETEND TO CRASH   RUN LEAP

c

𝗫 𝗫 𝗫 𝗫 𝗫 𝗫 𝗫 𝗫 𝗫   𝗢 𝗢 𝗢 𝗢 𝗢 𝗢 𝗢 𝗢 𝗢 𝗢 𝗢

↓ THESE CHILDREN GO TO THE OTHER SIDE FOR THE VERSES ↓

3.15

There are five verses preceding the refrains. The simplest choreography is to have the class choose five different locomotor movements to do individually during the verses, running quickly to their partners for the refrains. Try to include level and direction changes.

A possible outcome:

Verse 1, run and leap—refrain

Verse 2, roll—refrain

Verse 3, jazzy walk backward—refrain

Verse 4, crab crawl sideways—refrain

Verse 5, any locomotor movement we have not done—refrain

Another possibility for the verses is for the class to choose partner activities (see chapter 7), staying with the same partner throughout the dance. It is important that if they choose an activity that involves totally different positions, like Wheelbarrow, they do the activity for two verses with each person having a chance to do both positions.

A possible outcome:

Verse 1, Wheelbarrow—refrain

Verse 2, Wheelbarrow with partners in switched positions—refrain

Verse 3, partner roll—refrain

Verse 4, Horsie—refrain

Verse 5, Horsie with partners in switched positions—refrain

A more difficult choreographic possibility for the verses is to have partners choose their own five activities. (It is prudent to have the partners jot down their sequence because when they see the others, they tend to forget their own.) A lot of excitement is added if the partners include various props, making sure they have the equipment readily available so there is no break in the flow of the dance.

A possible outcome for one partner group:

Verse 1, partner ball pass (ball quickly rolled away)—refrain

Verse 2, synchronized run and leap—refrain

Verse 3, Horsie with a rope (p. 132)—refrain (rope draped around waist)

Verse 4, Horsie with a rope, partners in switched positions (rope quickly tossed aside)—refrain

Verse 5, partners pull out scarves that were hidden in pockets and twirl—refrain

This last version of the Jig Along Dance would be suitable for fourth through sixth graders. It requires a lot of forethought and partner cooperation—it also results in a spectacular dance.

Three More Dances

Following are three dances for your portfolio; all are choreographed to traditional songs and all are favorites. The Eensy Weensy Spider Dance is a beginning dance sequence for preschool to second grade. The Yankee Doodle Dance is an intermediate-level dance for second grade on up, and Camptown Races Dance is an advanced dance for fourth through sixth grades. For music, use any tape or CD version you have, or simply have the class sing the song as they dance.

Eensy Weensy Spider Dance

"The eesnsy weensy spider climbed up the water spout"—spider crawl (quickly stand at the end of the phrase).

"Down came the rain"—from standing, shake the entire body while lowering to sitting; "and washed the spider out"—sit and spin.

"Out came the sun and dried up all the rain"—stand, arms held wide to the side, and turn four beats one way and four beats the other way.

"And the eensy weensy spider climbed up the spout again"—spider crawl.

Once the dance is learned, add partners. The spider crawls become partner spider crawls (see p. 42), with one child over the other; for the last phrase the children reverse these spider crawl positions. Partners hold hands to shake down together for the "rain" but let go in order to spin on their seats. They return to holding hands for the "Out came the sun" spin. This partner format makes a charming first dance for very young children.

Yankee Doodle Dance

To start, children stand on one side of the room; they have their sides to the front of the room.

"Yankee Doodle came to town"—skip forward (four beats).

"Riding on a pony"—gallop forward (four beats).

"Stuck a feather in his cap"—jump backward (four beats).

"And called it macaroni"—twist down (two beats) and straighten to face the front (two beats).

"Yankee Doodle keep it up"—face straight front and side-slide in the direction of the skips (four beats).

"Yankee Doodle dandy"—side-slide the other way (four beats).

"Mind the music and the steps"—side-slide the first way again (four beats).

"And with the girls be handy!"—run and leap back to the starting place (four beats).

I normally divide the class in two, with each half on either side of the room. The sides take turns dancing the verses and at the end join together to take a formal bow.

Camptown Races Dance

Children start by standing in one or two lines midway in the room so there is plenty of room to move forward.

"Camptown ladies sing this song"—four beats of skip forward.

"Doo da. Doo da"—four beats of jump, hop; jump, hop.

"Camptown racetrack five miles long"—four beats of skip backward.

"Oh, doo da day"—four beats of jump, hop, jump, full turn jump. (These 16 beats are repeated.)

"Going to run all night!"—four beats of four side-slides to the right.

"Going to run all day!"—four side-slides to the left.

"I bet my money on the bobtail nag"—four beats of swing torso and arms right two beats, swing left two beats.

"Somebody bet on the bay"—four beats of jump, hop, full turn jump.

On my tape the entire dance repeats; you can divide the class so that each half does the dance once, or they can all do the whole thing twice. It is very fast and quite strenuous. What makes this dance difficult is the small, quick, precise footwork; an especially tricky transition is going from the full turn jump immediately into the next step without missing a beat.

Closing Thoughts

It is only chapter 3 and you are feeling overwhelmed? Let's back up. After introducing the idea of traveling movements, all that is needed are the 12 basic locomotor movements. These basic movements will offer ample coordination work and are the steps used for most of the dances presented. A standard warm-up uses the following locomotor movements in this order: skip, jump, hop, hopscotch, baby and crab crawl, roll, side-slide, jazzy walk, run and leap. The children will not get tired of this progression. Later, when you are ready, have the side-slides change sides and then try out a straddle roll. Of course you will want to introduce some tumbling moves like a somersault and one-knee back roll. Then, how about a one-legged skip or a leap turning in the air? How about a study or a dance? Don't fret; go at your own pace.

Chapter 4

Nonlocomotor Movements

Nonlocomotor movements are those that stay in one place. Generally children do not like them as much as locomotor movements. The challenge in teaching nonlocomotor movements is to expand the children's thinking so that nonlocomotor movements become an exciting part of their movement vocabulary. Like locomotor movements, nonlocomotor movements can be categorized into basic movements and variations. This chapter presents a catalog of nonlocomotor movements and variations, along with several studies combining movements.

Introducing Nonlocomotor Movements

I teach the concept *nonlocomotor* in relation to locomotor, so it is important that locomotor be clear before we begin. "You know what locomotor means, right? Good. Now I have a question for you: Non means not, so what do you guess nonlocomotor means?" (As I say the word nonlocomotor I shake my finger "no.") Even preschoolers will shout brilliantly: "Not locomotor!" I answer, "Right. Now, what could 'not locomotor' mean?" Again, either immediately or with some prodding, they will conclude, "Not locomotor means not going anywhere." Too many negatives; I shift the emphasis from "not moving" to "moving in one place."

"How in the world can you move but stay in one spot?" Some children understand immediately and some look up in blank dismay. This is a judgment crossroad. It is much better for children to figure out "logic" problems for themselves. I make a snap decision whether the children are simply not concentrating, in which case I will wait and prod ("Come on. What can you possibly move while staying right here?"); whether they need a hint ("Could you figure out one part of your body that can move without the rest of you going anywhere?"); or whether they are truly stumped ("I'll show you some ways to move in one spot and then you think of some different ways").

Once they get the idea of how to move in one place, I ask the children to think of many different nonlocomotor movements. They will mostly jump, hop, and run in place. I accept everything as long as it is in place. We try all the movements out, saying the word nonlocomotor while moving. The next step is to alternate locomotor and nonlocomotor movements in order to make the distinction clear. This is done in the Free Traveling Structure. "When you hear the piano, do a locomotor movement; when you hear the drum, do a nonlocomotor movement. What do you do when the sound stops? Right, freeze." I use this introductory alternation to suggest nonlocomotor movements that they have overlooked. If the children do not understand a movement, I demonstrate it. I am not fussy how the movements are done, but insist the children move exactly where they stopped.

Suggested Progression

Locomotor (piano sound)—nonlocomotor (drum sound)

1. Skip—swing in various ways
2. Hopscotch—spin in various ways
3. Run—shake going up and down
4. Jazzy walk—strike various body parts
5. Any locomotor movement—nonlocomotor movement with just arms
6. Any locomotor movement—nonlocomotor movement with just torso
7. Any locomotor movement—any nonlocomotor movement

We spend two or three lessons exploring the children's own nonlocomotor movements. Often children are limited in thinking of nonlocomotor movements; their movements are repetitive and half-hearted. Most often children simply do locomotor movement in place, for example, running in place (more on that later). At this stage I want to expand their thinking rather than impose new movements. There are three ways to increase nonlocomotor movement vocabulary without introducing specific movements:

1. Suggest an isolated movement.
2. Suggest a change of level.
3. Suggest a change in size.

Isolated movements are actions limited to one part of the body. It takes a great deal of focused energy to lift one shoulder and not the other, to wiggle toes but not fingers. Isolation of movements is good for concentration and coordination as well as exploring a range of motions. "What ways can you move just your head? Just one shoulder? Seat? Torso? Move just your eyes and keep everything else still . . . No, your eyes, not your head. Move just one leg, but don't let your arms or anything else move. Move just your hips. Pick one part of your body and move it. Pick two parts of your body and move them one after the other. First body part . . . Second body part. Can you move them at the same time? Great."

How precisely isolated these movements are, of course, depends on the age and ability of your class and how rigorously you want to pursue the idea of precision. As long as the children are concentrating, I am satisfied with the results.

Changing levels, that is the height of the body position, quickly eradicates the stationary locomotor movement syndrome. A run in place done on the lowest level becomes something like a shoulder stand pedaling movement; a skip done on sitting level becomes a kicky, swingy movement. Further, changing levels makes the most ordinary movements come to life; for example, a nonlocomotor movement shake going from air level down to lowest level, and back up, becomes exciting to watch and to do. "Do a nonlocomotor movement on the lowest level. Do the same thing on air level. What could you do on the knee level? Sitting level? Do a nonlocomotor movement and change levels without ever stopping the movement. Terrific!"

Most children do nonlocomotor movements all one size: medium. A change either way, smaller or bigger, enlivens almost any movement. "Do the nonlocomotor movement swing. Make it smaller and smaller until I can barely see it. Now make it huge so that the swing is your whole body. Bigger! Bigger!"

➡ REAL LIFE

When I tell the children to make a movement so small I can barely see it, they love to "trick" me: The children make the movement so miniscule as to be invisible. They tell me, "But I am moving. Look at my big toe!"

These techniques—isolation, level changes, size changes—are used initially when the children work on their own nonlocomotor movements and later when they work on specific nonlocomotor movements. The techniques fit into a lesson most easily as a warm-up activity. You can alternate one technique, for example isolation, with locomotor movements in the Free Traveling Structure:

1. Gallop—isolated movements (leg, arm, hip, knee)
2. Crawl, roll—isolated torso, head, shoulder
3. Side-slide, kicks, run leap—choice of three isolated body parts to move in sequence

Or you can create a more complex warm-up using all three of the techniques alternated with locomotor movements:

1. Skip—isolated movements (shoulder, head, hips, and so on)
2. Jump, hop, hopscotch—contract and stretch changing levels
3. Jazzy walk, run, run and leap—swing changing sizes

Following are examples of how I introduce specific nonlocomotor movements. I often use studies within these preliminary lessons, so I include some initial studies here. The next section presents a catalog of nonlocomotor movements, their leading variations, and additional studies.

Introducing Shake

The children sit in Perfect Spots. I ask them, "What does shake mean?"

"Wriggling."

"Shaking the rug out."

"Giggling with my body."

"Being tickled."

"Right. Those are great pictures!"

We work with shake using the three techniques mentioned previously: isolation and change of levels and size. "Let's shake our hands. How about just our arms? Legs. Torso. Put all the shakes together into a whole-body shake. Harder! Let's shake on the lowest level. Sitting level. Knee level. Standing. Can you shake at air level? Yes, you have to jump and shake at the same time. Now let's do a shake that is so tiny I can barely see it. Where did it go? Now shake so hard that it tingles. Bigger! Now let's do a shake that changes levels and never stops. Go all the way from air level through lowest level and back up. Keep going. Great."

Shake is easily understood and just as easily done, so it makes a good first nonlocomotor movement. The only thing to watch is that the torso shakes along with the arms and legs. I usually conclude this introduction with a short study. A beginning study might use shake within the Diagonal Structure. The children pick one locomotor movement to do to the middle of the diagonal. In the middle they shake, going to the lowest level and back up to air level without stopping the shake. Then they do a different locomotor movement to the end of the diagonal. A possible result: skip, shake, run.

Introducing Swing

A swing is an arc-shaped movement, usually with a release of tension at the low point of the arc. It is such a useful movement that I often introduce it second. We work on isolated swings, whole-body swings, and swings on different levels.

Isolated Swings

"Swing one arm . . . Both arms . . . Swing a leg . . . Switch . . . Swing your hands . . . Your head . . . Can you swing just your torso? . . . Swing your hips . . . Pretty jazzy!" These individual body swings can combine to make interesting studies by themselves:

1. Children swing the right arm, front to back (beats 1 and 2); swing left arm, front to back (beats 3 and 4); swing right leg, front to back (beats 5 and 6); swing left leg, front to back (beats 7 and 8). Swing head, side to side (beats 9 and 10); swing torso, side to side (beats 11 and 12); swing hips, side to side (beats 13 and 14); shake the whole body vigorously (beats 15 and 16).

2. Have the children pick four parts of their bodies to swing. Swing each part for six beats, three beats for one arc and three beats to return. Remember your sequence.

Whole-Body Swings

"Can you swing so big that your whole body is swinging? . . . Bend your knees so that you touch the ground . . . Good." At this beginning stage I work with four basic full-body swings: front, crossed, side, and twisted. More full-body swings are described in the catalog.

1. **Front swing:** Children start standing with arms above the head. Arms, head, and torso drop forward; hands touch the floor as the knees bend. The torso stays lowered as the arms swing back and the knees straighten—that is one arc. The second arc lifts up; the knees bend, hands touch the floor, and arms, head, and torso reach out in front and up (see figure 4.1, a through f).

4.1   *a*   *b*   *c*   *d*   *e*   *f*

2. **Crossed swing:** Children start standing with arms and legs wide apart. Torso and knees bend as arms drop to the ground. Knees straighten as arms cross in front of the body, but the torso remains bent—this is one arc. The arc is reversed as the arms uncross and drop. The torso and knees bend, and then they straighten as arms end wide again (see figure 4.2, a through e).

For young children, I do the crossed swing to this image: "Pick up a kitten" (first arc). "Let her go" (second arc). For older children I simply say rhythmically, "Crossed swing and open."

3. **Side swing:** Children stand, leaning to one side, arms overhead. Everything—arms, head, torso, and knees—drops and straightens to the other side. That is one arc. The arc is

4.2   *a*   *b*   *c*   *d*   *e*

4.3

reversed to the other side (see figure 4.3, a through c).

4. **Twist swing:** Children stand with their arms held wide. Arms, torso, and head swing around to twist to one side and then to the other side. Ideally the hips work to remain facing front. In the twist swing, the arc shape is horizontal to the floor as opposed to what happens in the front, crossed, and side swings, where the arc is vertical.

One of my favorite studies sequences these four swings. We start with four front swings and up, four crossed swings and open, four side swings and back, and four twist swings and back—the last swing becoming a full turn around. We then do two of each swing, and then one of each. When doing one of each, work to smoothly blend the transitions between swings so that the study is fluid and lyrical. This study is not only pretty; it is also an excellent body warm-up. I use it often.

Swings on Different Levels

"Who can figure out a way to swing on the lowest level? . . . Swing just your legs on the lowest level . . . Can you swing your whole body on the lowest level? . . . How can we swing on the sitting level? . . . How about with your legs wide on the sitting level? . . . How can we swing on the knee level? . . . Standing level? . . . Air level?" Air level will be a swing jump, going into the air at either end of the swing arc. "Swing and change levels."

An interesting study results simply from doing a swing on one level and then changing levels and

freezing in a strange shape. The rhythm is swing one way (three beats), swing back (three beats), change levels (three beats), freeze (three beats).

Releasing the Swing Energy

One difficulty with swings in general is letting go of the energy at the bottom of the arc. Children often want to stay in tight control, but that negates the flowing quality of the movement. To encourage the risk of letting go, I ask the children to shout "Blah" as they drop into a swing. This sound forces a quick exhalation, which forces a muscular release. The children, of course, think it is funny, and anyone passing by will think it strange.

Introducing Contract and Stretch

Contract is a tight curling or rounding, and *stretch* is a vigorous expanding or opening. These are my favorite nonlocomotor movements, and they are also fun to teach.

The children sit on the floor gathered around me. "Contract means to curl up tight like a fist [I close my hands into strong fists], and stretch means to open wide, big, long [I open my hands wide]. Let's do the movements together and say the words at the same time." The children and I contract and stretch different parts of the body. Each time we shout out the word as we demonstrate the movement. We contract and stretch hands, arms, legs, faces (Faces? Sure—contract by squishing together your features and stretch by opening them wide), necks, and torsos. Torsos curl as if one has been "hit in the stomach" for contract and arch back for stretch. It is important to pay attention to the torso because children often neglect it. But the torso is, in fact, the center of the body physically and the core of any movement. Just as a strong body must include powerful back and abdominal muscles, a strong contract or stretch must include the torso to make a full statement.

After working with individual body parts, the children contract and stretch their entire bodies. To get variety, I ask for different levels: "Can you contract on the lowest level? . . . Stretch on knee level . . . Stretch one leg out and arch your back on knee level . . . Contract on standing level and lift one leg off the floor . . . Stretch with that leg extended out . . . Contract on air level . . . Stretch on air level . . . Wonderful!"

Putting Energy In

"This is a grown-up idea," I say. "Look at my hand [I loosely close my hand]. It is in a contracted position, but this is not a real contraction because it is not tight and hard [I clench my fist extremely hard]. The same goes for stretch [I show my hand open but not fully extended]. This is a stretched position, but it is not a real stretch because it is not pulled hard [I extend my hand completely]. So when you contract your body, let me see a real contraction, hard and tight and strong! Who can do that? . . . Great! Now let me see a real stretch; pull more, harder, pull your fingers, your toes, your nose, your eyebrows, your teeth . . . Fantastic! You look beautiful!"

Including Limp

It is a good idea to introduce limp with contract and stretch in order to release the tension. I do not plan a formal introduction for limp; I just include it with the contract and stretch: "Do a hard contract . . . Do a huge stretch . . . Fine, now let everything go and hang limp . . . Make sure your head and neck let go too."

Partners

Contract and stretch are great to do with partners. I ask the children not only to contract their own bodies, but to contract with their partners so that the two are like one ball. Partners usually hug or lean over one another. For the stretch, partners must touch and pull away. The sculptural designs

are especially beautiful if the stretch is done on two different levels; for example, one person stretches on the standing level while the other stretches on the lowest level, and the standing child holds the other's foot.

This partner contract and stretch can be expanded into a group contract and stretch: "You and your partner combine with another two people and all four of you contract . . . Now all four of you stretch . . . Hold on . . . Can you get on four different levels and stretch? . . . Beautiful. How about if a group of four combined with another group of four, and all eight of you contracted into one big ball? . . . All eight of you hold on to each other and stretch . . . Terrific!"

Including Equipment

The range of contract and stretch can be expanded with the introduction of equipment. Mats will allow the movements to extend into gymnastics forms: Contract can be done as a frog balance (a preliminary headstand with the knees perched on the elbows) and the stretch as a fully extended headstand. Contract can be a somersault and immediately extend into a cartwheel stretch. "How else can you show me contract and stretch on the mats?" Another valuable piece of equipment is chairs. I have seen beautiful studies using chairs. There is a danger in folding chairs, and I never allow a child to sit on the back of a chair. But for an older class, chairs can be very effective: "Create five different ways of contracting and stretching using your chair. Yes, you can be on it (be careful), under it, holding it, lifting it, moving it, or holding on to it." An example is seen in figures 4.4 and 4.5.

4.4

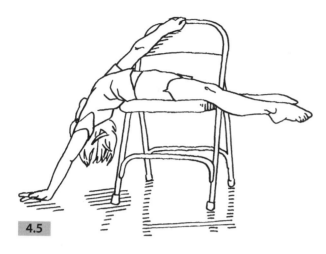

4.5

Introducing Strike

A strike is a punch or hitting motion. It can be done like a boxer's punch or like a "karate chop." The movement is hard and forceful. Children see so much striking on TV that they have no difficulty with this movement. After telling the children the meaning of strike, I ask them to strike with their arms, legs (as in a karate kick), torsos (the whole upper body vigorously bends forward), elbows, shoulder, head, and hips (a thrust to the side). Nonlocomotor movement strike is easy for children to understand. The only point to check is that they strike with energy and gusto.

> **⇒ SAFETY**
>
> Are you at all uneasy about the strikes degenerating into play fighting? If so, we have lost the controlled tone established by the three class management organizations. At all times, fun is held within bounds of reason and structure.

A great study sequences these four strikes: (1) arms, (2) legs, (3) torso, (4) hips. Do four of each strike, then two of each, then finally one of each. Striking with each of the body parts once creates a nice jazzy rhythm: arm-leg-torso-hip.

Introducing Twist

A twist is a stretch in two opposite directions. I hold up an enormous piece of "candy" (a rock wrapped in paper): "You know how the ends of candies are twisted shut? To do that I have to turn this part [the center part of the candy] one way and the end of the paper the other way." I dramatically twist both sides. "This is a twist: One side goes one way while the other side goes the other way."

We twist arms, legs, heads, hands, fingers, mouths, and torsos. Arms and legs can be twisted singly from the joint socket, or can be twisted together like a pretzel. Twisting the torso is difficult for a number of children. To begin, I ask the children to lie down on their backs and roll their hips one way while their shoulders roll to the other side. Once they feel the movement lying down, we do it standing up. After exploring the twist with individual body parts, I ask for several simultaneous twists: arms and legs, torso and head, fingers and toes, torso and arms, and legs and head. We then try a few full-body twists: "I hope you will be able to untangle yourselves!"

An introductory study sequences three twists and adds a shake: twist the right arm and come back (beats 1 and 2), twist the right leg and come back (beats 3 and 4), twist the torso to the right and come back (beats 5 and 6), and shake out (beats 7 and 8). Repeat the sequence with the left.

Spiral Twist Fall

A special use of twist is in the spiral twist fall (also called spiral twist sit). A fall in dance is a controlled lowering of the body (see falls in the catalog of nonlocomotor movements later in this chapter). This specific fall is beautiful and extremely useful for putting together sequences (see the Pachelbel Canon Dance, p. 194).

The children start in Perfect Spots. They stand with their legs wide, facing the back of the room. Keeping the legs where they are, the children twist around so that they are facing the front of the room. The crux of the movement is that the feet stay in place but the torso, hips, and feet pivot around. When the torso is completely twisted (facing front), the legs bend until the person is sitting. There is a danger of the back knee hitting the floor hard. Two refinements prevent that from happening: (1) The back foot changes its weight to the top of the foot, and (2) the back knee does not directly lower to the floor but rather slides under the standing leg. The legs end up tightly crossed one over the other (see figure 4.6, a through c).

4.6

Do not attempt to verbally explain this move. Have the class follow you visually. Begin with just the pivot to face the front of the room. Pull strongly front before lowering to the sit position. The control for the spiral twist fall comes from pulling the weight forward onto the front thigh. Ideally, the movement is tightly controlled so that it can be done in slow motion and stopped at any point. It is most dramatic, however, when done quickly.

Introducing Bend and Straighten

A bend is a folding of two straight sides, as with a book or a piece of paper. It is a hinge-like action. To straighten is to unhinge or align the two sides. Of the nonlocomotor movements, bend and straighten are the hardest to do correctly. I hold up a piece of cardboard: "Bend means folding two straight sides [I fold the cardboard]. Straighten means putting the sides in one line [I straighten the cardboard]. That is pretty clear, huh? Now, I have a tough question for you: What is the difference between contract and stretch, and bend and straighten?" The idea is that contract is a rounding or curling while bend is a folding of two straight sides; stretch is an extended lengthening while straighten is purely an alignment of the two sides. If your class answers in any coherent form, congratulations! They understand a great deal about movement and about how their own bodies can move.

We bend and straighten isolated parts of the body, hinging from elbows, knees, wrists, and ankles. Arms hinge at the shoulder, and legs hinge at the hip joint. These are relatively simple hinges. The difficulty comes from the full-body hinges. Usually full-body bends are done with the torso bending at the hip joint and remaining straight. The arms can remain by the side of the body or, harder, can reach front as in figure 4.7.

4.7

If the children are having a lot of trouble, have them bend their knees, straighten their torsos forward, and then work to straighten their knees. This particular bend and straighten is excellent for back strength. Another full-body bend and straighten is done on knee level. The torso and hips remain absolutely straight while hinging back (see figure 4.8).

4.8

This is excellent for strengthening the thighs. As the children have pointed out to me, a true straighten for this knee hinge would be falling flat on one's face. For a simple introductory study, have the children bend and straighten the right arm (beats 1 and 2), bend and straighten the left arm (beats 3 and 4), bend and straighten the right leg (beats 5 and 6), bend and straighten the left leg (beats 7 and 8), bend and straighten the torso (beats 9 and 10), and jump turn ready to begin again (beats 11 and 12).

Introducing Spin, Turn, or Twirl

To spin, the body rotates in space, remaining in place. Very often we see dances with spins as locomotor movements, but technically that kind of spin is combined with a walk or leap. Children are familiar with spinning, so I do not make a special verbal introduction. "How many ways can your body spin?" The children will immediately think of spinning on their seats. We extend the exploration to all levels: abdomen and back, knees, feet, and in the air. Once the children have spun on all levels, ask them to twirl changing levels without stopping the movement.

Turning from air level through lowest level without stopping creates a beautiful ministudy in itself. Specific beats for the turns complete the study. The beats can be kept the same, for example three beats for each turn. Or each spin can get a different number of beats, for example

1 beat for air level, 7 beats for standing, 2 beats for knee, 5 beats for sitting, and 10 beats for the lowest level. The movement should flow through the level changes.

One-Foot Standing Twirl

It is easy to do a standing-level turn by taking a few steps to turn around, more difficult to do it by balancing on the ball of one foot while twirling around. This one-foot twirl is dance studio work, but most children enjoy trying it. Here are a few tricks for accomplishing this turn:

- Step immediately up to the half-toe (metatarsal) rather than swooping up.
- Keep the body aligned and stretched up (easier said than done).
- Use less energy than you think necessary.
- Keep the standing leg, the leg you turn on, straight. (I do not attempt to teach a perfected one-foot twirl except in experienced dance classes.)

Fraction Jump Turns

Air-level turns (jump turns) are not only exhilarating but also useful for work on fractions. The class stands in Perfect Spots. I show the traditional pie cut in fourths and ask the children what jumping in fourths would mean. Most children see that it means taking four jumps to get completely around. (If not, I tell them.) I demonstrate, exaggerating stiff, precise quarter-turns: jumping to face one side of the room squarely, the back of the room, the other side, and the front of the room. The class then does quarter-turn jumps. For older classes, I include right and left directions: quarter-turns to the right and then to the left. Half-turns are next. Children jump twice, first facing the back of the room and then jumping to face front. Again, older children are asked to go to the right and left. Full turns are complete turns in the air. These can also go to the right and left.

These fraction turns combine nicely into a pattern. The children stand in Perfect Spots: four quarter-turns, two half-turns, one full turn—with no hesitation between any of the turns. Older children do the pattern twice, going once to the right and once to the left. We work on going faster and faster while keeping the turns very precise.

Rotation or Circle Turns

A different type of turn comes from individual body parts rotating or circling around. Arms, legs, the head, shoulders, upper torso, entire torso, and hips can all rotate from the joint. This kind of movement is good for limbering up and for isolation control. It creates a jazzy effect.

Combining a few of these rotating turns makes an interesting study. The children start standing. The head circles; when it reaches its starting point, the upper torso (waist up) rotates; just as this circle is complete, the entire torso (hips up) rotates. This completed movement propels the entire body to twirl on one foot back to starting position. There are no specific counts. The quality is loose, almost rag doll limp, and each turn propels the following one, like a pebble causing concentric circles in water.

Fish Turn

The fish turn is a dramatic spin of the legs under a stationary, sitting torso. Start by lying down,

abdomen on floor. Throughout the move, clamp legs together with toes pointed, like a fish tail. The legs swing to the right, pulling the torso into a sitting position; the legs swing to the front with the torso facing front; the legs swing to the left and then back to the original lying-down position. Practice slowly at first, clearly differentiating the leg positions; then smooth out the entire turn so it looks like one flowing circle of the legs under the torso (see figure 4.9, a through c).

Although the fish turn is initially difficult, I have taught it to third grade on up. It is part of the Pachelbel Canon Dance, an advanced study found in chapter 12.

Final Notes on Introducing Nonlocomotor Movements

Even after introducing shake, swing, contract and stretch, strike, twist, bend and straighten, and turn, one problem persists: Many children still think of nonlocomotor movements as stationary locomotor movements. Their creative efforts consistently lean toward running or jumping in place. It is time for my "true nonlocomotor movements" speech.

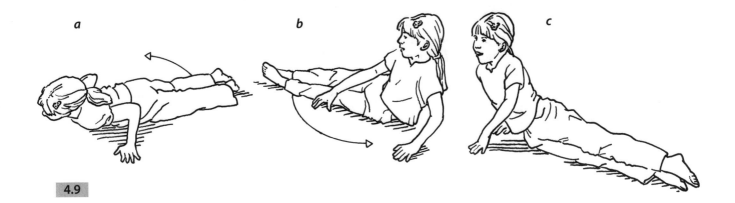

a   b   c

4.9

"I have a grown-up idea to tell you. Running, jumping, and skipping in place are technically nonlocomotor movements because they do not go anywhere, but they are not true nonlocomotor movements. What I mean is that running is usually a locomotor movement and it is the technicality of doing it in place that makes it become a nonlocomotor movement. The same goes for jumping, hopping, skipping, and so on. There are some movements, however, that are never locomotor movements by themselves. These movements are shake, swing, contract and stretch, strike, bend and straighten, twist, and turn. These are true nonlocomotor movements. Yes, you could do these moves and go somewhere, but you would have to add a locomotor movement like walk to do that. If you understand this, great! If you don't, don't worry about it."

The other problem with nonlocomotor movements is that, for some reason, these moves bring up the bugaboo of dance. I have had two kinds of disconcerting experiences with this word. In dance classes the children do beautiful dances with a prop or a movement problem and then ask me, "When are we going to dance?" The opposite problem occurs in schools where I teach "perceptual-motor coordination" to intermediate grades. If I say something like "Now we are going to do the Fall Dance," the class gasps in horror as if I had said the word "sex."

I think the whole thing is ridiculous. I think it is unfortunate that children do not know when they have created a dance and just as unfortunate when children cannot move if they think they are doing something "sissy," like dancing. What I do is use the word when it is appropriate and not use it when it is not. I call my school classes "movement classes," explaining that we do all sorts of movements: gymnastics, dance, physical education, and play. Later, when it is appropriate, I explain that a dance has a beginning, middle, and end and usually is repeatable. If the students create a dance, I call it that. Generally I find that if I am relaxed with the word the children will eventually become relaxed with it too.

Combining Nonlocomotor and Locomotor Movements

It is a milestone when the children understand and feel comfortable with both locomotor and nonlocomotor movements, because they have completed the groundwork of their movement foundation. It is time to put the two kinds of movement together.

"Do you know what locomotor movements are?"

"Yes."

"Do you know what nonlocomotor movements are?"

"Yes."

"Good. [I lift one hand.] Pretend this is a locomotor movement. [I lift the other hand.] Pretend this is a nonlocomotor movement. Who can figure out how to put them together? [I clap my hands together.]"

The usual response is silent disbelief in the possibility. A few children will come up with an interesting solution: They do a locomotor movement first and then do a nonlocomotor movement second, for example walk-walk-walk-swing-swing. This is excellent thinking, and I praise the solution highly. However, I persist in asking for a locomotor and nonlocomotor movement occurring at the same time. Occasionally, I will attempt one hint before giving in and showing an example. "Remember, they do not have to be in the same parts of the body." Hopefully, someone will figure it out; that child is congratulated, praised, and applauded.

Table 4.1 lists some combinations of locomotor and nonlocomotor movements that work well. The combinations are clearer if the nonlocomotor movement is done first and then the locomotor movement is added to it. Use the Free Traveling Structure to work on these.

Locomotor and nonlocomotor combinations also provide an extra challenge when used within

Table 4.1   Nonlocomotor/Locomotor Movement Combinations That Work

Nonlocomotor	ADD	Locomotor	Additions/Notes
Swing your arms	+	Skip	Can be done backward
Swing your arms	+	Gallop	
Gently twist your head "no"	+	Jump	Can be done backward or sideways
Gently twist your head "no"	+	Locomotor jump	Can be done backward or sideways
Shake one leg	+	Hop on the other leg	Change legs. Can be done in the turning direction
Contract and stretch	+	Roll	Contract while on the back and stretch while on the tummy
Wiggle the shoulders	+	Seat-scoot	Can be done backward
Gently shake your head "yes"	+	Crawl	Can be done in all directions
Shake the hands	+	Run	Can be done in all directions
Contract and stretch	+	Walk	Can be done in all directions
Swing the arms cross and open	+	Side-slide changing sides	
Strike	+	Walk	Possible to change levels
Bend and straighten arms	+	Jump	Can be done in all directions
Twist in the arms, rotating back and forth with the shoulder joint	+	Jump with legs wide, second-position feet	(An African dance movement)
Wiggle in the hips	+	Walk	
Contract and stretch	+	Skip	Hard and an excellent coordination problem. (I usually shout out something like "shades of Isadora Duncan." It is my favorite combination.)
Clap the hands	+	Run and leap	(I usually take a hammy bow.)

a Brain Catcher game (see chapter 10). As an example, the game might include (1) nonlocomotor swing in the arms plus locomotor skip, (2) nonlocomotor contract and stretch plus locomotor roll, and (3) nonlocomotor wiggle in the hips plus locomotor walk. These combinations are a great deal harder to remember than three single movements. Several skills are involved in grasping a Brain Catcher like the one in this example. First, the children need to understand the movement language well enough to quickly form a mental picture; and second, they need to sequence and retain these pictures. These are important mental as well as physical skills.

CATALOG OF NONLOCOMOTOR MOVEMENTS

Following is a catalog of nonlocomotor movements. I have distilled the list into nine basic nonlocomotor movements with numerous variations for each. Another section provides a list of the basic body positions used in dance; these are not movements but are included here because they are stationary. Like the catalog of locomotor movements, the list is not exhaustive but hopefully will make movement more accessible and comprehensible. These movements are not standards; do not feel compelled to introduce, let alone master, them all. They cover an enormous range of difficulty and can be performed with varying degrees of polish.

❶ Shake

Shake incorporates wiggle, wriggle, vibrate, thrash, and flick. It is a wavering, alternating motion that can be done whole-body or in just one part.

Variations

1. Isolated body parts: Hand, arm, leg, torso, seat.
2. Whole body. (Check that the torso is included.)
3. Levels: Air, standing, knee, sitting, lowest.
4. Vibration: An extremely tight, quick, small shake usually done in one part of the body like an arm or leg.
5. Flick: A small, quick shake, usually of the hands.
6. Tantrum/Thrash: A wiggling, kicking shake, usually done on lowest level. A tantrum is best accompanied by appropriate sounds.
7. Size: Small, big, growing, diminishing.
8. Energy: Limp, strenuous.
9. Partners: Shake hands, feet, heads, seats, elbows, and so on.
10. Combined with locomotor movements: Roll, crawl, jump, hop, run, and so on.
11. Wiggle: Essentially the same as a shake. Generally a wiggle implies a slower shake usually in one part of the body—for example, "Wiggle your hips."

❷ Swing

A swing is an arc-shaped movement usually with a release of tension at the midpoint of the arc. Swinging, either whole-body or with one body part, has a lyrical waltz-like quality.

Variations

1. Isolated body parts: Arm, leg, head, hips, hand, and so on. Arms and legs can be swung either bent or straight.
2. Front swing: Arms start above the head. Arms, head, and torso drop forward; hands touch the floor as knees bend. The torso stays lowered as arms reach back, and knees straighten. That is one arc. To come back, the knees bend, hands touch the floor, and everything reaches up. (See p. 50.)
3. Crossed swing: Arms and legs start wide. Torso and knees bend as arms drop to the ground and cross in front of the body; the torso remains bent. That is one arc. The arc is reversed as the arms uncross and drop; the torso and knees bend and then straighten as the arms open wide again. (See p. 51.)
4. Side swing: Arms, head, and torso all lean to one side; arms are above the head. Everything drops and straightens to the other side. That is one arc. The arc is reversed. The side swing can also be done with hands clasped. (See p. 51.)
5. Circle swing: This is like a side swing that continues around to outline an entire circle. The body leans to one side, arms overhead. The body drops and swings to the other side, then reaches up and around to the original side. The circle swing can be done with isolated body parts (head, head and torso, arms, legs) or with the whole body. Arms can be clasped together or apart.
6. Fan swing: This is a specific circle swing done with the leg. The child starts standing, legs together. The circling leg crosses over the other leg, opens wide, and returns to the starting position. The fan swing can be done lying down, resulting in a straddle roll. (See p. 38.) The child starts lying on his back on

the floor. The circling leg crosses the other leg, reaches up, and opens wide. As the leg returns to the side, the body rolls over.

7. Figure 8 swing: This is like the circle swing extended to a figure 8. The figure 8 can be done vertically with the arms and torso or horizontally with a leg.

8. Twist swing: The child starts standing with arms wide, feet and hips stable. The arms swing around to the back, twisting the torso. That is one arc. The arc is reversed to the other side. It is difficult, but better, if the hips work to remain facing front. For young children I sometimes use the image of a helicopter; we start slow and swing faster and faster.

9. Body wave: I am not sure this is truly a swing, but it is an arc-shaped movement and comes closest to the swing category. The body wave is like a reversed front swing. The hips start by pushing forward. The waist then pushes forward, then the upper back, and finally the head. The movement is a ripple through the body. The arms meanwhile move in a circle: They start overhead and then move forward, down, and back and up. The torso and arms flow together in one fluid movement (see figure 4.10, a through c).

13. Levels: Lowest, sitting, knee, standing, air. Virtually all swings can be done on all levels.

a. On the lowest level ask for swings of legs and hips as well as arms. Check that the swings do not deteriorate into shakes.

b. A difficult swing on sitting level is done with the legs wide. Start with the torso erect (a difficult position for most children). The hands clasp, and the torso drops over one leg and swings to the other leg. (Try to reach forward at the midpoint of the swing.) The arc is reversed by swinging back to the original leg. This is a good stretch for the inner thigh.

c. A pretty knee-level swing moves from sitting level to the knees. Start sitting with the right leg straight and the left leg bent or with both legs bent to the right (see figure 4.11, a and b). Swing forward and lift. Place the left hand near the seat and finish the swing by pushing up to the left knee, the right arm continuing the movement up. At the high point of the swing, the head reaches back and the hips push forward for a strong stretch of the entire torso (see figure 4.11c). Of course, do the swing with the legs on the other side.

4.10   *a*   *b*   *c*

10. Size: Huge, big, medium, small, tiny.

11. Energy: Limp, strenuous.

12. Combined with locomotor movements: Skip, gallop, jump, side-slide, walk.

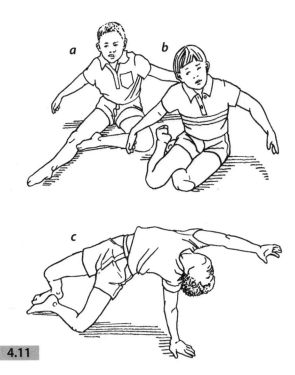

4.11

d. On standing level, check that the torso and head let go and drop into the swing.

e. For a good air-level swing, add a jump at both ends of a front swing. In other words, as the torso drops and the arms reach back, jump, and as the body straightens up, jump. Watch that the torso remains bent during the first jump. This air-level front swing is an excellent exercise for the seat muscles.

❸ Contract and Stretch

Contract is a tight curling or rounding; stretch is a strenuous expanding. These moves can involve the whole body or parts of the body and can be done fully, tightly coiled, or partially (shaped like the letter "C"). A typical modern dance (Martha Graham-style) contraction is an intense partial contraction of the torso.

Variations

1. Isolated parts of the body: Arms, legs, torso, hands, face, neck, fingers.

2. Combined body parts: Arm and leg, hand and torso, torso and leg, and so on.

3. Whole body.

4. Levels: Air, standing, knee, sitting, lowest.

5. Tempo.

6. Size: Partial rounding, full rounding.

7. Dynamic quality: Percussive, sustained.

8. Energy: Limp, strenuous. Unless otherwise specified, a contraction should have a great deal of energy.

9. Partners:

a. Contract together like a ball. Stretch apart holding on to each other, preferably on two different levels.

b. Contract and stretch in opposites; that is, while one person contracts the other stretches.

10. Combined with locomotor movements: Walk, jump, skip, roll, and crawl.

❹ Bend and Straighten

Bend is a hinge-like folding of two straight sides; straighten is an alignment of sides. The image is like a book: When the book is open the sides are essentially straight; the book can "bend" in varying degrees.

Variations

1. Isolated body parts: Arm, leg, hand, finger.

2. Combined body parts: Arm and leg, torso and knees, hands and feet (while sitting).

3. Whole body: Hinge from hip joint or from knees.

4. Pliés: A special bend and straighten. Pliés ("plee-ays") come from ballet but are an integral part of all dance. Essentially plié means to bend and straighten the knees, but certain additional conditions make plié difficult. To be correct, a plié must be done with (1) heels on the floor; (2) arches lifted; (3) torso perfectly aligned; (4) weight centered, usually between the big toe and second toe; (5) knees pushed back, if the legs are in a turned-out position; and (6) most important, energy—a plié is a burst of controlled energy (figure 4.12).

4.12

Pliés can be done in any standing position; see "Positions of the Body" later in the chapter. They can also be done sitting or lying down. It is excellent technique work to do pliés sitting or lying down to check the exact placement of the feet and the execution of the bend. For example, when one is lying down with the legs up, a first-position plié starts with the heels touching, feet flexed as if standing on the ceiling, toes angled toward the side of the body. When one is bending, it is important that the knees push out toward the sides rather than drop forward. It is often easier to see mistakes and correct children in this upside-down position.

5. Levels: Air, standing, knee, sitting, lowest.
6. Tempo.
7. Dynamic quality: Jerky, percussive, sustained.
8. Combined with locomotor movements: Walk, jump, hop. (On the whole, bend and straighten does not combine easily with locomotor movements.)

⑤ Bounce

Bounce in the body is similar to the bouncing of a ball. It is a drop-like movement with a split-second release of energy and a slight reverberation.

Variations

1. Isolated body parts: Head, shoulder, elbows, knees. Note: Bouncing knees might look like pliés but they are quite different. When done correctly, a plié smoothly elongates the muscles into a bend and then, with completely sustained energy, pulls into a straightened position. A bounce is a shrug, with a loose, letting-go type of energy.
2. Isolated body part—torso: Bouncing is very basic modern dance vocabulary. The torso can be either slightly contracted or bent completely over during the bounce.
3. Whole body: A whole-body bounce is a small jump.
4. Levels: Air, standing, sitting, knee, lowest.
5. Size.
6. Tempo.
7. Combined with walk.

⑥ Strike

A strike is a punching motion. It can be done like a boxer's jab or like a karate chop. A strike of the leg comes very close to a kick.

Variations

1. Isolated parts of the body: Arm, leg, torso, hip, elbow.

2. Combined body parts: Arm and leg, arm and torso, elbow and hip.
3. Levels: Air, standing, knee, sitting, lowest.
4. Size.
5. Tempo.
6. Combined with locomotor movements: Walk, jump, crawl, and so forth.

⑦ Twist

A twist is a stretch in two opposite directions.

Variations

1. Isolated body parts: Arms, legs, head, shoulders, torso.
2. Combined body parts entangled: Arms together, arm and leg, both legs.
3. Whole body.
4. Spiral twist sit: A specific whole-body twist (see "Introducing Twist" earlier in the chapter). The children start standing with legs wide. The feet remain in place but pivot as the torso twists completely around. The legs then bend to end up, with the person sitting, in a tightly crossed position.
5. Size: Partial twist, full twist.
6. Dynamic quality: Percussive, sustained.
7. Tempo.
8. Levels: Air, standing, knee, sitting, lowest.
9. Combined with locomotor movements: Walk, jump, hop, skip.

⑧ Spin

A spin, turn, or twirl rotates the body. It can be done whole-body or with body parts, fully or partially.

Variations

1. Isolated body parts turning or circling. What is the difference between this and circle swing? Just about nothing. This is one of the problems of categorizations. Generally, if the circle movement has a flowing, lilting quality, I call it a swing; if it is evenly controlled I call it a turn. Of course, we could always make up a new category just for circles. My point is that there

is nothing sacred about these categories. They are simply a method of organizing movements in order to understand and use them more efficiently.

2. Whole body.

3. Body part leading the turn. That is, a turn can originate with an arm, a leg, the head, torso, hip, elbow, whatever.

4. Tempo.

5. Levels: Air, standing, knee, sitting, lowest.

6. Partial or full turns.

7. Fraction turns: Dividing the circle described by a turn into equal parts.

8. Fish turn: Rotating the legs, held together, under a sitting torso (see earlier section on introducing turns).

9. Dynamic quality: Percussive, sustained, jerky.

10. Combined with locomotor movements: Walk, jump, hop, skip, leap.

❾ Falls

Falling in dance is quite different than in ordinary life; here it is a controlled lowering of the body. The control comes from an equalization of tension between gravity and a pull in the opposite direction. A fall usually connotes a lowering to the floor, but any shift from one level to a lower level is technically a fall.

Variations

1. Teeter-totter fall. Start standing very straight. The head and torso lower as one leg lifts, as with a teeter-totter. Hands are in front of the body to help catch the fall. When the head is as low as possible, place hands on the floor and "walk down" to the abdomen; that is, the foot stays in place and hands walk forward until the body is lying flat (see figure 4.13, a through c).

The important elements of this fall are (1) keeping both legs straight and (2) lowering the torso while one leg lifts high.

a b c

4.13

2. Back fall:
   a. Sitting back fall. This fall can start standing or on the knees. Pull the weight forward by reaching forward with the arms. Slowly, with control, lower seat to the ground and rock back to the lowest level.
   b. One-knee back fall. Start standing level. The arms reach front to pull the weight forward. The body is gently lowered to one knee and one foot (see figure 4.14).

4.14

Then the body is lowered to sitting with one foot on the floor. From there the back can be lowered to lowest level. Reversing the one-knee back fall is a good way to get up.

3. Side fall. Start on the knee level. To fall to the right side, lift arms overhead and reach to the left. Keep the weight pulling left while lowering the seat to the right side of the feet. After the seat is on the floor, place left hand to balance torso and lower right side to the ground (see figure 4.15, a through d).

The process is reversed for the left side. This fall can also be done from standing level. The process is essentially the same as from the knees. Reach arms overhead and pull left; the body arches right as the right knee is lowered to the right of the feet. The left hand reaches across the body and takes some of the weight as it aids the torso lowering to the ground.

4.15

4. Spiral twist fall—same as spiral twist sit. Start standing with the legs wide. The feet stay in place but pivot as the torso and hips twist completely around. The knees then bend and the body is lowered to sitting.

5. One-leg side fall. Start standing, keeping the weight on the left leg, and point the right foot diagonally forward. Put the right hand near the seat and stretch the left arm front. Look over the right shoulder at the right hand. This is the starting position (figure 4.16a). To fall, lift the weight up by pushing the hips forward and by stretching the left arm front. The forward push of the hips is crucial. Slide the right leg out while lowering the right hand to the floor. The left knee should not touch the floor at this point. Once the right hand is on the floor, lower the seat and then the left knee to the final position (see figure 4.16b).

4.16

"But my right foot won't slide! It keeps sticking to the floor." Keep the weight on the left leg. The right foot has almost no weight on it until the very end. Further, keep the right foot sharply pointed for easier sliding. "It looks scary!" This is an illusion. The fall is controlled by the right hand lowering to the floor, and it is not far from the floor to begin with. Before attempting the one-leg side fall I often have children practice just bending their knees and placing their right hand on the floor behind their seat. This is essentially the fall, except that one leg is kept straight while lowering. Do not forget to look at the right hand; this takes away some of the scariness. To fall to the other side, reverse all positions. This is a very dramatic fall. It looks as though the person is falling into the splits. This is not so, but the breath-catching quality is there.

6. Lunge fall. A very simple fall. Start standing and take a long step forward, bending the front leg. This is a lunge position. Bend the torso and put the hands on the floor on either side of the front foot. This step and bend is done quickly. From the bent position it is easy to lower the seat to the ground, shifting the weight back and ending on sitting or lowest level.

Positions of the Body

The five positions described next are not movements. They are some of the basic body positions common to most dance—a first position is the same in a ballet class in Moscow, a modern dance class in Paris, and a jazz class in San Francisco.

Standing-Level Positions

1. Parallel feet: Toes point straight ahead (figure 4.17a).

2. First position: Heels touch, toes point diagonally out (figure 4.17b).

3. Second position: A step wider than first position (figure 4.17c).

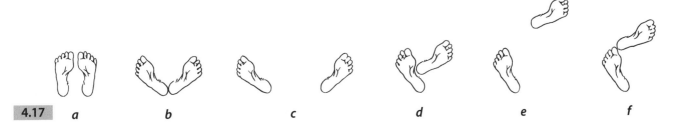

4.17   *a*   *b*   *c*   *d*   *e*   *f*

4. Third position: Heel touching instep, both feet turned out (figure 4.17d).

5. Fourth position: A step forward from third position (figure 4.17e).

6. Fifth position: Heel touching toe, both feet turned out (figure 4.17f).

7. Half-toe: This elevated stance can be done in any position. The metatarsal remains on the floor while the heels lift.

Knee-Level Positions

1. One knee and one foot on the floor.

2. Both knees on the floor.

3. Both hands and knees on the floor.

4. Both hands and one knee on the floor, the other leg usually stretched straight back.

Sitting-Level Positions

1. Crossed legs (traditional "Indian Style").

2. Soles of the feet clapped together.

3. Triangle position: Both legs bent to one side, toes of one foot touching knee of the other leg (see figure 4.18).

4.18

4. Both legs tucked tightly to one side (see figure 4.19).

4.19

5. One leg straight and one leg bent forward (see figure 4.20).

4.20

6. One leg straight and one bent back (see figure 4.21).

4.21

7. Wide stride: Both legs straight and wide (gymnastics straddle position).

4.22

8. Both legs straight and together (gymnastics piked position).
9. One leg bent and one foot on the floor (see figure 4.22).

Lowest-Level Positions

1. Legs and/or arms together; legs and/or arms wide
2. The back on the floor, arms and legs lifted straight or contracted.
3. The stomach on the floor, arms and legs lifted.

Other Positions

1. **Shoulder stand:** Head and upper back on floor, hips lifted and held with hands, legs lifted and usually straight.

2. **Push-up position:** Hands and feet on the floor, torso and legs "straight as a pencil." It is possible to bend and lift the hips into a "high push-up position."
3. **Bridge:** Hands and feet on the floor with the torso stretched into a vigorous arch. Hands are twisted behind shoulders to lift into this back bend. Head should be off the floor and dropped back.
4. **Frog balance:** Preliminary headstand. Head and hands on the floor with the head forward of the hands. Knees rest firmly on the elbows; torso is lifted.

Note on teaching a frog balance: Begin by placing masking tape in a large triangle (approximately two feet on each side) with the point of the triangle forward (^) on a mat. Tell the children that they will be able to balance on their heads only if they make a triangle position out of their hands and head. Position your (or a volunteer's) hands on the bottom points of the triangle and the top of the head at the top. Make the arms sturdy by pushing down on the mat. Slowly lift one knee onto one elbow and then gently place the other knee on the other elbow. Remove the tape and show how the head and hands can form the same triangle without tape. Have the children practice. Ninety-nine percent of the children that can't execute the frog balance do not have the head forward of their hands in a triangle position.

5. **Headstand:** Hands and top of head on the floor, torso and legs usually lifted straight up.
6. **Handstand:** Hands on the floor, body lifted up usually in a slight arch.

Nonlocomotor Movement Studies and Dances

We are finally ready to put together some of these movements into dance sequences or studies. There is not much difference between a dance and a study; it is a question of intent and execution. The purpose of a dance is an artistic expression, often with an emotional undertone;

unless specified as percussive, moves flow one into the other. A study is a demonstration of an intellectual challenge; the moves often stay distinct. However, I have seen studies turn into beautiful dances and dances executed like studies.

Teacher-Taught Combinations

1. **Eight Plus Eight Dance:** This is a well-worn dance. I am fond of this dance because it encompasses numerous concepts. It could be used as a culminating study for locomotor and nonlocomotor movements, for levels, and even to introduce the idea of canon. Also, it is pretty.

Children start in Perfect Spots, standing, arms overhead. Front swing down and up (beats 1 and 2), shake body down to sitting (beat 3), spin on seat (beat 4), contract lying on side (beats 5 and 6), stretch up to one knee—other leg extended (beats 7 and 8). This is the nonlocomotor eight-beat section.

The children then have eight beats to move, doing any locomotor movement they want, ending in their exact spot by count 8.

Once the children know the moves and counts, have half the class do the locomotor section while the other half does the nonlocomotor part at the same time. Repeat several times.

2. **Swing and strike:** Children start in Perfect Spots, standing, arms overhead. Front swing and come up (beats 1 and 2), strike one arm and then one leg (beats 3 and 4), side swing and return (beats 5 and 6), strike one elbow and one hip (beats 7 and 8). This is a tricky coordination problem.

3. **Swing and shake:** Children start in Perfect Spots, standing, arms overhead. Front swing and jump (beats 1 and 2), swing up and jump (beats 3 and 4), shake down to sitting (beats 5 and 6), spin once on the seat and get up (beats 7 and 8).

4. **Isolated contractions:** Children start in Perfect Spots, standing, arms down. Contract right arm and hold it (beat 1), contract left leg and hold it (beat 2), contract head and torso while balancing on right foot (beat 3), stretch everything out (beat 4). Repeating on the other side, contract left arm and hold (beat 5), contract right leg and hold (beat 6), contract head and torso while balancing (beat 7), stretch everything out (beat 8).

5. **Body wave warm-up:** This is an excellent warm-up for the back and legs; I use it often. Children start in Perfect Spots, standing, arms overhead. Front swing and up (beats 1 and 2), body wave swing (beats 3 and 4), repeat front swing and up (beats 5 and 6), repeat body wave swing (beats 7 and 8). Roll torso down, ideally palms flat on the floor (beats 1-4); bend knees and straighten back forward parallel to the floor, arms stretched forward (beats 5-8); straighten knees while holding flat back (beats 1-4); round from the base of the spin up, ending in a straight standing position (beats 5-8).

6. **Fluid turns:** This is another of my favorites. Children start in Perfect Spots, standing, arms wide. Spiral twist fall to sitting; spin on seat; throw legs under and spin halfway around, ending on the abdomen (like half a fish turn); lift up to sit in the triangle position; lift seat and spin on knees; stand and spin standing; jump turn. Do not use counts for this study. The children do it in their own time, moving smoothly and fluidly.

7. **Jump pattern:** Any number of nonlocomotor jumps can be sequenced into a pattern; these patterns are often a good first study. Here is an example: Starting with the feet in fourth position, jump switching legs (four beats), close and open legs (four beats), jump side to side (four beats), jump and shake down (two beats), do a small preparatory jump and jump turn (two beats).

8. **Nonlocomotor movements included in traveling patterns:**

   a. The Monster Rises. Children start in groups ready to move on the diagonal. They run to the middle of the diagonal and freeze in a strange shape; drop limply to the floor; contract on lowest level; start to shake (first small and then getting bigger and bigger) and shake up to standing level, arms up; front swing and up, ending the swing in a stretched jump; leap to the end of the diagonal.

   b. Swing, return the swing, contract, stretch, shake, travel somewhere. In rhythm: swing-2-3, swing-2-3, contract-2-3, stretch-2-3, shake-2-3, go-some-where (six measures of three).

   c. Waltz walk (three beats), waltz-walk turn (three beats), spiral twist fall halfway down (three beats), twist back up (three beats), side swing (three beats), swing to the other side (three beats), run (three beats), leap and hold (three beats) (eight measures of three). Put this to some lovely waltz music for a lyrical piece.

Group Problems

1. Ask the children to pick four nonlocomotor movements, each on a different level. Each movement will get six beats. To make this harder, ask for each person to do the same sequence but not in the same order. For example, one person could do air-level jump turn, standing-level spin, knee-level contract and stretch, and sitting-level swing, while another person could do the exact same moves but in the reverse order.

2. Have children pick five different parts of the body, then do a nonlocomotor movement with each part but without repeating any movements.

3. Children pick three different nonlocomotor movements and four different locomotor movements. Have them alternate locomotor and nonlocomotor movements and fit the sequence into the room in an interesting way.

4. Within 20 beats, students fit in four different nonlocomotor movements.

Closing Thoughts

Most children (teachers too) are not drawn to nonlocomotor movements as much as to locomotor movements. It is time to expand our thinking. Nonlocomotor movements develop flexibility both physically and mentally: A pattern like the Eight Plus Eight Dance warms up the back, torso, and joints, as well as the mind. Start with an introduction that alternates locomotor and nonlocomotor movements and then develop just one move fully—contract and stretch is especially useful. Really explore that move with isolated body parts, levels, sizes; use props and partners, tempos, and dynamic qualities if you are up for it. Then put it into a pattern, like the Eight Plus Eight Dance, and see if your students do not respond to the fluidity of sequenced moves—which is dance. You do not have to cover all the nonlocomotor movements and certainly not all the variations; you do not need to tangle with difficult moves, like the spiral sit or body wave. But it would be wonderful if children saw movement encompassing more than their feet.

Chapter 5

Levels

Level means height. The ability to use, recognize, and differentiate vertical space is an essential element of movement. Level is a simple yet extraordinarily useful concept.

When I was younger I introduced level like this, with the class standing in Perfect Spots: "I am going to teach you a new word: *level*. I am not going to tell you what it means; you'll have to guess." With the children imitating me, I demonstrated the five basic levels: air level (jumping), standing level (one or both feet on the ground), knee level (one or both knees on the ground), sitting level (seat on the ground), and lowest level (torso on the ground). The children and I went up and down through these five levels several times. "What do you guess level means?" Usually children saw that level means high and low or going up and down. If not, I told them. I am very fond of this guess-what-the-word-means type of introduction. (You see it again with introducing symmetry, as discussed in chapter 11.) The children are engaged and internalize the concept more readily. But sometimes our energy or our backs do not make this type of introduction possible.

Now that I am older I introduce level like this: "Have you heard the word level before?" Usually the children immediately think of levels in a video game (heaven help us). They will also come up with reading levels, level as even or not bumpy, and levels in an elevator. This multiple-meaning work is excellent in itself, especially for English learners. "In movement class, level means height

and we use 5 levels: air, standing, knee, sitting, and lowest." What about squatting, tiptoe, high knee, or low knee level? I realize that the 5 levels I have listed are arbitrary. There could easily be 8 levels or more. If a class can remember and use 8 or 10 levels, all the better. Just the same, if a class would do better with 3 levels to start (low, medium, high), that is fine. The goal is for the children to differentiate and use vertical space.

After the children go through the different levels with me, I ask them to find the levels without me. I call out levels nonsequentially: "Air level . . . Lowest level . . . Knee level . . ." and so on. I go fast and often play with the change from air level to lowest level. If we have the time, I'll try to trick them by doing a different level than the one I call: "I am going to trick all of you! I am going to call out a level but do something different. Do the level you hear, not the one you see. Can you do it?"

Once the idea of levels is clear, we do nonlocomotor movements using levels. We shake, swing, contract and stretch, twist, bend and straighten, and turn on all levels. Here is an example of exploring levels with contract and stretch: "How would you contract on the lowest level? Right, you need to get on your back or side . . . Good . . . Now stay down there and stretch . . . Contract sitting up . . . How about stretching with your legs wide? Lift your torso and stretch your legs into pointed toes . . . No, you're scrunching, stretch harder . . . harder . . . Great! Contract and stretch knee level

. . . Can you stretch so hard on knee level that you grab your heels? Contract standing level . . . Lift one leg while stretching on the standing level and balance . . . Pull everything. Who can figure out how to contract air level? Right, you have to jump and tuck in the air . . . Can you stretch air level? Yes, it is like a cheerleader yell. Hooray!"

If the concept *nonlocomotor* has been taught, I use the term while working with levels; if it has not been taught, we just do the levels. Teaching movement is a juggling process. I want to teach one concept but need another concept in order for the children to understand the first fully. The result is that I teach what is necessary at the time. For example, I usually teach nonlocomotor before levels but the order could just as easily be reversed. When exploring nonlocomotor movements I use levels and later formally teach the term and concept. This juggling process involves two factors: (1) Use what you need even if it has not been taught, and (2) do not consider that using an idea is the same as teaching it. After exploring nonlocomotor movements on all levels, we begin combining movements into studies.

Nonlocomotor Level Studies

The following are simple studies using only one nonlocomotor movement and keeping the levels in sequential order:

1. Shake on all levels. Shake down through all the levels and back up again without ever stopping the shake: eight beats down and eight up, four beats down and four up, two beats down and two up.

2. Swing on all levels. Do four swings on each level from highest to lowest. Change levels quickly so that there is no break in the swing rhythm. Do two swings on each level with no rhythmic break.

3. Combine studies 1 and 2. Shake from highest to lowest level (10 slow beats—2 beats for each level), turn and get up (2 beats); swing twice on each level from air level to lowest (10 slow beats), turn and get up (2 beats); repeat the shake.

4. Twirl on each level: Jump turn, one-foot twirl, spin on knees with or without hands, spin on seat, spin on tummy or back. Twirl through all the levels without stopping the movement.

5. Contract and stretch on each level. Contract and stretch four times on each level, changing quickly so the rhythm is unbroken. Contract and stretch twice on each level, once on each level. Finally, contract on one level and stretch on the next level, for example contract lowest level and stretch sitting level, contract sitting level and stretch knee level, contract knee level and stretch standing level, contract standing level and stretch air level.

6. Combine studies 4 and 5. Twirl from air level to lowest level without a break; contract on one level and stretch on the next higher level as explained for the preceding study; repeat the twirls back down.

7. For young children, up to third grade, rock on all levels using the Rocking Song. (See p. 17.)

• **Lowest level:** The children lie on their backs and rock from side to side. For a more difficult lowest-level rock, they lie on their abdomens and rock forward and back. Do this back-and-forth rock with legs and shoulders lifted off the ground, arms free, or with hands holding ankles as in figure 5.1. This is very strenuous; do it only a few times.

5.1

• **Sitting level:** Children sit with legs crossed and rock from side to side. For a more difficult sitting-level rock, stretch the legs wide and rock forward and back. During rocking forward, the head goes as close to the floor as possible; during rocking back the legs lift, still wide and straight, hopefully touching the floor in back of the head. This is an excellent leg and back stretch.

• **Knee level:** The children rock sideways. The seat is lifted and the hands help push from side to side.

• **Standing level:** The children stand with legs apart and rock from side to side. Each rock is a balanced tilt with the opposite leg lifted. On the word *still* the children stay in that one-legged balance and become "still on the inside" so they can stay balanced longer (see figure 5.2).

5.2

• **Air level:** The rocking is done as on standing level but with an added hop. This hop, of course, makes the final landing balance much harder.

8. Waves. Starting on lowest level, smoothly roll, rise, twirl, and turn through all levels like a wave rising out of the ocean, and jump breaking on shore. Have the wave recede down through all levels back to the spot from which it started. The movement can be structured to beats, for example 8 beats for the wave to break, and 13 beats to recede back to the original spot.

In these initial studies I use only one or two nonlocomotor movements. The level changes move sequentially from lowest to highest or from highest down, and the rhythmic structure is simple. Changing one or more of these factors makes the study more difficult. But it is possible. Remember:

1. Tackle only what you feel ready to try.
2. The children need to be correct but not perfect.

3. Do each move for more beats or stop between each move until you feel comfortable with the sequence.

Following are studies that combine different nonlocomotor movements but still keep the levels in sequence:

1. Shake air level; swing standing level; contract and stretch knee level; spin sitting level; kick legs in the air lowest level. Do each movement for four beats.

2. Two jump turns (four beats); standing strikes, arm-arm-leg-leg (four beats); contract and stretch on the knees (four beats); swing side to side sitting in a wide stride (four beats); have a temper tantrum on the lowest level (eight beats).

Children love this temper tantrum. They wiggle, kick, thrash, and shout. My only restriction is that they must stop exactly on beat 8. They therefore must control the yelling in order to hear the counts, but I do count very loudly. If the children do not abide by the restrictions, we do not do it, at least for the time being. Children love the opportunity to have a safe tantrum.

3. Shake on the lowest level (three beats); bounce seat on the floor (three beats); twirl on knees—use hands to push off but try to complete the twirl without hands (three beats); twist standing (three beats); use the momentum of the twist to jump turn (three beats).

4. Karate kick and jump (beats 1 and 2), contract and stretch standing (beats 3 and 4), spin on the knees (beats 5 and 6), shake hands and feet while balanced on the seat (beats 7 and 8), have a temper tantrum lowest level (beats 1 to 8).

Level studies are easier to do than to read about. The progression of levels provides a scaffolding on which to hang movement changes. Even young children readily remember the levels in sequence; then each movement change rests on its own step. And there is a wide range of possible performance results. Inexperienced classes will simply do the first-level movement, stop, do the second level, stop, and so forth. That is fine. More experienced classes need to eliminate any hesitation between level changes. These final two studies combine movements and mix up the level sequence:

1. Jump once, melt to sitting, spin and tuck legs under to end up on the abdomen, pull seat back and lift to the knees, lift one knee to plant the foot firmly on the floor, and stand. If done to counts, this is an eight-beat study: jump—1; melt—2; sit—3; spin and tuck legs—4; end on abdomen—5; pull seat back to heels—6; plant foot—7; stand ready to repeat—8.

2. Fluid levels. (1) Sit and spin; (2) throw legs under the body to lie on abdomen; (3) pull up to knees; (4) side fall (p. 65); (5) roll to back; (6) rock back (legs overhead) and immediately roll up into a sitting balance; (7) place one knee and the other foot on the floor; push to a standing position; (8) jump and sit, ready to start again. Ideally this is done smoothly, one movement flowing into the next.

Locomotor Level Studies

Locomotor movements generally break down into the following classifications: air-level locomotor movements leave the floor such as jump, hop, hopscotch, skip, gallop, side-slide, leap; standing-level locomotor movements, for the most part, keep a foot on the ground such as walk, jog, run; knee level has the knees on the ground such as crawl; sitting level has the seat on the ground such as seat-scoot; and lowest level has the torso touching the floor such as sliding on the abdomen or back, rolling. The children can figure out most of this categorization. Sometimes children come up with movements that do not fit the level categories, for example crab crawling or walking on hands.

> ⟹ *REAL LIFE*
>
> The children love to stump me when we determine what level a locomotor movement falls under. I may make an approximation:"Crab crawl looks pretty much like an upside-down knee level to me."Or I will throw my hands up:"I have no idea what level walking on hands would be, do you?"

Simple locomotor level studies can be done using the Diagonal Structure. Divide the diagonal in half and do one level for the first half and another for the second. For example, run to the middle, pretend to get tackled, and roll from the middle to the end of the diagonal. Following are a few more locomotor level studies:

1. Spider crawl (four beats); tuck roll (two beats), then stretch on knees (two beats); repeat the tuck roll (two beats) and stretch (two beats); low, mean-looking walk (four beats); turning walk (two beats) and stretch jumps (two beats); repeat the turning walk (two beats) and stretch jumps (two beats).

The count is six measures of four beats. The quality is like that of the hunter and the hunted. The spider crawl and the low walks are done with a mean, aggressive, hunter look. The rolls and stretches and the turning walks and jump stretches are done in the manner of a little hunted animal running away. (You could include the vocabulary *predator* and *prey*.) After the children know the study very well, add appropriate sounds and have the groups begin four beats apart.

2. Leap (four beats), roll (four beats), run (four beats), balance in a one-legged shape (four beats).

3. Jump (four beats), walk (four beats), walk on knees (four beats), seat-scoot backward (four beats), collapse to lowest level. There is no extra time for the level changes.

Here are some possible group problems. Groups are three to five children.

1. Make up a sequence using five different locomotor movements on five different levels.
2. Make up a pattern using one locomotor movement done on five different levels.
3. Going across the diagonal, use three different locomotor movements on three different levels in 20 beats.

Closing Thoughts

Levels open up a gold mine of movement ideas. If a group of students brings you a deathly boring study, tell them to use level changes. If your locomotor movements are getting too repetitious, use level changes. If a pattern is too easy, use level changes. Sound miraculous? It is.

Chapter 6

Awareness of Space

Spatial awareness is a battered phrase. Everybody is teaching it, but few people know what it is. The phrase has fallen into the nebulous mire of jargon. Awareness of space is actually a set of specific, somewhat mundane skills. These skills encompass (a) how we see ourselves moving through space (direction) and (b) how we see the space through which we are moving (floor pattern).

Clarifying Spatial Awareness

It is worth taking a moment to clarify the difference between *direction* and *floor pattern*. *Direction* distinguishes which plane—front, back, or side—is leading the body. I identify four directions: forward, backward, sideways, and turning. (Some dance teachers include an up and down direction, but I see that as a function of level, chapter 5.) *Floor pattern* distinguishes the lines created by the body moving through space—a diagonal line, a circle, and an intricate design are examples of floor patterns.

This distinction between *direction* and *floor pattern* is one I prefer to keep straight. Sometimes the two words are used interchangeably: "Go in the diagonal direction." "Go in the direction of the stage." These two sentences use the word *direction* in different ways, which could cause confusion. When a child brings up this confusion, I demonstrate: "Look, I can move on a diagonal line in the forward direction; I can go on the same diagonal line in the backward, sideward, or turning direction; or I can move in all four directions on this one line. The diagonal line is from here to there; the direction is which part of my body leads me there."

Children do not understand their relation to space. When running across a room, most children have no thought of the line they have created, nor do they perceive that a distinct plane of their body has led them. (In fact, after you introduce directions, a number of children will not know how to move forward.) Understanding and being at ease with the body moving in different directions, and understanding and visualizing the spatial design a movement creates, are keys to a greater control of individual movement and to an expanded movement vocabulary.

Direction and *floor pattern*, each with its own underlying skills, constitute my definition of spatial awareness.

Directions

Before a child can move clearly backward he must know with certainty where his back is, from the back of his head to the bottom of his heels. Before a child can feel at ease with right and left, she must clearly sense two separate sides running the length of her body. Before children can move in different directions, they must be introduced to the planes of their own bodies. Therefore, these are the directional skills:

1. Knowing and differentiating front, back, and side
2. Moving clearly forward, backward, sideways, and turning directions
3. Distinguishing right and left sides of the body

Walk Down Your Front

Walk Down Your Front is good for

• introducing front, back, and side; and

• leg stretch and arm strength.

To begin work finding front, back, and side, we do Walk Down Your Front. For children who are uncertain of right and left, I do Walk Down Your Front and the following exercises without mentioning right and left; as they mirror me, I ask for "this hand" and the "other hand." After right and left are introduced, I do these exercises again using the proper terms.

The children stand in Perfect Spots. The "face-front" component of Perfect Spots is crucial here. The first few times we do this exercise the children and I do it together, with the children imitating me. Later, the children follow my verbal instructions.

We start standing with hands on top of our heads. "Walk down your front," I say. Hands walk, step by step, down the front of our bodies; knees are kept straight but not locked. Reaching the feet, I ask, "What is at the front of your feet?"

"Toes," they decide.

"Glue the front of your feet as you keep walking front."

Keeping the toes in place and the knees straight, our hands walk forward on the floor until the body is completely stretched out in a push-up position—the weight is on the hands and toes, and everything else is lifted off the floor. I then say, "Walk up your front." (Warning! Do not, as I did the first time, say, "Walk back up your front." Complete confusion.) If done correctly, that is, legs straight, toes in place, body stretched as much as possible, this is an extremely good strengthening exercise.

After walking down and up our fronts, we run down and up our fronts.

"Walk down your back." We begin at the back of the head and walk down. Arms and hands must shift around to keep going below the shoulders. Knees are kept straight until hands reach the heels. We then glue the heels, bend the knees, and keep "walking." The body will end outstretched in a reverse push-up, seat off the ground.

"Walk up your back . . . Run down your back . . . Run up your back."

Children enjoy this exercise. If you have the time and inclination, do different locomotor movements down and up the front and back, for example the hands can skip, hop, "tiptoe," stomp, tickle. After front and back, we move to the sides. (Reminder: If the children are shaky on right and left, simply ask for this or that mirrored side.) "Raise your right arm." Since the children are in Perfect Spots, it takes only a few seconds to check every arm. The left arm is kept down, "glued to its side." We begin with our right hands on the top of our heads and slide down our right sides. Check that the children slide strictly down their sides and do not waver to their fronts. Slide all the way down to the right foot. "Glue the side of your right foot and keep sliding to your right side." This is tricky. Ideally, the body ends in a side balance on the right hand and foot, everything else off the ground. For young children, I ask for a side balance with the body resting on the floor; later we attempt the harder balance.

"Slide up your right side . . . Raise your left arm . . . Slide down your left side . . . Slide up your left side."

"Do you know where your front is? Do you know where your back is? How about your right side? Left side?" Ten to one the children will be touching the appropriate place as they shout, "Yes!"

Stationary Exercises Using Directions

After Walk Down Your Front, we do stationary exercises that use directions. It is important that the children feel how to move forward, backward, sideways, and turning with nonlocomotor movements before they attempt directions with locomotor movements.

1. **Bouncing torso.** Bounce the torso eight times to the front, eight to the back, eight to the right side, eight to the left side, and eight times turning (circling around). Then bounce four times in each direction, two times in each direction, and one time in each direction (going around four times). Go faster and faster with the ones. (You probably remember this one from your high school gym classes.)

2. **Kicking.** Kick legs (alternating right and left leg) eight times to the front, eight times to the back, eight times with the right leg to the right side, eight times with the left leg to the left side; four times in each direction; two times, one time in each direction (done four times). This is an excellent conditioning exercise as well as directional study.

3. **Shaking hands.** Shake hands in front of the body, shake hands in back, shake the right hand to the right side, shake the left hand to the left side, shake hands all around. Combine directions—for example, one hand shakes in front while the other hand shakes in back, one hand shakes in back and one to the right side.

4. **Looking.** Look in front of you; keeping the body facing front, look in back of you, look to the right, look to the left, look all around.

5. **Hip thrust.** Push your hips to the front; pull your hips to the back; push your hips to the right side; push your hips to the left side; swing the hips all the way around. Pretty jazzy.

6. **Jumping.** This is good for future locomotor movements using directions. Jump four jumps front, four jumps back, four jumps to the right, four to the left, four turning (ideally the turning jumps are full turns), making sure to end up facing front. Do two jumps in each direction and then one in each direction. (Watch that the feet stay together rather than separating into a gallop.)

7. **Rolls.** On mats, roll once front (forward somersault), roll back (backward roll), roll once to the right (log or cat roll), and roll once to the left. Spin on the knees and stand ready to start again.

8. **Stretches.**

a. Stretch front: Arms and torso reach forward. From a standing position, the back stretches parallel to the floor with the spine working to remain as straight as possible; that is, the person has a "flat back." Make sure the knees do not lock but stay slightly bent. Hold for a few seconds and then drop the torso down to the floor to rest. This is a basic dance warm-up; often a ballet barre (a table works as well) is held to help stretch the back into the correct position.

b. Stretch back: Head and neck reach back; arms rest on the hips. Ideally, the back arches high in the upper spine so that the lower back is not stressed. Hold for only a few seconds and watch that the abdomen stays tucked in.

c. Stretch side: With arms above the head, arms, neck, and torso, strenuously pull diagonally to the side rather than drooping toward the floor. Hips remain straight, not thrusting to the opposite side. Stretch right and left, holding just a few seconds each side.

d. Swing torso all the way around ready to start again.

9. **Tantrum legs.** Children sit in Perfect Spots. Ask them to have a temper tantrum with only their legs. Legs kick, shake, push, hit the floor. Have the tantrum with the legs in front, in back (they have to lie on their abdomens), to the right (they sit up and balance on the left hip as both legs thrash to the side), to the left, and all the way around. How about adding the appropriate tantrum sounds?

10. **Combinations.** Once the children are at ease transferring one movement to all four directions, it is time to combine movements. These combinations help prepare the class for future dance sequences.

a. Bounce torso side to side while you shake your hands to the front.

b. Jump forward while you look backward; jump backward while you look forward; jump right and look left; jump left and look right.

c. Kick alternating sides as you bounce your torso front and back.

11. **Strike.** Strike front: arms, legs, elbows, head, torso. Strike back: legs, seat, arms, elbows. Strike side: elbows, legs, hips. Then pick a different strike to do in each direction. For example:

a. Strike one arm to the front, one leg to the back, one elbow to the right, and the hip to the left.

b. Strike the torso front, elbows back, hip right, leg left.

c. Strike head front, seat back, leg right, arm left.

12. **Sequential patterns.** Just as the strike patterns just described used different strikes in each direction, any of the movements listed can be combined in a directional sequence. Examples:

a. Bounce torso to the front; look to the back; kick right; kick left; jump turn.

b. Sitting down, have a leg tantrum with the legs in front; cross the legs "Indian style" and strike elbows to the back; open the legs wide and stretch right, then left; spin on seat.

c. Jump front; kick one leg back; hip thrust to the right; stretch left; turn around.

d. Shake hands in front; strike seat back; look to the right; kick left; turn around.

e. Step-hop front; one-knee back roll back; remain on knee level and strike arm to the right; stand and turn; end with a hip thrust to the left.

f. Reach up, reach down, clap right side, clap left side, stretch diagonally right (right arm stretches up while the left foot lifts a little), stretch diagonally left (left arm stretches up while the right foot lifts a little), shake, and turn around. The result is a great cheerleader-like pattern: "Up, down, right side [clap on the word "side"], left side, diagonal, diagonal, and turn around." I have used this rhythmic pattern to reinforce some social studies concepts: "North, south, east, west, northeast, northwest, equator line."

Ninety percent of the time I mirror what I ask the children to do. If I cannot figure out the mirror I do it with them, that is, with my back to them. It would be very rare for me to face them and stretch to my left while the children stretched to theirs. This would happen only as a game in which the objective was to see if they could stick to their own direction while I seemed to move the opposite way.

"You are not being honest with the children," said a stern sixth grade teacher. Why not? If a child figures out the mirror and complains that I am going to the "wrong" side, I congratulate him: "You are absolutely right. I am doing it like a mirror facing you so that it looks the same." The child who figures out the mirror is way ahead, and the child who does not, needs the visual support that mirroring provides. As long as I am honest with the child who figures it out, I think I am playing fair.

However, mirroring is sometimes difficult, especially for new teachers. (You can always tell a brand-new aerobics teacher—she is the one saying "right" while going to her right. All the visual learners are mirroring her, and all the aural learners are following her verbal instructions.) Do not fret over this. If you need to turn your back, peek around often. If you forget to mirror and the class goes both ways, it is not the end of the world. You could actually make a lesson out of it.

If you have explored directions using generic sides, at some point it will be time to teach right and left. Frankly I do not think right and left are earthshaking concepts. They are simply terms. Children need to memorize these terms for report cards and other activities. (Come to think of it, I realize that in the frenzy of establishing standards and norm testing, there has been a de-emphasis on perceptual-motor skills such as laterality; I have not seen "knows right and left" on report cards for quite some time.)

As a child I could never keep right and left straight until my mother happened to buy me a ring. It was put on my right hand. My grades suddenly showed I knew "laterality." I remembered that "ring" starts with "r" and that therefore this must be my right hand. Years later, after the ring had to be sawed off my finger, the only way I knew my right was to feel where my precious ring had been.

My point is that right and left are only words. I am not de-emphasizing true laterality, but that is more than right and left. True laterality is knowing clearly where the side of the body is, knowing the entire area that is side, knowing where side is at all times, knowing that there are two different sides, and knowing how to move distinctly sideways. That one side is called "Herman," "right," or "this" and the other is called "Sam," "left," or "that" is much less important. Tying on a yarn "bracelet," marking a letter on the hand, putting on a small piece of tape—all are fine beginnings to sensorially memorizing the right hand. I certainly recommend a little turquoise ring.

When I am faced with an entire class that needs introduction to right and left, I use the following procedure. The children stand in Perfect Spots. "The arm that is closest to the chalkboard side of the room [I mirror the children] is our right arm. Raise your right arm." I check every arm quickly. If a child raises the wrong arm, I individually take her right arm and shake it vigorously for a couple of seconds. "This is your right arm." The vigor is more than good-natured fun. There must be a sensory memory in the arm, and a little tingle never hurts. This is done quickly and playfully so as not to interrupt the flow of the lesson.

"Shake your right arm . . . Swing your right arm . . . Contract and stretch your right arm . . . Strike, circle, wave, bend and straighten, twist, and reach for the sky with your right arm." Watch that the children do not try to change arms. The right arm should be tired; this is important for the muscular memory. "OK, shake everything out and spin around . . . Now face front and lift your right arm . . . Fantastic! Shake everything and spin around again . . . Let's see how fast you can raise your right arm . . . Great!"

We do this entire procedure on different days only with the right. After several reviews I ask the children to show me their right arm in more difficult ways: "Face the back of the room and raise your right arm . . . Go on the stage. Where is your right? . . . Lie down on your belly, facing front, and raise your right arm . . . Twirl around and, while spinning, raise your right arm."

Once the children know their right, I do not do the same with the left. Rather I start alternating movements: "Raise your right arm; raise your left . . . Shake your right arm; shake your left arm . . . Shake your right leg; left . . . Thrust your hip right; thrust left . . . With your right hand touch your left foot; with your left hand touch your right shoulder." And so on. We then repeat Walk Down Your Front and some direction exercises using the terms right and left. We also work on sensing the entire side with Right and Left Bug.

Right and Left Bug

Right and Left Bug is good for

- clarifying right and left sides and
- teaching parts of the body.

Right and Left Bug is a great deal of fun for pre-schoolers to third grade. Older children actually like it too, but I introduce it by asking them if they want to pretend they are young children.

The children stand in Perfect Spots. Raising my arm, wiggling my fingers, and making a buzzing sound, I say, "This is the right bug. The bug is flying around." The children wriggle and fly their right hands insect fashion, making buzzing sounds; the left arms are relaxed at their sides. This is the time I double-check to make sure all the children are using the correct arm.

"And the right bug, flying around, lands on your head." (Right hand lands on the head.) "It travels down your right side . . . Hello, right ear." (Wiggle right ear with right hand. Children say the "hellos" with me.) "Hello, right shoulder." (Right hand tickles the right shoulder; shoulder wiggles.) "Hello, right armpit!" (Right hand tickles the right armpit. My face hams exaggerated surprise and the children usually jump and scream.) "Hello, right side of my waist." (Right hand tickles right waist.) "Hello, right hip." (Right hand lands on right hip; hip wiggles.) "Hello, right knee." (Right hand wiggles right knee.) "Hello, right foot." (Right hand tickles right foot.) "Now shake that right bug off your right side!" (The right arm and leg shake vigorously—as if trying to get rid of a bug; the left side works to remain still.)

The process is repeated on the left side. At the end of the left side, I say, "Shake the left side . . . Shake the right . . . Left . . . Right . . ." We go faster until everything is shaking. Right and Left Bug is much requested, with the armpit being a definite high point.

Cops and Robbers

Cops and Robbers is good for

- preparing for sideways locomotor movements and
- teaching side-slide.

After the children are at ease using front, back, and right and left sides with nonlocomotor movements, we go on to directions with locomotor movements. Traveling sideways is much more difficult than traveling in the other three directions. Therefore I like to prepare for this difficulty with a preliminary exercise: Cops and Robbers.

The goal of this exercise is to help children move straight side rather than diagonally forward. Cops and Robbers is one of the most frequently requested exercises.

The children start standing in Perfect Spots. "You know those old-time movies where the robbers crack open the safe and take the money?" (Using exaggerated gestures, you and the class pretend to crack a safe, take the money, and stuff it into a bag.) "And then the cops come and—oh, no—there is nowhere to go but out the window." (Pretend to gingerly step out a window.) "The ledge outside this window is a thousand feet up." (Pretend to be scared, high in the air.) "Well, the cops are coming, we'd better step slowly along the ledge. Keep your back flat against the building. Step right, together [right foot steps right, left foot slides to meet it, that is, a slow side-slide] . . . Right, together, right, together . . . Uh oh, the cops are coming this way. We'd better go to our left [a little faster to the left: left, together four times] . . . Uh oh, here they come. Go right! [right, faster, four times] . . . Uh oh, left! [left, three times fast] . . . Uh oh, right! [right, three times fast] . . . Uh oh [extremely fast, left twice, right twice, left twice, right twice] . . . Uh oh, jump!"

This exercise teaches or reinforces the locomotor movement side-slide. After introducing Cops and Robbers I often say, "The movement you were doing along the ledge is called a side-slide. Can you show me that locomotor movement? Straight sides now."

Locomotor Movements Using Directions

Now we are ready for more general work with locomotor movements using directions. The children sit on the floor. "If your front is leading you [I pull myself by the front of my shirt], you are going forward. If your back is leading you [I pretend to be pulled by my back], you are going backward. If either side leads you [I pretend to be pulled by one side, then the other], you are going sideways. If your whole body is leading, then you are going in the turning directions. So we have four directions: forward, backward, sideways, and turning directions." Just for fun (and memory), ask the children to rattle off the four directions as fast as they can: forwardbackwardsidewaysturning. A definite tongue twister.

The children try out locomotor movements in these four directions. Generally I use the Free Traveling Structure. I do not use the Free Traveling Structure (1) if the room is too crowded or (2) if the children are too rambunctious and I am fearful of the backward movements. In these cases the children go from one side of the room to the other or use the Diagonal Structure.

It is important that the locomotor movements picked for this introduction be simple (a skip sideways is too hard for now) and feasible (no backward leaps). Here are some good locomotor movements for beginning direction work:

- Walk: forward, backward, sideways, turning. The side walk can be either a slow step-together or a grapevine (step, cross front, step, cross back).
- Jump: forward, backward, sideways, turning. Attempt a full turn for each of the turning jumps.
- Run: forward, backward, sideways, turning. Watch that the sideways run does not turn into a side-slide. It is most easily kept a run if the knees lift high.
- Crawl: forward, backward, sideways, turning.
- Using mats, roll forward (somersault), backward, sideways (log or cat roll), spin on knees to standing; repeat.

"Help!" I'll hear from teachers. "My children move forward, backward, and turning OK, but I can't get them to go straight sideways. It always looks frontish." Yes, I certainly know what they mean. Sideways locomotor movements are hard. Here are three techniques for working on straight side movements:

1. Have the children keep their toes on the lines created by the floor tiles or floorboards. Whatever locomotor movement they are doing, tell them to move slowly until they have the idea of going straight side and then to speed it up. This approach is good for mature, motivated classes. They want to go sideways, and they are willing to work on their own to do it.

2. For classes that do not really care if they ever move sideways or not, I work from Perfect Spots. In addition to doing Cops and Robbers, we jump, hop, walk, run, and crawl sideways, doing

the movement an equal number of times to the right and left sides. I use this Perfect Spot base because the children are facing front. As long as they remain facing front, the locomotor movement will be straight side.

As soon as a few children have the idea, I use peer pressure. "Ron, Janice, Eileen, and Javan, your sideward locomotor movements are getting so good I want to see if you can do them going anywhere in the room." Then to the class: "We'll keep practicing from our Perfect Spots here in the front of the room and let those four children try the movements in the back of the room. Greg, you want to join the kids back there? Well, let me see you jump straight side . . . Great, OK, go ahead. Shauna, you want to join them? Let me see you move straight side first . . ." When about half of the class is working independently, I have everyone try it. Moving sideways takes quite a bit of concentration. Once the children want to do it, they generally can.

3. Another technique uses one cleared wall. Have the class begin by literally walking against the wall, heels touching the baseboard. "You are walking straight side. Do you think you could take a step or two away from the wall and keep that straight side feeling? Fantastic! [If not fantastic, "Nope, the straight side is gone. Let's go back to the wall."] OK, let's try a jump. Put your back as close to the wall as possible as you jump sideways. Now take a few steps away. Can you jump as straight? Great."

After doing several different locomotor movements this way, I ask the class to pretend their backs are against a different wall, and we do several locomotor movements. If the children can move straight side pretending their backs are against each of the four walls, they are ready to do sideways movements anywhere in the room.

Once the class has some experience moving freely in four directions, I use the Diagonal Structure to observe each child carefully. I check run, walk, jump, and crawl in the forward, backward, sideways, and turning directions. This assessment tells me if we need to review or can go on to

1. more difficult locomotor movements,
2. beginning directional studies,
3. mixing directions with other concepts,
4. direction problems, and
5. full-scale direction studies.

Let us take a brief look at each of these five applications.

More Difficult Locomotor Movements Using Directions

If the four directions are precise with simple locomotor movements, it is time to attempt more difficult directional movements. These can be done in the Free Traveling Structure as a warm-up or in the Diagonal Structure for clearer visibility.

1. Skip: Forward, backward, sideways (made feasible by crossing the skipping leg), and turning.
2. Gallop: Forward, backward, turning. Sideways gallop is a side-slide. Side-slide changing sides.
3. Hopscotch: Forward, backward, sideways, turning.
4. Sliding on the floor: I recommend forward on abdomen, backward on back, sideways on side, and spin by rolling. (If you are using the Diagonal Structure, cut the diagonal in fourths and do the four directional slides on one diagonal. If you attempted to do one full diagonal for each of these four movements it would take all day.)
5. One-legged skip: Forward, backward, sideways, turning. If the class is having enormous difficulty with these (they are hard), have them do a regular skip backward and then immediately try the one-legged skip backward. The same with the other directions—turning is very tricky.
6. Run leap: Forward, sideways. Just for fun you can attempt it backward. For turning leaps, run forward and turn in the air midleap.
7. Jazzy walk: Forward, backward, sideways, turning.

Beginning Direction Studies

The children are now ready for an initial direction study:

1. Run forward to the middle of the diagonal; stop; fall down and slide on your back backward to the end.

2. Jazzy walk turning to the middle of the diagonal; leap forward to the end.

3. In Perfect Spots, four hops forward on the right foot; four hops backward on the left foot, four jumps sideways; four jumps turning returning to the starting spot.

4. Starting at one corner, make a rectangle, doing one move for each side of the room: gallop forward, side-slide changing sides, jump backward, run and leap turning in the air (see figure 6.1).

5. In Perfect Spots, five steps forward, four steps to the right side, three steps to the left side, two jumps backward, spin around ready to start again.

Mixing Directions With Other Concepts

The directions concept is now clear and solid; we can start mixing it with other concepts. I use the Free Traveling Structure and give instructions that to the untrained ear sound like an alien language.

1. Do a locomotor movement, air level, in the backward direction; do a nonlocomotor movement that continuously changes levels; then repeat the locomotor movement but do it in the forward direction.

2. Do a locomotor movement, standing level, forward direction; when I call change, change directions.

3. Start standing level, do a locomotor movement in the forward direction; when I call change, change direction and level.

4. When you hear the piano, do a locomotor movement in the turning direction, lowest level; when you hear the drum, do a locomotor movement, backward direction, knee level. Alternate sounds. (For more of these sound-change problems, see "Brain Catcher," chapter 10.)

5. With a partner, have one of you on standing level and one on sitting level; have one of you going forward while the other moves backward. You have to keep touching as you move.

6. With a partner, pick two levels and two directions. When I say change, change levels but keep your directions. Remember you have to continue touching your partner.

7. Again with a partner, get on two levels going in two directions. Now keep the levels the same but change directions.

8. Get into groups of three, each of you on a different level and each going in a different direction. You have to hold on to each other. Can you move?

These concept mixers are great warm-up activities. Within 10 minutes, the children's bodies are warmed up, they have reviewed a great deal

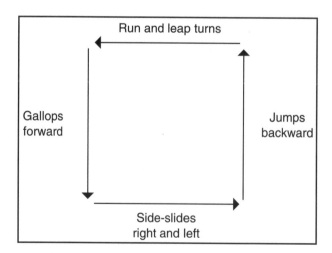

6.1

of information, their energy (if not released) is at least channeled, their brains are working, and they are focused into movement class. And, by the way, it's fun.

TROUBLESHOOTING

If the children know what you are saying but cannot seem to do it, you are probably saying the instructions too quickly. Pause at the end of each phrase so that the children can visualize each section.

Direction Problems

In addition to mixing with other concepts, directions can be used to create some challenging coordination problems. These direction problems are similar to the concept mixers but are more specific. Direction problems are given totally verbally (sometimes it takes great restraint to keep from moving) so the children figure them out by themselves. I almost always use the Diagonal Structure.

1. One-legged skip with the leg in front, forward direction.
2. One-legged skip with the leg in back, forward direction.
3. One-legged skip with the leg to the side, sideways direction.
4. One-legged skip with the leg in front, backward direction.
5. One-legged skip alternating the leg front and back, turning direction.
6. Kick to the back, move forward direction.
7. Kick to the front, move backward direction.
8. Kick side to side, move sideways direction.
9. Kick two times to the front and two times to the back, move turning direction.
10. Shake hands in front of you while side-sliding sideways; shake hands in back while side-sliding. Side-slide changing sides, alternating shaking hands in front and in back.
11. Skip backward while looking from side to side.
12. Skip turning and contract and stretch at the same time.
13. Hopscotch forward while your partner jogs backward; stay together. Switch in the middle of the diagonal.
14. Roll sideways while your partner spider crawls forward over you. Switch in the middle of the diagonal.

Full-Scale Direction Studies

The final component in this section on directions is a full-scale study:

1. Run forward to the middle of the diagonal; jazzy walk backward from the middle to the end of the diagonal. Across the second diagonal, hopscotch sideways to the middle; skip turning from the middle to the end. Keep both diagonals moving at the same time with no disasters.

2. Lowest-level slide on abdomen in the backward direction; sitting and knee-level move in the turning direction; standing-level move in the sideways direction doing a grapevine; air-level run and leap in the forward direction. Each direction gets a specific number of beats, possibly four or seven beats for each directional phrase, with no additional time to change.

3. One one-legged skip with the leg in back, forward direction; one one-legged skip with the leg to the side, sideways direction; one one-legged skip with the leg in front, backward direction; one waltz walk, turning direction. Each move is three beats; therefore the sequence is four measures of three. Repeat several times. Very difficult.

4. Four kicks to the back, moving forward; four kicks to the front, moving backward; four kicks to the side moving sideways, one small preparation jump and one jump turn. This pattern can be done in Perfect Spots—in which case the children move to one side for two beats and to the other side for two beats. This allows them to remain approximately in one spot. Or, the pattern can be done on the diagonal—in which case the body has to turn to execute the different directions on one line.

5. The Row, Row, Row Your Boat Dance is, if I do say so, a great dance. Start standing in Perfect Spots. The children learn this pattern: three jumps forward, five steps backward, four

side-slides to the right, four side-slides to the left. Done in Perfect Spots, the sequence forms an **L**-shaped floor pattern, as shown in figure 6.2.

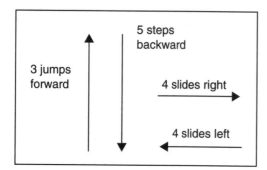

6.2

The pattern is practiced until it is easy. Children then get into groups, ready to move on the diagonal. With a grin I present this problem: "The pattern you have just done—three jumps forward, five steps backward, four slides to the right, and four slides to the left—can be done so that it takes you completely across the diagonal. It will travel from this corner all the way to the other corner. How can you do that?"

It is still amazing to me to find so many children so stumped. Most children think it is the size of movement and proceed to take enormous jumps forward and tiny steps backward, but it will not work. Inevitably one child will get the idea of turning his body around, although it often takes two or three children to figure out that they must turn their bodies on the backward steps and both of the side-slides. The resulting pattern looks like figure 6.3.

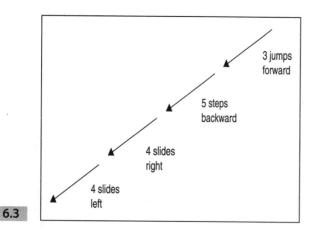

6.3

Once the children understand the pattern, do it to the song "Row, Row, Row Your Boat." The song consists of two phrases of eight beats; each phrase is subdivided into fours:

1	2	3	4	1	2	3	4
Row,	row,	row your boat,		gently	down the str-		eam

1	2	3	4	1	2	3	4
Merrily,	merrily,	merrily, merrily,		life is	but a	dr-	eam.

The movement pattern fits the large phrases, but it breaks up the even fours within the phrases with 3 + 5 and then 4 + 4. I find this more exciting than a straight phrase matchup. If your class is having too much trouble, just change the movement pattern to four jumps forward and four steps backward (the slides are the same), and this will fit the phrasing exactly.

As you know, "Row, Row, Row Your Boat" is a round, or canon, with the second part coming in eight beats after the first. It is wonderful to do the movement sequence as a canon too; as in the song, groups come in eight beats apart. The canon can be done using the diagonal or, for more excitement, using a floor pattern like the one in figure 6.4.

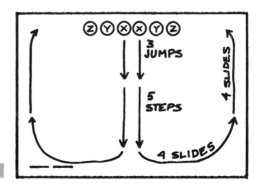

6.4

In this floor pattern the children are lined up so that they meet their partner in the middle of one side of the room. They do the three jumps forward and the five steps backward in a straight line, moving together. For the side-slides, they separate and curve around to their respective starting places while the next two children start the jumps. Therefore in figure 6.4, children labeled "Y" start their jumps while children labeled "X" start side-sliding. This culminating study requires precision and concentration; it is an excellent math lesson as well as concentrated work on spatial awareness and self-reliance. It takes patience to set up. But after the first few disastrous tries, the children will suddenly get the idea and the whole thing will miraculously fall into place.

Middle

At this point the children are relatively at ease moving in space. They know where their front, back, and right and left sides are, and they can move in the forward, backward, sideways, and turning directions. Before we go on to spatial designs we need to find one point in space—the middle.

The concept *middle* is not hard in itself. The trick is to make clear what it is we are finding the middle of. I hold a piece of yarn about a yard long: "The middle is where it is the same length on either side. [For older classes I say it is halfway between one end and the other.] Let's guess where the middle of this piece of yarn is. [One child picks.] We can check to see how close Yolanda is by folding the yarn and seeing if both sides are the same." (The child who picked the middle holds that point tightly while I match the two sides.) Usually the children are surprisingly accurate. If they are not, comparing the sides will show this and I'll say, "See if you can find a point that makes the sides equal (or equivalent)." We do this several times with different children picking the middle.

If you can spare the time, it is wonderful to linger here for a short while. Divide the class into partners, give each partner set one piece of yarn, and ask them to take turns guessing and checking the middle. It is hard to believe how much children love to do this guessing game over and over.

We then pick other lines in the room and find their middles. The lines have to be clearly defined. Do not ask for the middle of a wall yet, because that is a plane. We find the middle of one side of a door, one side of a window, the floorboard on one wall, one side of the chalkboard, the edge of the piano, one side of a poster. This is similar to finding diagonals throughout the room.

The children judge the middle simply by sight. With a clearly defined line, they are usually quite accurate. If they are off by too much or if you want to do a more comprehensive lesson, this is a perfect time for work on measuring. "Mitchell picked this point as the middle of the edge of the stage. How could we measure each side, from that end to the middle and from this end to the middle, making sure they are the same?"

"Get a ruler," is the most common reply.

"Yes, that is one good way. What are some other ways we could measure?"

I wait them out. With a hint, they will come up with different ways of measuring: hand spans, foot spans, paces, children lying down lengthwise, arm spans, pieces of yarn, book lengths, and so on. We pick one method to follow. Sometimes I will select two different methods and check to see if the middle is the same. When it works well, the creative thinking and problem solving stimulated by this lesson make me glow for the rest for the day.

Once the children feel confident finding the middle of lines, we go on to the middle of parts of their bodies. This is a good step between finding the middle of lines and finding the middle of planes. "Where is the middle of your arm? . . . Your leg? . . . Your whole body? . . . Your face? . . . Bend your arms in the middle . . . Bend your legs in the middle . . . Bend your body in the middle . . . Can you go somewhere like that?"

For the middle of planes—walls, floor, and rooms in general—the children need to realize that they are finding the middle of two lines. For example, they can find the middle of the floor by intersecting the two diagonals or by intersecting the center of the perpendicular lines traversing the width and length of the room. For young children, I stick to the idea of finding the middle of an area by intersecting both diagonals. (I think it is a mistake, however, to simply state that the middle of the floor is where the diagonals cross. Although it is clear to us, most children will not include the intermediate step of recognizing that the two diagonals cross at their middles. To them it will be another theoretical formula that works, but they are not sure why. It is better for them to light up with the discovery that the diagonals cross at their middles.) For older children I mention both ways of looking at it. When finding the middle using widths and lengths, it is clearest if one child stands in the middle of the width of the room and another stands in the middle of the length and they walk and meet. This is an excellent preparation for graph work.

The children have actually worked with the middle of the diagonal before this lesson. When using the Diagonal Structure, I sometimes ask one group to start when the group ahead reaches the middle. The children have also used middle in numerous studies. In these cases the middle has been clearly marked with a taped "X." Now that the concept middle is formally introduced, I take the mark away and see what happens. If the children can use middle without the marker, I congratulate them and put middle in the bag of known, usable, concepts.

Floor Patterns

Floor patterns are spatial designs made by locomotor movements. How wonderful that we are here! This is one of my favorite topics, and this unit is one of the largest and most important in my movement program. Floor patterns primarily concentrate on spatial awareness. These are the skills required to create and read a floor pattern:

1. The child can visualize the line a locomotor movement creates in space; for example if I run a circle, the child can "see" the circle even though there is nothing there. Visualization is extremely important to develop because it is actually the foundation of comprehension; if a child can "see" a story in her mind, she will be more likely to understand it.

2. The child can create and follow a map. This particular skill requires

    a. transferring images from two-dimensional paper to three-dimensional space;

    b. memorizing lines and movements;

    c. augmenting a line representation to room size; and

    d. conceptualizing the design as a whole, for example, seeing how one line fits with another.

3. The child can recognize and create different line shapes: straight, curved, wiggly, zigzag, looped, spiral. This is foundation work for writing, especially cursive.

4. The child can identify the front, back, and right and left sides of a room.

If all this were not enough, floor patterns can be used to teach or reinforce innumerable language and math concepts, and they help develop overall concentration and self-reliance. Sound too good to be true?

Floor patterns cover such a broad range of topics that I have broken the material up into three sections: (1) maps, (2) line shapes, and (3) additional work.

Maps

My introduction of maps sometimes does not ever get to the map itself. I begin with a spatial problem, putting a large piece of paper (12 × 18 inches) on the floor and saying, "Arrange yourselves so that you and everyone else can see this paper." I wait—as usual this is the hardest part. If the children are having a lot of trouble, I nudge them by complimenting the people in front who are sitting far enough from the paper that those in back of them can see. Eventually they get the idea and sit in a loosely formed circle with people behind either kneeling or standing. Why bother? It would be so much more efficient, not to mention less noisy, to get them organized yourself. I bother because this is an extremely important lesson in cooperation, spatial awareness, and peer group organization. Arranging the children yourself eliminates the self-responsibility required to actively go after a lesson; it is their job to find a place where they and everyone else can see. For me to seat them would be to forsake the bigger lesson of active learning and cooperation for the immediate goal of a floor pattern. Moreover, if I seat the children now I will have to seat them in the future, and in the long run that is much more time-consuming. Enough—on with maps.

We begin with a room representation, which is a stylized drawing of what is in the room. At this beginning stage, I include some identifying marks to show each corner and most walls—in future lessons I will draw only a few objects. Figure 6.5 is an example of a beginning room representation.

Starting at the top and going clockwise, this figure shows the stage, piano, chairs, my desk, a cabinet, two tables, a double door, more chairs, and a side door. Although the drawings are abstract, the children know what the symbols

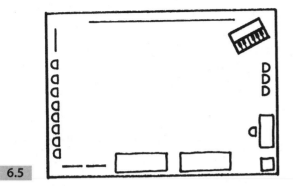

6.5

stand for because I identify each as it is being drawn. (Technical note: Use one dark color to draw the objects in the room.) Children like this room representation and often ask you to include all sorts of details like the tiles on the floor, the clock, the flag, their shoes. I go along with them for a short while because for most children the idea of representing a space is brand-new and very exciting. However, do not draw anything in the middle of the room. Now we are ready to go to the floor pattern.

I keep this first floor pattern as simple as possible, using the "cinch approach." I want the children to say, "This is a cinch." "Great. That's because you're so smart," I say to them. "Wait until you see where this 'cinch' will lead," I think to myself. For older and more mature classes I go faster rather than exclude steps at this stage.

I place a red "X" in one corner of the room representation, as in figure 6.6. "If I were standing here in the room, where would I be?"

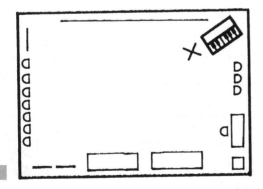

6.6

In this example the children would have to conclude, "by the piano." I choose one child or several children to stand at the appropriate spot and then rejoin the group. If the children have any difficulty transferring the "X" from the paper

to the room, check to see that the room representation is complete and that they understand it. If there is any doubt, start over, go slower, and draw another map in greater detail.

It is time for the first line of the floor pattern—keep it straight and simple. Curved, wiggly, and angled lines require specific attention. Also there is more chance of success if the line goes to a clearly marked spot in the room rather than an undefined area. Even if the concept middle has been taught, I do not use it unless there is an identifying mark. So, keeping it straight and ending at an identified spot, I draw the first line. It is drawn with the same color marker as the starting "X," and the locomotor movement (in this case "run") is written in the same color on the line, as in figure 6.7.

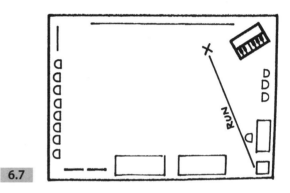

6.7

"Where does the line go?"

"To the cabinet."

"Anthony, start at the beginning 'X' and run the red line."

With a young class, several children try out the red line. With older classes, I move immediately to the next line. The second line starts where the first ended and is a different color, as in figure 6.8.

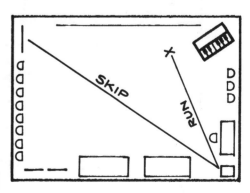

6.8

"Where does the green line end?"

"At the door."

"The double doors?"

"No, the door by the stage."

"Right. Alice, start at the beginning 'X,' run the red line, then skip the green line."

Staying faithful to the "cinch approach," the third line might be the last. It starts at the end of the second line and is drawn in a different color. I am fond of having the last line end where the pattern started, but that is not necessary. Another child demonstrates the movement in the room. Figure 6.9 shows a possible completed floor pattern.

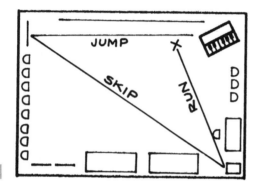

6.9

Figure 6.10, a through d, show other examples of initial floor patterns.

When this first map is completed it is time to watch everyone do the pattern. If your class is small enough and the room big enough, it is possible to do the floor pattern half the class at a time. If not, divide into groups, as in figure 6.11.

6.11

In a different initial map, the children line up at the appropriate side, as in figure 6.12.

That is our first map. Does it seem terribly mundane, plodding, and simple? Just wait: In subsequent maps, two changes occur—the room representation gets less detailed and the floor patterns get longer and harder.

Figure 6.13, a through c, shows how the room representation gets less and less detailed: The children might want to know why you are drawing less. I tell them it's because they do not need

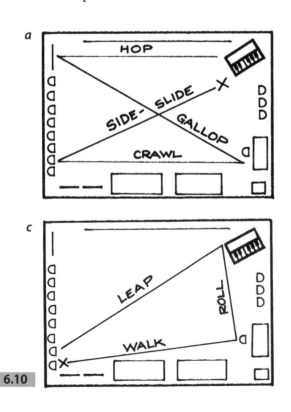

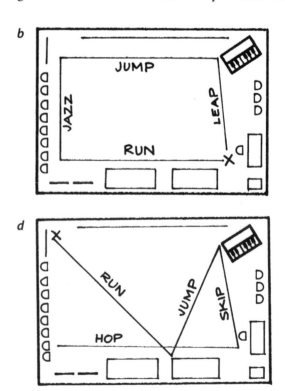

6.10

as much detail: "James, would you know where to go if I asked you to stand in this corner? [I point to a corner of the paper that has no identifying mark.] See, you know where everything is just from one or two things drawn."

Until I introduce specific line shapes, I keep the lines straight. But that does not mean that these floor patterns cannot be challenging. Figure 6.14, a through f, show examples of other straight-line floor patterns.

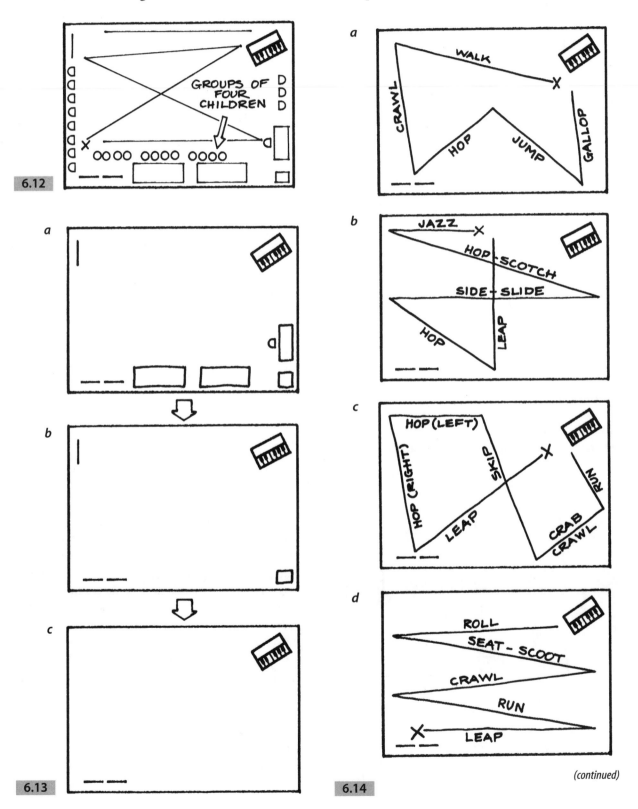

(continued)

e

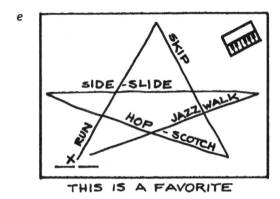

THIS IS A FAVORITE

f

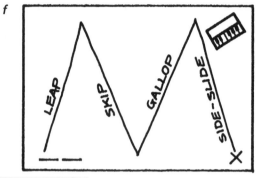

6.14   (continued)

Straight-lined letters and numbers are fine at this point; I de-emphasize their academic importance and just treat them as shapes (more on number and letter floor patterns in chapter 11). If you are doing a shape that requires backtracking, draw the line twice and mark the beginning and end of the line so that the children backtrack to the place where they started, for example the middle line of the letter "E" shown in figure 6.15.

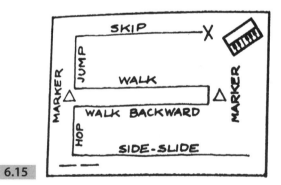

6.15

Write the locomotor movements on their lines in the same color as the line, for example write "skip" in green on the green line. This might be more for you than the children, but it does help keep everything orderly. However, do not always use the same color line to identify a particular locomotor movement—for example, skip is not always green. This would cause problems later and would detract from the inherent memory work.

Finally, make sure the starting "X" is in the same color as the first line so you can tell which way the pattern goes.

Even at this straight-line stage it is a good idea to let the children create their own floor patterns. Before setting them out on their own, we do three things:

1. The children practice putting the room representation straight.
2. We do a "helping floor pattern."
3. We do a spelling warm-up.

Putting the Room Representation Straight

In preparation for their own patterns, I draw a number of simple room representations on 12-by 18-inch construction paper (for a class of 30 I would make 10). I used to photocopy the room representation on ordinary paper, but through the years I found that the larger, thicker paper worked better and was worth the small investment of time. Do not let this stop you, though; if you prefer to print 100 room representations and be done with it, that is fine. In the initial floor patterns I drew the room representation while the class watched. Now the children are presented with an already drawn representation, and they have to figure out how it fits within the room.

The children gather around me on the floor, and I show one of the already drawn representations: "This is a picture of our room. Here is the piano, the door, my desk. If I placed the paper like this [turned upside down] the room would be upside down; the piano would be way over in that corner. Linda, can you turn the paper straight the way things are in the room? . . . Yes, very good." (Or "No, the piano goes in this corner.") "Omar, you try it." (I shake the paper and turn it a couple of times so it will be "mixed up" and then hand it to a child to lay straight "the way things are in the room.") Ideally I would have every child practice putting the room representation straight. Since this is not possible, I pick the ones I think might have trouble later.

A "Helping Floor Pattern"

"Now we are ready to make our floor pattern. Rachel, pick a color and put an 'X' where you want the floor pattern to start. It can start anywhere—in any corner, in the middle of any side, in the middle of the room. [She draws a starting "X" and continues with the first line.] Now write what locomotor movement you want in the same color on the line; I'll help you spell if you want." (She writes the movement.) It is helpful to have a chart of the basic locomotor movements easily visible (table 6.1).

"OK, now I have the $64,000 question [I know this really dates me]: Where does the second line have to start?" Stop and steel yourself! It is not obvious to the children that the lines have to connect. Teaching them to connect lines is the main reason it is necessary to have this helping floor pattern before they make their own. The children raise both index fingers. Have them say the word connect and touch the two fingers together; repeat several times. "Now, where does line 2 have to start? Right, it starts where line 1 ended. Joe, pick a different color and draw line 2—no, don't put an 'X,' that was to mark where the whole pattern starts—and write the locomotor movement in that color . . . OK, Patsy, you draw line 3. Where does it have to start?" We do this painstaking procedure for four lines. "Do you think you can make your own floor patterns?" If they answer "no," believe them and start over. A "yes" means we are ready to move on.

Spelling Warm-Up

Around this time of creating initial patterns, it is practical to do a spelling warm-up. Put up a chart of basic locomotor movements (see table 6.1). Spell out the movement names, and have

Table 6.1 Chart of Basic Locomotor Movements

Skip	Side-slide
Hop right and left	Baby crawl
Jump	Crab crawl
Hopscotch	Roll
Gallop	Jazzy walk
Jog	Run and leap

the class call out the word and execute the movement. Simple, but this will free you from a lot of individual spelling help.

First Group Floor Patterns

We are ready to create floor patterns. Divide the class into groups of four and ask the groups to sit in a small circle. Give each group a drawn room representation and a set of markers or crayons. "Make a floor pattern that has four straight lines, each a different color, each a different locomotor movement." I almost always start with groups of four making a four-line pattern because (1) the social arrangements are simplified with each child drawing one line, and (2) the assignment is long enough to be interesting but easy enough to allow success. For older or more mature classes, I would still divide the class into groups of four; but I would assign a six- to eight-line pattern and have them draw their own room representation.

I found it works best if the helping floor pattern immediately precedes the children's own patterns. Therefore, if we made a helping pattern at the end of one class, I would start with a spelling warm-up and then do another quick helping floor pattern before setting them out on their own.

When the group floor patterns have been drawn and checked, the children practice them. Yes, all the groups end up practicing their patterns at the same time. Yes, it is a bit confusing and noisy, but a group that can practice and perfect its pattern despite all that distraction certainly has had a study in concentration. Plus, I do not know a way around it. I ask the groups to know their patterns well enough to perform without the map. We then watch each other. When groups are performing, I hold the map and play appropriate music on the piano or drum. If a group does not move according to the pattern they have drawn, I emphasize the difference rather than say that one is right and one wrong. They can change either the map or their movements as long as the two end up corresponding.

As the children become more at ease with floor patterns, two changes occur simultaneously: I introduce line shapes, and the assignments get harder.

Line Shapes

Straight, wiggly, curved, spiral, zigzag, and looped are the line shapes we work on (see figure 6.16, a-f).

6.16

I used to methodically teach one line shape at a time, but more recently I have found a trick that allows me to approach all six shapes at once. I will tell you my secret weapon and then describe how to approach one line at a time if that is needed.

The trick is ropes. Start out the lesson with free time and guided movements using jump ropes, ending with partner Horsie (see chapter 9). Keep those partners, and have them work together with one rope to demonstrate the line shapes you show on a chart. "How fast can you make a straight line with your rope on the floor? . . . Great. Now make it into a curved line . . . Don't shake it, but arrange it so that it looks like a wiggly line . . . Yes, some of you made bigger wiggles and some smaller; both are fine. Now it will get harder. Pinch each curve of your wiggly line and you will have a zigzag."

→ TROUBLESHOOTING

Two notes: First, many children will pinch only one side of the wiggly line so that instead of a zigzag they end up with a scallop; show them that both the top and bottom need a sharp corner. Second, the plastic ropes will not retain a pinch; tell them to just pretend.

With second grade on up, go on to the looped line. If the children have a great deal of trouble,

slowly manipulate their rope to show them how the line has to backtrack on itself to make a loop. Let them watch your hand twist the rope into loops. Then shake out the loops you made and have them try it on their own. End with the across-the-age-span favorite, spiral lines. Even the youngest preschooler can wind his rope into a spiral. It does not matter if the spiral is tightly or loosely wound.

The ropes are put away and the class immediately gathers for a floor pattern that uses these very line shapes. For example, figures 6.17, a through e, shows a pattern of four line shapes.

If you want a more thorough approach to line shapes, it is possible to explore each line on its own. Since I teach each new line in about the same way, it will suffice to describe how I teach one: the wiggly line.

The Conceptual Approach to the Wiggly Line

The children stand ready to move on the diagonal. If possible, each child moves individually; if the class is too large or the time too short they move in small groups. First we examine the picture of a wiggly line. Then, without comment, the children run the line. I mutely watch the results, allowing all interpretations. Usually there is a pattern to

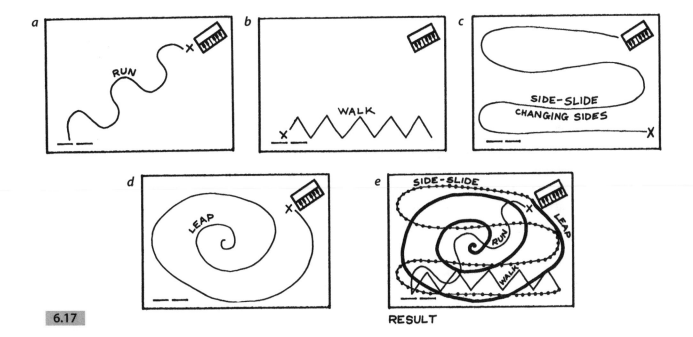

6.17

RESULT

the "mistakes"—namely, the curves are shallower than the curves in the picture. Showing the picture of the wiggly line, I say, "This red line is the line I asked you to do. Most of you did a line that looks like this yellow one." As I say this I draw a yellow line like the one in figure 6.18.

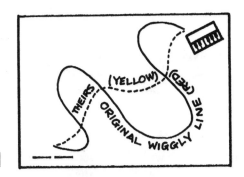

6.18

We talk about the differences between the two lines: "The red has bigger hills." "The yellow is more straight." The point here is not that one is right and one wrong, but that the two lines are different. I ask them to run the red line again and we repeat the process of comparing the visual representations if need be.

Once they can demonstrate approximately the line they see, we play with the whole idea of wiggly lines.

1. We can use more difficult locomotor movements: skip, skip turning, side-slide changing sides, waltz walk.

2. We can make the wiggly line go to different places in the room, as in figure 6.19, a through c. Because the children did the first line from sight, they usually have no

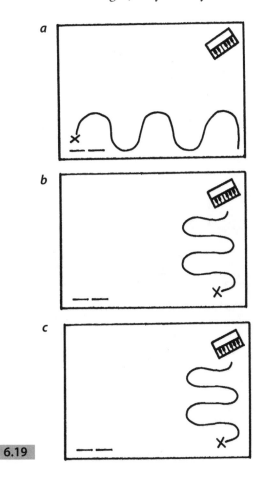

6.19

trouble with this place transference. If they do, simply repeat the process of drawing what they did in relation to what they saw.

3. In some classes we try different types of wiggly lines, with the wiggles getting larger or smaller, for example. The possibilities are endless.

I prefer this conceptual method of teaching line shape. Even though it is quite abstract, most young children do surprisingly well. Because the children learn the shape without demonstrations or physical markers, the idea is immediately internalized and applicable.

The Marker Method of Teaching the Wiggly Line

If you teach special education or have a very immature class, the conceptual approach might not work; there is nothing wrong with using markers. Here is the progression I use for teaching the wiggly line with markers:

1. Put tape numbers on the floor (tape is better than paper taped down because the paper will inevitably get demolished). The children run around them to achieve a wiggly line, as in figure 6.20. It is better to have the children run around the numbers than on them because if they run to each number, the line ends up angled.

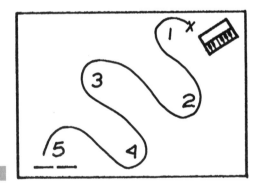

6.20

2. In the following lesson I replace the numbers with markers; cones are ideal but anything—shoes, chairs, books—will do. The children run the wiggly line using the markers. "Can you run the exact same line if I take away a marker?" I proceed to take away one marker at a time. The children run the line each time another marker is removed. Take the markers away in a random pattern, leaving the first marker until last.

The problem with the marker method is that the lines are set. It is difficult to transfer the idea of a wiggly line to the other diagonal or across the middle of the room. It might be necessary to go back to the movable marker stage for a newly placed line. But this approach, especially the backtracking, is extremely valuable for children with visual perceptual problems.

We are ready to use the wiggly line in a floor pattern like figure 6.21.

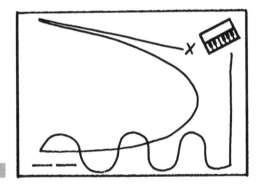

6.21

The techniques I use to teach the wiggly line are basic to all line shapes. However, here are a few additional notes on some peculiarities of the other shapes.

Curved Lines

The difficulty with the curved line is that children are not sure how deep to make it. It works best if the curve goes near a wall or other identifying object; that is, figure 6.22a will work better than figure 6.22b.

The children know they have to go very close to the side of the room. I mark the point at which the first curve ends and the second one begins. Markers can also be used to indicate shallow curves, as in figure 6.23.

Once curved lines are understood, all letters and numbers become feasible floor patterns. Children love to do their own names; at this stage each letter is a separate map. "Mary," for example, takes four floor patterns as shown in figure 6.24, a through d.

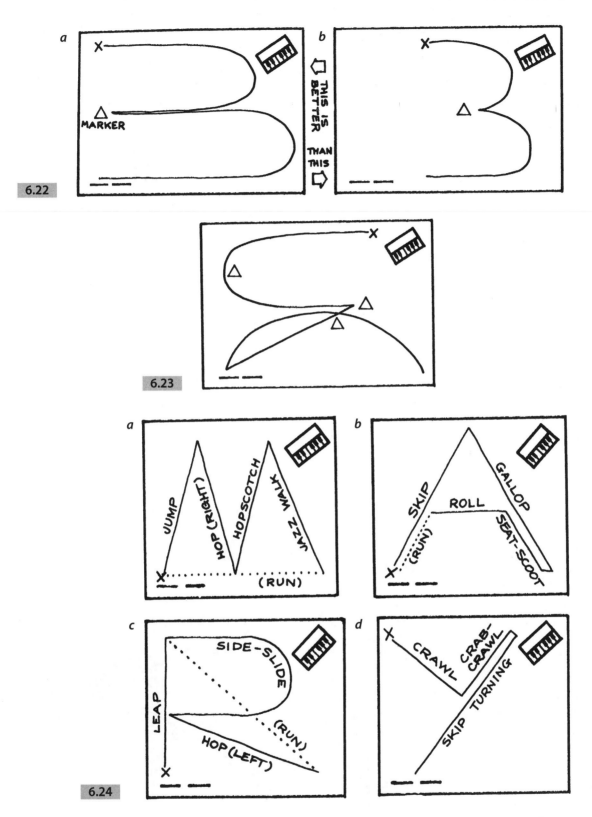

6.22

6.23

6.24

Mary does these four patterns in sequence, remembering all the line shapes and locomotor movements. Quite an accomplishment. Two or three children each moving her own name simultaneously create an interesting dance. Groups can work together on words of their own choosing—*love, U.S.A.,* or whatever might be appropriate.

Spiral Lines

Most children prefer the spiral line to any other. It looks more difficult than it is. If you want your

6.25   IS EASIER TO MAKE CLEAR THAN THIS

class to follow the shape exactly, a simple spiral works better than a many-layered one. That is, figure 6.25a will be done more precisely than figure 6.25b.

But, as long as the spiral gets smaller (or bigger if the children are going out from the center), I am not fussy about the number of circles.

Because a spiral line gets smaller and smaller, it is natural to make the movement littler and lower, possibly ending in a contracted shape. The spiral line can make grand finales because the entire class or group ends in the center of the room. Some possible climaxes:

1. Do a fast locomotor movement for the spiral line; as each child reaches the center he takes a strange shape and freezes. This works best if the children that follow have to touch two other children and also use a different level.

2. As children reach the center of the spiral, they stand very stiff and proceed to "boil down to a cooked noodle." I drape limp children gently over one another, forming a giant plate of "spaghetti" (see chapter 10).

3. Place several mats in the middle of the room. Divide the class into groups of approximately six. As the children reach the center they assume their prepared place in a simple gymnastics pyramid (see chapter 12).

4. Do you know the theater game Machine? One child starts a simple, repetitive, machine-like motion, for example, one arm moving up and down. A second child fits her machine-like gesture into the rhythm of the first, for example punching her arm forward as the first arm is moving down. One by one new children join the first, adding a related movement until the

group forms one united mechanism. The effect is heightened if the children add machine noises with their movements. Machine is a fascinating conclusion to a spiral line using either large groups or the whole class.

Zigzag Lines

The zigzag line is one of the two hardest lines (looped being the most difficult). In actuality, a zigzag line is an angled wiggly line, but those sharp corners are a challenge. Practice just the percussive shifts of focus by providing an image—military marching and robot walking seem most effective. Then put that shift into the zigzag line, trying to make the line segments of equal length, as in figure 6.26. I do not worry about whether children make the precise number of line segments shown in the drawing.

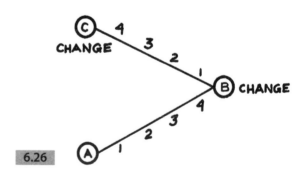

6.26

Looped Lines

Looped lines are hard; I rarely introduce them under second grade. The difficulty is that children want to make them wiggly, that is, they will not cross their own line. They will tend to do figure 6.27a rather than figure 6.27b:

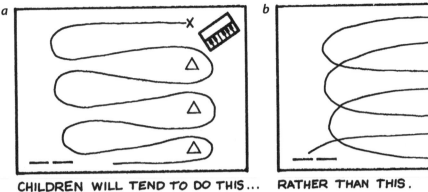

6.27   CHILDREN WILL TEND TO DO THIS... RATHER THAN THIS.

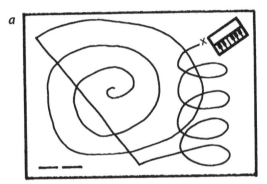
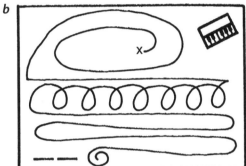

6.28

If this happens, it is a good time to use the conceptual approach described for the wiggly line and compare what the children did with what was drawn.

With these six lines introduced we can create varied and wondrous floor patterns, like those shown in figures 6.28, a and b.

Group Work

Throughout and after the introduction to line shapes, it is beneficial to include group work for creating floor patterns. We talked earlier about preparing a class with a helping floor pattern and about their initial straight-line designs. Following are some more difficult assignments:

1. Draw a floor pattern using four different line shapes, each a different locomotor movement, each going in a different direction. I enjoy and assign this problem the most because it necessitates a clear understanding of the difference between direction and floor pattern. It is a bit of an undertaking. I break up the assignment into two stages:

The children first draw floor patterns using four different line shapes, each using a different locomotor movement, as in figure 6.29.

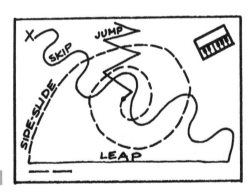

6.29

When the children are ready to add the directions, I take a few minutes to clarify the problem:

"Each time you move in space [I walk across the room] you do three things at one time: One, you use a locomotor movement. What movement did I just do?"

"Walking."

"Right. Two, you make a line shape. What shape did I do?"

"Straight line."

"Great. Three, you go in a direction. What direction did I go in?"

"Forward."

"You are terrific. Every locomotor movement has these three things going on at the same time: movement, line shape, direction. See if you can tell what I am doing." [I jump a wiggly line in the backward direction.]

"Jumping . . . Wiggly line . . . Backward."

"Yes, well done. Now you try out some problems. Hop a wiggly line in the sideways direction . . . Skip a spiral line in the turning direction. Hard! . . . Walk a zigzag line in the backward direction."

"Now let's go back to the floor patterns you made. So far the patterns have different line shapes and different locomotor movements. Now each line will also include a different direction. Decide which line you want to be forward, backward, sideways, and turning; make sure you can do it. It is a good idea to have the most difficult line move in the forward direction."

Generally half the class will understand and I scurry around helping others. It is worth the trouble. Once a child understands this problem and can perform the resulting pattern, he has an enormous grasp of both directions and floor pattern.

2. Draw a floor pattern using five lines, each a different line shape, a different locomotor movement, on a different level. Plan ahead. Do not do a long, complicated line, like a looped line, with a roll or a crawl. Give those lower-level movements a line that is feasible, like a short straight or zigzag line.

3. Draw a floor pattern using four different line shapes, each a different locomotor movement on a different level, each going in a different direction.

4. Draw four to seven lines. Each line must combine a different locomotor movement with a nonlocomotor movement, for example skip plus contract and stretch, jump plus shake.

5. Draw four to seven lines, each a different locomotor movement. Include a 10-second nonlocomotor movement in between each line.

6. Pick six locomotor movement cards at random. Make a floor pattern that uses those six movements.

7. Draw a floor pattern of four lines. Each line must combine two or more locomotor move-

ments. Examples are two jumps and two hops for one line; run, leap, fall, and roll for another line. No locomotor movement can be used twice!

8. The much requested Christmas tree floor pattern, figure 6.30.

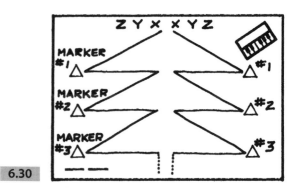

6.30

The children start together at the top of the tree ("X" and "X"); partners start on either side ("Y" and "Y," and "Z" and "Z"). Have the class get partners, and you set up the arrangement. Children skip four beats to the first markers and then side-slide four beats to join each other (you can add a "high five" here). They repeat the skips and side-slides to the second and third markers. Finally they jump four beats for the stem and run on the outside of the tree (tinsel?) to take their place at the end of their line.

Take the time and have the patience to watch each partner group perform the entire tree. Then have groups begin eight beats apart; that is, group 2 starts when group 1 begins skipping to the second marker. If they have it, try four beats apart. This makes a wonderful demonstration for the annual winter assembly.

Additional Activities

Floor patterns are an enormous well of movement ideas. Here are a few additional activities they have spawned: individual maps, artworks, tumbling patterns, Voice Box, and designs. (Work on symmetry using floor patterns is discussed in chapter 11.)

Individual Maps

I have drawings of about 40 different floor patterns. These patterns use all the line shapes and are quite difficult. To add to their difficulty, I do

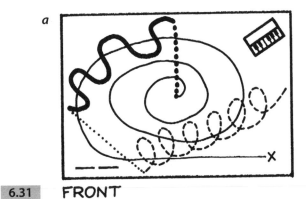

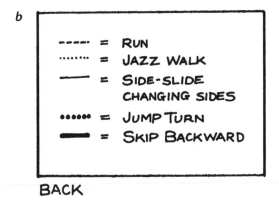

6.31   FRONT   BACK

not write the locomotor movement on the line but make a legend of color-coded lines on the back, as in figure 6.31, a and b.

Each child or pair of children is handed a floor pattern. Soon everyone is doing a different pattern all at the same time. When a child or pair is finished, either I or another child checks; if it is perfect the child or pair gets a new map to figure out.

Artworks

Floor patterns make wonderful art projects. Sometime when you have time, let the children draw their own room representations in as much detail as they want. As long as they keep the picture aligned, I allow anything and everything drawn, in as many colors as they want.

When the children are ready to add their floor patterns, I ask them to draw their conception of the movement: "How would a run look on paper? A jump? A skip?" There are amazing results when a child attempts to draw a skipping line going in a looped shape. This is obviously more art than movement. Since the goal is beauty rather than clarity, I am not my usual strict self.

Tumbling

Why not combine floor patterns and tumbling? Place a long line of mats in the room. The children make group floor patterns incorporating various gymnastics moves on the mats as one line within their pattern, as in figure 6.32.

⮕SAFETY

Have all the children start their tumbling at the same end of the mats. This way when they are practicing their patterns, there will be no disasters.

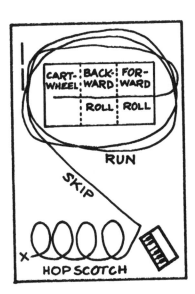

6.32

Voice Box

I have decorated a box, large enough for a child to fit into, and labeled it the Voice Box. On one side is a hole sized for a small face. With this box we play a language game. One child leaves the room while the rest of the class and I make up a difficult floor pattern. We move through it several times so that everyone (except the absent child) knows it. One person is picked to go into the Voice Box with the floor pattern; the rest of the class sits down. The child who is outside is retrieved and the game begins. The child in the box, using no other aid than her voice, must command the other child to do the floor pattern:

"Start at the door."

"Which door?"

"That door."

"Which one?"

"The one over there by the side of the stage . . . OK, now run a wiggly line . . . No, not to there, to the other side . . ."

I diabolically enjoy putting a timid child in the Voice Box with a bossy child as the mover. The problem, as you have probably noticed, is that only two children can play at one time. The other children enjoy watching, but I dislike having them sit for so long. I have not figured a way around that, so I rarely use the game. But I include it because it is an excellent language activity and you might have a special, smaller class or a time period with part of your class that it would work well in.

Designs

Doing abstract designs spatially is the most advanced stage of floor patterns. I have done this activity only with older dance studio classes. These floor patterns are simply designs. I draw some and the children can draw their own; sometimes I find interesting designs in magazines and art books, as in figure 6.33, a through e.

The children fulfill the design in any way they want. This is really a launching point for their own choreography, so I do not concern myself if the design is not actually recognizable.

Room Directions

When the children are at ease with floor patterns, it is time to clarify the idea of room directions—the front, back, and right and left sides of a room. If the children are clear with directions in their bodies they will have no trouble with this. The children already use "front" in Perfect Spots. "The front of any room is simply the wall we pick to be front. We already have the chalkboard wall as our front. Face front. The wall in back of you is the back of the room, the wall to your right is the right side of the room, and the other is the left side of the room.

"Now I have some tricky instructions for you":

1. Face front and point front with your right arm. Face back and point to the front of the room with your right arm.

6.33

2. Point right with your right arm; point right with your left arm; point right with your left arm and hop to the right side of the room on your left foot.

3. Face back and move toward the front of the room. What direction are you traveling in?

4. Move toward the back of the room in the forward direction; move toward the front of the room going in the sideways direction; move toward the right side of the room going in the backward direction; move toward the left side of the room going in the turning direction.

5. Make your feet point right; make your arms point left; move backward toward the front of the room.

Closing Thoughts

One piece of paper and a set of markers will produce attentive, well-behaved, enthusiastic classes. Phenomenal. Directions and especially floor patterns open up an enormous arena of lesson possibilities. They incorporate a lot of movement with a stunning array of academic skills. And because the focus is directed on the map, lessons are very easy to control. As you will see in the lesson plans, floor patterns can integrate many concepts into a culminating whole. On top of that, children love them. Floor patterns are not exactly a pedagogical panacea but are definitely close.

Part II

Building on the Basics

art II is flashier than part I. We have the cute, get-the-camera moments of partner activities, the excitement and exuberance of obstacle courses and stations, the flash and glitz of prop activities, the academic importance of the In and Out and Opposite Games. Part II offers a myriad of valuable activities. You will be tempted to start here: "Oh, my kids will love this. I'll try it." They will love it, and it is possible to start here. Being a teacher for as long as I have has made me a pragmatist. Any movement is better than none, and many of these activities can stand by themselves—the "Activity Finder" in the front of the book will help you choose activities appropriate to your purpose. Also, there is the hope that one move will lead to another and that as you experience success with various movement activities, you will backtrack into the conceptual base underlying them.

However, I have two concerns about starting with activities at this point. If you don't understand the concepts before starting the activities, you will lose some of movement's depth. A six-part ball sequence is great no matter what, but when the study is created with an understanding of locomotor and nonlocomotor movements, levels, and directions, it becomes richer both physically and intellectually. More importantly, I worry that you will not enjoy yourself because your class will be out of control, or verging on out of control, and you won't have a vision of what you want your movement program to become. Without class organizations like the Free Traveling Structure and Perfect Spots, class management might be tenuous at best. If you are on pins and needles about your class pushing the limits of control, you will work too hard. When other academic pressures encroach, I am afraid you will not come back. But you know what is best for you. Ideally I recommend laying a groundwork of class management organizations and basic movement concepts, with activities resting on these principles. However, if the activities entice you into trying movement with your class, that is terrific. Pass out the balls and have a ball.

Chapter 7

Working Together

One of the major goals of movement class is encouraging children's feelings of self-worth and empathy for others. Self-worth and empathy flow together as an unbroken circle: It requires a degree of self-esteem to reach out to others, and at the same time, reaching out increases our sense of self-worth. Children come to school with varying degrees of social skills, but all children benefit from learning how to foster friendship. Learning to make friends is as valuable as any intellectual or physical pursuit. Movement class can do a great deal to foster friendship by

1. offering specific partner and group activities,

2. coaching children on social skills, and

3. creating a tone of friendship and cooperation in class.

Partner and group activities usually involve touching one another. Children want and like to touch, but they often transfer physical warmth into teasing, fighting, and giggling. I think it is important that children get the OK to touch and feel close to one another. The movement activities in this chapter promote appropriate touching.

Fostering Friendship

During the first six weeks of movement class I use several or all of these partner and group activi-

ties any number of times, depending on the class needs. Throughout the year we come back to a few of these activities just for the fun of it, or if there is an influx of new children. Generally, the partner activities are used as lesson warm-ups in the Free Traveling Structure, and the group activities are used either for creative studies or as part of the locomotor movements in the Diagonal Structure.

All partner and group activities start with my "partner lecture." The class is gathered near me: "This is how we get partners in movement class. If someone touches you, or looks like they intend to choose you as their partner, you must be their partner. [I pretend to choose a student as my partner.] Now maybe Alicia, in her heart, does not want to be my partner. Maybe she is thinking, 'Yuck, I don't want to be Ms. Kogan's partner; I want to be Alex's partner.' That is fine, but I absolutely will not see that on her face or in her actions. She can feel what she wants but her face will be friendly [I exaggerate a friendly smile], and her actions will be cooperative [I exaggerate welcoming arms]. There are no 'no's here." Another formality I adhere to is having partners bow and say "thank you" when they separate. Whether the partners were together for a 10-second handshake or for a 10-minute warm-up, they need to acknowledge one another before moving on. One final point is clarifying the phrase *brand-new partner:* "When I ask you to get a brand-new partner you have to go with someone you have not been with today. If Alicia was with Karla and then went with Victoria, she cannot go back to Karla that day. Got it?"

Of course saying it will not make it happen. The first time someone says "no" or runs away from a potential partner, you need to come down hard, with full authority, "Out! You cannot act like that here." If people forget to say "thank you," call them back. If they do not get a brand-new partner and attempt to just pair up with friends, give them the "stern eye." It is worth the time and energy. They will understand very quickly by your attitude and actions what standard of behavior is required of them. Two factors ease the class into the desired behavior:

1. We start small with just a handshake.

2. The partner activities are so much fun that they are worth some social discomfort.

Partner Activities

Partner activities are movements that need, well, two people. Working in twos is very different from working in a group; there is an intimacy—however brief—that opens us up to one another. The social skills needed for partner work center on a sense of acceptance of another and the expectation of being accepted. Group work encompasses broader skills like the ability to take and receive ideas, negotiate, and balance standing up for oneself with bowing to group decisions. Friendships start in twos, so we begin there.

Partner Shake

Partner Shake is essentially a name-learning activity; therefore, I use it mainly in the first two weeks of class. This activity uses the Free Traveling Structure. "When you hear the piano sound [as always, any sound will do], do the locomotor movement I call out. When you hear the tambourine sound, find a partner and shake his or her hand. Make sure you know your partner's name . . . OK, bow and say 'thank you.'" Partner Shake can be as simple as that: alternating locomotor movements with shaking different partners' hands. Every Partner Shake is with a brand-new partner.

If you want to complicate the activity, alternate locomotor movements with different kinds of shakes. Table 7.1 is a possible progression.

Nonlocomotor Movements With Partners

In an activity very similar to Partner Shake, children do an individual locomotor movement and then get a partner to do a nonlocomotor movement. The structure is again Free Traveling, and the children switch partners each time. Doing nonlocomotor movements with a partner works better if the concept nonlocomotor has been introduced. Figure 7.1, a and b show partner contract and stretch. Table 7.2 shows a possible progression.

Levels and Directions With Partners

Using the Free Traveling Structure, children begin by getting partners and moving on various

Table 7.1 Sample Progression for Partner Shake

Sound	Locomotor movement	Partner Shake
1	Skip	Shake hands.
2	Jump, hop, hopscotch	Shake ankles.
3	Baby crawl, crab crawl, roll	Shake heads (if lice is not a concern).
4	Jazzy walk, side-slide	Shake elbows.
5	Run, run and leap	Shake backs.
6	Any locomotor movement	Shake any two different body parts, for example foot to shoulder, knee to hip. At the end of the shake, ask the children to hold their position and go somewhere together.

7.1

levels together, for example both children on knee level. Then partners have to move on two different levels while holding on: "Move together with one person on the lowest level and the other on air level. How are you going to hold on? . . . Now, one person on standing and one on sitting level. Are you traveling?" At the end, I ask the children to pick their own two different levels, hold on, and move. For example, two children might pick sitting level and air level. When I say

"Switch," they change to the level their partner was on. Switch faster and faster.

Directions with partners: Reinforcing the concept directions parallels the work just described with levels. The children hold on to each other by one hand and go in the direction I ask: forward, backward, sideways, turning. I then ask for two different directions: "One of you forward and the other turning . . . Hold on! . . . One sideways and one backward." At the end they choose two different directions.

Combining Levels and Directions With Partners

It is quite a challenge to mix levels and directions with partners. Here are a few examples:

- "One of you on the lowest level and one on standing level, one going forward and the other backward. Hold on. Are you getting anywhere? Switch."
- "One of you on knee level and the other on air level, one going sideways and one turning."
- "One of you on sitting level and the other on air level, one going backward and the other sideways. Terrific."

Table 7.2   Sample Progression for Nonlocomotor Movements With Partners

Sound	Locomotor movement	Followed by the nonlocomotor movement	Notes/Variations
1	Skip	Swing	Hold both hands and do large, vigorous swings.
2	Hopscotch	Contract and stretch	Contract with your partner into one tight ball: not two separate little contractions, but one big one. (Children have to hug each other or fold over one another.) Stretch by holding on and pulling away from each other (figure 7.1, a and b). If levels have been taught, ask the children to stretch on two different levels. This partner contract and stretch is very beautiful, and the children enjoy it tremendously. Another possibility is contract and stretch in opposites. When one person is contracted, the other is stretched; they switch faster and faster. The partners have to hold on to one another throughout.
3	Gallop	Strike	Partners face one another. Without touching, one partner does the nonlocomotor movement strike: legs, elbows, torsos, head, and hips. The other partner reacts as if struck—falling, ducking, rolling, dodging. Switch every four strikes.
4	Leap	Bend and straighten	Partners bend and straighten in opposites; that is, when one is bent the other is straight. They have to hold on to one another throughout.

In all these challenges children can touch side by side or they can circle their partner. In the third example, one child sitting and moving sideways while the other moves air level backward, it is more feasible to stay together if the air-level partner circles around the sitting one, touching his head or hand.

Bag a Partner

For children who are reluctant to touch or who consistently transfer physical warmth into fighting or giggling, I have a sneaky partner prop: bags. Onion, potato, and peanut bags are sometimes available at old-fashioned grocery stores—if not, they are easy to sew.

Each child gets a bag to explore freely. After about 10 minutes I move away from the persistent two-legs-in-the-bag jump by offering other suggestions: one leg in the bag, one leg and one arm, a head and an arm, even one leg and a head as in figure 7.2.

7.2

The next step is to take away half the bags; those without bags find partners like magic. I call out combinations of body parts for the two children to put into the bag: "Put in one of each of your legs . . . One of each of your arms . . . All four arms . . . Both heads . . . All four legs." At the end I often ask one partner to put one leg and a head in the bag while the partner carefully leads her around the room; of course they switch.

The power of the bags is that they offer an excuse for closeness. "It's not me, it's the bag that is forcing me to be close to you." Most of the time, children simply forget to be shy. Other props, like balls, ropes, scooters, and the parachute, also foster partner activities. These are covered in chapter 9, "Props."

Strictly Partner Movements

The following movements can be done only with a partner. These activities are usually done in the Free Traveling Structure as a warm-up (except for Leaping Logs, which must be more carefully controlled).

1. **Side-slide.** Partners stand front-to-front, hold both hands, and side-slide.

2. **Back-to-back side-slide.** Partners stand back-to-back, link elbows, and side-slide.

3. **Wring Out the Dishrag.** Partners stand facing one another holding both hands. They lift one arm, forming a bridge, and both go under at the same time, twisting their arms around and ending up back-to-back. They then return by forming another bridge and backing under it at the same time, ending up front to front again, as in figure 7.3, a and b.

Once they get the idea, they can flip around over and over in one continuous motion. I still do not know why it is called Wring Out the Dishrag.

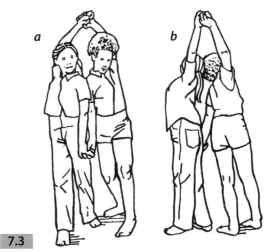

7.3

4. **Sitting down and getting up.** Partners stand back-to-back, elbows linked, and sit down. Then, without using hands on the floor, they get up. (The trick is to push against your partner rather than lean forward.)

5. **Sitting spin.** Sit back-to-back, elbows linked, and spin.

6. **Seat-scoot.** Partners sit facing each other, holding both ankles, and attempt to travel.

7. **Dragging.** One person lies down on his back, hands behind his head. The partner lifts his ankles (not pant legs, because they can come

off) and takes the lying-down child for a ride. I sometimes begin this activity by having children practice lifting and gently lowering their partner's legs. Only when they can demonstrate careful lowering of the legs do they get the OK to begin the ride. Of course they switch.

8. **Roll.** "There is a secret way to roll, holding your partner with both hands and never letting go. Can you figure it out?" This initial roll is hysterical. Children roll on top of one another, get entangled among each other, and generally cause small-scale havoc. Can you figure out the secret? (See figure 7.4.) Note: If you have an extra child and do not want to do the roll yourself, have the child join a group by holding onto another child's feet, making a chain.

7.4

9. **Standing spin.** Partners stand facing each other, holding both hands, and spin. The spin works best—that is, it's fast and exciting—if the children keep their feet close together, take little steps, and lean back.

This partner spin, simple as it is, demonstrates a great deal about a child: Does she let herself get spun? Does she do all the spinning? Does she look like a straw in the wind? Sometimes I find myself shouting, "Come on, Harriet, pull your own weight!" If it looks as though it is getting dangerous, stop that partner group. Remember to have the children spin the other way.

10. **Partner spider crawl.** One child positions his spider crawl perpendicularly on top of his partner's crawl, creating an 8-legged spider. Ideally both children should be in spider crawl positions (hands and feet) but if the bottom child is large he will have to lower to a baby crawl (hands and knees) position.

11. **Wheelbarrow.** One child puts his hands on the floor, the other lifts his legs at the ankles, and they walk.

⇨ *SAFETY*

Wheelbarrow, an old-fashioned partner activity, has come into disrepute lately because of possible back strain for the person walking on her hands. If it is done for a short while—8 to 16 beats—and the person on her hands remains straight rather than arching her back, I see no problems.

12. **Horsie.** One person gets on their hands and knees and the other person rides as on a horse. When I introduce this activity I choose the smallest child in the room, get on all fours, and have the child ride on me. Then I say, "Now we will have to switch places. Even if you are much bigger than your partner [indicating myself in comparison to the petite child], you still have to ride. Just keep some of your weight on your thighs so you don't kill your horse" [and I demonstrate]. (More about size differences in a moment.)

⇨ *SAFETY*

This might be a good time to consider how much play you want and can tolerate. If the "horse" is running or bucking a bit but the tone is playful and both children look as though they are having fun, I close an eye and move on. If there is any sense of disrespect or danger, I take a strong stand. You always have an "Out!"

13. **Hopping.** Partners stand front-to-front; each lifts a leg, and the partner holds it. Both children have to hop. Switch legs.

14. **Leapfrog.** One partner crouches while the other jumps over him. They continuously switch.

15. **Leaping Logs.** In the 20 years over which I have used this exercise, no one has gotten hurt. I, however, have nearly fainted. The idea is simple: One child rolls and her partner leaps over her both in the direction of the roll and coming back, as in figure 7.5.

This partner activity needs extremely clear traveling lines; I find it works best to move across

7.5

the room, partners switching in the middle. As partners line up on one side of the room, I send each pair off myself, making sure there is plenty of room around them. That is the key. An accident is less likely with one's partner than with someone else who is getting too close. When the children have reached the other side, they wait until everyone has had a turn before crossing the room again.

> **➡ SAFETY**
>
> As I said, I have never had a child hurt doing Leaping Logs. If you are too nervous about the leaps going both forward and back, have the leaps only cross back, opposite the direction of the roll; the leaping child then runs around his rolling partner to leap back again.

Mirror and Shadow

Most people have done Mirror in drama and dance classes, group therapy, or education courses. Two children face each other; one moves slowly and smoothly while the other, her mirror, attempts to follow the movements precisely. The mirror's job is to move with the mover and not as an afterthought. The mover's job is to make the movements slow, predictable, and feasible. There is no touching or speaking, and the roles switch frequently.

Shadow extends Mirror into locomotor movements, like Follow the Leader. This brilliant idea comes from my friend and master teacher, Ruth Bossieux. One child follows the other anywhere in the room, moving in whatever way the leader chooses. The leader can move as fast and as crazily as he wishes; his shadow tries to keep up

the best he can. Of course, the partners change roles frequently. Shadow is an excellent activity to follow Mirror; the children can release all the controlled energy needed for the sustained Mirror movements.

Lifting

"I am going to show you a way to lift somebody so that you could lift me, or your mom or dad." This is an attention-getting statement, and true too. Lifting is at the apex of partner work; it requires a good deal of sensitivity, mutual trust, and cooperation. Once mastered, it is a lot of fun (even learning how to lift is fun), and it gives many children a boost in their feelings of self-esteem and physical power. I do lifting in two stages: Stage 1 is easy and can be done with young children; stage 2 is harder and should be limited to third grade and higher. It is better if children master stage 1 before going on to stage 2.

Stage 1

Two children sit on the floor back-to-back. They slowly rock forward and back. As one child rocks forward, the other child leans back, resting completely on the forward child's back. The child who is forward slowly pushes up (lifting the back and head of his partner), and the process is reversed. It is simply a rocking forward and back done with a partner. Check that the children are going slowly and carefully and that the person leaning back lets go of her weight and truly rests her back and neck.

Now they are ready for the stage 1 lift. One child leans forward as before; the legs are in any comfortable position and the hands are on the floor, ready to brace the child if he should stretch farther forward than is comfortable. The leaning child pushes up on the back of the forward child so that his whole weight is resting on the other. They stay like this for a short while (10 or 15 seconds) and slowly reverse positions (see figure 7.6).

There should be no pain if (1) the children are around the same size; (2) the lifted child, the one on top, truly relaxes, straightens his legs, and lets his head and arms go; and (3) the lifting child, the one on the bottom, braces himself with his hands. The bottom child will feel a strong stretch, especially if his legs are in wide stride,

7.6

but he should not feel any real pain. If someone does, stop—something is wrong. In addition to all the social benefits, this partner lift is a good stretching exercise for the back and legs.

> ➡ **SAFETY**
>
> Two mistakes are common in the partner lift. In one, the top child is not resting evenly on the bottom child's upper back. In the other, the bottom child's elbows are straight—that is, she is not allowing any push forward at all; this puts too much strain on the elbows and back.

Stage 2

Now for the real thing: the standing lift. Figure 7.7 shows what it looks like.

7.7

Here is how to execute it: Partners stand back-to-back. At the beginning, partners need to be about the same size (height is more a factor than weight); later, as already noted, size will hardly matter. The child who is going to lift does three things:

1. Links elbows with his partner
2. While upright, bends his knees so that his seat is below the other child's seat—this is extremely important and in fact is the crux of this whole process

3. Hinges up, that is, straightens his knees and bends forward at the same time, thereby lifting the other child

The most important thing is for the lifted child to be high enough on the lifter's back that the lifted child's seat is on the lifter's lower back as opposed to her partner's seat. Secondly, it is necessary for the lifted child to relax; a tense, rigid body is almost impossible to lift. The top child needs to let go of her neck, arms, and legs, breathe deeply, and enjoy. The lifting child also needs to relax and take the weight in her knees as well as her back. The two children hold this position for a short while and change places.

Again, this is a good stretch, but it should not hurt. If it does, something is wrong. Ten to one what is wrong is that the lifter (the one on the bottom) did not bend her knees enough. Consequently she did not go low enough, and thus the top child did not get placed high enough on her back. Start again.

When the children are just learning to do this standing lift, I have them all in partners and adjust any wildly mismatched sizes. I allow only one partner group to try it at a time so that I can supervise them completely. I certainly would not want someone getting hurt, or even unusually scared, just when we were working on building trust. Once a partner group has it (both children are able to lift and get lifted), then they can work on their own.

Watch out that the bigger children do not do all the lifting and the smaller ones just get lifted. Many bad feelings about our bodies start in childhood—"I'm too big"; "I'm too fat"; "He'll never be able to get me off the ground"; "He doesn't want to be my partner." If the child is actually large, I will lift that child until the other children learn how to do it and are able to lift him. If you have a bad back or for other some reason cannot lift, why not show some older children how to do it and have them help you? If you can, let some competent lifters lift you. The kids will love it, and you might too.

Partner Obstacle Course

A fabulous way to practice social skills with a partner is through a partner obstacle course. You will find details in chapter 8, "Obstacle Courses and Stations."

One Left Over

All these partner activities assume an even division of children. It will never happen. I cannot explain it, but even if they start out evenly divided, something will occur—for example, one will get sick or be called out. You have two options for the remaining child: You can be a partner, or that child can join two other children to form a group of three. Generally, I recommend having the leftover person join a group. Your attention needs to span the class as a whole in order to spot any potential problems. But if you have the energy and inclination, kids love to work with their teacher. If the same child seems to be the one left out again and again, then I often put her with a partner and relocate a very social child into a group of three. Most of the partner activities can be done in threes; but if a particular activity cannot, we take a little extra time to take turns. Under no conditions do I eliminate a child from an activity because he is an inconvenient number.

Group Activities

Group activities expand social skills into a larger arena. When working in groups, children learn a great deal from one another; they also learn how to juggle cooperation and compromise while holding on to their own ideas. This type of ability to interact is exactly what employers are looking for in their employees. Examples of creative group assignments are presented throughout this book, working with all movement concepts, props, and floor patterns. Following are a few more ideas for specifically promoting group unity. These are done in the Diagonal Structure.

1. Group spin. A group of children holds hands to form a small circle and spins (like a small merry-go-round). This is obviously a takeoff on the partner spin, but it is more exciting when done in a group.

2. Cancan. The children hold shoulders and do their version of a cancan dance (see chapter 3). If the activity is treated with enough silliness, even boys like this one.

3. Horse in the Corral. One member of a group of three gallops forward while the other two people hold hands around him and side-slide.

4. Carrying. Any method of two people carrying a third is fun and often requested. The easiest carry is with one person lying down on her back and the other two people each carrying one arm and one leg.

A more complex carrying is the seat carriage. Each carrier holds his own left wrist with his right hand. The two carriers then hold each other's right wrist in order to form a solid square between them, as shown in figure 7.8, a and b. The third person gently gets on for a seated ride, as in figure 7.8c.

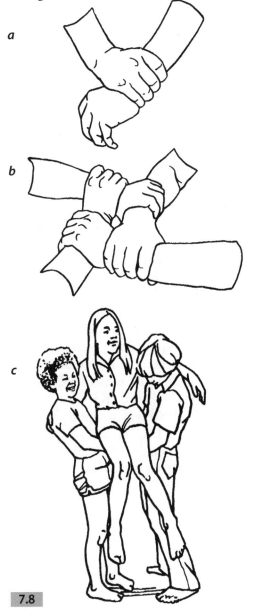

7.8

In all rides, every person in the group gets a turn. Rides take longer than you might expect, and they are noisy and a bit chaotic. I do not think there is much you can or should do about this; I am just giving a small forewarning.

Closing Thoughts

The most significant contributor to children's working together is the overall tone of the class. The feeling a class projects mirrors itself in the children. If the general tone of the class is warm, caring, and trusting, the children are likely to display those qualities with each other. No partner or group activity can overcome an unfriendly atmosphere.

Innumerable factors make up the emotional quality of a class. I want to touch on three:

1. Sensitivity to body image
2. Taking the time to lavish praise
3. Taking the risk to show some humanness

It is very important to be sensitive to the children's developing views about themselves. From third grade on, sometimes even younger, children begin to compare themselves with others, and many become hypercritical about themselves. The biggest issue is fat. What we as teachers can do is limited but not insignificant. First, we must not allow even a hint of peer disparagement. We cannot wait until partner activities to set this tone in the class; it must start on day one. On the whole, the children's attitude will reflect your feelings, so be careful not to sacrifice the child for the lesson: If a child is not very coordinated and is taking longer to do something, throwing off the pace of your class, train yourself to relax and enjoy his effort. Second, we must require a community effort of helping one another, including setting up the room, teaching one another steps, and encouraging all endeavors.

How does this sensitivity to body image translate to partner activities? The "partner lecture" is a good start. No matter how we feel, we act in a way that helps and encourages others. If I hear a child put herself down, I will usually say something like, "You are perfect for right now." No child is left out. If she is truly too big for some of the activities, either I will step in or I will make other arrangements. For example, during Wheelbarrow, if I truly think the standing child cannot safely hold the legs of the bottom child, I will take one leg or have a third child take one leg. But I do not make a big deal of it. "You are perfect for right now."

Most teachers are friendly and caring, but we sometimes get caught in the rigors of curriculums and the push and pull of schedules. It is very easy to fall into the trap of a perfunctory "Good work" and let it go at that. I believe that we should praise more, and more enthusiastically, than we criticize. That means taking the time and expending the energy to call home about a job well done, write a note about a new achievement, twirl a child in the air for displaying self-reliance, or shake hands with a child for showing a sense of fair play. Of course this lavish praise can take place only within a framework of sound discipline. All this requires a lot of energy, but I have found that the more praise is lavished the less criticism will be needed.

Although it is sometimes embarrassing, I think it is important to show some of our human side. That means apologizing when necessary, admitting mistakes, and revealing some feelings, both good and bad. If we want children to care about each other we must teach them that there is a common bond between people and that, as an example, that bond exists between teachers and students. If we approach each child with care and respect and demand care and respect back simply because we are all human beings, then the children are likely to start treating each other a little better.

Chapter 8

Obstacle Courses and Stations

Obstacle courses are sequenced movement activities. Once a course is set up, the children proceed through the activities essentially on their own. I cannot begin to express how wonderful, how fun, how valuable, a good obstacle course can be. Stations are separate activities shared by small groups of children—like academic centers in the classroom. Groups remain at one station for a period of time until the entire class rotates to the next station.

Obstacle Courses

Obstacle courses require work to set up and take down, but the benefits definitely outweigh the effort. There are many reasons why obstacle courses are valuable to movement class. Here are six of them:

1. An obstacle course sets an exciting tone for the class. It is usually the first activity I present to fourth through sixth grades. At this age children are often swaggeringly timid. They come in full of bluff and bravado because they have not the slightest idea what movement is about. They are not sure if it is going to be "sissy," if they are going to make fools of themselves, if they will be able to do it, or if their feet are going to stink when their socks come off. An obstacle course leaves little time for worrying, is certainly not sissy, and is most definitely fun. It tells the class that you are on their side.

2. An obstacle course acquaints children with the room as a moving space and introduces them to a lot of equipment. If you have a very limited number of props, five balls, two hoppities, four scooters, six tires, and four jump ropes, these few paltry pieces of equipment become the ingredients of a fabulous course.

3. An obstacle course can be a sneaky way of getting your rules across. For example, one can emphasize no gum during class by including a skip around a wastebasket and getting rid of any (pretend) gum; one can portray that the stage is off limits until a dance is perfected by tiptoeing in front of the stage. In addition, if the course is exciting, children will be incredibly motivated to act correctly.

4. Ironically, an obstacle course is both exhausting and relaxing. For you, the work is concentrated in setting up the equipment, especially the first time when the children do not know how to help you. Once the course is set up, however, you just need to warm up the class and then spot the balance beam. It is a very easy lesson. For the class, the lesson will completely tire them out but causes very little stress. It works well at any time but is absolutely the perfect lesson for standardized testing time. It also calms post-Halloween and pre-holiday hysteria.

5. An obstacle course is the best way to assess your class. You can check individual children very quickly without putting them on the spot

of feeling watched. Within an obstacle course you can easily assess balance (both dynamic and static), visual perception, motor planning, gross motor coordination, eye-hand and eye-foot coordination, strength, flexibility, and agility. In addition, you can get a fair assessment of concentration, memory, attention span, mastery, and overall attitude toward authority. In part III of this book, which presents lesson plans, a grid of possible assessments is included with each obstacle course lesson.

6. An obstacle course is an excellent medium for teaching and reinforcing relationship words. *Over*, *under*, *around*, *through*, *beneath*, and *between* become real and meaningful through kinesthetic experience. Have I convinced you it is worth the trouble to set up an obstacle course?

Let us not get carried away. There is a danger of overdoing obstacle courses. I know of a school that wanted a movement program and discovered the obstacle course as an easy and controlled lesson. They had a course ready to go along the sides of the multipurpose room; teachers simply had to pull the equipment away from the walls and they were in business. Every week the children did the same obstacle course.

Can you guess what happened? It took several months, but the children grew bored and became half-hearted and listless. Wouldn't you? I like to present an obstacle course about every six weeks. After we have been working hard exploring general movement activities and academic skills through movement, it is nice to take a break and change the pace with a course. Once a course is presented, it is very important to repeat that lesson the next class time, and preferably the next two times; it always works better the second and third times. But do not do an obstacle course more than four times in a row. After another six to eight weeks, set up a different course. In addition to providing these periodic breaks from "regular" movement classes, obstacle courses are excellent for initiating a movement program for older grades and releasing stress during testing periods.

So, what do these obstacle courses look like? Figure 8.1 is an example of a beginning, simple course.

I would use a course like this only with preschool to first grade. In the course shown, the children are told the instructions aurally, usually with a demonstration the first time:

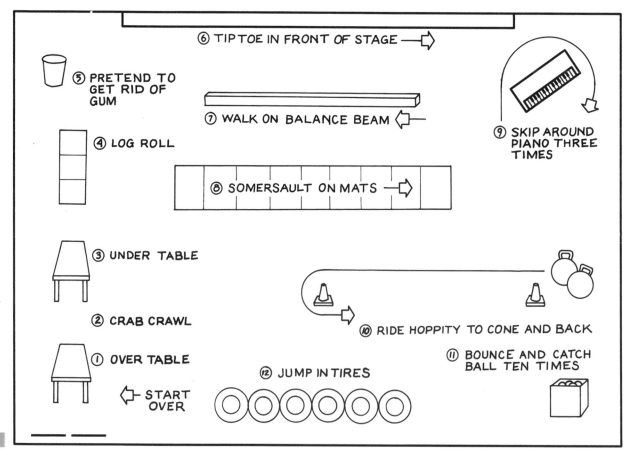

8.1

1. Climb over the table.
2. Crab crawl between the two tables.
3. Crawl under the table.
4. Log roll on the mat.
5. Pretend to get rid of gum.
6. Tip-toe in front of the stage.
7. Walk on the balance beam.
8. Somersault on the mats.
9. Skip around the piano three times.
10. Ride a hoppity from one cone to the other and back.
11. Bounce and catch a ball 10 times.
12. Jump in the tires. Start over.

As you watch your class, several things will become clear:

1. During this obstacle course you will be able to see how generally coordinated the children are. Did they leap easily over the table or did they clutchingly crawl over? Could they do a somersault? How far could they jump?

2. You will have a clear picture of the intellectual development of your class. How many instructions did they remember the first time through? How precisely did they do the three times around the piano? Were they comfortable with the words over, under, between, around?

3. You will have a good idea of the general attitude of your class. Did they clean up after themselves? Did they follow the sequence or try to skip some parts and repeat others? Did they deal considerately with their classmates or try to race in front of other children? Just as an obstacle course will teach you a great deal about your class, it can be used to teach your class a great deal.

The Greatest Obstacle Course

Many years ago I worked for an innovative recreation program in Richmond, California, run by my friend and mentor Gertrude Blanchard. She not only allowed but encouraged me, with the help of other staff, to create the greatest obstacle courses of all time. Figure 8.2 is an example of one of these courses.

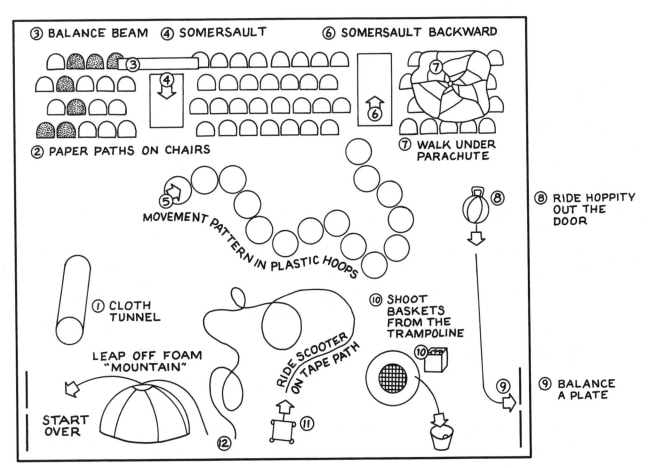

8.2

All instructions were written and taped where the numbers are indicated on figure 8.2 of the course:

1. Child goes through cloth tunnel (staff member makes it shake and wiggle).

2. Three paths are set up by taping colored paper to the backs of chairs; each piece of paper indicates a step. Red is the hardest with several chairs between steps, blue is medium hard with two chairs between steps, and green is the easiest with steps on adjacent chairs. The children pick their path and follow it, walking on the appropriate chairs.

> **SAFETY**

"Gad, isn't that dangerous?" asks my teacher friend, Pat, about the chair paths (number 2) in the Greatest Obstacle Course. It is a curious thing about "dangerous" activities. In all my years of teaching, no one has gotten hurt on the "dangerous" activities. In the case of the chair paths, we warn the children to step on the front part of the seat so the chair will not fold up. It has worked fine, especially since a child does not have to choose the hardest path unless he wants to. Children almost never elect to do something that is too dangerous for them. If they want to do something—not out of bluff but genuine desire—they are usually ready to do it. And I believe that danger-within-reason is important for children, and adults as well. It gives people a feeling of exhilaration, a sense of excitement and challenge. Why be shortchanged by preconceived limitation?

3. A balance beam is placed like a plank across the aisle separating rows of chairs. The children cross the beam, with a staff person to help, if needed.

4. Mats are set on the inclined aisle (this is an auditorium), and the children somersault down the mats.

5. Plastic hoops are arranged in a color pattern. For example, one red, followed by three blues, followed by two yellows, and so on. Each color represents a movement: jump in the red, hop in the blue, step in the yellow. The children have to figure out the resulting movement sequence.

6. Children somersault backward uphill on mats placed in a second aisle.

7. Children walk on the chairs under the parachute.

8. Children ride hoppities out the door.

9. On a little porch area, children try balancing a plastic plate on a pole and spinning it.

10. Children jump on a mini-trampoline while shooting baskets (tennis balls thrown into a waste paper container).

11. Children ride scooters on the taped line.

12. Children run and leap off a large foam "mountain" (a rounded incline mat). They start over.

Other Obstacle Courses

I consider an elaborate obstacle course like the The Greatest Obstacle Course almost a work of art. Unfortunately, most schools do not have the staff or equipment to do a course like that. Still, ordinary materials are available to make your course more intricate. Old tires, large boxes, of even the free sponge that comes with some facial creams, all have valuable obstacle course potential. Sometimes you can even use surprise textures: Make a hand-sized hole in the lid of a box and put in a bowl of cold, cooked spaghetti with water (gelatin is also a good choice); the children stick their hands in as part of the course. (Have a damp towel handy.) If there is a stage in the room where you hold class, you can place the balance beam a couple of feet from the edge and have the children pretend they are a thousand feet high as they cross the beam; or with double- or triple-thick mats on the floor, have the children jump off the stage.

We begin preparations for the obstacle course on the mats. After a thorough warm-up (emphasizing neck, back and leg stretches, abdominal exercises, and push-ups), we work on basic tumbling moves, such as bridges, shoulder stands (see "Blastoff" in chapter 2), somersaults, one-knee back rolls (see discussion of rolls in chapter 3), and frog balance (see "Positions of the Body" in chapter 4). We then combine these stunts into a gymnastics routine. This is my favorite: Do one somersault, jump in the air, sit down and push up into a bridge, contract, lift up into a shoulder stand, do a one-knee back roll, and end in a frog balance (or a headstand if the frog balance is solid). I tell the class that this routine will be

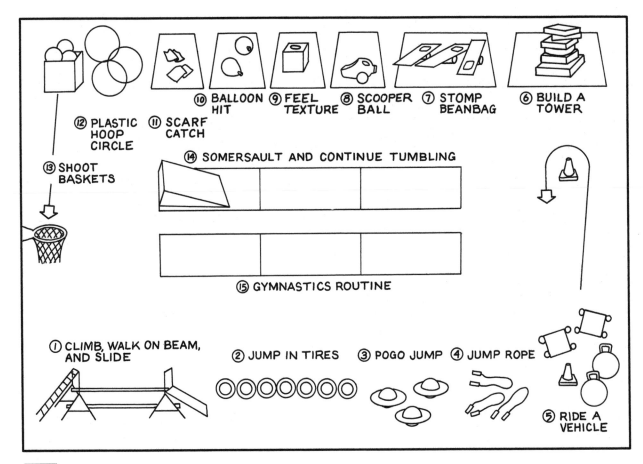

8.3

the last activity in the course, so they can practice it again and I can help them individually if necessary.

Figure 8.3 is an example of a typical obstacle course I use.

The obstacle course above moves the children through 15 activities:

1. The stegel is set up with two balance beams: one on the lowest and one on the medium level. The child climbs the ladder, walks across the balance beam of his choice, and slides down the slide on a scooter. (The scooter slide is great fun for second grade on up. Have the children hold the scooter so they cannot roll over their own fingers, and have them lift their heels off the floor.)

2. Jump (not step) in the tires.

3. Practice riding pogo balls.

4. Do 20 jumps with a jump rope.

5. Ride a vehicle, either a scooter or hoppity, from one cone to the other and back, then ride the other vehicle.

6. Stack some foam shapes into a tower and karate-kick it down – of course clean up the foam pieces before moving on.

7. Stomp on a foot stomper, catching the beanbag 10 times.

8. Throw and catch a soft ball with a scooper 10 times.

9. Stick a hand in the surprise texture box (and wipe the hand on a towel).

10. Hit a balloon with different body parts 10 times.

11. Throw and catch scarves, preparing for juggling, 10 times.

12. Attempt to keep a plastic hoop circling around waist for 10 seconds.

13. Take 10 tries at shooting baskets with a ball.

14. Somersault down the incline mat and continue on the row of mats doing rolls of their choice.

15. Practice the gymnastics routine taught at the beginning of class. Start over.

Tips for a Smooth Course

There are a number of ways to facilitate a smoothly running course:

1. In the course shown in figure 8.3, I situate myself between the balance beam and the mats where the children are practicing the gymnastics routine so that I can spot the beam and still help individual children with their gymnastics moves.

2. It is imperative that the children replace all equipment immediately when they complete an activity. If the course looks sloppy, it will be done in a sloppy fashion.

3. If a piece of equipment needs to be in an exact spot, mark the spot with a piece of tape. In the course shown in figure 8.3, I might mark the places for the cones with an "X" so the cones remain the correct distance apart.

4. Since the children are trained in the Free Traveling Structure, it should be easy to reverse the aural cue so that when you beat the drum, or use some other loud signal, they freeze immediately. Test them once or twice.

5. The children should have a set cue for starting on their own—for example, "When the person in front of you gets to the top of the ladder, you start." This allows a safe distance between children and frees you from that task. Be strict about this.

6. For the very first time with the very first course, it is probably a good idea to have everyone in line, waiting to start at the same place. From then on, certainly with second grade on up, have groups of children start at varying places so that there is little waiting. You need to make it clear that no matter where they start, they keep the order of the course. Once older classes are competent at dealing with obstacle courses, I simply tell them to start wherever they like.

7. As with the course shown in figure 8.3, keep the activities in a circular pattern around the room so that there is no question of what comes next.

8. If there is a big bunch-up in traffic flow, try to make that activity move more quickly. For example, if there was a tie-up at the foot stompers, I would lower the number of stomps from 10 to 5. If there was a tie-up at the vehicle ride, I would put out more vehicles or limit the activity to one ride.

9. If you have an activity that has a nebulous time frame, for example balancing a plastic hoop or spinning a plate on a pole, suggest a time limit like 10 seconds and watch. I like to put the responsibility for traffic flow on the children. "If it looks like there are a lot of people waiting behind you, then you need to take a shorter turn; if there is nobody waiting, then you can take a longer time if you want. Be considerate."

10. Allow enough time. The warm-up will take at least 15 minutes, and you need 30 minutes to teach the course and run through it several times. Allow time for the children to complete the course at least three times. The second time you present the obstacle course it will move much faster, so you could take longer for the warm-up and include Circus at the end.

Cleanup

How about setting up and cleaning up? Once the class has seen a course, the students will be glad to help you set it up in the future. My preference for setup is to do it at recess with about six reliable students. If this is not possible, have the class sit on one side of the room and assign one specific task to every two children. For cleanup I often use this assignment method, although by the end of the year I expect to be able to simply say, "Perfect cleanup."

Circus

At the end of the second or third lesson with this obstacle course, it is wonderful to play Circus. The children are forewarned that they will have an opportunity at the end of class to show one trick from the course. After they complete the obstacle course several times, they all sit on one of the rows of mats. I indicate to five children to stand where they will show a stunt. For example, they might want to show their balance on the beam so they would stand by the balance beam;

they might want to show a gymnastics routine so they would stand on the other row of mats; they might want to show a scooter ride or a basketball throw so they would stand in the appropriate locations. Generally children choose different stunts, but if most choose the same it is fine. Since there are only five at a time, things move quickly. I announce, "Ladies and gentlemen, we are now going to have a five-ring circus!" And the children perform their selected accomplishment. We all clap and cheer (no matter what), and then five other children perform until everybody (I do not allow refusals) gets a turn. This is a nice way to close the time with one particular obstacle course.

Partner Obstacle Course

There is one more obstacle course I want to describe: the partner obstacle course. In this course every activity is done with a partner; the children stay with the same partner throughout. Figure 8.4 shows a possible partner course.

This course might look intimidating. It is not as hard as it looks, and the time investment will be worth it. This is one lesson that should not be missed. We start on the mats, as in the previous course, and do a strenuous gymnastics warm-up emphasizing neck and back stretches, abdominal exercises, and push-ups. The children divide into partners with one person standing behind the other. Group 1 does a gymnastics routine like the one mentioned earlier—somersault, bridge, shoulder stand, one-knee back roll, frog balance or headstand. Each child tells her partner if she wants help on the frog balance or headstand. If she does not, her partner respects that; if she does, her partner gently lifts her legs to help her balance. Of course they switch places several times.

I then gather the class near me and show two signs: one with the word *cooperation* and the other

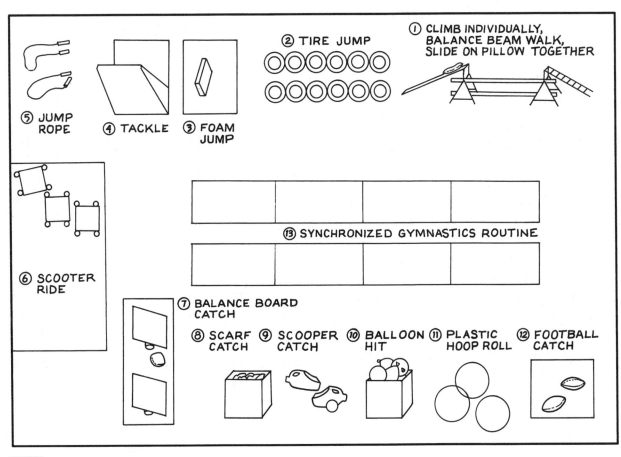

8.4

with *compromise*. We talk about cooperation and generally agree that it means being nice and helpful. "But what does compromise mean?" I offer a demonstration. I place two children about 6 feet apart. "Dan and Ricky want to shake hands but are too far apart. How could they do it? Dan could walk over to Ricky or Ricky could walk to Dan; that would be cooperative because it solves the problem, but that is not compromise. For compromise, both Dan and Ricky have to give in a little. [I motion for the two boys to walk toward each other.] See, one does not do all the giving in; they both come halfway. Get it? Throughout this course you will be with a partner and you will have plenty of opportunities to practice cooperation and compromise. For example, you will have to cooperate seeing who will climb the ladder first. You'll have to compromise on the balance beam if one of you wants to walk faster and one slower. How could you compromise those two speeds? Right, both could walk medium, or they could walk fast for half the beam and slow for the other half. Good thinking."

There are 13 activities included in this partner obstacle course:

1. Partners climb the ladder individually. Once they get on the adjacent balance beams they walk together holding hands or holding a "connector." (The connector can be a ruler or a plastic tube. Sometimes older children are reluctant to hold hands and any type of bar eliminates the whole issue. One person walks the bar back for the next pair.) Partners then slide down the slide together on one pillow (and put the pillow back).

2. Partners hold hands (or another connector) and jump in the tires at the same time.

3. One child holds the foam pillows the desired height and his partner jumps; they switch places.

4. One child holds the incline mat up and his partner tackles the mat; they switch places.

5. Both children jump using one rope.

6. Partner scooter ride. You are not going to believe this one. One child sits on a scooter, holding the sides and lifting his feet. His partner holds the sitting child's ankles, lowers his back so the legs are not lifted too high, and gives his partner a ride on the scooter.

⮕ SAFETY

The two crucial elements for a safe Partner Scooter ride are: first, clearly designate a separate area for this activity (cones or tape delineation are fine); second, make sure the child providing the ride keeps the sitting child's legs low or he will tilt him off the scooter. The rides can be exciting and can include twirls, but of course cannot be wild.

7. With two balance boards facing one another, partners throw and catch a beanbag five times.

8. Partners throw and catch scarves five times, or – a recent favorite – one person dumps the whole box of scarves on the other and then they switch.

9. Partners each hold scoopers and throw and catch one ball 10 times.

10. Partners bat one balloon back and forth 10 times.

11. Partners roll a plastic hoop back and forth 10 times. If you want, have them take turns ducking through it while it is rolling.

12. Partners throw and catch one foam football 10 times (and only 10 times).

13. Partners make up a synchronized gymnastics routine on the mats. You can specify the number of moves for the routine, four for younger classes, seven or eight for older. Start over.

There are two more, somewhat sophisticated, activities that can be included in a partner obstacle course: Trust Walk and Massage. These are possible with mature, older, preferably experienced classes. In Trust Walk, one person puts a scarf on like a blindfold and his partner carefully, with unwavering attention, walks him throughout the room. It is crucial that the blindfolded child never gets hurt or even scared. The leader can take him onto the mats and around the other activities, can take his hand to hit the piano once or twice, can ask him to touch various objects and guess what they are. Of course the two switch roles. If you notice that the blindfolded person is peeking a little, I recommend "not seeing" that. In Massage, the partner does just that (no, no oils or shedding of clothes). One child sits on a chair; the other stands behind her and kneads her shoulders and upper back. Of course they switch places. Ignore all giggles.

This partner obstacle course is the culmination of the partner and group activities worked on throughout the year. Some partners will need coaching on how to get along and how to take turns. But most will take to the activity immediately. Put your remaining child into a group of three and tell them to figure out how in the world to do it.

Stations

Stations are separate activities that are used by small groups of children. They can be used as an addition to classroom work—for example, "When you finish your math papers you can go to the reading or the puzzle station." Or they can be used with the entire class. In this case, the room is divided into a number of activity areas—I prefer five areas with four to six children at each station. The children rotate activities so that everyone has a turn with every activity. For a 45-minute class using five stations, that would be about 7 minutes per station.

Movement activities can be used in stations, even in a small room. The stations I use most commonly are balance beam, tumbling, jump-hop, scooter line, and some form of eye-hand practice. The setup is similar to that for an obstacle course except that there is much less equipment out. The children stay at their station, repeating the activity until it is time to switch to the next. Figure 8.5 shows a possible setup for stations.

There are five stations shown in figure 8.5:

1. Plastic hoops are laid in a line (taped together) and the children practice various jumps and hops.
2. Children ride scooters on the taped line.
3. The children practice tossing beanbags into a container.
4. Children practice walking in various ways on the balance beam.
5. Children practice tumbling moves.

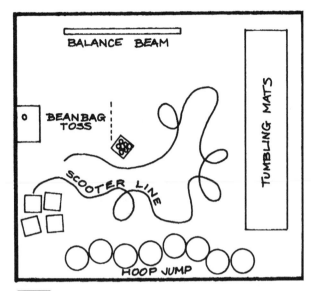

8.5

Many movement programs use stations as their main format. Stations are excellent for physical development: coordination, strength, agility, balance, and perceptual awareness. However, stations do not lend themselves to work with concepts, and since I am partial to the conceptual approach, I use them infrequently. Concepts provide a much richer approach to any subject—knowing the conceptual background creates a deeper understanding than simply following a recipe. Working with movement concepts provides opportunities for enormous personal, academic, and social growth as well as physical exercise. It is very exciting for me and, I believe, for the children. However, stations have their place. They are (1) an easy entrance into the world of movement, (2) a good workout, and (3) an excellent option to keep in mind for, say, substitute teacher lesson plans.

The key to stations is the correct number of repetitions. Children need to have the same stations repeated often enough to master the tasks, but the stations should not be repeated to the point of boredom. As with obstacle courses, I prefer two or three lessons in a row with stations and then a long break before new stations are presented. I find that stations are the most useful as a lesson plan for substitute teachers and for times when everyone needs a mental break.

I would use stations more frequently only when working with children who have motor problems. An ideal arrangement is to have these children twice a week. Once a week they participate in movement class with their peers, and another time during the week they return for "special work." Stations are perfect for this "special work" because it is easy to work with individual children in stations and the children get the repeated practice they need. When accompanying general movement classes, stations can be used throughout the year.

Notes for facilitating stations:

1. For young children, preschool to first grade, you will need two or more helpers. Moms and older children are fine for this. For second grade on up, helpers are nice to have but not essential.

2. Each station needs a written chart of activities (examples of charts for balance beam, tumbling, jump-hop, scooter line, and eye-hand coordination work follow in the upcoming sections). If you do not have a sequence of activities developing mastery at a station, the children will not sustain interest.

3. Teach every item on every chart.

4. Sometimes have the children do the charts in the reverse order so that they get to practice all the tasks.

5. Establish an aural cue (drum or tambourine) for stopping; since the children are trained in the Free Traveling Structure, they should have no trouble with this.

Balance Beam

The balance beam is perfect for station work because

- it takes very little space,
- the children need little supervision—group members can help each other, and
- almost all children greatly benefit from work on the balance beam.

On the beam, children improve balance, control, coordination, and perceptual awareness. This work is crucial for children with motor problems and is valuable for children who are coordinated. The balance beam is wonderful also because it is self-corrective. No one needs to tell a child he fell off the beam; by the same token, it is clear when a child has mastered a task.

Possible activities for the balance beam:

1. Walk forward.
2. Walk backward.
3. Walk sideways, right side leading.
4. Walk sideways, left side leading.
5. Grapevine—step side, cross the other leg in front, step side, cross the other leg in back.
6. Walk turning.
7. Walk on the balance beam while balancing a beanbag on the head.
8. Walk to the middle of the beam; stoop and pick up two beanbags laid on the beam; stand and walk the rest of the way.
9. Walk forward on the beam while bouncing a ball on the floor.
10. Crawl.
11. Jump over the balance beam. (Young children or children with motor problems jump forward over the beam; other children jump sideways.)
12. Hop on the beam; change feet in the middle.
13. Skip.
14. Leap.
15. Walk to the middle of the beam; balance on one foot for 10 seconds; walk to the end of the beam.
16. Walk to the middle of the beam and step over an obstacle, for example a yardstick held at knee level.
17. Walk to the middle of the beam and stoop under an obstacle, for example a yardstick held at shoulder level.
18. With a low-level beam, try jumping rope.
19. Make up a sequence of five moves to do on the balance beam.

Tumbling

Tumbling is another essential station. As with the balance beam, it does not require too much space, and all children benefit from tumbling practice.

On the mats children improve strength, agility, coordination, and control. In addition, work on tumbling often promotes children's feelings of self-worth. Somersaults, backward rolls, cartwheels, headstands, and handstands are scary. A child who comes close to conquering these stunts glows with pride.

Tumbling does require careful supervision, however. When I work alone I position myself by the tumbling mats and keep an eye on the whole room from there. If I have helpers, I still supervise the tumbling station. Closely watch rolls that go over the head; make sure the children round their necks so that only the back of the head touches.

Possible activities to include on a tumbling chart (young children do 1-7):

1. Log roll.
2. Cat roll.
3. Baby crawl.
4. Crab crawl.
5. Spider crawl.
6. Inchworm crawl.
7. Forward roll or somersault.
8. Backward roll or one-knee back roll.
9. Cartwheel.
10. Round-off.
11. Bridge, contract, shoulder stand.
12. Bridge walk.
13. Frog balance.
14. Headstand.
15. Handstand, forward roll.
16. A gymnastics routine made up of six different moves.

Jump-Hop

Among children with motor problems, 99% need work on jumping and hopping. Most of these children do not push equally with both feet while jumping, and most have trouble hopping on one side. Even coordinated children gain a great deal of strength and agility from practice with jumping and hopping.

Set up a plastic hoop pattern or a line of bicycle tires. The line can be straight (easier) or can wiggle (harder) as in figure 8.6, a and b. Have the tires or hoops touching one another, and tape them together.

Possible activities to include at a jump-hop station:

1. Jump.
2. Hop on the right foot.
3. Hop on the left foot.
4. Alternate jump and hop.
5. Bounce a ball while jumping.
6. Throw and catch a beanbag while jumping.
7. Jump over every other tire or hoop.
8. Jump in and then side to side out of each tire or hoop.
9. In each circle, jump to prepare and then jump a full turn.
10. Make up a jump, hop, step sequence.

Scooter Line

If you have three or more scooters available, a scooter line is a great station. Children love it, and it makes for excellent work on visual perception. Even simple play on scooters promotes balance,

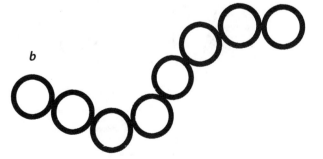

8.6

coordination, and strength. If you do not have scooters available, set up the line anyway and have the children follow it doing different locomotor movements.

Set up a line design with tape or paint as in figure 8.7. (If you leave masking tape on overnight, you will need a putty knife to remove it.)

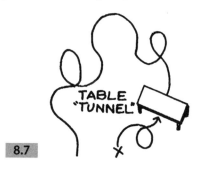

TABLE "TUNNEL"

8.7

Two rules with the scooter line:

- The children start when the child ahead has gone through the "tunnel."
- Under no condition can a child stand on a scooter.

Possible activities to include at a scooter line station:

1. Ride the scooter on your tummy.
2. Ride the scooter on the knees.
3. Ride the scooter on the seat.
4. Ride the scooter on the back.
5. Ride the scooter and spin while following the line.
6. With a partner, push or pull the scooter.
7. Ride a hoppity on the line.

8. Skip on the line.
9. Gallop on the line.
10. Leap on the line.
11. Make up a routine of different moves while still following the line.

Eye-Hand Work

Eye-hand work means practice in placing an object as the eyes direct. There are a number of ways to practice this skill. Because children need general practice rather than specific repetition with eye-hand work, I like to vary this station often.

The most easily controlled eye-hand work is a beanbag toss. The children simply practice tossing beanbags into a container. It is more fun if you can make or find a stand-up receptacle, as seen in figure 8.8, a and b. Children can also get partners and toss the beanbags to each other. For more beanbag activities see p. 143.

With enough room, the eye-hand station can use balls. Here are possible activities for a ball station:

1. Toss the ball into a container.
2. Bounce and catch the ball with two hands.
3. Dribble the ball with the right hand; dribble with the left hand.
4. Dribble the ball and alternate hands.
5. Roll the ball with the feet.
6. Bounce and catch the ball off a wall.
7. Throw the ball into the air and catch it.

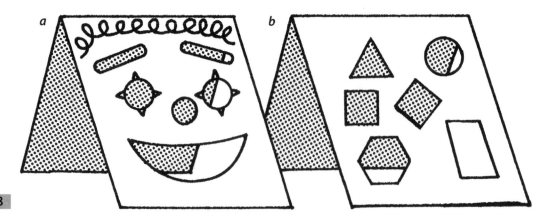

8.8

8. Throw and catch a ball with a partner.

9. Practice shooting baskets.

10. Bounce a ball while keeping a balloon in the air.

Some schools have small bowling sets, and these are good fun. (When using a bowling set, tape "X"s where the pins should stand so that the children do not spend their entire time arranging the pins.) Other possibilities for eye-hand practice are a ringtoss game and, for mature classes, a game of marbles.

Other Possible Stations

1. Jump ropes. You need enough ropes for one per child at the station. Give children a goal to shoot for—for example, "See if you can get to 500 jumps today; if you step on the rope, keep going." Note: Concrete floors are very hard on the feet. If possible use mats; if you have a wooden floor on the stage, use that for the jump rope station.

2. Patterning station. This station is for older children. Have pattern blocks or color paper squares available. The children create a pattern and represent each color with letters, numbers, food, toys, and movement. For example, red-red-blue-green-green-green could be translated into movement as jump-jump-spin-skip-skip-skip. They practice the movement patterns and ideally show their finished sequence to the rest of the class before moving on.

3. Small-motor coordination station. Here are a few of the many possible small-muscle coordination activities:

a. Sort beans with tweezers. Have three or four different kinds of beans on a small plate. The child sorts the beans using hand tweezers.

b. Use an eyedropper to count how many drops of colored water fit into different-sized containers.

c. Trace the inside of a form. Tracing a form with the pencil pushing out against a frame is easier than tracing by pushing the pencil in. An easily available form is a plastic puzzle in a frame that one lifts the pieces out of. For this activity the child uses the frame; for the next activity the child uses the puzzle pieces.

d. Trace a puzzle piece form.

e. Make a design out of pattern blocks. The child traces and colors each block in the design, cuts out the shapes, and then recreates his design with the paper forms.

Closing Thoughts

Especially to beginning teachers, those stations look awfully good, don't they? They are easy to set up, easy to control with charts, easy to justify, easy to understand. True. If stations are your entry into movement—and I know several teachers who began that way—that is fine. But they simply will not work after a while: They are too predictable and they do not encompass the mental challenges and creative outlets that concept work provides. Obstacle courses and stations are like carrots in a stew: they are colorful and tasty, and it is nice to have plenty of them, but they are not the meat.

Chapter 9

Props

Props are heaven sent. They spice up a class, bring concepts together, make great shows, embolden the timid, restrain the rambunctious, utilize memory and sequential skills, and build coordination and endurance. Plus, these miracles are wrought from objects easily acquired: balls, scarves, ropes, plastic hoops, marbles, balloons, parachute, chairs, or whatever works.

Tips for Working With Props

Why, then, are props so rarely used? Many teachers worry about the chaos that a prop can produce. They are right. Props are exciting and unleash enormous exuberance in children. Balls flying about, scarves whipping every which way, dozens of hands grabbing the parachute—nightmarish visions! These can, but need not, become real. Your primary defense against prop chaos is the establishment of the Free Traveling Structure (chapter 2). If you have trained your class to freeze when the sound stops, this control will extend to include the prop. "You know that when the sound stops you have to freeze; if your ball gets away from you, you still have to freeze your body and keep your eye on the ball." Your second defense is the general tone of your class. If a child does not follow instructions or if the prop is not being used appropriately, he must be put out. Your gut level sense of what is appropriate is correct. Do not imagine you are doing him, or the rest of the class, any favors by being so "nice" that you lose consistency. I do not mean harsh or rigid, or

even unwilling to allow possible exceptions, but the tone of the class is "We can have fun only if the rules are followed by everyone all the time." This expectation of good behavior is projected by your actions more than words. If a child is hurling a ball across the room, a thousand words will not accomplish nearly as much as silently removing the ball. One final consideration is planning how to distribute and put away the prop. I will give you a few tricks for passing out and collecting equipment, but I am sure you have great ideas if you prepare for these transitions.

What follows is the basic formula for working with any individual prop, that is, props like balls or scarves with each child having one. All activities are in the Free Traveling Structure unless otherwise noted.

Provide Free Time

Free time is essential. The children will not want to follow your instructions until they have had time to explore the prop on their own. This is very similar to what happens in any good math program, in which children are given time to explore the math manipulatives before doing any problems with them. Free time typically lasts 10, possibly 15 minutes; the key is to terminate free time when the children have exhausted their ideas and are ready for yours.

Do not be afraid of free time. If the children are being too rough, stop them. If their attitude is not completely cooperative after a warning, take the prop away. Do not use too many words, do not make a fuss, and do give the cooperative children a fabulous time. Also do not be afraid that free time is wasted time. The children are accomplishing many things: They are exercising, they are exploring their creativity, they are working on coordination skills, and they are having fun. But the bottom line is that they will not be receptive to new ideas until they have fulfilled their own intentions. I plan for at least two consecutive lessons with a prop; three is better. Each lesson begins with free time, but the length of the free time can get shorter.

Introduce Guided Movements

Guided movements are activities done by the class as a whole. These can be your ideas—"Dribble the ball with just your right hand . . . Just the left hand . . . Alternating hands." Or the ideas can be gleaned from the class—"Let's do Isabelle's idea with the ball. Show us, Isabelle." Generally I offer 10 to 20 guided movements at a fairly fast pace.

The purpose of guided movements is to expand the children's thinking about the prop; that is, a ball does not always have to be moved with just hands or feet. This expanded range of movement promotes divergent thinking, which is the basis for creative problem solving. Questions like "How many different ways can you move this ball?" are exactly the same sort of questions used to teach thinking skills, for example "What could you do with a six-finger glove?" Further, working with a prop in nontraditional ways frees and relaxes children to simply play. They do not have to worry about everyone lined up behind them watching them throw a brick. Like learning to improvise on an instrument, guided movements build coordination without stress.

In addition to offering specific ideas, you can have children explore new movements by incorporating general concepts. For example, they can use different parts of the body, tempos, directions, levels, and locomotor and nonlocomotor movements: "Move your plastic hoop and change levels. Keep your balloon in the air while moving slowly, now quickly. Move your ball while doing a nonlocomotor movement." These kinds of suggestions steer the children away from stereotyped movements.

Note: If a class is extremely timid or inordinately rambunctious I reverse free time and guided movements. That is, I will begin with my ideas and then allow them free time. But the general rule is: If a class does not want to do guided movements, they have not had enough free time.

Conclude With a Prop Study

Ideas are put together in an ordered, remembered progression. Prop studies can be created by the class as a whole, by small groups, or by individual children. Studies range from three to seven sequenced movements, each movement done for a phrase that is, say, 8 to 16 beats long. For example, the class sits gathered with the ball in their laps, their hands off the ball. (If they touch the ball, I take it and return it after we create the study.) "What shall we do first with our ball? OK, Steven, we'll run and bounce. What shall we do second? Good, Marilyn, roll it with our heads. Now what was the first thing? . . . Second? Good. What shall we do for the third? . . ." The activity continues like this until we get to the desired sequence length. I ask the children to close their eyes and say the sequence before we try it. Then we practice. The first attempt might include my help or my asking the class to shout the upcoming movement; then I ask the children to do the study without any help. The final stage is for the class to divide in half and perform for each other.

This progression works best in three consecutive lessons. In the first lesson we have free time and guided movements. The second lesson includes a shorter free time, guided movements, and setting up the study; and the third lesson again starts with a short free time and proceeds to a few guided movements, perfecting the study, and performing it.

One last note about props in general: If you do not have enough room or enough props for everyone to work at the same time, have half watch and half work. This arrangement is certainly not ideal, but it can work if the halves switch quickly and often. For example, when I was doing a demonstration lesson in a classroom with the furniture pushed to the sides, I divided the class in half (not boys and girls for this) and had the watching half sit on the desks, ready to jump down in a flash. We did free time with the moving half and then switched; we did guided movements and switched; and so forth. No one sat for more than 10 minutes, and they actually enjoyed watching each other. This half-and-half arrangement does offer more control, but in addition to taking longer, does not tire the children out. So I would not voluntarily choose it.

Balls

Balls are good for

- larger-muscle coordination,
- eye-hand and eye-foot coordination,
- sequencing and memory skills,
- endurance, and
- partner work.

Balls are an excellent first prop. Every child is enticed by a ball. My preference is very durable, 6-inch rubber balls. But I have worked with every type of ball imaginable—if need be, you can get a class set of used tennis balls.

There are several ways of passing out the balls. You can call the class in groups of various sorts: their reading groups, color of shirts groups, number-of-letters-in-first-name groups.

➡ *TROUBLESHOOTING*

You can form groups with many commands, but what will not work is long and short hair. When I tried that, I found that it was too relative. A boy with short hair went with the long hair group because, as he said, his hair was long for him. The discussion was interesting, though.

If you have the time, it is fun on occasion to throw the balls to individual children and see if they can catch them. I use this option infrequently since it takes a bit of time. My favorite way to distribute balls is to dump the box over and have the children scrabble for them.

Free time lasts 10 to 15 minutes but is not entirely free. I do not allow the balls to be thrown hard against the wall or to be kicked across the room. The children can do a controlled kick like a soccer dribble.

Following is a list of guided movement ideas:

1. Bounce catch the ball; walk and bounce catch; run and bounce catch.

2. Chase: Bounce the ball and run after it yelling, "Come back here!" This is obviously

for young children, but older ones actually love it.

3. Dribble the ball with one hand; with the other hand; with alternating hands; through the legs.

4. Soccer dribble: Roll the ball with just the feet, keeping it under control. Do not kick it into the air. Move backward.

5. Roll the ball without hands or feet. A possible solution is seen in figure 9.1.

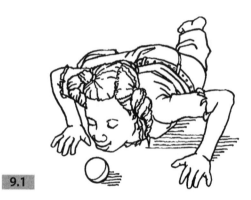

9.1

6. Jazzy walk while carrying the ball without using hands.

7. Roll with the ball under your chin or between the ankles.

8. Put the ball between the knees and "Ride 'em cowgirls and cowboys!"

9. Put the ball behind one knee and hop; switch legs.

10. Put the ball between the feet, sit and spin.

11. Use the ball as a drum.

12. Start with the ball on the floor and tap it continuously until you get it to bounce.

13. With the ball between the ankles, jump up and catch it in your hands.

14. Bounce the ball with your hand and swing your leg over it; change legs.

15. Throw the ball gently from hand to hand and skip at the same time.

16. Throw the ball high and catch it; spin and catch it; see how many claps you can do before catching it.

17. Gently throw and catch the ball while running and leaping.

18. Spin the ball on the ground; spin the ball on one finger (like the pro basketball players).

19. Spin the ball and try to imitate it; bounce the ball and imitate it.

When the children have explored a number of movement possibilities with balls, it is time for a study. The goal of a study is sequential memory. At first we practice the study while I call out the movements. Next, I say to do the first move, the second move, and so on, accompanied by the piano or drum. Finally, the sound is the only signal of movement change. Following is a list of study ideas:

• (1) Play Chase with the ball. (2) Sit and spin with the ball between the feet. (3) Move the ball with just your feet.

• (1) Soccer dribble, backward direction. (2) Run and basketball dribble, forward direction. (3) Move the ball using no hands or feet. (4) Throw the ball high in the air and see how many times you can clap your hands.

• (1) Dribble the ball and shoot baskets. (2) Roll with the ball held under your chin. (3) Skip while throwing the ball gently from hand to hand. (4) Jazzy walk and carry the ball without hands. (5) Run and leap while throwing and catching the ball. (6) Do anything you want except what you just did. (This is a nice way to structure improvisations, and it also provides an extra memory problem.)

• (1) Bounce the ball while changing levels at all times. (2) Alternate one skip and one gallop while throwing and catching the ball. (3) Put the ball between your ankles, jump it into the air, and catch it. (4) Bounce the ball and swing your leg over it; switch legs. (5) Spin the ball either on the floor or on one finger. (6) Bounce the ball and follow its movement exactly with your body.

• Create a sequence of five different locomotor movements with five different ball moves. Possible result: (1) Run and dribble. (2) Skip and throw and catch the ball. (3) Crawl and roll the ball with your nose. (4) Roll while holding the ball between the knees. (5) Gallop and kick the ball.

• In groups of four, pick three to seven ball movement ideas and put them in a remembered sequence.

If you would like to review or teach the idea of a canon, or round, balls are a great way to do it. We touched on the idea of canon in the Row, Row, Row Your Boat Dance in chapter 6: One group starts the sequence and subsequent groups come in later. With a prop like balls, simply choose three or four distinct phrases and assign each phrase the same number of beats. Have one group start and the following groups do the study beginning one phrase later. It is easier if the room is divided in half as well as the class; but once they have it, mixing up the groups anywhere in the room makes for an excellent challenge. The phrases in the following sequence work well because they are simple and quite distinct. Each group comes in eight beats apart:

1. Run and dribble (eight beats).

2. Sit and spin with the ball between the feet (eight beats).

3. Jazzy walk and carry the ball without hands (eight beats).

4. Jump with the ball between the knees (eight beats).

An entirely different use for balls is in partner work. These ideas can be used as warm-ups, or they can be part of a group of guided movement ideas, or they can be included within studies.

• Partner pass. Two children play catch with one ball. First they sit and roll the ball. (Yes, even sixth graders like this. They suck their thumbs and carry on like babies but love doing so.) Then they kneel and bounce pass the ball; then they stand and bounce pass the ball. Finally, they continue to pass the ball but move at the same time. They run, skip, gallop, roll, seat-scoot, jump, and leap continuously while passing the ball back and forth. For older children I sometimes add another ball so that there are two balls to be passed while they are moving.

This partner pass can be very useful to reinforce the concepts near and far when teaching Perfect Spots or at any time. Have the partners start sitting close to each other, legs wide stride, as they start rolling the ball; then say, "Oh, that's too easy, go farther." They keep going farther until they are across the room and the balls are crisscrossing one another. Later have the students do the same near and far work when passing the ball while standing.

• Partner carry. Without using hands, partners hold a ball between them and go somewhere. They can hold the ball back-to-back, front-to-front, foot-to-foot, forehead-to-forehead, or even hip-to-hip. Then, ask for two different body parts to hold the ball, for example head-to-hip, seat-to-tummy, foot-to-hip.

Balls can be used as warm-up, as an end-of-class treat, for studies, and for partner work. I have on occasion dumped all the balls in the middle of the room and said, "Find a ball and move it." Make sure the doors are shut and have a ball.

Scarves

Scarves are good for

- fantasy play,
- large-muscle coordination,
- sequencing and memory skills,
- partner work, and
- juggling.

Scarves are equal to balls in all-around usefulness, but they are a little harder to find. In the past I have bought crepe-like material and searched out garage sales for beautiful, unique scarves, but now I limit my scarf box to the 2-foot-square sheer juggling scarves available in most sport and educational catalogs. I prefer the juggling scarves because they eliminate the commotion of choosing a special scarf—they are all the same size and come in only three colors. They are light enough to float and not long enough to trip anyone. Also we can use them for juggling. If you have a collection of different scarves, distribution will take longer. Also you will need to factor in some trading time and then close it with, "This is the scarf you have for today." If you have the juggling scarves, the distribution needs no special attention.

Free time with scarves will ideally trigger the children's fantasy play. If they are ballet dancers and Ninja Powers, let them be. When the children stop pretending to be matadors and start acting like bulls, it is time for guided movements.

Guided movements can extend their range of ideas by including concepts: "Move your scarf on the air level . . . Move it on the lowest level . . . Change levels . . . Do nonlocomotor movements with your scarf . . . How many locomotor movements can you do with your scarf? . . . Can you change directions?" Or you might present specific movement ideas such as these:

1. Throw and catch the scarf; jump, throw, and catch.
2. Throw and catch the scarf with different body parts—head, shoulder, elbow, knee, back, toe, and so on.
3. Throw the scarf with your hand and catch it by lying down quickly, trying to gauge where to be so that the scarf lands on your tummy.
4. Twirl yourself and the scarf.
5. Circle the scarf and gallop.
6. Circle the scarf and roll.
7. Drop the scarf and pick it up with your toes. Wave it and hop. Switch legs.
8. Hold the scarf in your toes and spin on your seat. Spin the other way.
9. Hold the scarf taut in two hands and side-slide.
10. Run and leap while throwing the scarf forward and catching it.
11. Have a sword fight.
12. Be a matador and a bull. Switch roles.
13. Be a bride and a groom.
14. Be ballet dancers. (Yes, boys too.)
15. Do Jazzy Scarf. Wear the scarf in a cool way and jazzy walk.
16. Do Magic Scarf. "The scarf is going to be magic; it is going to stay on your torso without being held." I demonstrate by arching slightly and running very fast. The air pressure keeps the scarf up. When doing Magic Scarf, children need to all go the same way; and if the scarf starts to slip down, have them stop and lift it so they do not slip on it.
17. Do Magician Scarf. Children stuff the scarf in a fist or a pocket or shirtsleeve and say, "No scarf. Ta da, here it is!" (I feel compelled to say the kids came up with this one; it seemed ridiculous to me, but whenever I

have introduced it to other children, they have loved it.)

18. Be Superpowers. Tuck the scarf in your shirt collars like a cape and become Super Girls and Super Boys.

19. Juggle. Believe me, if I can juggle, anyone can. With two scarves, one in each hand, throw the right one diagonally up and then the left one diagonally up, making an "X" in the air, and catch them with opposite hands. Make sure the scarves go high and that the children do not simply circle them hand to hand. After this two-scarf "X" add the third scarf, starting with two scarves in the right hand and one in the left. The process is the same as with two scarves but it is faster with three scarves.

20. Lie down and put the scarf over you: "Now, children, it is time to go to sleep. Pull up your blankie and take a nap."

After free time and guided movements, it is time for a scarf study:

• (1) Gallop while making a circle with your scarf. (2) Spin on your seat with the scarf in your toes. (3) Do Magic Scarf.

• (1) Throw the scarf in the air and catch it with different parts of your body. (2) Pick up the scarf with your toes and shake it. (3) Hold the scarf in two hands and side-slide. (4) Jazzy walk with the scarf. (5) Pull up your blankie and take a nap.

• (1) Run leap throwing and catching the scarf. (2) Sword fight. (3) Be ballet dancers. (4) Be matadors and bulls (switch). (5) Be Superpowers. (6) Throw the scarf up and catch it by lying down, gauging where it will land on your tummy.

• Make a floor pattern using different line shapes (see chapter 6). Do the pattern with the scarves held high in the air.

• In groups, choose six different ways to move the scarf and put them into a remembered sequence. Use locomotor and nonlocomotor movements, levels, and directions.

• This is a dramatic study for older children that I have done only with experienced dance studio classes. (1) Hide your scarf (in sleeves, pant legs, pockets, etc.). Walk shyly, slowly pulling out the scarf. As the scarf appears, become more and more free and make your movements larger until the scarf is completely out and you are doing enormous leaping and twirling movements. (2) Do nonlocomotor movement twirl, changing levels at all times. End in a shape and freeze. (3) For those who want to do individual dances, the scarf becomes whatever they choose: a costume, "freedom," "happiness," "a weight," "entanglement," or simply an abstract design element. The soloists leave the stage area when they are finished. The other children remain frozen while the soloists perform. (4) The children who did not solo prepare a simple unison movement pattern, which moves them off the stage.

• As with the balls, a scarf sequence can be used to create a canon. Again, the phrases should be simple and distinct and should have the same number of beats. A good sequence for a canon: (1) Twirl (eight beats). (2) Gallop and circle the scarf (eight beats). (3) Roll and circle the scarf (eight beats). (4) Jump, throwing, and catching the scarf (eight beats).

Scarves can also extend into partner work. Children can throw and catch bunches of scarves to each other and—their idea, not mine—take turns dumping scarves on one another. Trust Walk, mentioned in connection with the partner obstacle course (chapter 8), is an entirely different way to use the scarf. One child (second grade on up) turns a scarf into a blindfold, and her partner takes her on a safe walk throughout the room. The leaders can sit the followers down or move them about, have them touch various textures or even people. But the leader must, at all times, take care to ensure the safety and trust of her partner. These activities fit in most easily within an obstacle course, though the Trust Walk can make a lovely lesson ending. (Note: Trust Walk fits in exquisitely with the story *Through Grandpa's Eyes* by Patricia MacLachlan, published by Curtis Brown, in which a young boy tries to experience his grandfather's blindness.)

At the end of a scarf lesson, even the youngest child folds and puts away his own scarf. I do not yield on this point; I refuse to clean up after children unnecessarily. If your class needs a lesson in folding, ask them to lay the scarf flat on the floor: "Fold two corners to two corners . . . Turn the scarf (lengthwise) and fold two corners to two corners . . . Now we will make it smaller. Fold two corners to two corners . . . Turn . . . Fold."

Ropes

Ropes are good for

- large-muscle coordination,
- strength,
- partner work, and
- line shapes in floor patterns.

You do not have to wait until your class is old enough to jump rope; this fabulous prop has many applications beyond jumping. Any type of rope will do as long as it is long enough for the child. I prefer the softer cloth ropes to the nylon or plastic ones, but at the moment I have a hodgepodge of all different kinds of ropes. Handles are nice, but they do not last very long.

For safety, free time with ropes needs to be essentially in Perfect Spots. I say "essentially" because if some children want to try jumping while running, I let them if the space allows. For the most part they practice in their spots. During the free time I generally sit the entire class down and demonstrate how to jump rope. I do this even with older classes, and I show the whole class because I have found that many intermediate children actually do not know how to jump rope but are too embarrassed to say so. I start with the rope behind me, swing it in front, and step over it. When starting out, it is best to simply step and not jump. Then the step gets faster and faster until it looks like the standard one-foot-leading rope jump.

Following are some guided movement ideas for ropes:

1. Jump backward.
2. Add a swing in the rope between jumps.
3. Hop (switch feet).
4. Hot Pepper (jumping very fast).
5. Lay the rope in a straight line on the floor:
   a. Walk on it as if it were a tightrope "a thousand feet off the floor."
   b. Jump side to side over the rope.
   c. Football run—feet on either side of the rope, run with knees up the length of the rope and back.
   d. Crazy walk. (A special education teacher told me that this movement is especially good for integrating the two sides of the brain.) Children start with both feet on one side of the rope and cross the outside leg over. That is, if the rope is to the right of the feet, the left leg will cross the right and step over the rope; the right will swing around and cross in front of the left and step over the rope. The walk has a "drunken-sailor" look.
6. Close the rope into a circle on the floor:
   a. Jump in and out of the rope circle forward and back.
   b. Jump in and out side to side.
   c. Straddle the rope and then jump in with both feet—open and close.
   d. Put the preceding moves into a pattern—forward, back, side, side, open, close (each move is a jump).
   e. Run around the rope.
   f. Put the hands in the rope circle and kick the legs over—this is a beginning cartwheel.
7. Jazzy Rope. Drape the rope around your neck and twirl the end as you jazzy walk.
8. Broken Leg. Hold one foot in the rope as if it were a long sling and limp around saying, "Oh, I broke my leg." Switch legs.
9. Snake. Shake the rope behind you while yelling, "Yeek, a snake is following me!"
10. Microphone. Microphone and the next two ideas, Telephone and Horsie, are especially wonderful. Use the handle of the rope (or just fold a part of the rope if there is no handle) and pretend it is a microphone; give a speech or sing a song. Yes, everyone at once.
11. Telephone. Children get partners and have a telephone conversation. You can use both the ropes or get rid of one.
12. Horsie. This is such a favorite, even with the older kids if they trust you (see figure 9.2). Put one rope away so that partners have one rope between them. One person is the horse and has the rope around her waist—not neck. Her partner holds

9.2

the ends of the rope, not the handles (I think that's how I lost most of mine). The "horse" does a fast gallop and the "rider" keeps up. Switch. (For a remaining child, there would be two horses.)

13. Make line shapes. In chapter 6 we talk about using ropes to demonstrate straight, curved, wiggly, zigzag, looped, and spiral lines before attempting them with movement.

14. Using one rope for each partner group, stand very close either front-to-front or back-to-front, and jump rope together.

The first time I introduce ropes I run through most or all of these guided movement ideas. It takes almost the whole lesson. Ropes then are used as a fast-paced warm-up, are included in obstacle courses, or are used for a prop study. Here are a few suggestions for studies:

• (1) Jazzy walk circling the rope. (2) Regular rope jumping. (3) Side-to-side jumping over a straight rope. (4) Snake.

• (1) Broken Leg. (2) Start standing in the rope circle on the floor; jump in and out forward and back, side to side, open the legs to straddle the rope, and close the legs back in the rope. (3) Microphone. (4) Hot Pepper. (5) Horsie.

• Like balls and scarves, ropes can be sequenced into a canon. A possible progression: (1) Regular jump rope (12 beats). (2) Walk the rope in a straight line like a tightrope (12 beats). (3) Jazzy Rope (12 beats). Groups come in 12 beats apart.

• In groups, create seven different ways to move with the rope.

Chinese Ropes

A totally different kind of rope is called a Chinese jump rope. These are elastic circle ropes approximately 2 feet in diameter. They are great for stretching. Often a child gets so intrigued with the shapes the rope can make that he stretches much harder than he would otherwise. This is my goal. "Make your rope into a triangle . . . A square . . . A rectangle . . . A circle (impossible!) . . . Pentagon . . . Hexagon . . . A tangled mess . . . Make your rope as long as possible . . . As taut as possible . . . Make it as big as possible . . . Use only your legs to stretch the rope . . . Move your shape to standing level and go somewhere . . . Roll, keeping the rope taut . . . Change levels and move."

Chinese jump ropes elicit wonderful partner activities:

1. Horsie can be done the same way as with the straight ropes.

2. With a partner, using no hands, make a triangle (or any other shape you might be working on) out of the rope and go somewhere. Take the rope away, and see if you can get your bodies in the same positions. Go somewhere again.

3. With a partner get your rope as round as possible. Spin.

4. In groups of three, using one rope, make a star shape out of your rope. Rise and fall.

5. In groups of four, three people get ropes. These ropes are stretched across and through one another until a maze is created. The fourth person jumps in and out of the maze without touching a rope. If she touches, it is someone else's turn to jump, and the child who jumped takes that person's place holding the rope. The maze can slightly stretch and contract while the child is jumping.

Any of these, or the children's ideas, can be sequenced into a Chinese jump rope study. Here are a few suggestions for studies:

- (1) Make your rope as big as you can and go somewhere. (2) Make your rope as small as you can, without using hands, and stay in place. (3) Make your rope as long as you can and go somewhere.

- (1) Make a triangle with your rope. (2) On a different level, make a rectangle. (3) On a different level, make a square. (4) On a different level, make a pentagon. (5) On a different level, make a star.

- (1) Stretch your rope as big as you can with just your legs; get on the lowest level and go somewhere. (2) Stretch your rope as long as possible using one leg and one arm. Do a non-locomotor swing. (3) Make your rope as wide as possible using both arms and legs, sitting level. Can you spin?

Once a Chinese jump rope study is clear, I might ask the children to repeat the study without the rope to see if their bodies can remember the shapes solely on their own.

Plastic Hoops

Plastic hoops are good for

- coordination and
- sequencing and memory skills.

As with ropes, free time with plastic hoops needs to be essentially in Perfect Spots. One favored activity is rolling the hoop, and that will take the children out of their spots. Here are some guided movement ideas:

1. Spin your hoop in the traditional around-the-waist position. (I personally cannot do this to save my life; the kids have a good laugh seeing me try, and it frees them to fail at it too.)
2. Spin the hoop in different ways—around the neck, around an arm, around a leg with the other leg hopping over the twirling hoop as in figure 9.3.

9.3

3. Swing the hoop over the body like a stiff jump rope.
4. Roll the hoop like a wheel. With the proper flick of the wrist, you can roll it so it comes back—another stunt I cannot do.
5. Roll the hoop and duck through it.
6. Put the hoop flat on the floor, jump in and out, skip around, leap over.
7. Plastic hoops can be used for patterning sequences. The hoops generally come in three colors. Place them on the floor with each color representing a movement. The children work out the resulting pattern, as in figure 9.4. Two tips: (1) This is harder than it seems, so make the color pattern simple and obvious—rarely use a color just once in a row. Try it out yourself first. (2) Put the hoops very close together and tape them down. This initial effort will pay off in that the hoops will not be scattered by a faulty hop.

I generally use hoops within obstacle courses and stations, but they make fine warm-up activities and interesting studies. Sequencing any of the moves just explained can create a hoop study, or a group can figure out four to seven different ways of moving the hoop. As with the Chinese jump ropes, it is a good challenge to ask for the study to be repeated without the hoop.

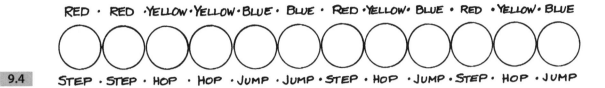

RED · RED ·YELLOW·YELLOW·BLUE· BLUE · RED ·YELLOW· BLUE · RED ·YELLOW· BLUE

9.4

STEP · STEP · HOP · HOP ·JUMP · JUMP ·STEP · HOP ·JUMP·STEP · HOP ·JUMP

Balloons

Balloons are good for

- coordination,
- sequencing and memory skills,
- sport skills, and
- abstraction.

The longer I teach the more I love balloons; I am hardly ever without a package of balloons in my schoolbag. It is worth buying the expensive, round balloons in order to reduce the pops. A few miscellaneous tips:

1. Blow the balloons up yourself or use some reliable help. Even older children who say they can blow up balloons often cannot and you are stuck with flat, wet balloons. However, do not blow up 30 balloons yourself in 10 minutes.

2. Devise in advance a place where you can keep all those balloons enclosed. The best place is a stiff mat standing up like a "house." Big garbage bags and large boxes also work.

3. Do not put the balloons near a heating vent. (I can smile now thinking about the situations that bring these suggestions to mind.)

Free time should definitely give the children ample opportunity to explore their balloons. I tell the class that if their balloons should accidentally pop, they simply pick up the pieces, throw them away, and take another balloon—have several extra balloons ready. "If, however, I even suspect that you made it pop, you will not get another."

Here are some guided movement ideas with balloons:

1. Jump as you hit the balloon; see if you can get it to touch the ceiling.

2. Keep the balloon up using different body parts—head (this is an especially good coordination activity), shoulders, knees, elbows, hips, seat, toes. (You can also use more challenging body part words like thigh, calf, forearm, and wrist.)

3. Rub your balloon on your hair and see if it will stay up on the wall. (A lesson in static electricity.)

4. Put your balloon between your knees and "Ride 'em cowgirls and cowboys."

5. Put the balloon on the ground and move it without touching it. (It is delightful to see kindergarten children puzzling over this problem.) Older children can also keep the balloon up in the air by blowing it.

6. Balance the balloon on the palm of your hand. Then balance it on one finger (do not bounce it.)

7. Punch the balloon as if you are mad at it. This will not pop the balloon as long as one does not hold the end of the balloon while punching. It is a sad commentary that this punching appears to be a needed outlet for almost all students.

8. Carry your balloon without using hands. (When I was pregnant, guess where most children decided to carry theirs?)

9. Bounce the balloon like a basketball. Can you shoot baskets?

10. Punt the balloon and then catch it yourself and do a football run.

11. With your hands clasped together, bat the balloon like a baseball. Run and field it.

12. Hit the balloon forehand and backhand as in tennis.

13. Try three volleyball moves—dig with two hands, set up with hands clasped, and spike.

14. With a partner, bat one balloon back and forth without letting it touch the ground. I like doing this partner batting before

putting the balloons away because the children have to give up one of their balloons and share the other balloon. This loosens their personal attachment to the balloon in general, making the final collection a bit easier.

Balloon studies are very effective for movement shows. Sequencing any of the ideas listed will work fine.

Here are a few more suggestions for studies:

• (1) Jump, hitting the balloon as high as possible. (2) Move the balloon without touching it. (3) Kick it. (4) Keep the balloon in the air with just your head. (5) Balance the balloon on one finger.

• Pick three to seven sport activities to do with the balloon and put them in a remembered sequence.

• Using balloons in a canon is very beautiful. Try to have some phrases with the balloon up and some with it down; as with the other props, the phrases should be distinct and all the same length. Here is a possible progression: (1) Keep the balloon in the air with different body parts (eight beats). (2) Move the balloon on the ground by blowing it. (3) Bounce the balloon. Repeat the sequence once; have groups come in eight beats apart. Make sure the children and their balloons remain motionless when they wait to start or if they are waiting for the group after them—this is an excellent self-discipline challenge. The clarity of the canon structure amid the festivity of the balloons makes this study very effective.

• A totally different way to use balloons is having them not blown up. For these activities the less expensive balloons work fine. Each child picks his preferred color. "How many ways, without tying them, can you make the balloon move?" The children will stretch the balloons in various ways, blow them up and let the air out—making them "squeak"—and, best of all, blow them up and let them fly. I let the class have about 10 minutes of free time, depending on how long I can stand it.

Then I ask the children to imitate the balloon movement with their bodies. This will not work if they are still playing with their balloons, so I ask them to put their balloons in their pockets or someplace where they will be able to find them later. I then demonstrate using one balloon. (Since the balloons are used for such a short time, why bother giving each child her own balloon? It works better. That period of free time before the children imitate the balloon makes the movements come alive. Also most children really appreciate the gift.) I demonstrate these actions with the balloon and the children reproduce the movements with their bodies:

a. Stretch the balloon long and let it snap. The children reproduce that action in their bodies by pulling themselves into a long, narrow stretch and then quickly contracting. This is done with isolated body parts—arms, legs, torso—and then with the whole body. The whole stretch and snap is done on different levels.

b. Blow the balloon up and slowly let the air out. Since it takes several breaths to fill the balloon with air, I expect the children to show a jerky, wide stretch and then a slow, even release. This is done with various wide shapes, on all levels. (This is not a bad time for a quick language lesson on inflate and deflate and prefixes "in" and "de.")

c. Blow the balloon up and let it fly. At first most children just shake wildly. I ask them to stop and actually look at the path of the flying balloon. The balloon usually spins several times, leaps up, and dives down. We talk about how we could approximate these movements in our bodies. Then I set the flight pattern—for example, "Three spins, leap up, and land," or "Spin twice, bounce off the floor, and slide land," or "Loop around, hit a wall, bounce off the floor, leap up, and land." In other words, we watch the balloon a few times, talk about its typical flight pattern, and then follow the verbal pattern that I call out. This is a foreshadowing of abstraction work that we will consider at the end of this chapter.

As with any prop, these ideas can be sequenced into a study. Here are a few possibilities:

• (1) Stretch long and snap contract, lowest level. (2) Blow the balloon wide and slowly let the air out, standing level. (3) Blow the balloon up again and let it fly—spin, spin, leap up and land.

• (1) Stretch and snap contract five different parts of your body. Each stretch is 8 beats long, and each snap is 1 beat long and then held 1 beat. (2) Stretch wide and slowly release twice, each on a different level; each stretch and release is 13 beats long. (3) Blow the balloon up again and let it fly, making up your own pattern, for 16 beats.

• Divide into groups of four. Pick five movements your balloons did and put them in a pattern. Use voices sometimes if you want. All group members do not have to do the same movement at the same time; it is interesting to juxtapose two different movements—for example, two people fly while two people stretch and snap arms and legs. However, I do require that the group as a whole have a remembered sequence.

Scooters

Scooters are good for

• coordination,
• visual perceptual work, and
• partner cooperation.

Scooters look like square skateboards. They range from 1 to 2 feet square and are made of wood or plastic. They are available from most sport and educational catalogs. Although they are expensive, you do not need many. Four to six scooters would allow you to include them within an obstacle course or stations; if you can afford enough for half a class, that is ideal. Any size and type of scooter will work.

Even with scooters, I allow free time. The trick is to have enough space for them. If they are part of an obstacle course, make sure the scooter area is large and clearly marked off. Children can lie on their tummy or back; they can sit or kneel. They absolutely cannot stand on the scooter. Guided movements include using the different body parts on the scooter, spinning, and pushing off a wall.

The best thing I have found to do with scooters is a scooter line. Tape a large design on the floor. (I must warn you that removal of masking tape left on overnight will require a putty knife. There is another, expensive, tape that does not

adhere so unyieldingly; generally it is blue and available in hardware stores. It would be possible to paint or chalk a line outside, but asphalt will badly scratch those lovely scooter wheels. Problems. I generally use the scooter line within an obstacle course; I use masking tape and remove it immediately after use even if this means putting it on again the next week or the next day.) The scooter line should include loops and uncrossed circles as in figure 9.5.

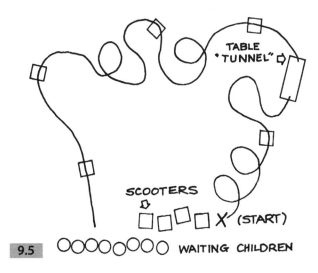

9.5

The children ride their scooter any way they wish (except for standing) and follow the line. You need a signal for the next child to start so as not to have traffic jams. Say, for example, "When the child ahead goes under the 'tunnel' you start" or "When the child ahead completes the first loop you start."

Children who miss the loops entirely or who do not backtrack their loops show warning signs for visual perceptual problems. Doing the scooter line is a good remediation in itself.

Children love moving on the scooter line, not only with scooters, but simply using locomotor movements: walk, run, skip, gallop, hopscotch, jazzy walk. Doing various locomotor movements on the line is great preparation for riding the scooter on it.

With partners, the scooter ride has one child sitting on the scooter and his partner pushing or pulling him. If the leading child takes the sitting child's legs, make sure that the leader bends down so the legs are kept low; if the legs are raised too high, they will topple the sitting child off the scooter. Partners can also both ride together in any number of ways. And then there is the wonderful group scooter train made from three or more scooters linked together.

Parachute

A parachute is good for

- class tone,
- coordination,
- perceptual skills, and
- cooperation.

When you introduce the parachute you need to be ready for two repercussions: (1) For the rest of the school year you will get daily requests for it, and (2) while using the parachute your class will be in controlled chaos; the parachute is so exciting that the children's excitement verges on the volcanic. You need a sturdy, 24-foot-diameter parachute; these are found in most educational and sport catalogs.

Ocean

The parachute is spread out with the children standing, spaced around it, holding the edges. The children shake the parachute vigorously. Put a ball in and see who can catch it as the ocean careens it up. Then put half the class (a girl and boy division is fine) on top of the ocean. They can walk, "swim," roll, crawl, or just sit there (see figure 9.6).

> ➡ *TROUBLESHOOTING*
>
> It is very important to have the children barefoot when walking on parachutes: Shoes would definitely rip it, and socks are much too slippery.

It feels wonderful and just a bit scary. Do not let any children pull the edge hard so as to try to make the children on top fall. Have the children who are on the chute stay closer to the center of the parachute rather than near the very edges so as to avoid undue strain on the material. Of course, they take turns. Ocean is the best activity to start with because shaking the parachute hard is tiring work and releases a lot of tension-excitement.

Whooshing

Whooshing is not so much an idea by itself as basis for several other ideas. The parachute is spread out; children stand spaced around it, holding the edge. The parachute needs to be loose rather than taut. With the count, "1, 2, 3 Whoosh!" everyone lifts the parachute so that it mushroom-clouds up. At this point the children will want to (1) let go, which will cause the parachute to flutter away to one side; or (2) move back as they hold on, which will cause the parachute to lose its billowy fullness.

Therefore before doing the Whoosh, impress on your class to hold on and stay put. The children will need some practice whooshing and

9.6

letting the parachute gently float down at its own speed.

Young children will need helpers to get the parachute up into magnificent whooshes—moms or a few older children would be great. I might mention that recently I have asked for more help from older children. They are wonderful aides in activities involving the parachute, gymnastics, and some small-group work. Generally, it works out fine if the older children are the "troublemakers" in their own classrooms. This is an extraordinary situation. When they come into a movement class of kindergarten children, they are not only older and wiser but they are successes. They can do things that the little ones cannot do yet. For many of these older children the admiration they get is unfortunately rare, and fortunately very effective. They almost always come through. They turn out to be good helpers, good teachers, and good example setters. I had one child, the biggest and toughest of the rough crowd, help with headstands and parachute activities. Stone (his real name) taught with such firm gentleness that I think of him often when I need inspiration.

Hamburgers and French Fries

The parachute is spread out; children stand spaced around it, holding the edge. I divide the class into alternating groups by calling half "Hamburgers" and half "French Fries." This is simply another form of walking around assigning "1" or "2" to the students. If the class is very big, I might add a third division, "Milk Shakes." The children whoosh the parachute up. When it is up, the Hamburgers let go of the edge and go under. They do whatever they want, staying under as long as they can, but they have to return to their original places before the parachute lands on them. It is important that they go back to their original places so that the children are always in alternate groups and therefore are spaced fairly evenly around the parachute. It is then the French Fries' turn.

What about children who stay under the parachute? If the children accidentally have the parachute land on them while they are scurrying out and the pace of the activity is going well, I ignore them. If the children deliberately stay under the parachute, slowing down the fun for the rest of the class, I have them lose their next turn.

One variation on Hamburgers and French Fries is to have the children stay under the parachute and let it land on them. After the parachute has covered them up (not before, so we can be surprised), they take a strange shape and freeze. The French Fries and I then whoosh the parachute up and see what they look like. If you have taught the word *connected* (perhaps while doing floor patterns), sometimes ask for all the children under the chute to be connected to each other. The children stay in their weird shapes as long as they can and then scramble out before the parachute lands on them again.

Another variation on Hamburgers and French Fries is having the children run around, under the parachute, as many times as they can before it lands on them. They must run in the same direction, and I indicate that before we whoosh.

Trap

Now that you have finally gotten the class to allow the whooshed parachute to gently come down at its own speed rather than pulling it down, it is time to introduce Trap. The children are divided into alternating groups like Hamburgers and French Fries. One group whooshes the parachute up, the other group goes under, and the first group quickly pulls down the edges so the others are trapped. The children under the parachute try to get out, and the others try to keep them in only by holding the edges. Be careful that the trapping children are not too rough with those underneath. Then I say, "OK, let them all out. Who made it? Great, it is time to switch."

Merry-Go-Round

Do Merry-Go-Round only on a day when you have taken your vitamins. The parachute is spread out; children stand spaced around it, holding the edge. Four to six children sit in the middle, on top of the chute. The rest of the class is equally spaced around the parachute pulling it taut—it works better if they all use the same hand. While pulling the chute tight, they run quickly around, creating a merry-go-round effect. The children in the middle can just sit there or they can try to stand or walk, but they need to stay pretty much in the center or they will stop the merry-go-round. Of course everyone has a turn.

Shark

A second grade class thought of this. It is really silly, and I would be embarrassed to include it if the children did not love it dearly. The parachute is spread out on the floor and the children sit around it with their legs underneath. We pretend we are at the ocean with our legs in the water, the edge of the parachute in our laps. Meanwhile, one child is chosen to go under and become the "mean, child-eating shark" that pulls children under the parachute with her. A child who has been pulled in becomes a shark too until everyone—including me—ends up under the chute. Then we come out and do it again. I told you it was silly.

Ms. Monster

This idea is as much fun for the people watching as for those doing it and therefore is a good one for a school demonstration. The class is divided in half; one half is the audience and the other becomes Ms. Monster. This monster is created when children go completely under the parachute and, as a unit, move the chute about the room. It works best if the children under the parachute stay on the lower levels, and it is imperative that they do not step on the chute but push it forward in front of them. (If they step on it, it will tend to turn inside out.) The children who are under the parachute toward the back work to remain under and not have the chute leave them behind. Ms. Monster can come out from behind pianos or the edge of the stage, and moves to the center of the room.

Often I combine this activity with a bit of review. I'll say, "Hello, Ms. Monster. Thank you for coming to our school. Could you show us the concept locomotor? Yes, I see you are moving to another place. Good. Now, could you show us the concept level? My, look at you moving up and down. [The children move at their own speed through all the levels, creating a striking billowing effect.] Great. Now, Ms. Monster, do you know what nonlocomotor means? [For nonlocomotor, the children, still under the parachute, sit or lie down and stick one leg out from the edge, holding it high in the air. The legs do a nonlocomotor movement like shake, twist, or contract and stretch. It is extremely funny to see the parachute with legs sticking out, moving in various ways.] Thank you. How about the concept direction? [This requires more organization. One child at the designated front of the parachute sticks out his head; one child at the back of the parachute sticks out his seat; and the parachute, as a unit, moves forward and backward.] Well, thank you, Ms. Monster; for our final concept, could you show us focus? [The children stick their heads out of the edge, focus on something or someone, and move toward that object or person. This is just a sneaky way to get them out, ready to switch groups.] Good work, Ms. Monster."

Flying

If two or three children take one side of the parachute, lift their arms high, and run very fast, the whole parachute will lift and billow and look very beautiful. If you have a clean, dry, outside area, it is OK to fly the parachute there, but I much prefer a large room.

Rock and Wave

Rock and Wave uses the fly activity just described. The children are frozen in bizarre shapes all around the room—they are the rocks. Two children fly the parachute—they are the wave—over the rocks. As they do, for the instant the parachute is fleetingly over them, the rocks quickly change their shapes. The effect is of the rocks having been one shape and miraculously becoming another. Rock and Wave is exciting to watch and fun to do, but it takes some work to get there.

I begin without the parachute. The children get in Perfect Spots on the lowest level and assume rocklike shapes. It would be beneficial to bring some rocks in and have a discussion about how they are gnarled or craggy. "I will say, '1, 2, 3, Change!' On the word 'change' you change your shape and change your level." The level change is important; otherwise the shape change will not appear very distinct. We practice level and shape changes, moving quickly and freezing immediately. This might be a lesson in itself. It certainly is a good review of levels.

"Now that you can change levels and shapes so well, I will not tell you when to change; the parachute will tell you. When the parachute goes over you, change levels and shape. So, we will see you one way, the parachute will hide you for a second, and then we will see you a different way." I walk around and glide the parachute over the children, reminding them to change. After they get the idea, I ask two children to fly the parachute over the rocks. If the parachute goes over only a part of the rock, only that part changes shape.

Later, ask the children to get partners and make one rock shape out of the two of them. When the parachute goes over them they have to change level and shape simultaneously, but each may wind up on a different level. It is at this point that I have gotten some great rewards as a teacher. Not only have the shapes been marvelously creative, but the partner work, the freedom of touching, the closeness, the cooperation, and the joy on the children's faces assure me it has all been worthwhile. These partner rocks can join and make rocks of four people, eight, and even the whole class.

At the end, I sometimes add a variation. The rocks become individual rocks again. I become the wave, that is, I hold one end of the parachute high, ready to fly. As I go over a rock the child gets up and comes with me under the parachute as in figure 9.7.

9.7

The children cannot use their hands to slow the parachute down. I start very slowly, picking up one child at a time, and then speed up until the whole class is running, trying to stay under the parachute as I fly it around the room. Exciting and exhausting.

Mushroom

This is the best ending for parachute work. The children whoosh the parachute up. At its peak they quickly pull it down behind them and sit on the edge. With the whole class under the parachute, sitting on the edge, the air is captured. The children immediately scoot toward the middle. This pushes the parachute up into a tentlike house or mushroom. The feeling inside the mushroom is marvelous: warm, safe, united. One child said it felt like church. If you want, while under the parachute, tell a story or a continuing story in which you start, one child continues, another goes on, and so forth. But the story needs to be fairly short—a mushroom stays up about half a minute.

Putting the Parachute Away

Putting the parachute away requires preplanning. The children will not want to give it up. Their reactions will range from moaning, to diving under it, to just holding on. It is essential to prepare for putting it away. Here are a few suggestions, from the straightforward to the sneaky.

1. The children roll the parachute from the edge into the middle.

2. "Drop the parachute, take a step away, and sit down." The children sing and sway to the Rocking Song on the sitting level. I ask them to do it again on a different level while I whisk the parachute away. The children calm down with the song, and I have a moment to get the chute into its box.

3. With the children sitting around the parachute, I say in a singsong voice, "Now, boys and girls, it is time for your nap. Pull your blankie up and go to sleep." Children pull the edge of the parachute up, like a blanket. After a moment, "Now I am going to pull the blanket off and you show me how you are sleeping." I pull the parachute away—quickly stuffing it in its box—and the children remain lying on the floor.

Children love the opportunity to act younger. Third to sixth grades especially, when they feel safe, adore acting like babies. They pout and cry about their blankies being taken away, suck their thumbs, and wave their arms and legs. I think it is good for them to act babylike. In the intermediate grades they spend so much of the time being "cool" and acting older that it is nice for them to have time to act younger. I am tolerant of most of the commotion but still insist on putting the parachute away.

4. Play Rock and Wave and fly the wave right into its box.

5. Play Mushroom and forewarn the class, "When the parachute comes down it is time for socks and shoes. No hassles, OK?"

6. Play the variation of Hamburgers and French Fries in which half the class takes strange shapes and freezes. When the second half of the class is under, I say, "Instead of whooshing the parachute up, we are going to pull the parachute off to see what you look like. You stay frozen and I will 'unveil' you." Quite a hodgepodge of metaphors, but this unveiling technique is the most consistently easy method for putting the parachute away.

Foam Jump

The Foam Jump is a terrific way to end a movement class. It can also be included in a partner obstacle course. Collect 10 pieces of 2-foot-square foam about 4 inches thick. If at all possible, these pieces can be covered like pillows, ideally in different colors, but this is not necessary. The children line up at one end of the room. Put a long mat out and stack four foam pieces at the front end of the mat. The children take turns warming up their ankles by jumping over the short stack. For their second turn they can choose how many pieces of foam they want and ask for this number using a math equation. For example, "I want to jump six. There are four there, so add two more." The next person has to take it from the new height: "I want to jump five. There are six, so subtract one." Or, the child might say, "I want six, so leave it the way it is." This will take a bit of time: For a class of 25, plan for at least 15 minutes. What if a child picks a number of foams that is obviously too high? If I am not worried about her safety I will let her go ahead; if I think she might get hurt, I'll simply say that it is too high for this time.

A totally different way to use the foam is to place pieces horizontally on the mat. The children start leaping over two pieces of foam and then can ask for more as they did when the foam was stacked

vertically. What I love about the Foam Jump is that it is visible, personal, and real math.

Incline Mat

If you can afford to buy a large mat shaped like a wedge of cheese, called an incline mat in most catalogs, do not hesitate. It is an invaluable piece of equipment. Like the Foam Jump, the incline mat is a great way to end a lesson, or it can be included in an obstacle course. Start with the class lined up on one side. Place the incline mat so the children have to run up the diagonal and "fly" onto a flat mat. Then turn the incline mat around so that it slopes down from the children. Each child comes up and does a somersault down the mat. (Notes: The children stand on the edge of the incline mat, on their feet. They place their hands close to their feet, tuck their head under their legs, and roll. The downward slope makes the roll easier and more fun.) Once they are good at this slow somersault, let them take a running start into the somersault—it will start to look like a flip. Make sure you have good, thick, long-enough mats extending from the incline mat.

One more idea for the incline mat might make you blanch. Stand the incline mat up in front of a flat mat. Tell the class it is football season and have them look fierce, take a running start, and tackle the incline mat. For older classes or for very tall youngsters, have them scrunch down so that there is no danger of them hitting their head off the incline mat. Tackle is a definite favorite. (See figure 9.8.)

9.8

Other Props

Almost anything can be used as a prop, whatever strikes your fancy, whatever you have available. If you are not sure what to do with a prop, follow the basic formula of (1) free time, (2) guided movements, and (3) study. For guided movements, if you have no specific movements in mind, guide the students in general ways: different levels, directions, locomotor or nonlocomotor movements, size, tempo, use of different parts of the body. Also watch the children during free time and have the class copy any ingenious ideas. With this formula, your only limitation regarding props is storage space and money. Here I discuss a few miscellaneous props I have used.

Beanbag

Beanbags reinforce eye-hand coordination and overall conditioning skills. Like balls or balloons, beanbag activities move from free time to guided movements to remembered studies. Beanbag activities normally encompass throwing and catching:

1. Toss the bag hand-to-hand staying stationary or while doing locomotor movements.
2. Toss the bag with one hand, spin the body before catching, or catch the bag behind the body. (Make sure to use the other hand.)
3. Toss the bag to a partner using level changes, staying stationary or traveling.

The bag can also be used for work on balance:

1. Balance the beanbag on almost any body part: head, shoulder, chest, back, knee, toe, and so on.
2. While balancing a beanbag, shift levels or add locomotor movements, e.g., "Balance your bag on your head, sit and get up. No holding on to the beanbag with your hands." "Balance the bag on one shoulder while you side-slide; switch sides and shoulders." "What movement could you do with the beanbag balanced on your chest? Toe? Seat?"
3. Balancing a beanbag greatly increases the difficulty of body balances: "Balance the beanbag on your elbow while you balance on one foot. Can you lift to half-toe?" "Balance the beanbag on your feet while in a shoulder stand." "Choose five precarious balances and include a beanbag balance on a different body part for each one."

Beanbags can combine with other equipment for additional eye-hand coordination work. These activities are usually included in obstacle courses and stations. Beanbags can be used with foot stompers and balance boards, or tossed into wastebaskets, tires, and other receptacles (see p. 117).

Despite their benefits, I have difficulty with beanbags. The main problem is that even good quality beanbags keep tearing. We are constantly sweeping up tiny plastic "beans." Further, they keep getting stuck in crevices and lost behind the bleachers. Since most eye-hand coordination work can be done with balls, scarves, and balloons, my tendency is to include a few beanbags in obstacle courses and to use them mostly in combination with precarious body balances for an extra challenge.

Marbles

It all started with an enormous marble craze at school. I had encountered a pocketfull of marbles spilling on the floor, some shattering, and a child getting glass in his foot. I ruled that the children were to leave their marbles in their shoes during movement class and that any marbles I saw or heard were mine. In a few months I had collected hundreds of marbles. What to do with them?

I handed each child a marble. Free time carried the restriction that to prevent dropping, the marbles had to stay on the floor. For guided movements, the children moved the marbles on the floor in various ways: They used different levels, different parts of the body, different locomotor movements in different directions. One excellent foot exercise was picking up the marble with the toes, but not lifting it too high. Studies were done in groups of four: "Pick six different ways to move your marbles and put them into a sequence." At the end of class all the children went home with the marbles they had worked with. I felt a little like Robin Hood equalizing the marble wealth.

Feathers

When you can find them, feathers are lovely. They are available at craft and educational supplies stores (and from shedding birds). You need one feather per child. With feathers – like with balloons – the children find different ways of moving them and different ways of imitating their movement. When they imitate the feather, have them use isolated parts of their bodies: "Make one leg fall the way the feather fell. Make one arm stay in the air, the way the feather did when you blew on it. Make your torso spiral down like the feather." Have the children extend these movements into different speeds and sizes, different locomotor and nonlocomotor movements, and then sequence them into a study. This is a pretty, quiet prop activity.

Newspapers

When I was in my experimental dance phase, I brought in stacks of newspapers and asked the children to rip them, wad them up, throw them, and so on. It was not an especially successful prop in that the children's movement imagination did not seem to grow, but it was fun for one time. Newsprint, however, is very hard to wash off.

Plastic Garbage Bags

If they were not so expensive, large plastic garbage bags would be great props. Children run, filling the bags with air. The bags make strange, indescribable noises, depending on how they fill with air. They also can be punched, jumped in, and so on. The obvious restriction is that the bags cannot go near the children's heads. My objection to the bags is the expense. No matter how well they hold up to garbage, they do not last long with children.

Chairs

Ordinary chairs are the bases for marvelous studies. Any kind of chair will do. (If the chairs fold, spend a few minutes talking about safety. But I definitely prefer the nonfolding kind.) There are two basic approaches to moving with a chair: (1) Move it and (2) let it be stationary and move on, around, under, and through it.

Chairs are so taken for granted that children are at a loss thinking of what to do with them. When using chairs I therefore postpone free time and go right into guided movements: "Move your chair from one place to another. Move it with no hands. Use a different locomotor movement and move it. Use a different level. Fold your chair and move it. Shake your chair. Find a different way to position your chair, for example laying it down, turning it over. How many ways can you move under, around, over, and through the chair? Use the chair to find a strange way to contract and then to stretch." After work with guided movements, a few minutes of free time is appreciated.

One beautiful chair study came from a simple structure. Each child sequenced a contract and stretch on each level—except air level—using the chair. (Examples of this are shown in chapter 4.) The class divided into groups of five and decided how to arrange their chairs and how to organize their individual movements into a group study. In some groups everyone contracted and stretched at the same time; some groups moved one after the other; and other groups contrasted the movements so that some children were contracting while others stretched.

I have used chair studies several times for demonstrations because they are impressive even on a small stage. Here are some other chair studies:

1. In groups, pick seven things to do with your chair and put them into a sequence.

2. Each child finds a way to move the chair from one side of the room to the center. Staying in the middle of the room she does five different movements using her chair, and then moves the chair back to the side of the room in a different way. The children do their patterns all at one time. They do it once with the chair and then repeat their study attempting the movements without the chair.

3. The class divides into groups, and the groups put their chairs in any arrangement they want. They do different locomotor movements around the chairs without touching them. Then they move through, over, and under their chairs in various ways. "Now put one around, one through, one over, and one hide into a group study."

Costumes

There is not much to say about costumes except trust your class or do not use them. I have used costumes mainly in my dance studio classes. I have to know that they will be handled carefully without my constant scrutiny and that the children are sophisticated enough to do something with them other than giggle.

What to use for costumes is completely open. Most teachers are collectors at heart; this is just another area to think about. My costume suitcase includes old party dresses, the leopard skin one-piece pajama my mother sent, army boots, ballet shoes, the grass skirt my sister got in Hawaii, lederhosen, a fringed bikini, football shirts, a merry widow, some harem pants, red satin boxing shorts, various masks, costume jewelry, and all sorts of hats. In addition, I bring my scarf box, a box of safety pins, and an inexpensive full-length mirror if one is not already available. It is important that there be enough costumes for everyone.

On costume day I say, "Try on as many different combinations as you want. How does each costume make you feel like moving? Let me see even a short movement pattern before you exchange your costume." Then I open the suitcase. Do not expect to be able to give instructions for at least 15 minutes after you open the suitcase. It is possible to set some of these movement patterns into studies—once a delightful play spontaneously grew out of the costumes. Usually, however, I see costumes as a one-time improvisation. With costumes I have three recommendations: Sit down, ignore how fast your grass skirt is shedding, and enjoy watching the children.

Abstractions

Most props are passive; that is, the children's movement consists of making the prop move—for example, "Keep the balloon in the air." Some props are active and inspire imitation—for example, "Stretch like the balloon being blown up and fly like the balloon being let go." Imitating movement and then abstracting it to create new movements is an important part of choreography.

We touched on imitative movements with use of balloons that have not been blown up and with feathers, as well as in some of the ball activities.

These were casual foreshadowings. Sometime you might want a more direct approach to imitative movement and subsequent abstractions. Some props can specifically excite imitative movements. Anything can be used as long as it moves and it captivates attention. In my bag of movable props are a book; a windup car; several moving bath toys; a plastic squeeze toy that, when poked, "contracts"; the gears of a clock; a bottle of spray cologne; a push-button bottle of hand cream; a bottle of soap bubble maker; and (my favorite) a pronged olive picker—when the handle is pressed, three wire fingers come out and grab an imaginary olive.

This type of movement exploration is for older classes, fourth grade on up, preferably with some dance experience. The children gather near me on the floor. We begin with a demonstration; most often I use a book. Opening and closing it, I ask, "Can you move like this?" The children come up with numerous examples. We explore the hinge-like movement with isolated body parts, with the whole body, with a partner. I make sure the children note that they are using different levels, locomotor and nonlocomotor movements, and different sizes and tempos.

The next step is to demonstrate how to combine a number of these movement ideas into a pattern—choreography. Using as many variations on hinge movements as possible, I direct a short study. Here is one example:

1. The children move toward the center of the room, each doing a different hinge movement, for example both arms opening and closing, hinging at the elbow, hinging at the knee, hinging at the hip joint.

2. When they reach the middle of the room, the children assume positions using different levels and hinge robotlike from the hip joint. They move at varying speeds.

3. One by one, the children "break loose" from the robotlike hinge movements and do large locomotor movements plus hinge movements with their arms.

4. They regroup in partners and do a paired hinge movement that takes them off to the side of the room.

In this example I directed the class by calling out the movement changes and configurations. My purpose was to give the students a rich experience in the many ways movements can be organized and varied. The class then divides into groups, and each group picks their own movable prop. They experiment with imitative movements and create a study based on one of their abstracted movements. The beauty of using movable props for group choreography is that it stimulates creative problem solving and imaginative thinking, as well as teamwork and cooperation. How does one burst like a soap bubble or advance like a three-pronged olive picker? Such questions are stimulating challenges and occasionally result in beautiful dances.

Closing Thoughts

Are you raring to try some props with your class? Props are a fabulous addition to any movement program, and I encourage you to venture even a toe into this area. The formula of free time, guided movements, and studies will give you a sound framework from which to proceed, and the children will love you for it. I conclude with a few thoughts on criticizing creative efforts and on fun.

A great deal of the work with props culminates with the creation of a study by the children. When the children show me their creative efforts I am free in giving my choreographic criticisms. I do not think it "stifles creativity" in the least. All of us need to have our creative energies pushed now and then; if a sequence is dull, it does not help

the children for me to say "How wonderful!" In addition, new ideas often inspire others.

However, I do two things to lighten my authoritative hand: (1) Almost all of the time I make recommendations with the understanding that the children do not have to follow them, and (2) the tone of my class is such that I welcome a group saying "Don't watch us now" or "We don't want any ideas now." As long as they are working hard, I hold my tongue.

When they are ready for ideas, I give them. Generally what children's choreography will need is diversity: A group will get stuck with all locomotor or all nonlocomotor movements or with the movements all on one level, or with one configuration. Most children need to be encouraged to use more space and different tempos, and almost all need to move more varied parts of their bodies. Occasionally a group will need to repeat some movements so that the study is a tighter unit, but usually the patterns will need greater variety.

You can have a sound movement program without props, but it will not be great. Props are wonderful tools for working on basic skills: memory, sequencing, large-muscle coordination, eye-hand and eye-foot coordination, teamwork, and abstractions. Equally important, props are just fun. "Let's do Mushroom with the parachute and tell ghost stories." "Let's warm up with the balls." "Let me see you leap up and bounce off the wall like that balloon." This kind of "unnecessary" fun is important to children. It makes them feel good. It brings them closer to each other and to you. It says to them, "I like you and I like seeing you happy."

Chapter 10

Tricks of the Trade

Every subject has distinct problems and unique solutions. "Tricks of the Trade" presents a collection of miscellaneous teaching techniques, little discoveries that make teaching a bit easier. These gimmicks range from comforting the crying child to aligning posture, to heaping children on top of one another. These ideas are not crucial, but one or two might come in handy.

Are You Alive?

Are You Alive? is appropriate for young children and is good for

- calming a scared child and
- class tone.

Moving children are bound to fall down, bump into someone, or run into something. With young children this happens with regularity. If a child is seriously hurt, she of course needs care and sympathy. But often a young child will start crying when startled to find himself suddenly on the floor. When this happens, it is time for Are You Alive?

Are You Alive? is appropriate for young children up to first grade, those small enough to pick up. (As with any physical attention, if the child does not welcome being picked up, do not press it.) Pick up the crying child and sit her on a high place—a piano top is perfect, a table or chair will do. "Let's see if Cynthia is going to live." I gently shake one arm, "Is this arm alive? . . . Nope."

Taking the other arm, "Is this arm alive? . . . No." Gently shaking one leg, "Is this leg alive? . . . No." "Is this [the other leg] alive? . . . No way." Stroking the child's head, "Is Cynthia's head alive? . . . Uh oh, no!" Tickling the torso, "Is your torso alive? . . . Nope!" I pick the child up, holding her upside down by the knees, "I guess we'll have to take you to the dump." I walk around the room, find a soft "dump" place and gently lower the child (see figure 10.1).

Other children love to watch Are You Alive? (It takes only about 30 seconds). The only trouble is that you might have requests for it when not needed.

10.1

Jump Your Name

Jump Your Name is good for

- introduction of names and
- assessing first impressions.

This is a nice introduction activity for first to fourth grades. Children gather near me. "I want you to tell me your name but in a special way. Shout your name in the air! I'll show you what I mean." I stand and jump, shouting my name at the high point of the jump. "Would you like to do it?" Usually children do want to; if some do not, I pass them. I offer this option because this is an introductory game, and it is valuable to know who are the shy children. You will learn a great deal about all the children with this activity. Which children shouted their names at top volume? Who whispered almost inaudibly? Who got the timing of the name while in the air and who did not? Who landed on their seat rather than their feet? You will learn a lot about a new group of children, even their names.

The Stage

A real or imaginary stage is good for

- precision work,
- performance experience, and
- self-discipline.

If you teach movement in your school's auditorium and if that room has a stage, you have an invaluable tool at hand. If you do not have a stage, you can use the idea of a stage with almost as much ease.

I use the stage as a visible culmination of mastery. "When this study is perfect we will put it on the stage." If there is no physical stage, I simply divide the class into audience and performers, each taking turns: "When this study is perfect we will perform it." You can heighten the drama by announcing the performance with a grandiose introduction and by inviting a special guest, like the principal. The only way the stage becomes a source of enjoyment is if the children are not allowed on it unless they are performing a finished piece. What is perfected is, of course, a matter of personal judgment. If a kindergarten class remembers the movements and gets the basic rhythmic framework, I consider that "perfect." For a sixth grade class, "perfect" means exact counts and appropriate dynamic qualities in the movements.

The idea of designating the stage as a reward for completion came from a mundane problem. Children are fascinated by the stage; their first impulse on entering the auditorium is to play on the stage. This is not workable. A wild stage party would create havoc with the idea of an orderly class; and there are curtains, stored stage sets, lights, and other things that can be destroyed. It was clear to me that use of the stage had to be limited and clearly defined. Why not use the stage for its original intention? A stage is the end result of finished productions and, on a small scale, that is exactly what it is used for in my classes.

I have known of no child who has not liked the stage. Some may be timid, but they are still fascinated. Getting onstage is a sought-after reward. However, I do not use the stage competitively in the sense of child against child. I would pick some children to go on the stage and not everyone only if one or a few children had done something extraordinary. An entire class works to complete a study; if 90% have it, everyone performs.

Of course if there are performers, there has to be an audience. Most children do not know what it means to be an audience. I tell them: (1) An audience is absolutely quiet; (2) they give their full attention to the performers; (3) they clap at the end and never "boo." Meanwhile the performers are instructed to move silently backstage, get their starting places quickly, perform with gusto, and take gracious bows. Does it sound very formal? It is. If we are going to perform we might as well go all the way, and despite, or perhaps because of, the formality, the children love it. They love the process of mastering a study, elegantly mounting the stage, dancing their best, and receiving the adulation of the crowd.

Alignment

Proper alignment is good for

- correct centering of the body,
- balance,
- ease and grace of movement, and
- health.

"Forget everything your mom or dad ever said about standing straight, anything you ever heard about sticking your chest out and your shoulders back." That is the introduction to my method of teaching alignment. I call it *alignment*, rather than posture or standing up straight, because the associations with what is supposed to be straight are usually wrong. When children try to stand straight they curve their spines into swaybacks, puff their chests out, give themselves double chins, and stop breathing. That is why I ask them to forget all that.

Instead, I ask children to feel, with their fingers, the lowest part of the spine. With closed eyes (the better to feel with) they go up the center back, touching each vertebra, until they reach the back of the head. I ask them to pretend to hold the very top of their spine, at the back of the head, and pull up, as if lifting the body They pull their spine taller so that the whole body is elongated and "hook the top of the spine" up there as if they were hanging a coat. Hanging from the top of the spine allows the shoulders to drop rather than be forcibly pushed down. This is essentially the entire process of alignment: feeling the spine, pulling the body taller, and suspending the body weight from the back of the head. (At first, pulling the weight up from the back of the head makes people feel as though they cannot pivot their heads. They walk around like stiff-necked robots. The stiffness will disappear as soon as the alignment is internalized. The immobile neck is simply illusion. Gently take the head and move it from one side to the other, demonstrating that it actually can move while the body remains lifted.) To emphasize this feeling of lift I ask the children to pull their spines even further up, lifting their bodies to half-toe. The children are asked to stay there, that is, weight up and forward, while they lower their heels to the floor. The result should feel tall, light, catlike, ready to spring into action (see figure 10.2).

In general, this process of pulling the spine taller fixes most postures. Later, extreme cases of swayback (arched spine) or protruding ribs can be corrected individually.

The process of pulling up from the back of the head is different from what is often taught. In magazines and gym classes we are told to imagine a plumb line from the top center of our head down, putting shoulders on top of hips, on top

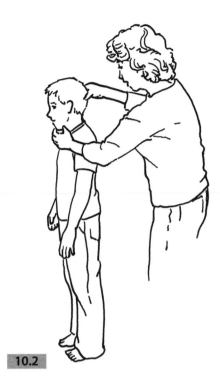

10.2

of the center of our feet. The dual instructions—center and down—simply do not work. If one pulls from the center rather than from the back of the head, the chin will automatically stick out, the neck will compensate by curving forward, the back will arch, the ribs will protrude, and the seat will pull back for balance. Perhaps it is fortunate that nobody can hold this position very long. In addition, this traditional approach pulls the energy down—head to shoulders to hips to feet. It is very important to pull the energy up. Almost anyone who is reaching up, extending, will have good posture. Consider an outfielder stretching to make a catch, a basketball player shooting, a dancer leaping—all pull up, all look wonderful.

Posture is more than looks; it is a state of mind. Regrettably posture is not emphasized the way it used to be. I remember (I am well aware of how much this dates me) when we were not allowed to slump in our seats. Now slumping is de rigueur. But a straight back—a real lifted, not forced straight, back—can change our mood, our brain function, our courage, our stance in life. Am I overstating? A number of years ago I had the privilege to work with a wonderful psychotherapist in a group setting. My job, when the time was right, was to fix the pattern of postural alignment that was holding back the client's development into a centered, relaxed, lifted stance. That was when I learned to pull the spine and reach up. What is amazing is that the effects of good posture can work from the outside in; that is, even if we are feeling low and droopy, lifting our spines will in fact lift our spirits. It is time for posture to make a comeback.

Turnout

Turnout is good for

- correct body positioning and
- hip joint flexibility.

Turn out is a dance term that means to turn the legs, from hip joint to toes, toward the outside of the body. Turnout is an integral part of ballet, modern, and jazz dance, though modern and jazz dance frequently use other rotations of the leg. In dance classes a great deal of time is devoted to turnout and its development. Exercises are done specifically to increase turnout, and extra care is given to see that it is used unless otherwise specified. In a general movement class, however, I emphasize turnout in only two areas: wide-stride stretches and pliés.

Turnout is necessary in wide-stride stretches in order to produce a careful, correct stretch that does not hurt the leg and in order to stretch the inner thigh. When the children are sitting in wide stride, I explain and demonstrate that when the knees and toes are turned to face one another it is called *turned in* and when they face out it is called *turned out*. We turn in and out several times to get the idea and to loosen the hip joint. I then ask for both legs to turn out and stay like that. Most often this is done before stage 3 of Blastoff in which the back rounds down with the legs in wide-stride position. Lowering the back while the legs are wide and kept turned out is difficult; almost all legs want to turn in. I ask the children to become their own teachers: "You be your own teacher and make your legs mind you. (I point threateningly at my own legs and the children follow suit with their legs.) You make you legs turn out even if they don't want to. If you can't round your back as low keeping your legs out, don't go as low." As we start to lower the backs, if a child's leg starts to turn in

I do not correct the leg. I say, "Henry, your leg is not minding you."

The emphasis on having the children make their own legs mind them is more important than it might seem. This is truly a case of self-discipline and self-responsibility. When the child becomes the boss of his own legs, it is a step toward the beauty of a body with inner force and control. The child decides what he is going to do and takes charge of the process. Later the idea of turnout can be relegated to muscular memory. But this process of decision, self-discipline, and internalization applies to many areas, from alignment to reading. If a child does not align her own body, or if a child decides not to read, no outpouring of instruction or reminders will do it.

In pliés, turnout is necessary for safety of the knees and proper use of the muscles. The knees have to pull back as the body lowers. Easier said than done. A first-position plié begins with the back perfectly aligned, legs straight and turned out, heels touching. (To get your own true turnout, start with feet parallel, that is, toes facing straight front. Tighten the seat, rock back slightly, and turn the toes out, equalizing the weight. Wherever they land is your own true turnout; do not maneuver the feet to turn out more.) The knees bend only to the extent that the heels can remain on the floor; turnout is maintained throughout with the knees lowering behind the big toes. The feeling is one of pushing one's pelvis forward while pushing the knees back, meanwhile keeping the torso ramrod straight. The grimace will come off later. A plié done correctly, with energy, is a magnificent exercise. Five or six perfectly done pliés will knock you out.

Wide-stride stretches and pliés are two of the areas in which I pay special attention to turnout. In more advanced classes, turnout becomes an integral part of the movement vocabulary and is incorporated into leaps, one-legged skips, extensions, and jumps.

Twirls

Twirls are good for

- tone of the class,
- children's feelings of self-esteem, and
- vocabulary review.

There are many good reasons for picking a child up and twirling him around: (1) It is fun. (2) it is a moment of closeness with the teacher as a person. (3) it is a special moment of individual attention, a moment in which the child is told, "I like you." However, if the child is hesitant, it is best to postpone the twirl until more trust is built up.

Very young children can be picked up in standard "baby style." As the child gets more adventuresome, I let go of the head and torso while holding firmly to the knees; the child twirls upside down. Medium-sized children can get "airplane twirls": Hold a wrist (not the hand because it can dislocate) and an ankle and spin the child as in figure 10.3. Make sure you have enough room for this twirl.

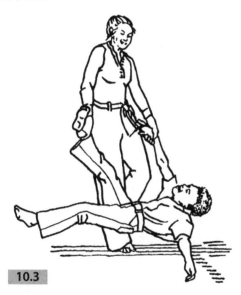

10.3

As the children get too big to lift, I use a special twirl that I developed. The child sits on the floor, knees bent, and holds her hands firmly under her knees. The child needs to be quite tightly contracted and the hands firmly held. I pick her up by the ankles and use the momentum of the body weight to swing her around as in figure 10.4. In this way I have twirled youngsters up to 100 pounds.

Ideally I would like the time, energy, and back strength to twirl every child, but that is impossible. Twirls can occasionally be used for review rewards: As the children finish taking off their socks and shoes and find their Perfect Spots, I ask, "What does locomotor mean?" Children in Per-

10.4

fect Spots with a quiet hand who answer correctly get twirled. I ask for definitions of all concept words introduced so far, with each correct answer getting a twirl. (Sometimes it is nice to switch and say the definition and ask for the concept word, e.g., "What word means moving in place?") But twirls are really best for special occasions like birthdays, leavings, and returns. Of course there was the time a group of children decided it was not fair that I did not get twirled . . .

Orchestra and Dancers

Orchestra and Dancers is good for

- memory and
- self-discipline.

Do this on a day when you can tolerate noise. Do you have percussion instruments available? You know, an old, dusty box with some drums, rhythm sticks, tambourines, bells, triangles, and cymbals? Divide the class in half: One half will be the orchestra and the other half dancers. Have the orchestra section explore the percussion instruments for a few minutes and then settle on one each. (Meanwhile the dancers warm up and practice locomotor movements.) Group the instruments into sections, that is, the drums, the triangles, the cymbals, and so forth—try to have at least five sections. Show the orchestra the conductor's (your) signal to start and to stop. It is extremely important for the orchestra to be under your direction. Then, with the class as a whole, choose movements that will correspond to each sound section; for example, the drum sound will be hopscotch, the tambourine sound will be skipping, the triangle sound will be rolling. When everything is set up, proclaim a grandiose introduction of Orchestra and Dancers. At first, direct the orchestra in the sequence that you have established—making sure that the sound sections stop immediately when you indicate. Have the sections play for various lengths of time, sometimes for a long time and sometimes for just a few seconds. Then mix up the order of the sounds. Finally have the orchestra all play at the same time—the dancers have to do try to do all the moves simultaneously! End the pandemonium and switch.

Brain Catcher Game

This game is good for

- memory,
- review of movement concepts, and
- visualization and problem solving.

"Usually when someone, especially a teacher, says something to you it goes in one ear and out the other. Now we are going to play a game where your brain has to catch the instructions as they come in your ears and hold them there. The game is called Brain Catcher." This is my introduction to a "game" that is simply a memory exercise.

To play the game I say a movement sequence and the children remember it. I use the Free Traveling Structure. For example: "Are your brains ready to catch these instructions?" For younger classes we all put our open hands in front of our foreheads ready to grasp the challenge. "When you hear the piano the first time, skip; when you hear the piano the second time, swing; the third time, run. Don't forget to freeze when the sound stops." This example is the most common form of Brain Catcher—it uses one (the same) sound a number of times. You can make it easier by adopting the appropriate rhythm for each movement, or harder by using the same or a noncommittal rhythmic pattern for all the movements.

Another form of Brain Catcher is to have many different sounds, each representing a different movement: "When you hear the drum—run; when you hear the bell—shake; when you hear the piano—skip; when you hear the tambourine—spin

on your seat." After the children have mastered the sound-movement relations in order, mix them up. In future games do not use the same sound-movement relationships; keep changing them. This form of Brain Catcher is reminiscent of Orchestra and Dancers.

One final approach to Brain Catcher is simply playing with memory work. For example, turn things upside down: "When you hear the sound, freeze; when you hear no sound, move. That's a switch, isn't it? OK, the first no-sound—gallop; the second no-sound—strike; the third no-sound—leap." Another astonishing mix-up: "When you hear the sound—move in silence; when the sound stops—freeze your body but start talking to someone; when the sound starts again go back to being silent. OK? The first sound—twist; second sound—roll; third sound—run."

I give sequences that are three to seven parts long (yes, seven; if you are like me, you might need to write them down to remember them yourself). I push classes to remember more than they think they can. What if they forget? Since the entire class moves at one time, someone usually has it and the rest pick it up. If it is truly too difficult I shorten the sequence and say it again. In subsequent Brain Catchers, I attempt (though I doubt the effort is fully successful) to continuously give new sequences even if the variations are minor.

That is the entire "game"—a perfect warm-up activity. Not only is it excellent work in memory and concentration, but Brain Catcher can be used to reinforce numerous concepts. With so many weighty purposes being served, I do not know why children like it so much. Following are some of the ways the game can review concepts.

To reinforce the concepts locomotor and nonlocomotor:

- (1) Locomotor gallop, (2) nonlocomotor contract and stretch, (3) locomotor jazzy walk, (4) nonlocomotor swing.

- (1) Nonlocomotor strike, (2) locomotor run, (3) nonlocomotor twist, (4) locomotor run, (5) nonlocomotor shake, (6) locomotor run, (7) nonlocomotor swing.

- (1) Any fast locomotor movement, (2) any nonlocomotor movement, (3) any slow locomotor movement, (4) any nonlocomotor movement, (5) any medium tempo locomotor movement, (6) any nonlocomotor movement.

To reinforce the concept level:

- (1) Air-level skip, (2) knee-level swing, (3) lowest-level roll.
- (1) Contract on lowest level and stretch on knee level; (2) do any locomotor movement that continuously changes levels; (3) contract on knee level and stretch on lowest level.
- (1) Any locomotor movement on knee level, (2) any nonlocomotor movement on lowest level, (3) any locomotor movement on air level, (4) any nonlocomotor movement lowest level, (5) any locomotor movement knee level. It is worth the time to point out the symmetry of a pattern like this:

knee	lowest	air	lowest	knee
locomotor	nonlocomotor	locomotor	nonlocomotor	locomotor

It is important not only to ask children to remember, but also to give them the tools with which to remember. Finding patterns is an important intellectual procedure in itself, as well as an excellent memory technique. We consider patterning further in chapter 11.

To reinforce the concept direction:

- (1) Run forward; (2) run backward; (3) run sideways; (4) run turning.
- (1) Jump backward; (2) skip turning; (3) crab crawl sideways; (3) leap forward.
- Using any locomotor movements, (1) go forward, (2) go turning, (3) go sideways, (4) go in the direction you did not go in before.

To reinforce and differentiate between tempo and size:

- (1) Do a locomotor movement very big and very fast; (2) do a nonlocomotor movement very small and very slow.
- (1) Run big in slow motion; (2) run small in fast motion; (3) swing big in slow motion; (4) swing small in fast motion.
- Pick any nonlocomotor movement and do it (1) big and slow, (2) big and fast, (3) small and slow, (4) small and fast.

To work on combined locomotor and nonlocomotor movements:

- (1) Jump and shake your head; (2) side-slide and swing your arms; (3) skip and contract and stretch; (4) leap and clap your hands.

To work on combining several concepts—the memory work here is not as much sequential as vertical, a layering of concepts:

- Do the nonlocomotor movement shake in the arms, plus the locomotor movement walk, standing level, forward direction, in the floor pattern of a zigzag line.
- Do the nonlocomotor movement swing in the arms plus the locomotor movement jump, air level, turning-around direction. Do the whole thing in a circular floor pattern. (This Brain Catcher emphasizes the difference between turning direction and circular floor pattern.)
- (1) Do the nonlocomotor movement contract and stretch plus the locomotor movement roll, lowest level, in the floor pattern of a straight line. (2) Do the nonlocomotor movement strike with your arms plus the locomotor movement run, standing level, backward direction, in a spiral floor pattern.

For problem solving:

- (1) Move with two parts of your body on the ground; (2) move with five parts of your body on the ground; (3) move with one part of your body on the ground; (4) move with seven parts of your body on the ground.

Rocking As a Relaxer

Rocking to relax is good for

- calming young classes.

Sometimes the immediate task is not to create movement but to quiet it. I like to calm a class down at the end of a lesson before sending them back to their room; otherwise children coming from movement class tend to explode onto the rest of the school. (This is especially true of primary children.) Luckily, there is the versatile Rocking Song. As explained in chapter 2, the Rocking Song can be used as the core of a lesson to teach the Free Traveling Structure and locomotor movements to young children (see p. 17). Here this same little song becomes a marvelous relaxer.

The Rocking Song works well for kindergarten through third grade; occasionally it can be used in fourth grade but certainly no older. I find that older children (fifth and sixth grades) do not need a specific end-of-class relaxer. The reason may be that they are generally more contained—"cooler"—than the younger classes. In any case, if they do need to be calmed down I use standard relaxation techniques like slow breathing or conscious relaxation of isolated body parts. For example, "Tense your fingers...Now let them go. Tense your hands...Now let them go...Tense your arms...Now let them go." But for the younger grades, Rocking as a Relaxer cannot be beat. It is the combination of repetition and the swaying motion that soothes the little savage beast.

Generally, I ask the class to get their Perfect Spots; this is somewhat of a calmer in itself. If I am in a hurry I ask the class to sit wherever they are. There are several ways the song can be used:

• Rising levels: The children sit and sing the Rocking Song as they sway from side to side. They repeat the song and movement on knee level and standing level. (Do not go to air level because it is too active and breaks the calm.) As they finish on standing level, with one foot off the floor, I say quietly, "Be still on the inside so you can balance like this forever."

• Fast and slow: This time the activity is all done on the sitting level. The children sing and rock with the song at a moderate speed. We then do it as fast as possible. Conclude by singing and rocking as slowly as possible.

• Softer: Sing and rock, sitting level, at normal speed and volume. Gradually get softer and softer (you can move down to lowest level, if you wish) until the song is "sung" silently.

Spaghetti

Spaghetti is good for

• class tone.

Spaghetti is the kind of activity that elicits groans of "Oh, no," but that children secretly love. I

know because they have told me so. What is it? Piling children up one on top of the other like a plate of noodles. Do I hear you groaning?

There are two ways to start Spaghetti—the end result is the same. The first way (easier to control; harder on your back) is to have the children find their Perfect Spots and lie on their backs. They are to be "limp as cooked spaghetti." "Now we'll make a plateful of spaghetti." I take one child by the legs and drag him gently to the middle of the room.

→ TROUBLESHOOTING

As with any physical attention, if the child does not want to be touched she can walk to the middle. In 36 years no one has ever shied away from being dragged, but we must always keep that option open.

I drag another child and place his legs over the first child's abdomen. The children get layered into a big heap as shown in figure 10.5. If a class is very giggly and tickly I ask them to rest their hands in back of their heads. Then we attempt to hold the spaghetti silent for 10 seconds.

10.5

Since I invariably do Spaghetti at the end of class, I conclude by saying, "Turn yourself into a meatball and gently roll to your shoes."

The other way to start Spaghetti (harder to control; easier on your back) uses the Diagonal Structure. The children move across the diagonal one at a time. They walk stiffly, like "uncooked noodles." When they get to the middle, they pretend to step into a pot of boiling water, slowly melting from the bottom up. The next child melts gently on top of the first and so on until the class is in a layered heap. Warning: It is necessary to guide a class through the layering several times before allowing them to do it alone; without direction they get carried away with football tackles and heaping players.

Why heap children on top of one another? It is fun, and the children like it. If that were not enough, it is useful for class unity, friendships, and group work, and it gets us away from "girls on this side and boys on that side" kinds of situations. Further, it sets a warm, friendly tone for the end of class. Spaghetti is great for all ages, kindergarten on up. I have done it with adults at teacher workshops—never could get those teachers to stop giggling for 10 seconds.

Closing Thoughts

To this day I need to picture a flat horizon for a millisecond before I remember how a horizontal line goes. I am sure all music students use F-A-C-E and E-very G-ood B-oy D-oes F-ine to start reading notes on the staff. This chapter provides such tricks for movement. I find alignment especially useful; turnout is important for studio work, and Brain Catcher can be an effective warm-up. These ideas are helpful but not crucial. You can live a long and fulfilled life without ever piling children on top on each other. On the other hand, if it is the perfect Spaghetti moment, nothing can beat it.

Chapter 11

Movement As an Academic Tool

Movement is an excellent tool for teaching academic skills. Throughout this book we have touched on general skills such as sequencing, memory, concentration, and visual awareness. In this chapter we focus on specific language and math skills. My hope is not so much to cover all possible needs of a class, but to present the techniques with which to apply movement to whatever needs arise.

Movement can teach academic skills in two ways. First, movement can provide concrete experiences involving the skill. For example, children can represent the division problem 20 divided by 3 by grouping themselves into six sets of three with a visible remainder of two; they can demonstrate *beneath* by crawling under a table or *mischief* by acting naughty. Second, movement can link a desired skill into a rhythmic framework that facilitates memorization. For example, children can enhance memory by spelling *necessary* out loud while skipping across the room; they can recite multiplication facts between locomotor movements. Whatever is learned kinesthetically has a better chance of being remembered and internalized.

Language Development

Reality shapes language and, conversely, language shapes reality. We understand text from the background knowledge we bring to it, while at the same time, text can change our very being. The more direct, sensory experience a child has with language, whether with letters, words, spelling, or literature, the more it will enrich his reality.

Letters

Anyone working with young children spends a great deal of time teaching letters. There are three ways to ingrain letters into muscular memory: making letter shapes, outlining letters, and creating floor pattern letters.

Almost everyone has, at one time or another, made letters out of body shapes: "Make your body into an 'A' [one arm across the knees] . . . Make your body into a 'B' [rounded arm and rounded leg]." It is not a bad idea and worth doing—but not overdoing. I have a few recommendations:

1. Make sure the letters are right. The only value in making letters is to teach them to children. If the children form a letter incorrectly there is no value in the exercise. There may be several correct ways of making a letter, but check to see that the rationale behind each variation is appropriate.

2. Have the child say the sound—I would ask for both short and long vowel sounds—while in the letter shape.

3. Do only a few at a time and do them fully. Maybe just do "A, B, and C," or "X, Y, and Z," or "p, d, and q." (Make sure the children see the room as if it were a piece of paper, with a distinct top and bottom, so that the relation of circle to

stem in the letters is correct.) Try the letters on different levels: "Make an 'X' on the standing level . . . On lowest level . . . On knee level . . . Can you make an air-level 'X'?" Ask the letters to move somewhere: "Make a 'Y' on standing level and go somewhere . . . Don't let the stem come apart . . . Make a 'Z' on knee level and crawl . . . Make a 'P' on air level and go somewhere." Make letters with a partner: "Get a partner and the two of you make one 'E' . . . Stay like that and go somewhere."

4. Start combining letter shapes into a study. Here are three examples of studies:

a. Do "A" on the standing level, "B" on the lowest level, and "C" on the knee level. Move smoothly from one letter to the other without stopping.

b. In groups of four, pick four letters and make each one on a different level. Move smoothly from one to the other with no stops or hesitations.

c. With a partner, pick three letters and make them together, that is, one letter out of the two of you. In between each letter you will have eight beats of free locomotor movements. On count 8 be back together because you will have only two beats to get into your next shape.

Making letters by outlining them in the air is coming back into style. Children draw the shape on an imaginary chalkboard. When I use this technique I have the children hold their hands together so that I can clearly see the shape they are attempting. Another possibility is to use a scarf as a paintbrush. The letters are made as big as possible, stretching high, wide, and low. Also the letters need to be made the same way as they are written; for example, an "A" starts at the top and goes diagonally down to the left, backs up to the top and goes down to the right, then crosses from left to right.

Once the children are at ease outlining letters with their hands in front of them, I ask for two types of variations:

1. A different part of the body

2. A different plane in space

"Outline a 'B' with your hands clasped in front of you . . . Now do the 'B' on the floor . . . Could you

outline a 'B' on the ceiling? Yes, it works better when you lie down. Outline a 'D' with your toes as the pencil . . . Make the 'D' in front of you on the floor . . . On the ceiling . . . Can you make a 'D' with your toes in back of you? Outline an 'S' with your elbow, your head, your seat, your little finger." Gradation in size is also possible: "Use your nose to make the biggest 'S' in the world. . . Use your right knee to make the smallest 'S' in the world . . . How about a medium-sized 'S' with your tummy?" When body parts like the seat, tummy, torso, eyes, and shoulder are used, the letters are difficult to distinguish and I am not fussy about the resulting letter outlines. These are mainly for fun. When hands, arms, elbows, toes, and head are used, I am medium fussy—at least I am on the lookout for scribbling.

My favorite way to reinforce letters is through floor patterns. It is best to introduce letter floor patterns after the children have had some experience with straight and curved lines at least. As with other floor patterns (chapter 6), we begin with a room representation. The pattern then moves the same way as the letter is formed on paper. For example, a "B" starts down with the straight line, backtracks up, and then curves twice, as in figure 11.1.

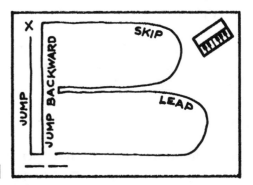

11.1

Most of the time I make the letters room size. Sometimes we play with the size gradation: "Make a 'B' as big as the entire room . . . Make a medium-sized 'B' . . . Keep the three locomotor movements you used and make a tiny 'B.'"

These floor pattern letters are an unlimited source of studies. In chapter 6 we talked about putting letters together into a complete word or name (see p. 94). Here are two more studies:

1. Pick four letters and make each a different floor pattern using different locomotor movements.

11.2

2. Pick a word and do one cursive floor pattern (as in figure 11.2; this is for older classes).

Best of all is combining these three letter-forming techniques—body shapes, outlining, and floor patterns—into one study. Here are a few examples:

1. Beautiful studies have come out of this simple structure: Pick a word and make each letter a different way. Although there are only three basic letter-forming techniques, each can be done in various ways. For example, body shapes can be done on different levels, outlining can be done with different parts of the body, and floor patterns can be different sizes. "Move smoothly from one letter to the next so that the pattern becomes one fluid dance." These can be truly lovely, especially if the children include different tempos and dynamic qualities.

2. Groups choose a word that has the same number of letters as the group size; for example, a group of five has to find a five-letter word. If you prefer, you can assign words, perhaps ones related to a spelling challenge or a social studies unit. *Moist, quiet, island,* and *ocean* are five-letter words that offer sound instructional possibilities and are frequently found on standardized tests. Each team member makes one letter in her own, unique way. The children make the letters one after the other, then repeat them simultaneously.

3. Pick three letters and make each one in four different ways.

4. Move your name.

5. Using voice and movement, tell the class a message.

→ TROUBLESHOOTING

Are you sensing an incongruity in this section on letters? My objection, and perhaps yours, is that the children who need letter recognition are too young to use most of these techniques while older children do not need to work on letters. I include the section because young children can work on the basic levels of body shape, outlining, and floor pattern letters and this work will do them good. The more extensive techniques are useful for choreography and might come in handy with older English learners.

Vocabulary Comprehension

With letter patterns we began to overlap into the area of words. Movement is a master at teaching words. A movement lesson can teach almost any word, even if the word is not about moving. I made this claim once at a teacher workshop, and one of the participants called me on it. "All right," she said, "if movement can teach almost any word, I'll pick a word and you create a lesson." I accepted the challenge with trepidation. She picked the word *and* and I sighed with relief. I shook one arm, "I am shaking my arm *and* [lifting a shaking leg] shaking my leg." "I am twisting my head *and* bending my knees." "I am swinging my torso *and* wiggling my fingers."

I was lucky; I had put myself on the spot. I do not believe movement can teach any word, but it can teach and develop a surprising number of words. Following are movement ideas for (1) relationship words, (2) problem words, (3) vocabulary words, (4) inclusive and exclusive words, (5) emotion words, (6) homonyms and antonyms. These examples may be useful in themselves, but more importantly, they will help you develop your own ideas about using movement as a language tool.

Education is at least 50% teaching words, their meaning and use. When a child knows a word in his body, that word becomes a reality; it is an internalized and usable part of his world.

Relationship Words

Relationship words describe the juxtaposition of one object to another: on, off, in, out, in front of, behind, beside, between, and so forth. These words are the glue that ties ideas together. They are crucial for text comprehension, following instructions, and testing skills.

The two best ways of teaching relationship words are an obstacle course and the In and Out Game. An obstacle course can easily reinforce most relationship words: over the table, under the chair, around the piano, on and off the foam, in and out of the box, between the bookcases. It is important to vary the courses so that the relationship words are not always associated with a particular object. The words should have a wide range of applications (including paper and pencil tasks, which are ideal to present immediately following a kinesthetic experience). Obstacle courses are covered in chapter 8; also see an obstacle course-like literature dance, the Bears in the Night Dance, at the end of this chapter.

The In and Out Game is a catchall for working with words. In addition to the three class management structures introduced at the beginning of the book, the In and Out Game is one of the most valuable activities presented. For young children or new English learners, it is a good idea to introduce some of the relationship words separately. For most second grades on up, I plunge right into the game itself. Following are techniques for working with individual sets of relationship words and then a description of the In and Out Game as a whole.

On and Off

Place mats around the room, close enough together that a child can jump from one to another but far enough apart that it is a long jump. "Jump only on the mats; don't touch the floor . . . Jog off the mats . . . Hop on the mats . . . Stand off the mats and swing . . . Roll on the mats . . . Skip off the mats." Simple—a good warm-up activity. The mats are fun because while on them the children are very close together holding on to each other "so they won't fall off," giggling and carrying on. Off the mats they have room to move freely with a lot of energy. For safety, choose movements that are rather small for *on;* for energy release, choose large movements for *off.*

What happens to the child who is off when she supposed to be on? It depends on the reason. Once in a great while a child will truly not under-

stand. She needs individual help with myriad off and on experiences: "Put your hand on the piano . . . Take it off . . . Put your foot on the chair . . . Take it off . . . Put your head on the desk . . . Take it off." This one-to-one work needs to be done outside of class. Most mistakes with off and on are caused by carelessness. This is when I revert to a competitive game: "Anyone off when they are supposed to be on and vice versa will sit out this round. You'll be able to play the next round." A new round starts when about half the class is out, and I usually play three rounds.

In and Out

Large boxes (from furniture or appliance stores) are wonderful for work with *in* and *out.* Have the children divide into groups of three to five and have one box for each group. "One child in . . . Come out . . . Three children in . . . Two come out . . . Three more go in. How many children are in the box now? [Oops, off on an arithmetic lesson.] One child goes in and the rest of the group gives him a ride. [Take turns so everyone has a ride.] Everybody get in your box . . . Can you stay in and go somewhere?"

Going in and out of boxes has produced some spectacular studies. These studies resulted from this simple assignment: Your box has to go from one side of the room to the middle; then you will do something, and then you will go to the other side of the room. Use some parts of your bodies in and some out of the box. I gave this study to grades three to six, and the results were incredibly funny. One box started from the side of the room with just feet, pointed every which way, showing from the bottom. In the middle of the room the box, with children in it, turned itself over so that the open side was on top. Disjointed arms, legs, and elbows emerged, proceeding to put on a show full of remarkably identifiable personalities. The box turned back over and walked off as it had come in. In other studies children cut holes in their boxes so that they could stick parts of their bodies out; the boxes looked grotesquely human. These studies certainly grew much larger than the original intention of working with in and out. (The biggest problem is storing these big boxes. If it is possible to nest some of them one inside the other, that helps.)

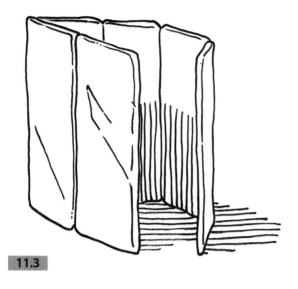

11.3

For younger children, mats can be used to differentiate between on and off and in and out. Stiff mats can be made to stand up like little "houses," as in figure 11.3.

The children stand the mats up and go in the house and then come out. Then they knock the houses down and stand on and off them. This game can be repeated innumerable times; young children do not seem to tire of it. Their favorite part, of course, is knocking the houses down.

In Front of, Behind, and Beside

Children who can find front, back, and side on their own bodies (chapter 6) will easily transfer these directional planes to objects. I explain that just as our bodies have a front, back, and sides, so do many objects: "If you stand by the front of something, it's called in front of; if you stand by its back, it's called behind; if you stand by its side, it's called beside.

We work with *in front of*, *behind*, and *beside* somewhat in the same way we worked with near and far to get Perfect Spots. "Go in front of the piano . . . Go behind a chair . . . Go beside my desk . . . Go in front of the chalkboard . . . Go behind me . . . Go beside Andrew." The trick is to pick objects that have a clear front and back and to make sure they are possible and the results are desirable. Sending the class to the front of an open piano was definitely regrettable; for a few more goofs see the "Real Life" section that follows.

⇒ *REAL LIFE*

Some instructions I wish I had never said. "Go behind the front door"—they all left. "Go behind the chalkboard"—it is nailed down. "Go behind the stage"—cluttered with lighting equipment.

Once the children get these one-part instructions, try two parts. The two-part instructions can either combine two objects or combine an object with the child's body. Here are examples with two objects: "Go behind the piano and in front of a chair . . . Go in front of me and beside my desk . . . Go behind Stephanie and behind the green box." Here are examples of an object combined with the child's body: "Put your back beside my desk . . . Stand with your front behind the piano . . . Stand with your side in front of the stage."

Between

You can foreshadow the In and Out Game working with just the word *between*. Scatter objects randomly throughout the room (tables, chairs, pillows, mats, cones, etc.) and ask the children to stand between two specified objects: "Stand between a traffic cone and the piano." As with the forthcoming game, you can limit the number of seconds the children have to get to their designated spot. Those that do not make it are out for that round, and we usually play three rounds.

Another way to reinforce *between* is with locomotor movements in the Diagonal Structure. Ask for groups of three. "If you line up side by side in your groups, there are two people on either side and one person between them. First group, the person who is between two people, raise your hand . . . That's right, Greg, you are between Antoine and Mark." If there is any question whether the children are clear on the concept, spend some time mixing up the children and asking who is between. Once that is clear (for most classes it is immediately), do a series of movements in which the between child does something special or different. The children take turns being the between person, and if the movement is especially fun we do it three times so that everyone has a turn.

1. **Seat Carriage.** This is the between favorite. The two side people make a hand square as shown

in chapter 7, page 111. Each child holds her own left wrist with her right hand and then holds her partner's wrist with the left hand. The between person sits on the hand square and gets carried across the diagonal. Obviously this locomotor movement has to be done three times.

2. **Directional cancan.** Children hold on to each other's shoulders. The two side people kick forward, and the between person kicks backward.

3. **Galloping in a basket.** The two side people hold hands and side-slide. The between person gallops within the arms of the side people.

4. **Directional running.** The two side people run forward and the between person runs backward, while all hold hands.

5. **The stretcher.** The side people walk sideways, each holding one arm and one leg of the between person, who relaxes and enjoys the ride.

6. **Counterpoint.** All the children learn a simple, even beat pattern, for example, walk (four beats), jump (four beats), skip (four beats). The side people do the pattern in the original order while the between person does it in reverse order. (In this pattern the jumps coincide, and that helps keep the group together.) The children have to move in concert. This is a good exercise in thinking for oneself.

The In and Out Game

We are ready for the unbeatable In and Out Game. This game reinforces all the previous relationship words plus many more, plus many geometry words. And the children love it more than the parachute. Amazing!

To set the game up, place two stiff mats standing up like houses (see figure 11.3) in various parts of the room. Scatter any other equipment available throughout the room: two or three mats lying flat, the incline mat, a stegel end, pieces of foam, chairs, boxes, plastic hoops, tires, foam geometric shapes, traffic cones, beanbags, tables, whatever. Pull the piano and your desk slightly away from the wall. The room will look like a total disaster, as in figure 11.4.

We start with a warm-up going over things but never touching anything except the floor. I do

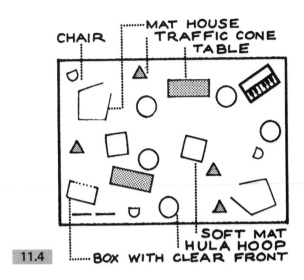

11.4

not put people "out" during the warm-up. We do various locomotor movements—skip, jump, hop, hopscotch, crawl, jazzy walk, run and leap—over any and all the equipment. Have the class travel essentially in a circular direction so that two children are not leaping over the same mat in opposite directions. Then the children sit on one side of the room and we demonstrate individually each word that will be used in the game. Here are the words and phrases I use:

> **over**—This is the only word done with locomotor movements; all the other words are done with stationary positions. *Over* is demonstrated by leaping over various objects without touching them, as in the warm-up. I use a piano or tambourine sound, as with a Free Traveling warm-up.
>
> **on top of**—Children stand on any object. Warn them to step directly on the pillows, because they can slip, and to only kneel (not stand) on folding chairs.
>
> **under**—The children can go under tables and chairs, mats, or even pillows and other smaller objects by lifting the object above their head if necessary—that is, they are under.
>
> **above**—I understand there is a subtle difference between on top of and above (above has more of a hovering quality), but I do not differentiate the actions. You certainly could.

below—Same as under.

beneath—Same as under and below.

in—The children can stand within the mat "houses" or in a plastic hoop, tire, or box. If the children who are in a standing mat knock it down, they are all out.

around—Children run circles around any one object.

in front of—Children stand in front of the seat of a chair.

behind—Children stand in back of a chair. In all these cases there can be several children at each spot, one in front of the other. In front of, beside, and behind do not have to be done solely with a chair, but whatever object you specify must have a clear front and back—for example, a mat will not do.

beside—Children stand alongside a chair.

between—Children are told to stand between two specific objects, e.g., between two tires. In this case they stand with one tire on one side and the second tire on the other side. The tires can be far apart as long as the children are on the invisible line connecting the two tires. Any designated objects will do; for example, children can stand between two mats or stand between a table and a cone.

through—I introduce through like this: "She was so strong from her karate lessons that she was able to smash her fist through a brick." (I punch my arm through a foam doughnut shape or a plastic hoop with exaggerated forcefulness.) The children then demonstrate examples of *through* using tires and hoops (stand them up), chairs (through the middle of the back, not under), cones (their fingers peek through the little hole at the end), the stegel (through the back, not under), and crates (fingers poking through).

These are the relationship words and phrases I use. There is no reason to use all these; young children or beginning English learners might do best using only seven or eight of them. But most third grades and above will handle these words and phrases easily and be up for more challenges. So I have extended the game to include geometric concepts:

horizontal, vertical, diagonal—Children get on a piece of equipment and either lie flat, stand straight up with arms raised, or tilt over in a slant. Be careful if you are using an incline mat: Lying down on the mat will not be horizontal, but diagonal, because the mat itself is slanted. On a chair, to be horizontal the children have to be lying straight, extended across the seat of the chair, arms overhead like a flying Superman—extreme abdominal exercise.

perpendicular lines—Children make a horizontal line connected to a vertical line in their own bodies while they are on a piece of equipment.

right, obtuse, and acute angles—Children sit with their legs directly in front of them, backs straight, for a right angle. (This of course would also work for perpendicular lines—very good if the children discover that.) With their legs in front of them, they lean back for the obtuse angle and bend forward for the acute. All of this is great abdominal work in addition to its academic applications.

symmetry and asymmetry—Children get on a piece of equipment and assume a shape that is the same on both sides to show symmetry, different on the two sides to show asymmetry. For example, to show symmetry a child could stand on a mat, both legs turned out and both arms twisted exactly the same way; to show asymmetry he might bend one arm and leg and straighten the other arm and leg.

parallel line—Children choose a line (this can be an edge of any piece of equipment) and make their arm parallel to that line (identical in alignment but not touching; equidistant). If you really want to challenge them ask for "parallel vertical lines" (the edge they choose must be vertical like the leg of the piano or the edge of a stand-up mat), "parallel horizontal lines," "parallel diagonal lines."

These are the words I use, but I am positive that you will come up with many more once you try this game out. The game is simple: Call out a word and have the children demonstrate it within a prescribed time. This time limit is what makes the game exciting. When we start out I count to 10 and, for young children and English learners, we stay there. How fast or slow you count is, of course, up to you, but you need to make the game fast paced. If children do not show the word within the time limit, or are moving past the last count, they are out. When children get "out" they have to sit on the side of the room; on the way they must—it is a part of the game—say with a shrug, "Oh, well, it is only a game." Sitting out is not as horrendous as it sounds because it is only for one round, and I usually play at least three rounds. The round ends when there are only a few children left—and they are all declared winners.

Here is how to speed up the ending of a round: (1) Cut the time in half, for example, to 5 seconds. (2) Ask for two words done at the same time. Examples are *on top* and *under* at the same time (a child can put one body part under and one on top or can move equipment so that she is on top of, say, a mat while under a pillow), *in* and *around* (shown with one foot in a tire and the other hopping around the tire), *in* and *under* (shown by getting in a tire or "house" while stooping under a pillow or cone), and *horizontal* and *vertical* (shown by perpendicular lines). You can devise other diabolical combinations. At the end of the entire game I say that all will be winners if they can do the final challenge; this is so everyone ends on a high note.

If children argue with any of the calls, tell them that the umpire's word (yours) is final. If a child starts sulking or cheating he gets a class warning. In my classes two warnings put the child out for the day. It is important to keep the tone of the game light and playful while revving the pace up to charged excitement. Three rounds could easily fit into 15 minutes—but factor in another 15 minutes for the warm-up and the introductory demonstration of each word.

Here are a few typical calls: "In, 1, 2, 3, 4, 5, 6, 7, 8, 9, 10; on top, 1-10. Uh oh, you didn't make it. Out. Under, 1-10; around, 1-10; get on something and show me vertical lines, 1-10. Sally, you are horizontal, out." Go on like this until half the class is out—then, "You are too good at this; now you'll have only 5 seconds. Through, 1-5. Oh, you three are out. Get on something and show me a shape that has symmetry, 1-5. Oh no, you didn't make it. OK, all of you will be winners if you can do the last thing: parallel lines, 1-5. Great! New round."

Brand-new English learners need to be partnered with more experienced children. But actually, many new English learners do just fine by watching and copying. If the whole class speaks little English, use fewer words and go a bit slower.

There are two methods of cleaning up:

1. Sit all the children on one side of the room and assign every two or three a specific task. When they complete that task they sit back down. This method is very controlled and is excellent for following verbal instructions—for example, "You two children fold the standing mats and put them away." But it does take a bit of time.

2. Once the children know you and you trust them, you can ask for a "perfect cleanup." I personally am very fussy that everything has an assigned place and that the children put the equipment away exactly the way it was. They do not call me a "neat freak" for nothing.

Problem Words

Problem words are particular words with which a class has difficulty. Each class has its own unique problem words. Here are a few examples of movement lessons used to teach word comprehension. These examples demonstrate four techniques of working with specific words: progression, opposites, vignettes, and physical objects. (Pantomime is a fifth technique; but I include it in the sections on sophisticated locomotor movements, homophones, and spelling.)

Progression

Here is a good, adaptable progression for teaching words:

1. Present the initial definition.
2. Explore the idea with isolated body parts.
3. Explore the idea with the whole body.
4. Play with the idea, adding other known concepts.
5. Create a remembered study.

The sequence moves from little to big, from less to more freedom, from a literal to a more expanded view of the idea. This progression can be used to teach just about any word.

Let us say a class has a lot of trouble with the words horizontal and vertical. We would start with a short verbal definition and then explore the two words with isolated body parts: "Make your hand horizontal to the floor . . . Make your hand vertical to the floor . . . Make your arm horizontal . . . Your arm vertical . . ." Continue with legs, torso, feet, and so on. "Can you make your seat horizontal? . . . vertical?"

From working with isolated body parts, we go on to whole-body positions on different levels: "Make your body horizontal on the lowest level . . . Sitting level . . . Knee level . . . Standing level . . . Can you make your body, or part of it, horizontal in the air?" For sitting, knee, and standing levels I accept any part of the body in a horizontal position. For example, on standing level a child might bend her torso straight forward, or even better, lift a leg back as she bends forward as in figure 11.5.

11.5

Vertical is easier, and we do it on all levels. For lowest-level vertical positions, I accept shoulder stands or prone torsos with raised legs and arms.

Now we are ready to incorporate other concepts: "Make your body horizontal on any level you want . . . Keep the shape and move locomotor, backward direction . . . Make your body vertical and change levels . . . Keep changing levels and go somewhere." Best of all, "Get into groups of three and lift one person so he is completely horizontal off the ground." (Children take turns holding the lifted child carefully, as on a stretcher.) "Lift one person so she is vertical off the ground." (Chil-

dren take turns lifting one child a few inches off the ground.)

Finally, a short study: In groups of three, make up four different ways to show horizontal and four different ways to show vertical. Move smoothly from one to the other and shout the word as you get in each position.

Opposites and Vignettes

Sometimes the best way to understand one word is to match it with its opposite. Let us take the word *comfortable*; it makes much more sense if we compare it to *uncomfortable*. "Twist so hard you are uncomfortable, strained, or hurt a little . . . Relax so that you are comfortable or at ease . . . Contract so hard you are uncomfortable . . . Relax and get comfortable . . . Stretch so you are uncomfortable . . . Now relax into comfortable."

For older children the idea of *comfortable* and *uncomfortable* can be expanded into social situations. Fifth and sixth graders identify easily with these images: "Walk as though you were uncomfortable or ill at ease in a brand-new school . . . In a scary place . . . Among a group of kids that don't like you . . . Walk as though you were comfortable with all your friends . . . Sit comfortably in a big, soft chair . . . Lie down comfortably on a warm, sandy beach."

Have you ever done vignettes? The children place themselves in a frozen picture depicting some idea. In the case of *uncomfortable*, four children might sit pointing accusingly at one startled child, or they might stand very crowded as if in a packed elevator. *Comfortable* could be staged as holding up an A paper or relaxing with friends. The pictures are set so that each child knows exactly where he stands and exactly what position he is in. The children move instantly into these pictures and freeze until I ask them to go on to the next.

Vignettes are a great structure for words that can be visualized. In this example, I asked groups of five children to set up two vignettes showing something *comfortable* and two showing *uncomfortable*. The vignettes were put in a sequence and performed on stage. A good show.

Physical Objects

We used physical objects when working with relationship words; objects can also be used to teach other words. Here is an example of using objects

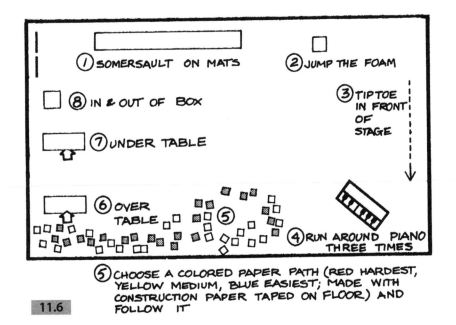

① SOMERSAULT ON MATS

② JUMP THE FOAM

③ TIPTOE IN FRONT OF STAGE

⑧ IN & OUT OF BOX

⑦ UNDER TABLE

⑥ OVER TABLE

⑤

④ RUN AROUND PIANO THREE TIMES

⑤ CHOOSE A COLORED PAPER PATH (RED HARDEST, YELLOW MEDIUM, BLUE EASIEST; MADE WITH CONSTRUCTION PAPER TAPED ON FLOOR) AND FOLLOW IT

11.6

to teach the word *reverse*. I work with the word *reverse* specifically to refer to going from the end to the beginning. In this way *reverse* and *backward* are differentiated. *Backward* is used to refer to a direction of the body, the back leading; *reverse* is reserved for opposite ordering. The best clarification of this differentiation comes from working with an obstacle course. I set up a standard course like the one in figure 11.6.

The children learn the course quickly and then I add the backward direction. When I stop the piano, the children stop and I call either forward or backward. The children continue the course in that direction. They are, however, still taking the obstacles in the same sequence. Next I introduce the idea of *original order* and *reverse order*. For original order the children do the course in the order first taught; for reverse order the children turn, wherever they are in the course, and go the other way in the sequence.

When I first introduce original order and reverse order the children do them only in the forward direction. Later, I combine original and reverse order and forward and backward directions. When I stop the piano the children freeze and I give dual instructions: "Go in the original order, backward direction." "Go in the original order, forward direction." "Go in the reverse order, forward direction." "Go in the reverse order, backward direction." This is pretty much self-corrective because someone going the wrong way is met by a rush of children going the other way. I speed up the change of instructions, going faster and faster, until the whole thing falls apart in laughter.

For younger children the distinction between backward and reverse order can be exemplified with use of a simplified obstacle course or a simple locomotor study. A locomotor study might be to skip one side of the room, jump one side, run one side, and crawl one side. "Do the pattern . . . Do the pattern, backward direction . . . Do the pattern in reverse order, that is, the crawl side first . . . Do the pattern in reverse order, backward direction."

Vocabulary Words

Let us look at two areas of vocabulary expansion:

1. In the classroom, the vocabulary words presented before a reading selection.

2. In movement class, words that specifically expand movement vocabulary.

Before every reading selection, I present approximately five words that I think might give the children trouble and we learn them through movement. Almost all words can be represented with some type of gesture in order to make them memorable. At this moment my class is reading *Borreguita and the Coyote*, by Verna Aardema (Harcourt Brace, third grade Signature Series). Before we began, I made cards, and the reading group crawled like ewes, bleating away as they frisked about the room. They braced themselves against the wall and then lay horizontally on chairs pretending to be a ledge. My goal is for the children to internalize the vocabulary so that it is remembered and usable. This type of movement activity inside the classroom certainly enlivens reading time. If you have more than one reading group, the second group will have a good challenge in concentration and then have an opportunity to play with the vocabulary words from their story. Some particularly memorable vocabulary words: *pelt*—we took recyclable paper, wadded it up, and pelted one another (shut the door); *debate*—we held a full-scale debate on whether the school day should be longer; *daintily*—we lifted imaginary teacups with raised, curled, pinkies; *coy*—we practiced batting eyelashes and saying things like "Oh, Ricky, you're so strong. Would you help me with these groceries?"; *tousle*—well, you can imagine what our hair looked like that day.

My favorite vocabulary work in movement class is with sophisticated locomotor movement words. "Sophisticated means grown-up. We are going to learn a number of new words; these are the kinds of words you will run into in high school and college books. The words are grown-up, but the movements are really easy." Following are the words I present; I am sure you will discover many more.

1. March
2. Tramp
3. Trudge
4. Plod
5. Stagger

   I tell a little story to cement these words: "You are in the army, and you get up for a 25-mile hike. You're feeling good and start out with a march—back lifted, knees high; you go along for about 10 miles and you don't have the same energy, so you tramp—like a march but with lower knees. Now you've gone 15 miles and you don't want to do it any longer; you trudge—back rounded, slower walk. At 20 miles you cannot think any more; you can only put one foot in front of the other, plod—eyes

almost closed, mouth gaping, back stooped. Finally you're almost done, you can barely make it, you stagger—almost falling.

6. Creep
7. Slink

   Creep and slink are sneaky, slow, silent walks.

8. Stalk

   Stalk is like a cat that freezes, then moves quickly and stealthily and freezes again; stalk usually ends with a pounce.

9. Strut
10. Saunter

    For strut and saunter we get ready for a party, putting on cool clothes and fixing our hair, and then walk very jazzy.

11. Amble
12. Stroll
13. Meander

    Amble, stroll, and meander are slow and enjoyable, as in walking through a beautiful garden on a lovely sunny day. Meander has a wandering quality—for example, streams meander.

14. Race
15. Sprint
16. Scamper
17. Scramble
18. Frisk
19. Dodge

    These six running words have subtle differences. A race is fast but has to contain some energy because races sometimes last a few miles. A sprint expends every ounce of energy. Scamper, scramble, and frisk are a light run, like animals running from the meadow to the barn. If your class is ready for more subtle distinctions, mention that scamper has the quality of a bounding rabbit, scramble has an element of panic, and frisk contains eager confidence. Dodge is a zigzag run, like a football player avoiding being tackled as he heads for the touchdown.

20. Limp

21. Hobble

    For limp, one leg is hurt; for hobble, both feet hurt as if your shoes are too tight.

22. Scurry

23. Bustle

    These run words usually have to do with being late. "Oh, no! My alarm didn't go off! I'm so late I have to scurry or bustle around trying to find my shoes and backpack."

24. Stride

    Stride—take big, strong steps—is how you enter the throne room when you are a king or queen. Or, if you are very mad, you might slam the door and stride out.

25. Prance

26. Trot

    These last two are jogs often associated with horses. When they prance, people move with the top of the foot pushing an imaginary ball and trot is what Barry Bonds does around the bases after he hits a home run.

We post the list of sophisticated locomotor movements in the gym and take several days to explore each of them; the children enjoy this pantomime. When we are done, it is time for a study: Groups of four create a floor pattern using different line shapes. The lines are assigned only sophisticated locomotor movements.

Inclusive and Exclusive Words

Inclusive and exclusive words, *only, both, everybody,* and *nobody,* demand physical attention because they are so abstract that they are sometimes non-functional. I am sure we have all experienced the hair-pulling frustration of saying "Everybody get a ball" only to have one child ask, "Do I get a ball?"

Only

"Move only your fingers." (I am strict about making sure that nothing else moves. This is good for muscular coordination as well as mental concentration.) "Move only one shoulder . . . Only your toes . . . Only your head . . . Only your eyes . . . Only your hips . . . Only your leg." "Take only one jump . . . Only three skips . . . Only two hops

. . . Only one leap." "Only the boys move . . . Only the girls move . . . Only the children with black hair . . . Only the children wearing red . . ." Simple but workable.

Because *only* requires a lot of control, do not work with it too long. It is better to have fewer examples and more precision. *Only* works well alternated with free locomotor movements in the Free Traveling Structure.

Both

After *only* is established, use it as a contrast to *both.* "Move only one arm . . . Now move both arms . . . Move only one leg . . . Now move both legs . . . Move only your head . . . Move only your hips . . . Now move both your head and hips . . . Move only your fingers . . . Move only your toes . . . Now move both your fingers and toes." I find that it works best to use two *onlys* before a *both,* so that the both results in precisely two movements rather than a jumble of activity.

Only and *both* are great to do with partners: "Only one of you skip . . . The other person gallops . . . Now keep your own movements, hold onto one another, and both of you move. Only one of you jump . . . Only one of you roll . . . Now stay together and both of you move."

Everybody and Nobody

Everybody and *nobody* are best done together, as in a game. "Everybody stand in Perfect Spots and swing . . . Nobody swing." For the nobody I instruct the children to stand still. This has to be initially pointed out: "If no body is swinging then you don't swing." If the children do something else instead, like shake or spin, I accept that, since no one is swinging. But that is quite sophisticated and rarely happens. "OK, nobody jump, come on, nobody jump." (I ham it up as if I expected them to jump and am surprised that they do not—this foreshadows the Opposite Game, which is coming up.) "Everybody jump . . . Everybody skip . . . Nobody skip . . . Now nobody run. Uh oh, I fooled you. Now everybody run."

Emotion Words

Emotion words would seem to be a natural part of movement class. The basis of a great deal of dance is emotional expression in physical form. The trouble with using emotion in the classroom is that it often ends up so trite. *Sad* is a limp head with a frown; *happy* is a wide-palm skip. I must admit that I have sometimes neglected emotion words just because I could not bear the results. I do not have a solution for this stereotyping. However, I do have four observations:

1. Emotional expressions turn out trite because they are untrue, not from the gut. Either the children are not in touch with their feelings or they are afraid to let them out. Dealing with the children's inhibitions creates a teaching dilemma: I do not want to criticize, but I do not want to accept their superficiality. Generally, I attempt some gentle prodding to engage their real feelings.

2. The children need to expand their emotion vocabulary: *Terrified* needs to look very different from *apprehensive*, and *mad* needs to be distinguished from *annoyed*. This subtly pulls us away from much of the stereotyping. Although younger children do not have the vocabulary expected from older students, they do know many distinctions—like between *joyous* and *OK,* or between *nervous* and *scared.* And this kind of work is excellent language development.

3. The children need to expand what movements, and movement concepts, they use to demonstrate an emotion. *Sad* does not always have to be a slow walk; it is quite a challenge to hopscotch, roll, skip, or run, sadly. When we attempt *sad* on different levels and in different directions, using locomotor and nonlocomotor movements, with partners, with different tempos and sizes, we are broadened physically and emotionally.

4. The children need many good examples of emotions: pictures, movies, performances, art. It is best to introduce emotion words in the Free Traveling Structure so no one feels too exposed. Later we can look at the words more closely with the Diagonal Structure.

For younger grades I use emotion words like: happy, joyous, curious, excited, sad, mad, annoyed, proud, scared, frightened, nervous, confused, lonely, and tired.

Older grades can build extensive emotion word vocabularies: melancholy, blue, down, exuberant, astonished, guilty, enthusiastic, amused, pleased, glad, cheerful, blissful, exultant, intimidated, glo-
rious, exasperated, sullen, determined, terrified, apprehensive, fidgety, exhausted, annoyed, furious, gleeful, mischievous, playful, loving, anxious, boastful, bold, timid, worried, concerned, uneasy, restless, fretful, fearful, vindictive, depressed, irritated, content, peaceful, delighted, surprised, and many words you encounter in literature.

If possible, it is worth taking a minute to set the scene: "You are walking to school by yourself. Another kid comes and purposely pushes you down; on top of that he takes your homework paper and won't give it back. He runs off laughing and you can't catch him." (Even though the children are reacting to the scene, rather than acting it out, it is important that the other child run off and not be caught; otherwise all the resulting movement will simply be a fight.) "How would you look? . . . How would you walk? . . . Run? . . . Sit? . . . Contract angry? . . . Stretch? . . . Twist? . . . Turn? . . . Can you skip angry? Use as many different movements as you can to show me anger."

Working with emotion words will be better after the children have tried it several times. Children need the time to build up confidence in themselves and trust in the class. I make few corrections. When I do, I use a light hand: "How could somebody who is angry giggle so much? Your joyous and your melancholy look an awful lot alike. Do that exuberant on different levels. Use both locomotor and nonlocomotor movement to show timid. Can you do excited backward?"

After exploring emotion words in the Free Traveling Structure, we do them on the diagonal. When working on the diagonal, I will often ask for the same locomotor movement or pattern done in different ways: "Skip as if you're happy . . . Skip sadly . . . Skip proudly . . . Skip determined . . ." We are then ready for studies using emotion words:

• Teach a simple pattern, for example, walk (four beats), contract (four beats), stretch (four beats), and gallop (four beats). The children divide into groups; each group picks an emotion and does the pattern appropriately.

• Teach a simple pattern, for example, run to the middle of the room, turn, fall, and roll. The children form groups; each group picks three emotions and does the pattern three times, each in a different way.

• Each group is given an emotion word on a card. They show that emotion in 5 to 10 different movements and put the movements together to form a continuous study. The children are instructed to use all known movement concepts: levels, locomotor and nonlocomotor movements, directions, and floor patterns, as well as tempo, size, and dynamic quality.

Homonyms, Homophones, and Antonyms

Homonyms, homophones, and antonyms can be an academic bore, but in movement class they are wonderful fun. Here I give a few examples of how to work with these words; again the particular words are not as valuable as the overall procedures.

Homonyms

Homonyms are two or more words that are spelled the same but have different meanings. Let us take a frequently tested homonym: *skip*. "What does skip mean?"

"To skip around."

"Yes, that is locomotor movement skip. Good. What other kinds of skips are there?"

"The guy that runs a boat." (The skipper of a boat.)

"Someone's name."

"Skip it."

"Great. The word skip has a number of meanings. You already know the locomotor movement skip. We are going to work with the kind of skip that means to pass over, as in 'skip it.'"

The children line up on one side of the room and I pick a volunteer. "Tina, shake hands with the first person in line . . . Now skip nine people and shake hands with the next . . . Skip three more and shake hands with the next . . . Now skip one more and shake hands with the next." Subsequent volunteers can shake feet, pat backs, twirl, and possibly hug people while practicing skip.

We then go on to a more abstract skip. In the example just presented it was visually clear what was skipped. Now the children will skip sections that they cannot see. The children learn a simple movement pattern, for example, jump (four beats), walk (four beats), skip (four beats).

They form groups and practice the pattern on the diagonal. "Group 1, do the pattern but skip the jump part." To do this, the group stands still for the first four beats and then resumes the pattern with the walk and skip sections. "Group 2, you skip the walk part." This group jumps four beats, stands still four beats, and skips four beats. "Group 3, you skip the skip part."

It would be useful after this experiential lesson to give a paper and pencil task involving *skip*. The multiple-meaning section of standardized tests is one of the hardest, especially for people learning English. The basic format is to present a sentence that includes a homonym; the children have to match another sentence that uses the word in a similar way.

For example: I was so happy I began to skip down the street.

In which sentence is skip used in the same way:

1. Skip problems 1 through 5.
2. I'd like you to meet my friend Skip.
3. I like to skip rope.
4. Do the locomotor movement skip.

Another example is the threesome *row*, *row*, and *row*. Show the word on a card and verbally distinguish the three kinds. I say, "Row, the boat kind," and the children pull at imaginary oars. When I say, "Row, the line kind," the children quickly line up. Row, the fight kind, has a different pronunciation, so I do not have to include a definition—the children gleefully pretend to have an enormous brawl.

Homophones

Homophones are two words that sound alike but are spelled differently. They are easily distinguished with pantomime. Generally I do not like pantomime in movement class. Too often children spend a lot of time jumping like frogs, growing like flowers, and swinging like elephant trunks, but they do not go anywhere from there. I suspect I have overreacted. My fear is that too much energy devoted to superficial imitation will sacrifice the energy needed to experiment with the children's own movement. True pantomime begins only after extensive training and requires an enormous movement vocabulary and fluency.

It is an art form I greatly admire. But elephants that look like dogs that look like mice are not close to true pantomime. However, given all that, pantomime is a fast and efficient way to see if a class understands the difference between two similar-sounding words. Following are a few examples. In all cases I show the words on cards and the class acts them out.

1. *Aisle* and *isle* present a good spelling problem. For *isle* the children essentially find Perfect Spots, pretending to be islands. For *aisle* the children line up in two rows, leaving an aisle between them—sometimes I ask two children to "walk down the aisle."

2. How about *fowl* and *foul?* When the card *fowl* is held up, the children act like chickens. For *foul* they enact a ball going out of fair play.

3. For *write* they pretend to energetically scribble; *right* gets a self-righteous pat on the back with a right hand. That covers homophones and homonyms in one swoop.

Antonyms

For antonyms, we begin with a verbal introduction of the word *opposite:* "Opposite means very different. What is the most different from, or opposite to, 'yes'? 'day'? 'left'? 'wrong'? 'high'? 'big'? 'happy'? 'rich'? 'ugly'? 'messy'? 'wonderful'? At this point, in young classes, I bring out Ms. Opposite. Ms. Opposite is a large cardboard puppet that I made: One eye is open and one is shut. Half of her mouth is happy and half is sad; she has short, light hair on one side and long, dark hair on the other; half her torso is covered with bumpy corduroy and half with smooth silk; half her skirt is red and half is green; one foot has a shoe on and the other does not. The joints are put together with butterfly tacks so they are movable; we can show one bent arm and one straight, a contracted leg and a stretched one, high and low, and so on. The children imitate all the puppet positions. Numerous movement activities are possible with opposites. The two best are Partner Opposites and the Opposite Game.

Partner Opposites

The goal of Partner Opposites is for the children to stay with their partners while demonstrating an opposite relationship. The children hold hands and show high and low, forward and backward, pretty and ugly, crooked and straight, heavy and light—and for older classes, stereotyped boy and girl. A good logic problem is to ask the children to stay together (not necessarily holding hands) while demonstrating fast and slow. One child can run circles around a slow-moving partner, or one child can run fast but almost in place while the other child moves slowly. Don't divulge solutions too soon.

The Opposite Game

The Opposite Game is another of the best activities in this book. The children sit in the middle of the room and I tell them that this is the day they have all been waiting for: They get to do the opposite of what their teacher tells them. Before starting, I set out the rules:

1. When I say "Game's over," the game is over. (I learned the importance of preestablishing this rule the hard way.)
2. When I tell you to move a certain way, move in the tracklike circle used for warm-ups but make the movement opposite. OK, we're ready for the game.

The joy of this game depends entirely on teacher "hamminess." "OK boys and girls, everybody stand up." (They stay seated.) Smiling with nervous embarrassment, "OK, all of you up, come on, let's get started!" (They lie back languidly.) "Fine, if you want to stay seated . . ." (They all stand.) "Oh, no, this is a terrible class. All right, let me see you straight, you know how I like good posture." (They slump or put their bodies in bent or crooked shapes.) "What is wrong with you? Do you call this straight? This is awful! Well, just stay crooked then." (They all pull ramrod straight.) "My goodness, this class is just terrible. Well, let's just start on the mat side of the room." (I walk to one side of the room, and the class runs to the opposite side.) "OK, we'll start on the other side." (I walk toward them as they run to the opposite side.) "We're going to start right here and you stay put!" (They gleefully run across.) "All right, let's do a really fast movement around the room . . . Why are you moving so slowly? Would you hurry up! OK, go slowly then."

You get the picture. In this way we normally go through the opposites described earlier plus high and low, light and heavy, together and apart, forward and backward, and any others that occur to me. At the end I wail, "This has been just terrible; I just can't stand it. Just move silently." Don't forget to say "Game's over!"

It is amazing how often shy, never-do-anything-wrong children request this game. Children will clamor for it daily; but I reserve it for an occasional special ending to movement class. It is possible to contain it in a classroom, but do not play it so often that it loses its punch. Many years ago the children in a dance class pleaded to do the Opposite Game for Visitors' Day, a demonstration class for friends and relatives. We started with the Opposite Game, not telling the visitors what we were doing. I could see some parents getting upset at their "unruly" children. I had to pretend to cough many times to keep from laughing and giving the game away. After a short while everyone caught on—great fun.

Spelling

The spelling problems that movement solves best involve those pure memory words that do not fit the rules, spelling connected to word comprehension, and word families.

Rhythmic Spelling

Do you remember how you learned to spell *Mississippi*? Most of us put it in a singsong pattern and learned it by rote. The same is true of *necessary*—"NeCeSSarY." Let us look at a mini-lesson on *said*. Since there is no phonic rule involved, I treat *said* strictly as a memory exercise. The children are lined up ready to move on the diagonal. We chant "s—a-i-d," a few times and then take turns shouting "s-a-i-d" while running across the diagonal. Twenty children calling out the spelling pretty well ingrains it, but just to make sure, I have each child yell "s-a-i-d" very fast, in the air, while jumping the foam.

Ought is broken into "o" (clap) "u" (clap) "g-h-t" (three stomps). The rhythm is

| o | u | g-h-t |
| clap | clap | stomp, stomp, stomp |

Once they have that, move across the diagonal: "o" (clap and jump) "u" (clap and jump) "g-h-t" (three leaps). The same rhythmic breakdown can be done with *ight*: "i" (clap and jump) "g-h-t" (three leaps). For the *ight* family of words, have the children shout the beginning consonant of a word and then act it out. For example: "R" (shout) "i" (clap and jump) "g-h-t" (three leaps) "spells right!" (students raise their right hands). Another example is flight: "F-l" (shout) "i" (clap and jump) "g-h-t" (three leaps) "spells flight!" (students fly to the end of the diagonal).

Spelling Plus Word Comprehension

Words like *turn* and *friend* can connect spelling and meaning. For *turn* the children pick five different ways to turn and accompany each with a loud "t-u-r-n." *Friend* is approached through partners: Each pair moves across the diagonal in a "friendly way" while shouting "f-r-i-e-n-d." Some results from previous years: One child gave another a piggyback ride and they shouted the spelling simultaneously; two held hands and took turns jumping, and with each jump the children shouted the next letter of the word; one pair did leapfrog, and the person jumping over spelled *friend* quickly in the air.

Movement can be incorporated in some very unlikely places, like helping children learn how to spell the 13 colonies. A sixth grade teacher presented this challenge, and it certainly tested my movement-can-teach-almost-anything ingenuity. We tackled the problem through pantomime and puns. I divided the class into 13 groups. Each group got a card with the name of a colony. Their instructions were simple: "Do the spelling of your colony so that it will be remembered." The only other suggestion I made was to divide large words into smaller pieces. One of the most ingenious results came from *Connecticut*: Two girls put their arms over each other's shoulder and shouted "connect—c-o-n-n-e-c-t"; they then pointed to their eyes and shouted "i"; they then pretended to cut, "cut—c-u-t." (Even I remember how to spell it now.) Another good example was *New Hampshire*: Three boys strolled out pretending to display new clothes, "new—n-e-w"; acted and sounded like pigs, "ham—h-a-m"; pretended to spray their underarms (as in a TV commercial for a deodorant called "Sure") "sure—p-s-h-i-r-e." Yes, the pronunciations were a little strange and the syllabification was way off, but the results were memorable.

Literature

Having started with letters and moved on to words, let us progress to the ways in which movement can enrich literature. The power of dancing stories is that the meaning literally comes to life. Words that might have been glossed over take on deeper significance, and the sequence of the story becomes clear. The children and I have two favorites: *Bears in the Night*, by Stan and Jan Berenstain, and *Where the Wild Things Are*, by Maurice Sendak.

The Bears in the Night Dance was designed for young children, preschool to third grade, but it has been repeatedly requested by fourth through sixth graders. The room setup looks a little like an obstacle course: In it are a stegel with a slide attached, a stack of five pillows on the edge of a mat, a table, the parachute partially spread out, two sets of two mats with a small space between them, tires randomly placed in one area, and the incline mat. In the middle of the room are two large mats, one on top of the other, as in figure 11.7.

The children, a third to a half of the class, lie between the mats as if they were in bed with a cover on them; the rest of the class sits on one side of the room and has a participatory audience role. "In bed," I say, and the children under the mats begin to snore. The audience section of the class chants an eerie "Whoooo," and the performers lift their heads as if surprised. "Out of bed," I call, and they get out of bed and start creeping toward

the stegel. They go to and through the window (the top of the stegel). I repeat this until they have all gotten to the window; then they go "down the tree" by sliding down the slide. "Over the wall"—they jump the foam wall; "and under the bridge"—they crawl under the table; "around the lake"—they run around the parachute. I repeat these first instructions several times so that the children catch up around the lake. "Between the rocks"—they squeeze between the two sets of mats; "and through the woods"—they walk around the tires as if the tires were tree trunks. I repeat these next instructions as often as needed so that the children climb "Spook Mountain" (the incline mat) together. "Whoooo," the audience yells. The performers scream and reverse the sequence as fast as they can: "Down Spook Mountain, through the woods, between the rocks, around the lake, under the bridge, over the wall, up the tree, through the window, and back in . . . back in . . . back in . . . bed!"

Following are a few detail notes: It is best to read the book the day before and tell the class that they will dance the story as told in the book but not exactly. I take a bit of liberty repeating some of the directions so that everyone catches up before jumping the wall and while running around the lake. Before we start, I rehearse the audience starting and stopping their "Whooo"

① "IN BED"
② "THROUGH THE WINDOW" AND "DOWN THE TREE"
③ "OVER THE WALL"
④ "UNDER THE BRIDGE"
⑤ "AROUND THE LAKE"
⑥ "BETWEEN THE ROCKS"
⑦ "THROUGH THE WOODS"
⑧ "UP SPOOK MOUNTAIN"

11.7

sound on my signal. And of course, we do the dance twice so the audience and performers can switch places.

The Bears in the Night Dance is simple because the equipment and wording of the story tell the children exactly what to do. The Where the Wild Things Are Dance is a bit more difficult because they have to remember the moves as for a dance. This dance was designed for third to sixth grades, but it can be done with mature younger classes. Wild Things starts with the whole class closely bunched up in the middle of the room, standing straight and looking solemn. I begin with Max "making mischief"; the tambourine sounds and the children literally make mischief for a few minutes. (See mischief ideas further on.) When the tambourine stops, they immediately freeze; three hits on the tambourine bring them running back to the middle of the room. I point threateningly and call them "wild things." The children put their hands on their hips and adopt a very sassy manner—"I'll eat you up," they shout. So Max is sent to bed; the children drop where they are and pretend to sleep. As the vines grow in his room, the children slowly lift and twist one of their limbs, then continue growing to standing. "Until his ceiling hung with vines and the walls became the world all around"—arms grow to a full extension overhead; on "world" the hands stretch open, and then the arms travel sideways down for "the world all around." The children stand and rock side to side pretending to be on a boat until they get "to where the wild things are," when they stop abruptly. The children then roar, gnash their teeth, roll their eyes and heads, and lift hands splayed like claws. When Max says "BE STILL!" the children point their index fingers as if instructing on "be" and immediately crouch, hands on knees, for "still." They stay crouched and stare into the audience's eyes. Then, in unison, they raise one arm and cry out with Max, "And now let the rumpus start!" The children dance like monsters, first individually, then with partners, and finally in groups of three to five. We create a real "rumpus" by having many different props going at one time. One or a few children ride hoppities; some ride

scooters; some run around throwing scarves or foam pieces; some play with plastic hoops, balloons, and/or balls. In addition, a few children go under the parachute that comes out of a corner of the room like a billowing monster. It all adds up to colorful confusion. When Max says, "Now stop!" the tambourine sounds and the children immediately freeze as they are. With three hits of the tambourine they get off or out from under any equipment and start walking with a rocking motion back to the middle of the room. Having regrouped in the middle of the room, the class shouts the concluding line about Max's supper, "and it was still hot."

Following are some detail notes: As with *Bears in the Night*, it is best if the story is read the day before. Talk about the word *mischief* and establish that it means naughty. Clearly differentiate between *bad* and *mischief*, clarifying that *mischief* is only a little bad and does not ever hurt anyone or destroy anything. Come up with some ideas of how to demonstrate mischief in the movement room: running screaming, giving rabbit ears, climbing the mats, banging once or twice on the piano, climbing the bleachers, and so on. When an audience is invited to watch the dance, a wonderful form of mischief is to climb into the audience and tickle them. Practice making mischief when the tambourine sounds and immediately freezing when it stops; this is an extreme test of the Free Traveling Structure. If the class cannot stop the mischief correctly, I recommend not going on. When doing unison work, for example with "the world all around" or "let the rumpus start," demand that the class truly move as one unit. At the end, when the rumpus is frozen in place, make sure the children leave everything as is when they start to walk back to the middle of the room and that they do not step on, or even touch, any of the equipment. As with most dances, the only way this dance is funny is if the class works precisely. It is the contrast between their stiff, solemn stance and the unexpected chaos of the "mischief" and later the "rumpus" that is startlingly humorous; stopping the hoopla exactly on cue makes the movements into a cohesive whole, creating a real dance.

Both dances offer enormous vocabulary development. I especially like introducing The Bears in the Night Dance after the In and Out Game (p. 161) because the dance applies the relationship words in a different context. This technique of working with words in various contexts enriches their meaning and makes them memorable. *Mischief*, *rumpus*, *gnash*, and *ceiling* will be fully activated vocabulary after the children have done The Where the Wild Things Are Dance. On a broader scope, the difficult precision work demanded by both these dances will help them on the continual quest for self-discipline and mastery work. Once polished, these dances make wonderful shows: The Bears in the Night Dance will need to be presented first in a show so that the equipment can be ready; it can be quickly dismantled after the dance. The Where the Wild Things Are Dance makes a wonderful, flashy ending to any performance.

Math

Math is logic. It is the ability to look at the world as an organized, quantifiable system. Some children have a natural affinity for the order and correctness of math while others find it foreign. As with language, all children benefit from personal, sensory experience with numbers, equations, and geometric shapes.

Numbers

Body shapes can form numbers, just as they can letters. In making numbers I like to use the quantity as well as the shape: 2s made by two children, 3s made by three children, 10 made by 10 children, and so on. The way to form the larger numbers is to line children up and see the number as if from above (bird's-eye view), as in figure 11.8. With young children these large numbers need teacher assistance.

Interesting patterns come out of number shapes plus quantity. For example, a group of six makes one 6 and then divides up the 6 any way they want. They could have six separate 1s, or three 2s (each made by two children), or two 3s (each made by three children), or a 4 and a 2 (made by a group of four and a pair of children). We put the pattern into an ABA form; that is, the beginning and

11.8

ending are the same with something different in the middle. The six children begin with their 6; they divide up and show one or two equivalences, for example, 3 and 3 and then 5 and 1; then they form the composite 6 again.

Like letter shapes, numbers can be outlined. Ask the children to clasp their hands together and outline the number shape in the air in front of them; with hands clasped it will easier to check if they are making the number correctly. The class can then attempt different parts of the body outlining numbers on different planes. With number outlines, I ask the children to make the shape the same number of times as the number; therefore we outline a 3 three times.

Floor patterns are as useful for number shapes as they are for letter shapes (see figure 11.9). Again I like to use quantity as much as possible, so for a floor pattern of a 2, I will ask for groups of two and we do the pattern twice. For older classes I also ask for two locomotor movements,

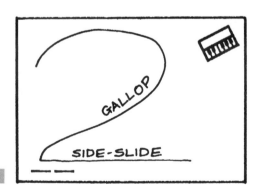

11.9

changing every two steps, for example walk-walk-jump-jump-walk-walk-jump-jump.

Combining techniques—body shapes, outlining, and floor patterns—creates some marvelous studies. You can ask the children to do the following, for example:

1. Do your telephone number, each number in a different way.

2. In groups of five, form a 5 out of all five of you. Break up and each of you do numbers in different ways that equal 5. Each group member does a number that in combination equals 5. For example, 1 + 0 + 1 + 3 + 0. Then rejoin and make the 5 again.

3. In groups of three, figure out a way to make a 1 in one beat, a 3 in 3 beats, a 7 in 7 beats, and a 13 in 13 beats.

4. In groups of four, pick a number and do it in as many ways as possible.

Geometry is especially well suited to movement activities. We discussed introducing horizontal, vertical, and diagonal in the In and Out Game and then reinforcing horizontal and vertical when exemplifying problem words. (Diagonal is probably solid because of the work using the Diagonal Structure.) It is always a good idea to extend these ideas to other applications (such as paper and pencil tasks and geo-boards), as well as to refer to them occasionally in other contexts. You might say, for example, "Put the book horizontally on the shelf; now place it vertically. Can you balance it diagonally?"

Angles

Angles were also introduced within the context of the In and Out Game. These also need wider applications, but I have found that children remember angles best if they are done sitting, with the angle exemplified by the hip joint. When working with any topic that requires an understanding of angles, my class is accustomed to dropping to the floor of the classroom and sitting with their legs straight in front of them, torso lifted vertically up, and calling, "Right angle." Bending over their legs, they call "Acute angle"; and hinging back while keeping the back straight, "Obtuse angle." I have not done it but would

foresee no problem in including the degrees, for example, "Right angle, 90 degrees."

Parallel and Perpendicular Lines

Parallel and perpendicular lines were also introduced in the all-purpose In and Out Game, but some wonderful additional activities can reinforce these concepts. Once the concepts are introduced with visual representations, I like to differentiate parallel from perpendicular. In the Free Traveling Structure, alternate locomotor movements with partner demonstrations of the two words as in the following example.

1. Students skip individually. Then they get a partner and show parallel lines on the standing level by standing equidistant from each other. One child remains standing. The other lies down or stands on one leg while tilting her body horizontally to show perpendicular lines.

2. Students hopscotch individually. They then get a partner and show parallel lines on the lowest level by lying down equidistantly. The partners then make a "T" with their prone bodies to show perpendicular lines.

3. Students run and leap individually. They then get a partner and show parallel lines on knee level by kneeling equidistantly. One child remains kneeling and lifts his arms up. The other child either lies down or gets on his hands and one knee with the other leg extended straight back to show perpendicular lines.

The next step from positions is moving in parallel and perpendicular lines. In the Free Traveling Structure, do one locomotor movement freely, then do the same movement forming parallel lines and perpendicular lines. For example: Do the locomotor side-slide; then ask for partners to side-slide together, not touching but remaining equidistant as they move; then ask the partners to side-slide making perpendicular lines across the room.

Parallel and perpendicular lines can be included in floor patterns, especially in work with geometric shapes. The ubiquitous floor pattern is perfect

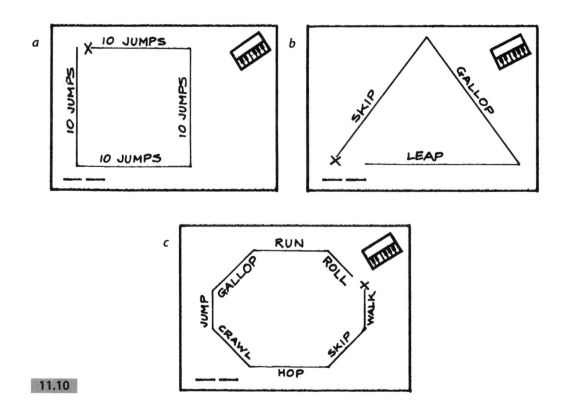

11.10

for teaching simple shapes: squares, rectangles, triangles, trapezoids, hexagons, and so forth, as in figure 11.10, a through c.

The shapes must be correct and exact or they will blur together. I am fussy that the angles are sharp, and I ask for military corners. Also it is important that any equal lines be executed the same length. You can make the two long sides of a rectangle one movement and the two short sides one movement, or you can have a different movement for each side as long as the sides measure equally. Doing a square with the same movement for each side, done for the exact same counts, is a concrete reinforcement of the concept of equal sides; but it is not much fun and is totally uninteresting to watch. A good study for geometric shapes is to give groups of children one to three designated shapes. The groups draw and perform their shapes without ever repeating a locomotor movement.

Circumference, Diameter, and Radius

Circumference, diameter, and radius can be quickly cemented by use of the parachute. Lay the parachute on the floor and take a step away. Show a card with *circumference* and identify it as the outside edge of a circle; ask for a few children to individually walk the circumference of the parachute. Do the same with *diameter* and *radius.* Then call out a child's name, hold up one of the three words, and have that child execute the walk until everyone has had a turn. (You do not have to wait until one child has completed her line before going on to the next as long as you can keep track that the lines are done correctly.) Spend a short time with this vocabulary work, because the class will be eager to do other parachute activities. When using the parachute for academic work, always plan for time to play with it.

Computations

There are two math activities I do regularly: group divisions and the Foam Jump. These are done without special emphasis; the academic results come from using them often. When I ask a class to divide into groups, ready to move across the diagonal, I follow a set procedure. I ask for a certain group division, for example,

"Get into groups of four." (When the term sets was popular it was "sets of four.") Only those children who are in groups of four can line up. If the class divides up evenly, I say, "Wow, this class divides evenly into fours" and we proceed to skip count by fours, pointing to each group as we go. If the class did not divide evenly, the remaining children stand aside: "Congratulations [I shake their hands], you are the remainders. Remainders get to pick any group they want to join." If the number of remainders was one or two, they would choose two separate groups to join; a remainder of three would form their own, smaller group. This whole procedure—dividing, counting, distinguishing the remainders—takes under 5 minutes. When it is done regularly the children become very comfortable with division, skip counting, and remainders. Also, since we all have to be remainders sometimes, it is nice to take the stigma out of it.

The other computation activity I use regularly is the Foam Jump. This game is described fully in chapter 9. The children line up on one side. Foam pieces are stacked in front of a mat, and the children formulate a mathematical sentence before they jump, for example, "I want to jump 6; there are 9, subtract 3" or "I want to jump 10; there are 6, add 4." What I love about the Foam Jump is that numbers become very real: Eight pieces of foam are clearly harder to jump over than four.

One more computation activity is doing sums with locomotor movements. "Do four jumps . . . Add two steps . . . The sum of both movements is what? Now do the four jumps and the two steps while I count the sum, 1, 2, 3, 4, 5, 6. On what count do you change from the jump to the steps? Great! Let's try another one: Hop seven times . . . Add nine skips . . . Add one jump turn . . . What is the sum of all those movements? Do them while I count the sum." You can add larger numbers, for example 10 steps, 12 gallops, 15 skips, or a longer series of numbers like one jump, plus two jumps, plus three jumps, plus four jumps, plus five jumps. You can count the sum or keep a steady beat on the drum and let the children count. This type of lesson needs to be kept short and light. Just slip one computation in when doing some other locomotor movements.

Patterning

Recognizing and creating patterns are important to both math and language development. They are a form of mental discipline that teaches children to think clearly and logically. Pattern continuation is a consistent component of standardized tests. This is an enormous subject—worthy of an entire book—but here I present a few suggestions.

Naming Syllable Patterns

Naming syllable patterns is a good activity for the beginning of the year. Gathered together on the floor, we pick several names and accent their syllables in three ways: clapping hands, slapping thighs, and snapping fingers. For example, we might do Harry (two claps), John (one slap on the thighs), Margarita (four snaps). We then put all the names together, ideally with no break in between, and move on to three different names.

It is also possible to include body movements with the hand gestures. In the sequence just mentioned, this might be Harry (two claps plus two walks), John (one slap plus a jump), Margarita (four snaps plus four hip thrusts side to side). Here are two more examples:

1. Kim (one clap plus a hop), Leticia (three slaps plus three skips), Jack (one snap plus a contract)
2. Randy (two claps plus two jazzy walks), David (two slaps plus two jumps), Cynthia (three snaps plus three swings)

Linear Patterns

There are any number of ways to create a linear sequence: using colored counting squares, Unifix® cubes, junk boxes (like collections of keys, buttons, bottle caps, and nuts, normally used for math sorting), pattern blocks, or simply paper squares in various colors. Let us look at paper squares as an example: The children create a horizontal pattern as in figure 11.11.

We can give this color sequence letter names, starting with "A," in which case this pattern would be A-B-B-A-B-B-A-B-B. We can assign different letters, for example, X-Y-Y . . . , B-O-O . . . , and so

11.11

forth. We can designate the sequence with numbers (e.g., 1-2-2 . . . , 18-300-300 . . .), food (e.g., apple-cookie-cookie . . .), toys (e.g., skateboard-video game-video game . . .), and movement (e.g., jump-step-step . . . , step-swing-swing . . . , strike-skip-skip . . .). In studies, groups of children first create a linear sequence and then represent it with letters, numbers, food, toys, sports, animals, and so on and finally with a movement pattern that they demonstrate.

Pattern blocks—those colorful math manipulative blocks that come in six geometric shapes—create beautiful designs. For linear sequences, the design must be one horizontal line with a repeated pattern, as in figure 11.12, a through c.

If a child creates a sequence that has many different blocks in succession, the subsequent movement work will be too difficult. I simply say that the work will be too hard and substitute some blocks so there are more of the same in a row. For example, figure 11.13a would be simplified to figure 11.13b.

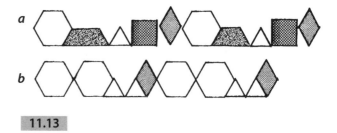

11.13

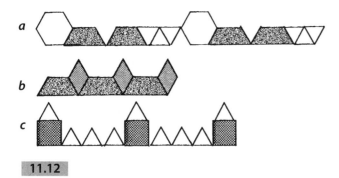

11.12

As with the colored squares, the children choose movements that represent their patterns. The block shapes may stand for any movements as long as a given block always represents the same movement and the movements are done precisely the number of times shown. The children practice their movement patterns until they can do them perfectly without looking at the blocks. Some examples are in figure 11.14, a through c.

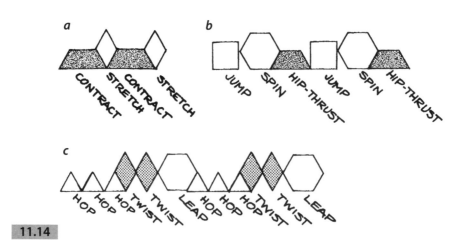

11.14

Patterns can be found almost anywhere: on a shirt, in books, on furniture. There are accidental patterns found on a walk—arrangements of fences, cars, buildings, cracks in the sidewalk, patterns on or formed by leaves and trees. The children like to surprise me with hidden patterns: "Look, our shoes make the pattern gym shoe—gym shoe—boot—gym shoe—gym shoe—boot." The trick with patterning is to do it less than the children want to. If kept light and gamelike, patterning is fun. If done too often or too intensely, patterning can become overwhelming and dull.

In the patterning work discussed so far, each item in the sequence represented one specific movement. Patterns can also be seen as larger forms, represented by figure 11.15.

11.15   A   B   A

In this pattern, traditionally called an ABA form, each geometric shape represents an entire phrase of music or dance. It is worth telling the children that patterns can be tiny, dot-dash-dot, or huge, earth-sun-earth. This type of larger form is very useful for transforming class studies into unified pieces. For example, if the children create an eight-beat study, say, a level study, have them perform the study for A and do free locomotor movements for 16 beats for B, returning to their original spots ready to repeat the study for A again. If the class has mastered a gymnastics routine (see chapter 8), have them perform the routine for A, move freely off the mats for B, and repeat the routine for A. The ABA form

11.16

can be extended into a rondo form, ABACADA, represented by figure 11.16.

This extended form is especially useful for

1. grouping the children's work into one whole and
2. tiring them out.

The class learns a simple study that they do for the repeated A-pattern. In between, each group presents its own completed study. The result is that the individual studies are sequenced into one whole. If A is represented by an entire gymnastics or exercise routine and B, C, and D are represented by different locomotor movements, the whole pattern covers a lot of movement. The class will get a terrific workout without even knowing it.

One specific larger form has been mentioned in connection with the Row, Row, Row Your Boat Dance (chapter 6) and prop studies (chapter 9). The larger form will be used again with the Pachelbel Canon Dance (chapter 12)—this is the canon or round. The form can be represented visually as in figure 11.17.

This representation shows a sequence of three phrases repeated once. The children are in two groups, with the second group starting one phrase later than the first. A canon can be done with any number of phrases and any number of groups, but it is harder than it looks. Also, in this example, each phrase is of equal length. Technically the

++++++++◆◆◆◆◆◆◆◆●●●●●●●●++++++++◆◆◆◆◆◆◆◆●●●●●●●●●
  ++++++++◆◆◆◆◆◆◆◆●●●●●●●●++++++++◆◆◆◆◆◆◆◆●●●●●●●●●

11.17

phrases could be of differing lengths, but I would not recommend that except for the most advanced classes. Movement canons are most clear when the phrases are very different. Here are a few examples; in each case subsequent groups come in one phrase later:

1. Skip—roll—jazzy walk
2. Somersaults on a mat—free locomotor movements off the mats—balance on one foot near the mat, ready to begin again
3. Partner run and leap—partner spin—partner Wheelbarrow—partner hop

Symmetry and Asymmetry

A specific form of patterning relates to symmetry (in which two sides match when folded) and asymmetry (where they do not). To teach these concepts I introduce the words but do not tell what they mean: "Here are two new words: symmetry and asymmetry. (We practice saying them.) I'm not going to tell you what they mean; you are going to have to guess." I position myself in a symmetrical shape and announce, "Symmetry"; taking an asymmetrical shape I say, "Asymmetry." After a few examples, I ask the children if they can guess what the words mean. Very often they will throw in other elements, for example, "Symmetry is straight and asymmetry is contract." Rather than just say "no," I show a contracted symmetrical position and a straight asymmetrical position. Someone will eventually conclude that symmetry means the same on both sides and that asymmetry means different-shaped sides. If the students give up, I simply tell them. Even if I end up having to tell them, children like this guessing game and are more receptive to the information than if it had simply been told to them.

We go on to make symmetrical shapes out of our bodies. In order to avoid the adjective form of the words, I say "Put your body in a shape that has symmetry." To get greater variety, I ask for different levels and on occasion ask the children to stay in their shapes, pick a locomotor movement, and travel.

The next step is making symmetrical shapes with a partner. I prefer partners taking shapes side by side so that we can identify the line of symmetry and what limbs are inside (close to

the line of symmetry) and what limbs are outside (farther from the line of symmetry). If partners are essentially just standing there, I will ask for one person to take a very asymmetrical shape and then for his partner to make it symmetrical by matching it, as in figure 11.18. This is also a good time to introduce or revisit Mirror and Shadow (chapter 7).

11.18

When the concepts of symmetry and asymmetry are understood, it is time to apply them to floor patterns. An example of a simple symmetrical floor pattern is seen in figure 11.19. The class divides into partners, each starting at an "X"; partners move at the same time.

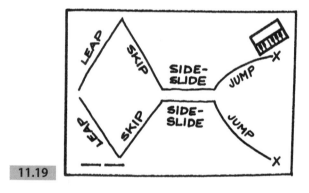

11.19

More examples of symmetrical floor patterns are shown in figure 11.20, a through c.

Asymmetrical patterns are formed by two sets of children doing totally different lines, as in figure 11.21. An interesting study on asymmetry is to ask that both lines be completed within the same number of beats.

Group studies using symmetry are done in groups of four; two children do one side while two do the other. The pairs actually move in parallel lines while executing the symmetrical design—and this differentiation is worth point-

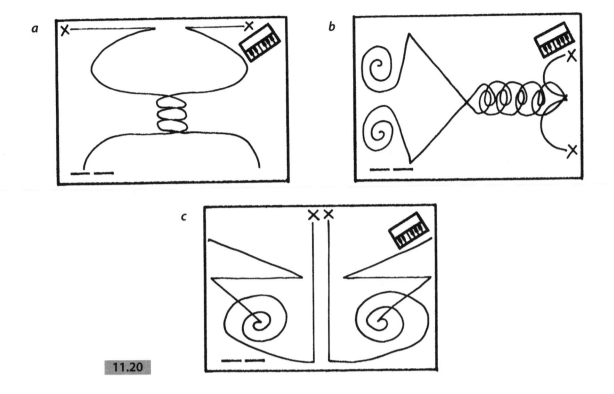

11.20

11.21

vocabulary development). This is a wonderful synthesis of many concepts. If the children have just completed a symmetrical floor pattern, especially using sophisticated locomotor movements, sit down and appreciate how far they have come: They have incorporated spatial design, visual perception, memory, muscular control, cooperation, language, social skills, and concentration. We have come a long way from that first floor pattern when they were saying, "This is a cinch."

Closing Thoughts

ing out. The studies could be done in partners, but there are disadvantages: (1) It takes too long to show everyone's pattern; and (2) if someone's partner is absent, the study cannot be shown. If there is an uneven division, say a group of five, the design can remain symmetrical by having two people do one line while three do the other side. My favorite assignment is for groups of four to design a symmetrical floor pattern using different line shapes and then do locomotor movements that I assign from the list of sophisticated movements presented earlier (in the section on

Traditional physical education classes have usually been mindlessly strenuous. Strenuousness I approve of, mindlessness I do not. Progressive dance classes are often fun but chaotic. Fun is great but chaos is unworkable. It is hard to reach a happy medium with movement. Children love it and get exuberant. If the teacher structures too much, the class gets rigid; and if not enough, it gets wild. The solution (yes, I will venture a solution) comes from two ingredients necessary for growth: goals and expectations. To me, that is the academic spirit.

The key to an effective use of movement is considering it a subject with clearly defined goals. A subject with goals makes the class purposeful and directed. Certainly there will be sidetracks and activities that are just for fun, just as in any subject; but there will also be direction and achievement. And these achievements will be clearly visible to the children as well as to you. When the class masters group symmetrical floor patterns, when they perform a dance flawlessly, when they remember a six-part Brain Catcher, they know themselves that they have grasped new information. Children have often told me, "I like your class because you teach me things."

Further, the expectations within the class need to be clear and need to reflect high standards. Just as we do not accept slipshod reading and incorrect math, we must know what we want from a movement study and get it. If the children are to stop in the middle of the room and they run three-quarters of the way across, the movement is incorrect and needs to be done again. If they are to shake for four beats and they shake for five, they need to be corrected. Corrections are best done nicely, even gently, but they need to be done firmly. We must know what we want in movement class, what is great and what is not so good, what is acceptable and what is not. Our expectations need to be clear both behaviorally and academically. When we say, "Excellent," it needs to be true. Movement is an invaluable tool as long as we make it a tool of the highest quality.

Chapter 12

Advanced Work

We have come a long way. The children know the fundamental language of movement: They are at ease with locomotor and nonlocomotor movements, levels, directions, and floor patterns. They have enjoyed working together and with props; they have used movement to reinforce some academic skills. Most importantly, the children are becoming at ease with their bodies and with basic movement vocabulary; they enjoy moving and are confident in their physical ability. We are ready to move on. It is time to attempt more difficult physical challenges, time to incorporate new and difficult concepts, time for longer and harder studies. The crux of more advanced work is not any particular element. It is a quality of richness, a multilayered mixture of concepts that turns movement into dance. Studies are no longer simply geared to teach an idea or practice a step—although they still do. They now become a form of communication, which is art. There are three basic areas of advanced skills: more difficult physical challenges, concepts, and dances.

Advanced Physical Challenges

Physical challenges require the body to be extended by demanding more strength, flexibility, and endurance in addition to greater coordination and control. Let us look at how physical chal-

lenges would apply to exercises, warm-ups, and movement sequences.

Exercises

As the children get older and more experienced, the exercises we do change in two ways:

- They become more strenuous.
- They become more pure exercises as opposed to rhythmic games and stories.

Here are a few examples of more difficult exercises:

1. **Back wave.** This is a marvelous initial exercise to warm up the back. Children sit with the soles of their feet together, torso rounded down "nose to toes." They pull the torso back ("as if you were socked in the stomach")—count 1; lift the torso straight up—count 2; arch (chest pushed forward, shoulders and head pulled back)—count 3; lean forward with the arched back as low as possible and then round to the original position—count 4. This progression can be smoothed into one continuous movement that looks like a wave. I normally do 10 back waves, starting slowly and gradually speeding up.

2. **Body wave warm-up.** See chapter 4.

3. **Leg stretches.** Sit with one leg straight and the bent leg forward (see figure 4.20 in chapter 4). Stretch over the straight leg, shoulders parallel to the floor, for eight beats and then open the torso

to the front and stretch for another eight beats. Swing over the bent leg, placing a hand near the seat, and lift the torso up to the knee level; hold for a few seconds and then swing back over the straight leg to sit down. Do the swing four times, preferably as one fluid motion. Switch the leg positions and repeat the entire sequence.

→ SAFETY

When I was young we always bounced to stretch but now that is a no-no. The contraction of the muscle while bouncing actually prevents a lengthening that is needed to increase flexibility. It is better to stretch by pulling and breathing into a relaxation of the muscle so that it can extend farther.

4. **"Killer" leg and back stretch.** Sit with legs in wide stride and stretch forward to prepare the legs and back. Lift the back straight up, lean sideways over one leg, grasp the hands together and swing low to the other leg, unclasp the hands and open the torso to the front (that is the killer part), and lift the torso straight again. Alternate sides six times.

5. **Abdominal contractions.** Start lying on the back. Contract the abdominal muscles and lift the back and legs so that the body is balanced on the seat. Hold for a few seconds and lower—with control—to the prone position. Start with 20 repetitions and work up to 100. It is possible to do these contractions angled to either side or with the torso twisted opposite the legs. At the end, push into a bridge-contract-shoulder stand, to stretch the abdominal muscles out.

6. **Abdominal crunches.** Crunches are small contractions of the abdomen done in five leg positions:

a. Lie down with legs bent, feet on the floor. The hands are behind the head, but do not push the neck forward; the head rests in the hands. The abdomen contracts causing the head and torso to lift up to about a 45° angle.

b. Lie with one leg bent, foot on the floor, the other leg crossing the first with the ankle resting on the knee (see figure 12.1); hands are behind the head. The torso lifts and twists so that one elbow touches the opposite knee, for example left elbow to right knee.

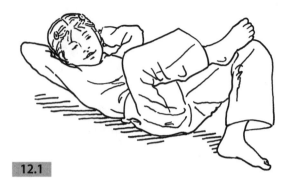

12.1

c. Repeat the preceding position with the legs switched.

d. Lie with knees close to the chest, hands behind the head. Touch both elbows to the knees; the lower abdomen gets a better workout if the knees move toward the elbows rather than the elbows moving toward the knees.

e. Continuing with the knees close to the chest, hands behind the head, twist and touch one elbow to the opposite knee and immediately switch to touch the other elbow to the other knee—both moves are counted as one. Do 10 crunches in each position (for 50 abdominal contractions) and work up to 20 in each position.

Of course movement class must be appropriately strenuous. Children need to be developed rather than arbitrarily pushed. Ideally this development results from the child's inner drive. Sometimes this drive needs to be activated: "Lie down, close your eyes, and picture the Olympic athletes. Do you think those incredible track stars stop running when they feel a little tired? Can you picture how hard a gymnast practices stretching every day? How many abdominal contractions do you think hockey or basketball or volleyball players do every day? Hundreds, maybe thousands. Doing eight of this or that, working half-heartedly, working only when you think I am watching you, will not get you anywhere. You need to push yourself. Feeling a bit tired or feeling your muscles strain a little will not hurt you—I'm not talking about real pain, that is a warning sign to stop—I mean the feeling that you would rather be playing video games. Push yourself beyond that. We have to raise your standards. We might not be Olympic athletes, but let's be the best that we can be." (I want to say right here that I used the "be the best that we can be" phrase way before the army did.)

Warm-Ups

More difficult warm-ups encompass strenuous exercises, more difficult steps, combinations of concepts, and a faster pace. By including more movements, the children are vigorously active for the entire 10- to 15-minute warm-up period. They are building up strength and endurance as well as reviewing a lot of movement vocabulary. Here are some examples:

Warming Up With Gymnastics

1. Sitting on the mats, warm up the neck with slow circles of the head in both directions, side-to-side tilts, and pressing the head forward with the hands gently to stretch the back of the neck.
2. Warm the back with 10 back waves as described earlier; then rock back and forth several times, stretching the legs to touch the floor behind the head and, using the forward momentum, touching the toes in front of the body.
3. Stretch the legs in a wide stride and then do the "killer" stretch described previously.
4. Do 100 abdominal crunches.
5. Do 20 push-ups.
6. Bridge-contract-shoulder stand three times.
7. Do continuous somersaults and jump up (make sure the somersaults all go in the same direction, so children cannot roll into one another).

Warming Up by Alternating Locomotor and Nonlocomotor Movements

1. Locomotor movement one-legged skip with the leg in front (switch legs); one-legged skip with the leg bent to the side (switch legs); one-legged skip with the leg straight back (switch legs). Sequence one of each of these skips: leg front, leg side, leg back. Do the sequence several times with the same leg lifted each time and then switch legs so that the other leg lifts.
2. Nonlocomotor movements contract, stretch, limp repeated on all levels, starting from the lowest and moving up to air level.
3. Locomotor movement jumping side to side and then jumping full turns, practicing turning right and left. Sequence four side-to-side jumps (beats 1-4), jump turn to the right (beats 5-6), jump turn to the left (beats 7-8)—repeat five times.
4. Nonlocomotor movement swing: four swings front and back, four cross swings, four side swings, four twist swings—the last twist spinning around ready to repeat. Repeat the sequence in twos and then do each swing once flowing into the next (see chapter 4).
5. Locomotor movement waltz walk and waltz-walk turns. Sequence two straight waltz walks, then one waltz-walk turn right, one waltz-walk turn left—repeat eight times.
6. Nonlocomotor movements bend, straighten, twist on all levels starting from the air level and moving down to lowest level.
7. Locomotor movements run and leap. Put a run and leap with the waltz-walk pattern: two straight waltz walks, one waltz-walk turn right, one waltz-walk turn left, two straight waltz walks, run-run-run-leap.

Warming Up With a Prop: Balls

1. Dribble and run; speed up to race, then sprint and dribble.
2. Dribble the ball with the feet; dribble and dodge.
3. Carry the ball behind one knee and hop, switch legs.
4. Put the ball between the ankles, jump it up, and catch it.
5. Put the ball between the knees and do 100 abdominal exercises.
6. Put the ball on the floor and, without placing weight on it, do push-ups over it.
7. Throw the ball up, spin, and catch it.
8. Throw the ball hand to hand and skip.

9. Throw the ball gently in the air and run and leap.

10. With a partner, sit wide stride and roll two balls back and forth.

11. With a partner, pass two balls and walk, jog, run.

Sequences

Sequences become harder in three ways:

- The steps themselves are more difficult; for example, a waltz walk is much trickier than an ordinary walk.

- There are fewer of one kind of movement; for example, one skip and one gallop is much more difficult than four skips and four gallops.

- The rhythm of the pattern is more complex.

In the catalog of locomotor movements, the more difficult steps are waltz walk, grapevine, bridge crawl, one-legged skip, straddle roll, kicks in the air, and stag leap. The more difficult nonlocomotor movements are hinges, spiral twist sit, and falls in general. These movements can be taught to beginners, but they require a great deal of control to do properly. Of course you can make any movement more challenging by adding a nonlocomotor movement or placing it in a pattern.

In choreographing for children I use the following progression of difficulty. Very young children do best with phrases rather than exact counts. "First we'll skip, then we'll jump"—the rhythm might be eight beats of skip and eight beats of jump, but the children do not have to count. They could do 10 or 6 skips within the phrase, but they change moves to a sound cue. For young children I would be loath to ever go under an eight-beat phrase for one movement, and I never ask for specific right and left steps. By second and third grade, children can count beats, but anything under four beats for one movement is quite difficult. (I am not saying not to do it. I have taught third graders hard dances, but I am aware that I am asking for a coordination stretch.) Also, at this level I rarely ask for right and left. One would think that fourth graders on up would welcome physical challenges—and they do—but

if the students have never had movement experience, some of these steps might be overwhelming. Even adults attempting a waltz walk for the first time get frustrated. The key for inexperienced older children is to have a few physical challenges and create the illusion of complexity: Use current music, have long sequences but keep the phrases four to eight beats long, put the sequence into a canon form, use props, and alternate sections choreographed by the students with unison sequences. Experienced older children want—I would say even crave—truly difficult sequences and concepts such as those described in the next section.

We can heighten the difficulty of sequences by the actual steps, by the number of beats per move, and also by rhythmic complexity. The easiest rhythms are twos, fours, and eights, probably because we are symmetrical beings. Simply using counts of threes or even more complex counts of fives or sevens greatly increases the difficulty. Adding any different accent shifts, syncopation, and breaks in established patterns also makes things trickier. This is not to discourage you from tackling such challenges, only to make you aware of the level of sophistication you are asking for.

➡ TROUBLESHOOTING

Several years ago a student teacher created a lovely dance using move changes every two beats and requiring specific steps right and left, but it was for a kindergarten class. She was disappointed they were not getting it; we reconfigured it into phrases of eight and used "this side" or "that side" and—voilà—they grasped it immediately. Understanding the inherent difficulty of movement sequences is similar to knowing reading levels; we need to be aware of our students' capabilities and extend them without causing discouragement.

Advanced Concepts

It is clear what makes physical activities advanced: a lot of strength, flexibility, or coordination. What constitutes more advanced concepts is more subjective. Focus and dynamic quality require a more subtle integration of the body and an enormous amount of concentration. Falls and balance can extend into almost dangerous territory. But these are exciting regions, and traveling to them will greatly enrich the children.

Focus

Focus means directing and controlling the eyes. It is easy to understand but difficult to do. What makes focus difficult is the consciousness needed to control one's eyes—it is somewhat like controlling one's breathing. We are accustomed to breathing and to looking unconsciously; to do so consciously, we must concentrate.

I gather the children near me on the floor and ask if anyone has heard of the word focus.

"What you do to a camera."

"You twist it [the focusing mechanism] on binoculars."

"When the focus is out the TV is broken."

"Good. In all these examples focus has to do with seeing clearly. Focus in movement means to look at something hard." As I say this, I focus on one child and point with my finger: "I am focusing on Andrew." I focus on and point at several different children.

The children then focus on and point at different objects and people. At this beginning stage, pointing is important because it helps the children remember what they are doing, and it helps you to see if they are focusing on what they think they are. For example, if the children are told to focus on the ceiling, often their fingers will point up while their heads look straight ahead. It is worth showing them what they look like. Once the children understand what focus is, we practice changing focus while remaining stationary: "Focus on me; focus on the ceiling; focus on the floor; focus on the clock; focus on the piano; focus on your neighbor's eyes [giggles]; focus on your own tummy; focus on your own big toe."

The next step is to focus while doing locomotor movements. The children get into groups of three ready to move on the diagonal. I place something attention-grabbing in the middle of the room. (If you are planning to work with a prop later that day, use that prop as the focal point. For example, if you are going to play with the parachute later, put it in the middle of the room; if you are going to work with scarves, dump the whole box of scarves in the middle of the room.) One of my favorite props is a bouquet of bright paper flowers sprayed with cologne. I ask each group to focus (eyes and fingers) on the flowers, walk to them, smell them, and continue walking to the end of the diagonal. They are never to lose their focus. This is not easy. From the middle to the end of the diagonal, the children will either have to walk backward or turn their head sharply back as in figure 12.2.

12.2

I ask the children who are waiting for their turn to help me check the focus of the children who are moving. After walking and focusing on a central object, we repeat the exercise skipping, galloping, and running. Do not do this, or any focus problem, for very long. It takes a lot of concentration to focus for even a few minutes. It is better for children to succeed in focusing while moving across the diagonal once than to do it several times and lose their attention. This is a good exercise to review quickly and often.

Once the children are relatively at ease focusing on a central object while moving across the diagonal, we go on to harder focus problems.

1. I stand at one corner of the diagonal: "Focus on me as you side-slide on the diagonal . . . Now focus on me as you side-slide changing sides." The children like to focus on me; I ham it up and make faces at them. When I am the focus point it is also easier for me to see if they are doing it right and to make a commotion if they are not: "Hey, here I am, look at me!"

2. Have the children focus on the ceiling as they tiptoe to the middle of the room; focus on the floor as they low-walk (bent knee walk) from the middle to the end of the diagonal. Later, use a quicker change of focus by having four beats of tiptoe with the focus on the ceiling, then four beats of low-walk with the focus on the floor. Then ask for two beats of each.

3. Have interesting objects in the corners of the diagonal in which the children are not moving, that is, objects A and B in figure 12.3. The children hopscotch on the diagonal; they focus on object A for their jump and on object B for their hop. Therefore, the focus changes every beat. Past the middle, they have to do it backward or turn their head. But do not worry—if they can do it just to the middle, that is great. This is extremely difficult.

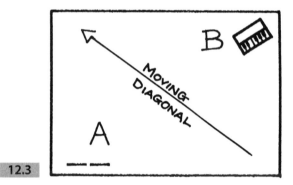

12.3

4. Place an interesting object (like yourself) at the end of the diagonal. The children focus on the object while doing a turning locomotor movement. I allow any kind of moving turn. This is the dance technique called spotting: The head turns as much as possible to keep the focus on the object and then snaps around to regain the focus without "seeing" anything else. So, with you as the focal point, the children look at you as long as they can twist their head, then whip around to immediately focus on you again. You might mention to the children that it is this technique of spotting that allows dancers to do those endless turns without getting dizzy.

5. Focusing is fun to do with a partner:

   a. Partners stand facing each other holding hands; they focus on each other's eyes and side-slide.

   b. Partners lie down on their bellies opposite each other and hold both hands; they focus on each other's eyes and roll.

   c. Partners stand facing each other holding both hands; they lean back a little and spin while keeping the focus on each other's eyes.

6. Focusing on one's own body while moving is a good coordination problem and provides interesting visual results:

   a. Focus on your own hand. Let your hand take you on a trip to the end of the diagonal. Your hand can go around you, above you, under you; all the while your eyes never lose sight of your hand.

   b. Focus on your own big toe as it leads you across the diagonal.

   c. Focus on your tummy, seat, elbow, or hip as it leads you across the diagonal.

7. Finally, include directed focus within a study. Pick a study the children have already learned. Incorporate several focus changes within the pattern. Later, pick one pattern and have the children individually decide where to include focus changes. It is very interesting to see the same pattern done with different focus changes.

There is a direct correlation between the ability to focus and attention span. Both result from self-discipline; they require an inner force to selectively pay attention and to ignore distractions. These are the very qualities that are necessary for any type of concentration. Children begin school unequal in their ability to focus, but focus is a skill that can be taught and developed in all children.

Dynamic Quality

Dynamic quality refers to the type of force projected in a movement. I distinguish three main dynamic qualities: percussive, sustained, and limp.

Percussive refers to moving quickly and sharply—percussive moves burst and freeze, jolting and stopping in a herky-jerky rhythm. Call out several movements and have the children do them percussively: contract, stretch, twist, strike, jump. The children then improvise their own percussive movements. Watch that the children do specific movements; it is easy for percussive movements to degenerate into a series of undifferentiated jerks.

Sustained refers to moving slowly and smoothly but with intensity. Call out several movements and have the children do them with a sustained quality: contract, stretch, bend, straighten, turn, step, fall. They then improvise their own sustained movements. Both percussive and sustained qualities use a lot of energy: Percussive movements burst with energy while sustained movements flow with a strong, constant force.

Limp quality is different in that the movements use as little energy as possible. Again the children try out movements I call out, doing them with a limp quality, and then improvise their own movements.

Now that we have distinguished the main dynamic qualities we are ready to use them in a study:

1. Teach a pattern that has specified dynamic qualities. For example, start standing and circle the arms with a sustained quality (beats 1-4); contract in a series of percussive contractions (beats 5-8); drop limply to the floor (beat 9 hold 10). Then balance on one knee and hand and stretch one arm and one leg with a sustained quality (beats 1-4); in that position, contract percussively (beat 5 hold 6) and stretch percussively while placing the extended foot on the floor—the result is a knee-foot position (beat 7 hold 8). Then do a series of percussive strikes (beats 9-12); stand and turn limply (beats 13-16). The pattern is actually quite simple, but adding dynamic qualities requires an additional element to remember and control.

2. Teach a basic, rather simple, pattern and have the children add their own dynamic qualities. For example, start standing and reach up, contract, fall back to the seat, rock back and then up to knee level, turn, and stand. The children individually designate a specific dynamic quality for each movement.

3. Do a semistructured improvisation using dynamic qualities. For example, do one movement percussively, do one movement sustained, do one movement limply, then go somewhere in no particular quality. The rhythm is percussive-sustained-limp; go somewhere-go somewhere-go somewhere stop. Repeat several times.

4. Do a group study using dynamic qualities. For example, pick three percussive, three sustained, and three limp movements and put them together in a remembered sequence.

Falls

"To fall means to lower your body. In movement class it does not mean to plop down and hurt yourself. You must control the lowering so that you never get hurt. There is a secret to this control: Whatever way your body is lowering, pull in the opposite direction." I demonstrate this secret: "I am going to fall back. Which way should I pull? Right, my arms, head, and torso all pull forward as I fall backward so there is no bump or jar. [I lower my seat to the floor and rock back.] If I want to fall to the right side, which way should I pull? Correct, I would pull my arms and torso to the left as my hips lower to the right. [I do a side fall, reaching to the left and falling right.] If I want to fall forward, which way should I pull? Correct, I should pull back. [I do a teeter-totter fall, lowering forward while pulling back with one leg.] This conceptual approach to falls opens up an enormous number of movement possibilities. The children try out their own ideas of possible falls under the condition that they absolutely cannot hurt themselves. The difficulty with falls is, of course, the control of energy. The child must stretch consistently throughout the movement or the body will collapse. If I see them getting sloppy, I instruct them to do their falls in slow motion.

After this general introduction, the children are ready to learn specific falls. I probably have introduced a number of falls throughout the year as I needed them for particular studies, but now they are reintroduced as examples of this overall concept. These are the basic falls:

1. Teeter-totter
2. Back fall
3. Side fall
4. Spiral twist fall
5. One-leg side fall
6. Lunge fall

Descriptions of these falls are found in the catalog of nonlocomotor movements, chapter 4.

Beautiful studies result from combining falls:

1. **Cat Dance.** This study is in two parts, each 12 beats long. The 12-beat sequences can stand by themselves, or the two parts can fit together.

Children start standing in Perfect Spots. Jump and land in a crouched position (the upbeat "and" for the jump, beat 1 for the landing); fall back onto the seat (beat 2); rock back (beat 3); rock up to sitting with the right foot and left knee on the floor (beat 4); lift the seat up without using hands, weight on the left knee (beat 5); lift to standing (beat 6); teeter-totter fall, ending on the abdomen (beats 7-10); pull seat back to ankles and lift body up to the knees (beats 11-12). Figure 12.4 shows beats 3 to 6.

12.4

From the knees, do a side fall (beats 1-2); roll once toward the back of the room (beats 3-4); curl up to the knees, facing the front of the room (beats 5-6); do a side fall to the other side (beats 7-8); roll once to the back of the room again (beats 9-10); curl up to the knees facing the front of the room and stand (beats 11-12).

These two 12-beat patterns join to make one long study. It is very effective to divide the class in half and do the study as a canon.

2. **Fall Dance.** Children start standing in Perfect Spots. Lift the left leg to a T balance (like the teeter-totter balance, described in chapter 4); contract while balanced on the right leg and shoot the left leg out into a low lunge position as in figure 12.5.

Fall to the side and roll once, straightening the legs wide for a second while on the back, and end on the knees. Do a side fall; roll back once again straightening the legs wide for a second,

12.5

and immediately push up to the knees and stand. Do a spiral fall; spin on the seat and shoot the legs back as the torso falls forward, ending flat on the abdomen. Lift up to standing (reversed teeter-totter fall) ready to start again.

There are no counts. The exact movements are not as important as the feeling of fluidity. The pattern should flow like waves continuously rising, falling, breaking and ebbing.

Balance

As with falls, I introduce balance conceptually before working with specific balances. And as with falls, the difficulty with balance work is that it requires a great deal of consistent control. Balance requires even more control than falls because it is a management of energy while the body is still. To be in balance, the body must be centered and the weight pulled up. It is easier to exert energy while moving than while standing still.

"Balance means being steady, not falling. Some positions are easier to balance in than others. For example, standing on two feet is an easy way to balance; standing on one foot is a little harder; standing on half a foot (the ball of the foot) is much harder." The children explore different ways of balancing. Ideally, they have access to mats as well as cleared floor space so that they can try some more precarious balances like headstands and handstands. After the class has had a chance to freely explore different balances, I guide them in two ways: with level changes and with the number of body parts.

1. **Levels.** On the lowest level, balance on just the tummy and then in a no-hand shoulder stand (shown in figure 12.6, a and b).

   On seating level, balance on just the seat; then try half a seat (figure 12.7)

12.6

12.7

2. Run very fast to the middle of the diagonal and immediately balance in a strange shape, and hold; skip turning twice, reach up and fall down to the floor, immediately balance in a strange shape on the lowest level, and hold.

3. Use tables or ballet barres, if available, to practice this pattern. Stand on the left foot, and contract the right leg, torso, and head. Stretch the right leg to the side while stretching the torso to the left, taking a sideways T position (figure 12.8, a and b).

12.8

On knee level, balance on two knees and a hand, one knee and one hand: "Try balancing on your right knee and right hand; now on your right knee and left hand. Which was easier, the same side or opposite sides? Switch sides. Now balance on just one knee. On standing level, balance on one foot and one hand; balance on tiptoes; balance on one foot with eyes closed and on half-toe, heel lifted.

2. **Number of body parts.** Balance on seven parts of the body, on four parts of the body, on three parts, on two parts, one part, on half a part.

We are now ready for studies using difficult balances. Here are three teacher-taught patterns:

1. One straight waltz walk, one turn waltz walk, balance on half-toe for three beats, one-legged skip with the leg bent in front, one-legged skip with the leg straight back, three runs and then a leap, hold the ending balance for three beats. Each move gets three beats; therefore the pattern is eight measures of three beats.

Keep the right leg outstretched, and lift the torso and head vertically. Put the right leg down and side-slide to the right. Turn once and repeat the pattern using the other leg. After practicing this pattern using a table or barre, try it balancing without any help. Very hard.

Following are two teacher-structured group studies using balance:

1. Divide the class into groups of four and give each group a set of cards with the numbers 1, 2, 3, 4. Each group must have a different-colored set of cards; for example, group 1 has four red cards, group 2 has four green cards, and so on. Each group tapes their four cards in four different places throughout the room. They then pick four difficult balances, one for each number card, that they will hold for 10 seconds. In addition, they choose different locomotor movements traveling to each balance point. Possible result: Skip to card 1 and balance on one foot for 10 seconds; leap to card 2 and balance on half a seat; side-slide to card 3 and balance on one knee and one hand; crab crawl to card 4 and balance on one foot with the torso tilted. (Of course

any gymnastics balances would have to be done on mats.) Watch each group individually and then have all the groups perform at the same time.

2. Divide class into small groups. Have each group pick four to seven difficult balances and put them together in a sequence. With this study I often introduce the idea of transition. The groups can make the transitions between their balances as long or as short as they want, but the transitions must be planned, interesting, and smooth.

Finally, if you are feeling brave, this is the perfect time to work with group pyramids. Pyramids are architectural formations, usually involving children balanced on top of each other. The most common pyramid is three children on hands and knees on the bottom level, two on top of them, and one perched above the rest. But the sculptural designs can involve numerous other balances, such as headstands and handstands, one-foot balances, and so on. Most often pyramids attempt a symmetrical design. Figure 12.9 shows a four-person "block" formation flanked on either side with (attempted) headstands.

Once you have covered the basics of safety and respect, divide the class into larger groups—groups of six or eight are best. Cluster three or four mats in several areas of the room and have each group attempt their own pyramids. I offer my services as one of the bottom blocks if I am needed, but you must do what your body directs.

After the groups have had a chance to explore various pyramid formations I ask for a set study.

This is my favorite: Pick five different precarious balances and put them into a remembered sequence. One balance has to be individual, one balance in partners, and one balance in threes; and there have to be two different pyramid formations. Make the transitions between positions interesting and smooth. This study takes quite a bit of time and is somewhat noisy. Once perfected it makes a spectacular show.

⇒ SAFETY

Before trying out any child-on-child balances it is important to talk about safety and consideration. Instruct the children never to place their weight on another child's lower back; their weight must be divided between the shoulder blade area and the tailbone area of the bottom child. Their weight also must be divided between two bottom children so that no one is carrying another's full weight. (Once in a while, if a child is very light, this rule can be bent.) The child balancing on top must move very gently and carefully and avoid stepping on the bottom person's calves. Be very careful of self-image here. Unless a child is truly obese, all children get a turn at balancing at least on the middle level.

Advanced Dances

Verbal descriptions of movements are long, boring, and usually unclear. I will, however, describe two of my favorite advanced dances, the

12.9

Partner Dance and the Pachelbel Canon Dance, because the results are worth the effort.

The Partner Dance

The Partner Dance is in two parts, each 16 beats long. The children need to learn all 32 beats perfectly in order to do the pattern as intended. It is especially important that they do each move exactly at its specified count.

Part 1

The children start lying on their abdomens, facing the back of the room.

1. The right leg bends and initiates the movement lifting the body up to a sitting position facing the front of the room while the legs bend into a triangle position (counts 1 and 2). Figure 12.10a shows the beginning of this first move.

2. The children place their left hand by their seat and push up onto that hand and their feet; the hips and the right hand reach up (counts 3-4). (See figure 12.10b.)

3. The children sit back down in the triangle position (counts 5-6).

4. They then lie back down on their abdomens, facing the back wall (beats 7-8). (Counts 5-8 reverse the moves done for counts 1-4.)

5. From the prone position, they curl their toes under and push their seats up, as in a high push-up position (counts 9-10), shown in figure 12.10c.

6. Starting from this push-up position, the left leg crosses in back of the right leg while the left arm lifts up—the children end up balanced on two feet and the right hand (counts 11-12) as shown in figure 12.10d.

7. The torso, left foot, and left hand return to the high push-up position (counts 13-14).

8. The right foot lunges close to the chest and the left foot comes in; the child sits down with legs tucked close to the body, facing the right side of the room (counts 15-16).

12.10

Part 2

The children start sitting with their legs tucked close to the body, facing the right side of the room—this is the position in which the first part ended.

1. The children lower to torso so that they are lying down with their knees bent (counts 1-2).

2. They push up into a bridge (counts 3-4).

3. They lower the bridge one part of the body at a time—head, shoulders, back, seat (counts 5-8). (Watch that the children take all four beats to lower their bridge. They will want to come down in two beats rather than four.)

4. They push with their feet so that they are sliding backward on their back while their hands reach up to the ceiling and pretend to tickle (counts 9-12), as in figure 12.10e.

5. The children sit up and spin on their seats (counts 13-14).

6. They lie down on their abdomens, facing the back of the room—the starting position of the first part (counts 15-16).

The movements are not actually difficult or beautiful. What makes this dance special is its execution. After the children know both parts very well it is time to put them together. The children get partners. One person lies down on his abdomen facing the back of the room (starting position for part 1) while his partner sits on his right, facing the right side of the room (starting position for part 2). It is important that the sitting child be a particular distance from the lying-down child. Have the sitting person lie down so that his head touches his partner's hip, and then sit up. That is the correct distance between the partners. The two children do the first and second part at the same time. If done correctly, the tickle section of the second part (beats 9-12) will slide under the partner's high lift, as shown in figure 12.10f.

When the partners have finished their respective parts, they should be in position to begin again and do the other part. This pattern is difficult to teach at first because it is long and exacting. However, when the children realize how it fits together with a partner, they will practice over and over until they have it.

The Pachelbel Canon Dance

The Pachelbel Canon Dance is a lovely, lyrical piece. Start standing in Perfect Spots, stretched tall.

1. The right leg fans—crosses and circles back—ending well behind the standing leg (count 1).

2. Keeping the feet where they are, pivot to face the back of the room and then continue the pivot, twisting all the way front (count 2).

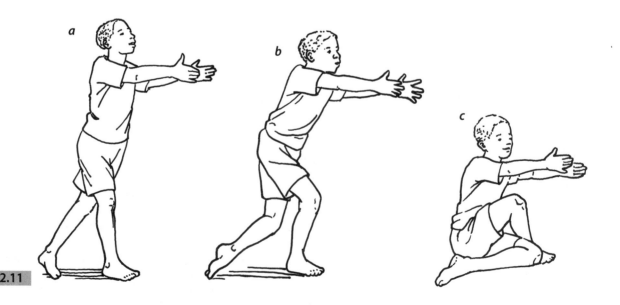

12.11

3. Staying in the twisted position, pull toward the front with the arms (count 3) and sit in a spiral sit (count 4) as in figure 12.11, a-c.

4. Spin on the seat once while untangling the legs (count 5) and do a one-knee back roll ending on one knee with the other leg stretched high (counts 6-8), as in figure 12.12.

12.12

5. Lower the torso to the floor and do a fish turn (counts 1 and 2).

6. Do one straddle roll (counts 3 and 4).

7. Sit up in a triangle position, facing the back of the room (counts 5 and 6).

8. Stand, ready to repeat (counts 7 and 8). Despite having exact counts, this dance flows as one smooth sequence. To perform it as a canon, divide into two groups and have the second group start eight beats after the first.

Closing Thoughts

Even if you waded through this chapter shaking your head "impossible," I applaud you for looking. This is advanced work, and a lot of it is geared toward the dance studio venue. But much of it is accessible if taken in small doses. I personally am very fond of the back wave and abdominal exercises described in "Advanced Physical Challenges," so I use them often, with second graders on up. Third graders and up have often warmed up with the gymnastics or ball sequence described in the section "Warm-Ups." First graders have created balance studies, and I just taught my third graders the Pachelbel Canon Dance. These advanced physical and mental challenges are paths to truly complex movement work, but you do not have to travel the entire path; just try a step or two.

Part III

Lesson Plans

Finally we are ready for actual lessons. If you haven't peeked already, you are probably wondering how in the world to structure the class management organizations, along with the movement concepts and skill activities into a coherent sequence. As in teaching other subjects, the key is juggling—keeping many goals in mind at the same time, both immediate and far-reaching. We begin with what is crucial and, from there, launch into several directions at once. For example, while establishing the three class management organizations, we also introduce props and studies, prepare for partner and group cooperation, and initiate some gymnastics skills that need time to develop.

Within this goal-juggling process, individual lessons have a rhythm of their own. The warm-up ideally offers a taste of the forthcoming meat of the lesson. There is a conditioning section and then a return to the central focus, culminating in a study that pulls together the ideas introduced. The lesson closes with a flashy finale that facilitates a wind-down to shoes. For example, a warm-up with ropes introduces the concept of line shapes. After some conditioning exercises, the core lesson develops these line shapes into a comprehensive floor pattern. The lesson closes with individual children jumping over the foam to their shoes. I understand that this is idealistic, but sometimes it actually happens.

Groups of lessons form their own rhythmic unit. Concepts build one on the other, culminating into a more encompassing goal. For example, many movement concepts, specific steps, and smaller studies combine to accomplish a mastered suite of dances. Once a unit goal is achieved, we can relax with a few lessons of simple physical fun such as an obstacle course. Then we are ready to tackle a new unit and culminating goal.

The lesson plans in part III will hopefully be useful in two ways. They can serve as specific models to be followed; and they can serve as generalized examples of how movement themes, concepts, and specific skills can be woven together. Do not worry about doing things perfectly or necessarily the way I would do them. Be safe, have fun, learn, try, sweat, and laugh.

Chapter 13

Framework of Movement Lessons

Armed with a foundation of movement education concepts and activities from parts I and II, we are ready to venture into actual lessons. The process of understanding concepts first, adding activities, and then formulating lessons is similar to the conceptual approach advocated for your students. This conceptual approach allows the greatest freedom and richness in the formation of lessons. I salute you for getting here and assure you that the results will be enormously rewarding.

Organization of Lesson Plans

The chapters that follow present 15 lesson plans for each of the three age categories: preschool to first grade; second and third grades; and fourth through sixth grades. The lesson plans are "true" in the sense that I have used them often, but they are somewhat unrealistic: They cover an enormous amount of material at breakneck speed. I chose to write these "packed" lessons for several reasons: (1) It seemed absurd to waste your time repeating this or asking you to practice that. (2) Some sophisticated classes—students with a background of sport and dance, coming from homes where they are taken to concerts and museums, enriched with intensive extracurricular activities—can handle the plans as they are. (3) The children who have had this movement program in previous years (e.g., a second grader who had movement in

kindergarten and first grade) will enjoy the greater challenge of these lessons. (4) Movement specialists and dance teachers might appreciate this pace, especially if teaching limited sessions. For most classes, teachers will want to keep the high energy of the lesson while developing the material more fully (see information on adaptations in "Lesson Plan Format" further on).

Therefore the lesson plans can be seen as a format to follow and also as more general guidelines to modify. As I tell my student teachers, "Keep a third, modify a third, and throw out a third." That is why an understanding of the concepts is so helpful; you have a sense of what areas you want to concentrate on for your particular class. Notice that the lessons do not begin to cover all the movements and activities in the book. My intent for this book was to present activities for the widest range of ability levels—from professional studio work to inner city inexperience—so there are many options to choose from. Do not begin to think that you need to cover close to everything that is offered.

But what is crucial to cover? Especially if you are brand-new, a bit of triage might be useful. It is imperative that you teach the three class management organizations: in order of importance, Free Traveling Structure, Perfect Spots, and Diagonal Structure. Locomotor and nonlocomotor movements, level, direction, and floor pattern are foundational. Some exercises, a few dances and studies, props, and games round out the curriculum.

Within any one class, you might consider this progression:

1. Free Traveling warm-up
2. Perfect Spots exercises and patterns
3. Free Traveling prop work, studies, or floor patterns
4. Diagonal Structure finale

This is a sound skeletal framework but, as you will see in the lessons, it certainly is not set in stone. Since it is impossible to teach everything at once, remember your basic juggling: Use what you need and cover more fully when you can.

Peppered in between the plans are short sections called "Reflections and Options." Because I want you to be able to fish rather than handing you a trout, I explain my reasoning in choosing the progression of lessons. These are insights into my thinking that hopefully will help you personalize the curriculum as a whole.

Practical Setup

I am assuming you will teach one 45-minute class, once a week. I personally squeeze in two 45-minute classes each week, and I will drop anything before I cancel movement. Having two classes a week is better for mental and physical conditioning and allows us the time to balance play, academics, and mastery. But once a week is fine; teaching movement is work to plan and set up, so do not pressure yourself too much. Half-hour classes would be the barest minimum, and hour classes would be luxurious; given the other curriculum constraints, 45 minutes is a good compromise.

The ideal room setup is a gym, multipurpose room, or dance studio. But how many of us have that? Use what you have; if it is warm and clean, it will be fine. If you need to move furniture or do a special cleanup, train your class to do most of it. They need to be part of the effort to value what is happening, and you have enough on your plate.

Lesson Plan Format

Following are the sections that each lesson plan includes. Feel free to use only the sections that pertain to your class.

1. **Lesson number, lesson title, grade level.** This information would seem self-explanatory, but there are some considerations. You do not have to follow the grade level assigned. The lessons for preschool to first grade start slowly and concentrate on safe, minute, incremental steps. The second and third grade lessons offer the most basic developmental organization of the material. The fourth through sixth grade lessons are geared toward older, more advanced, possibly less outwardly enthusiastic students. Let's say you have a second grade that is very timid; it would be reasonable to follow the preschool through first grade lessons, at least initially. A sharp first grade will do well with the second and third grade curriculum. If your third grade has had movement for a couple of years, they would do better with the advanced plans. And for a fifth grade that has never experienced movement, the second and third grade plans are a good choice. If you start with one progression and need to switch, fine.

There are 15 lesson plans per grade group, and teaching once a week for a year will require approximately 30. (One consideration in writing this book was to produce a book you could actually lift.) Some lessons need to be repeated; for example, obstacle courses are best repeated twice more. Most of the studies need more mastery time to complete, and within the lessons there are adaptations that develop the material more fully. Many teachers report that the conceptual approach allows them to expand the program with their own ideas. But if you feel you have covered the age-appropriate curriculum and want to move on, terrific.

2. **Teacher to teacher.** These sections are just me talking: This is tea in the faculty lounge, your personal coach, your cheering squad, your older sister helping you avoid having all 35 balloons burst because they were left near a heating vent. If you want to save this section for later (or never), that is fine.

3. **Student objectives.** These child-oriented objectives will help you focus on the goals of the lesson. This will aid with assessment (discussed further on) and will come in handy if you have to justify movement time to higher-ups.

4. **Materials.** The materials list is an idealized one. See what you have and with what you can make do; unless specified, the exact type, size, and quality are not crucial. For example, when

working with scarves, I prefer the 2-foot-square juggling scarves; but for years I worked with a box of enormously varied scarves—all lengths, shapes, fabrics—collected mostly from garage sales. Beg or borrow—if you have to, buy. Whenever possible, assemble the materials before class.

5. **Instructions.** Finally, the actual plans. These are step-by-step instructions, and for the most part the given order is necessary. If a dance or activity requires fuller explanation, the description can be found in the text. Use the "Activity Finder" on page xiii to refer to the initial introduction of activities and their application to lessons.

6. **Adaptations.** Three adaptations are presented: easier, harder, and English Language Development (ELD). Classes vary greatly; even in the same school, the maturity level of a grade changes dramatically from year to year. You have the option of working with the basic instructions in another grade grouping, as already mentioned, or looking at the adaptations to adjust the lesson. Further, you can dip in and out of the adaptations. That is, a class might need slightly easier lessons at the beginning but be ready for more challenging lessons once they get the hang of movement class.

English Language Development is a specialized adaptation for children who are learning English. Movement is (dare I say it?) the best medium for learning a language because of the physical connection with words. You remember the old introduction game in which a group of people form a circle and say their names by adding one to the other: Mary, Joe; Mary, Joe, Arthur, and so on. It is almost impossible to remember more than five names. When an identifying gesture is added to each name, the memory capacity easily doubles. So it is with movement. Further, if the gesture underscores the meaning of the word, for example if one lies horizontally to show horizontal, the depth of understanding as well as memory is intensified. But this can happen only if you speak in English. If you use English learners' primary language because it is easier or if you immediately translate so they do not have to struggle, they will not push themselves to learn English. It is hard to learn a new language, especially if many classmates speak the primary tongue; children need an incentive to actively grasp the second language. Movement class instructed in English is the perfect incentive.

7. **Assessment.** Most of the lessons conclude with an informal assessment on what has or has not worked within the lesson. I have noted any potential red flags concerning physical, cognitive, and social development. These are broad, sometimes sweeping diagnoses that will complement the assessment work you are doing in the classroom. An assessment of specific skills follows the three obstacle course plans—lesson 7 in the chapter on preschool through first grade, lesson 4 in the chapter on second and third grades, and lesson 1 in the chapter on fourth through sixth grades. These lessons present a grid of physical activities included within the obstacle course. Since children move through the course on their own and the course is repeated for two or three consecutive lessons, it is the easiest and most discreet way to assess each child. The activities can be sequenced into another obstacle course later in the year to mark progress.

It is hard to assess without clear expectations. Included is a checklist of the developmental skills that can be expected from the three age groupings.

DEVELOPMENTAL CHECKLIST

This list is culled from years of observation, but it is not exhaustive or definitive; children mature at their own speed. It is meant only as a guideline for standard growth that can be an aid as you define your expectations. This checklist includes categories in physical, social, and cognitive development.

Preschool Through First Grade

The younger the class, the wider the range of ability skills.

Physical

❐ Walk flat and on tiptoe

❐ Jump, with imperfect but visible two-foot landings

❐ Beginning hop, usually accomplished on one side

❐ Hopscotch with hop only on one side

- ❏ Beginning skip—possibly an unintentional one-legged skip
- ❏ Gallop
- ❏ Imprecise side-slide—diagonal more than straight side
- ❏ Run and gallop rather than run and leap
- ❏ Good oppositional crawl
- ❏ Log roll but not fully stretched
- ❏ Bridge
- ❏ Somersault accomplished by first grade
- ❏ Able to climb up stegel and turn body to climb down the other side by first grade
- ❏ Walk on low balance beam on own
- ❏ Ride scooter and hoppity
- ❏ Bounce and catch a 6-inch ball with two hands
- ❏ Follow a taped line but not necessarily cross back on the loop
- ❏ Able to change movements in phrases of eight

Social

- ❏ Confidence to separate from mom without distress
- ❏ Confidence to attempt supported new activities
- ❏ Ability to establish structures and confidence to break routines
- ❏ Desire to please a trusted adult
- ❏ Ability to follow three-part directions
- ❏ Ability to choose and be chosen by a partner by first grade
- ❏ Ability to share
- ❏ A balance between generosity and capacity to say no
- ❏ Ability to lead and follow
- ❏ Ability to express emotion
- ❏ Ability to "read" many social/emotional cues
- ❏ Capacity for strong emotional attachments

Cognitive

- ❏ Ability to focus for 15 minutes
- ❏ Resiliency to return to a task after failure
- ❏ Knowledge of letters and numbers and ability to read patterned books by first grade
- ❏ Ability to write name and short words
- ❏ Ability to see and understand patterns using *same* and *different*
- ❏ Ability to orient a floor pattern to the room and do a five-line floor pattern
- ❏ Ability to do straight, curved, wiggly, and spiral lines
- ❏ Ability to remember a four-part sequence

Second and Third Grades

All the previously identified skills plus the following:

Physical

- ❏ Equal landing jumps
- ❏ Full jump turns
- ❏ Hops equally well on either foot
- ❏ Hops and holds the other leg
- ❏ Hopscotch alternating hopping leg
- ❏ Straight side side-slides
- ❏ Side-slides changing sides
- ❏ Fully stretched log roll
- ❏ Tucked roll
- ❏ One-knee back roll
- ❏ Running somersault
- ❏ Bridge with one leg lifted
- ❏ Cartwheel

(continued)

❒ Frog balance

❒ Runs and leaps but legs not stretched

❒ Runs and turns in the air

❒ Runs and clicks heels in the air

❒ Dribbles ball

❒ Shoots baskets on standard hoop and makes 1 out of 10

❒ Jumps rope

❒ Walks on medium-level balance beam alone

❒ Follows scooter line precisely

❒ Knows right and left

❒ Changes movements in phrases of four

Social

❒ Able to work independently, with a partner, and in a group

❒ Able to offer ideas to whole class

❒ Able to listen from a distance

❒ Able to follow four-part directions

❒ Able to compromise

❒ Able to delay gratification for foreseeable goal

❒ Able to internalize rules

❒ Able to assume responsibility for concrete tasks

❒ Able to read most social/emotional cues

❒ Begins to form friendship bonds

Cognitive

❒ Is able to focus for half an hour

❒ Is able to self-correct

❒ Is able to read and understand text literally

❒ Is beginning to infer meaning in text

❒ Can write in logical paragraphs by end of third grade

❒ Sees and understands patterns using *same, different,* and *similar*

❒ Can draw room representation and do a seven-line floor pattern

❒ Can do straight, curved, wiggly, zigzag, spiral, and beginning looped lines

❒ Remembers a six-part sequence

Fourth Through Sixth Grades

Starting in about the fifth grade, there occurs a great divide. Those children that have integrated their bodies adequately will be able to do virtually any movement. But about this time many children actually regress: They gain a lot of weight, are reluctant to exert energy, and are wary of new physical activities. (One reason the obstacle course start is so enticing is that, with everyone moving at once, no one feels put on the spot.) The following list is geared to those youngsters who have continued to develop physically.

All the previously identified skills plus the following:

Physical

❒ Hurdle

❒ Hopscotch changing hopping leg plus hand clap and slap

❒ Tumbling rolls with legs in precise gymnastics positions

❒ Round-off

❒ Headstand

❒ Splits

❒ Precise gymnastics routines

❒ Jump rope tricks like crossing arms, changing hops, and Double Dutch

❒ Walk on high balance beam with a supporting hand

❒ Some stunts on the beam like balance on one foot, walk in different directions

❒ Run and leap with stretched legs

❒ Dribble in various ways, pass, and shoot baskets making 3 out of 10

❒ Able to change moves every one or two beats

Social

❒ Sensitive to social and emotional cues

❒ Able to empathize

❒ Able to delay gratification for a goal in the future

❒ Able to plan ahead

❒ Able to modify a reaction to a more tactful response

Cognitive

❒ Able to collaborate

❒ Able to assume responsibility for day-to-day issues

❒ Able to manage time and prioritize

❒ Can read with inference and deductions

❒ Can research and organize writing

❒ Can integrate many concepts into a whole, for example assignments using several concepts at one time

❒ Can remember an eight-part sequence

From *Step by Step: A Complete Movement Education Curriculum*, by Sheila Kogan, 2003, Champaign, IL: Human Kinetics.

If a child lacks a skill that is far below him, for example, if a fourth grader does not know how to turn backward when climbing down, we must not jump to the conclusion that he is developmentally delayed. Cultural over- and underprotection and lack of opportunities and experiences are the most likely causes. It is worth observing a child over a period of time before we form conclusions. I have seen children approach the balance beam and scooter with almost paralyzed terror; these youngsters have never swung on a swing, climbed a fence, swum in a river. Regular movement classes will open up a new world to them; it will not take that long for them to say, "I don't need your help."

The First Class

Like a good breakfast, the first class is imperative to a good start. We launch the curriculum and set the tone for the rest of the year. Because it is so important, let's look at the first class closely.

The Basic First Class

A typical first class includes three elements: establishing the Free Traveling Structure, teaching Perfect Spots, and working with balls. The Free Traveling Structure comes first because it is the most useful of the class management techniques and is workable immediately for a warm-up using locomotor movements. This locomotor movement warm-up lets us practice stopping on an aural cue, tires the children out, and allows a cursory evaluation of class skills. Starting with Free Traveling locomotor movements also conveys a first impression of movement class as energetic, fun, and hard (which is true). I teach Perfect Spots next in order to establish this management technique, and we do initial exercises using Perfect Spots. The first lesson concludes with a prop, usually balls, to test the Free Traveling Structure and to offer a flashy ending.

The first class starts with very few words and leaves no time to worry. "Hello, welcome to movement class. Sit down, take your socks and shoes off, put your socks in your shoes and put them under your chair. When you're done, come sit on the floor near me." The children work barefoot because shoes can be dirty, treacherous, or slippery. Socks alone, of course, are dangerously slippery. In addition, children have better sensory awareness and control when barefoot, and a lot of equipment can be used only without shoes.

We immediately begin with an introduction to the Free Traveling Structure. Teaching the Free Traveling Structure follows a progression of minute steps, each one increasing in the amount of control needed to succeed (see chapter 2). The teaching progression begins with the words *start* and *stop* combined with small, isolated movements. The sound cue is then transferred to the tambourine and the movements grow in size, although they remain nonlocomotor. The sound can then move to the piano or tapes, and the movements transition into locomotor movements. At each step the children have gained success in controlling their bodies so that they can stop when the sound stops. However, to teach a structure and not use it is like climbing a mountain and dismissing the view. We use the Free Traveling Structure to warm up with locomotor movements, which allows work on large-muscle coordination and endurance.

Teaching the Perfect Spots Structure follows a similar progression of gaining control (see chapter 2). The concept *near* is easier than *far*; the control expands from the class gathered together to individuals scattered to the outer reaches of the room. As with the Free Traveling Structure, once a structure is established it needs to be used or it has no purpose. In Perfect Spots we work on strength and flexibility exercises and on techniques and body positions that will be needed later on.

We end with a prop because that will engage the most reluctant mover, and balls are especially loved. Children have free time with the balls, and then we try some guided movements together (see chapter 9). If there is time we start a preliminary study. Working with balls in the Free Traveling Structure is a perfect way to cement that organizational form. It takes a lot of control for a child to stop moving both her body and a ball, and even more control to freeze and let the ball go. However, you have the power to take the ball away, and that provides extraordinary incentive. When the children have succeeded in controlling themselves and their ball in the Free Traveling Structure, they have accomplished an amazing feat, and this foundation will allow you to build a fabulous movement program.

The First Class for Younger and Older Children

The first class for very young children actually covers the same elements as just described but couches them in the soothing, repetitive Rocking Song (p. 17). The rocking lesson (p. 16) uses this song to establish the Free Traveling Structure. In essence we are replacing the progression using isolated and stationary movements with the rocking introduction. After that, we follow the same succession, introducing Perfect Spots and

concluding with balls. But the pace is slower and gentler; very young children like energy but become frenzied with too much rushing.

The first class for intermediate children is totally different. A fabulously long obstacle course is the best way to approach older, "jaded" children. This designation applies to most fifth and sixth grade classes and also to some third and fourth graders who have had movement for several years. If the students have a hip-slinging, what-can-you-teach-me look to them, it is a good idea to start with all the flash available: the balance beam set on the highest notch, balls, scarves, balloons, scooters on a line, hoppities, ringtoss, almost anything you can find that will grab them (see chapter 8). Start the class on the mats with an extremely strenuous warm-up (see chapter 12), and continue with a tough gymnastics pattern. Then quickly teach the obstacle course and let them go. Start groups of children at different places in the course so there is little wait time.

Of course the children's participation in this rollicking good time is contingent on their high standard of behavior. I have rarely seen a child able to resist; they will do anything, even behave, to be able to participate. That is why the obstacle course will work even before the class management organizations have been taught. The key for older children is to keep the pace terrifically fast and the movements challenging. The activities need to be beyond their easy reach. (You might gently whisper to the large, awkward ones not to worry, you will teach them later.) The fast pace and physical challenges are crucial to setting a tone that says: "I have something to teach you and this will not even hint of baby stuff." Upper elementary and middle school children want, more than anything, to look cool. They actually love to do "baby" things, like baby crawl with baby sounds and Horsie, but only after they have established their coolness. The way to make a class cool is to make it fast, hard, and flashy.

The obstacle course can be done for one to three lessons and then go on to the standard beginning lesson—Free Traveling Structure, Perfect Spots, balls—to establish the class management structures. This obstacle course introduction, therefore, is like a prelude to the basic lesson. If you do not have the equipment to start with the obstacle course lesson, begin with the "basic" plan, making sure that the pace is fast and the activities are challenging. The goal is to captivate the children and get them on our side from the beginning. Then we can teach them.

Discipline

The first class is a barrage of new ideas, experiences, and impressions. What the children actually learn about movement is less important than the tone set for the class. If the children believe, after the first class, that movement is a subject like reading or math, then you are set; if they think it is going to be recess for an hour, then you need to change your tone.

This movement-is-a-subject approach is crucial. If it comes down to a fast choice between allowing a child to join on his own terms and not allowing him to join—for example, if he will not take off his shoes or will not spit out the gum—I recommend not letting the child join. Movement is naturally fun. When the child sees all the other children skipping and running, he will join, especially if he is given a chance to save face. "I want you to join us now. When you get those shoes off, there is a spot for you right here."

Harsh? Perhaps. Necessary? Absolutely. If you do not build strong structural walls of control, you will never have the freedom to have fun in your movement house. You will constantly be patching up the crumbling restraints of discipline. A fun class is your best class management technique because the children will be on your side; but no matter how good the program, it cannot substitute for your unwavering commitment to appropriate behavior.

Discipline is an old-fashioned word conjuring up harsh images of drill sergeants and grim schoolmasters. Now we say "class management," "behavioral skills," or "motivational techniques." But we have strayed a little afield. Fifty years ago discipline rested 100% on the child. No matter what was happening to or around her, no matter how boring or inappropriate the class, the child was supposed to sit still and be quiet. When I first started teaching in the projects of Chicago

our primary job was to maintain order. We were allowed—I'd say encouraged—to keep the upper hand by swatting children with two rulers taped together. I remember a series of staff workshops on controlling a child by pressing a certain nerve in his neck. There is no doubt that things had to change, and they did. The 1960s and 1970s saw discipline travel from the children's burden to the teacher's responsibility; if the class was acting up, we were at fault because we had not approached them correctly. But like all pendulums, the discipline issue has swung out of balance. Teachers cannot replace poor parenting, teachers cannot motivate every single child, and teachers cannot produce (too many) miracles. What we can do is our very best, combining as much knowledge as possible with genuine care for every child.

Discipline—the cultivation of appropriate, attentive behavior—requires three factors:

1. We need to offer appropriate lessons, which, as Piaget would say, require moderate novelty. Each lesson must be based on a foundation of established skills while offering an exciting challenge. Both the foundation and the challenge are crucial. In my experience many teachers err on the side of not enough challenge. Children love play, fun, props, and parties, but more than anything they love the feeling of mastering "hard stuff." A feeling of "Look what I can do now!" is the most consistent ingredient necessary for control. A corollary to the appropriate lesson is the planning behind it. Children, as well as adults, love to come into a class knowing that the teacher is prepared, organized, and goal oriented. Of course there is the unexpected and spontaneous; but a hesitant, what-shall-we-do-today approach makes the class feel as though they are not important.

2. The children must know with certainty that you are on their side. As with good parenting being on a child's side does not mean—actually cannot mean—always giving her what she wants. Being on the children's side means wanting and working toward the best for them. As educators we need to keep the bigger picture in mind so that we constantly strive for their overall development. This is tough in our present culture of bubbled-in correctness. But it is the life skills of forming friends, pushing beyond tiredness,

learning determination, and taking responsibility and helping others that grow the child into a full human being. Our job is achieving a constant balance between the planned curriculum and the larger lesson.

3. In addition to planning challenging lessons and wanting the greatest possible growth from our children, we build discipline on the highest possible standards of respect between the children and ourselves and among the children. Then it is our exhausting job to hold those standards unwaveringly throughout the class.

Closing Thoughts

Enough. Let us get into the lesson plans. The chapter on each age grouping starts with an overview of the 15 lessons, showing the overall curriculum at a glance, and then presents the lessons. You are ready; jump in.

Chapter 14

Lesson Plans for Preschool Through First Grade

The focus of lessons for very young children is growth in small increments: step by baby step. Very young children often do not have the preconcepts to grasp an idea that seems obvious to us. For example, "Get a place where there is space all around you" involves several preliminary concepts—how near or far they are from an object. Further, since very young children are just starting to gain experience of the world, much of the curriculum offers a variety of introductions. The following table is an overview of the preschool to first grade curriculum.

Preschool Through First Grade Curriculum

Lesson plan number	Lesson plan name	Purpose/Notes
1	Rocking	We set the tone and establish the Free Traveling Structure. Children are introduced to locomotor movements and to balls.
2	Locomotor	Children work with a variety of traveling movements. They prepare for Perfect Spots and keep practicing the Free Traveling Structure. Ball skills are sequenced into a remembered study.
2.5	Reflections and options	I encourage you to schedule movement class twice a week, essentially repeating each class.
3	Mastering two class organizations	This is a consolidation lesson in which we perfect the Free Traveling and Perfect Spots Structures. We also perfect and perform the ball study.
4	Approaching partners	This is a preparation lesson: We prepare children for (1) nonlocomotor movements, (2) partner work, (3) the Diagonal Structure, and (4) a somersault needed for the gymnastics routine presented in lesson 7.
4.5	Reflections and options	I describe the "taste approach" in which children are introduced to just a tiny bit of what will be taught next. For example, we sampled partners in the preceding lesson and will explore partner activities in the next lesson.

(continued)

Lesson plan number	Lesson plan name	Purpose/Notes
5	Partners	Children try out a variety of partner activities and are introduced to the Eensy Weensy Spider Dance. This dance pulls together locomotor and nonlocomotor movements as well as partner work and remembered sequences.
6	Nonlocomotor movements	This is a more in-depth view of stationary movements. We perfect the Eensy Weensy Spider Dance and establish the Diagonal Structure. Notice that nonlocomotor movements were used long before they were formally introduced. We cannot introduce everything at the same time, so we use what we need at a given time.
7	Obstacle course	This lesson breaks the progression. By now we have established the three class management organizations—Free Traveling Structure, Perfect Spots, Diagonal Structure. We have covered the concepts of locomotor and nonlocomotor movements, partner skills, and remembered sequences. This lesson is a smorgasbord of coordination activities plus the first attempt at gymnastics; it is the perfect venue for individual assessments. Although it is strenuous, it gives us a moment to process all the information gathered so far.
8	Levels	We are back to basic movement concepts—here, vertical space. Children are also introduced to the idea of maps and allowed free creative play with the scarves.
9	Star floor pattern	We intensify the work with floor patterns in this more difficult five-line design. We also pull together some of the scarf exploration ideas into a study.
10	Creating their own floor patterns	This is a culminating lesson in that it integrates many strands: locomotor and nonlocomotor movements, floor patterns, and partner work extended into a group cooperative effort. The lesson also perfects the scarf study. Many accomplishments for this age group!
11	In and out game	Like the obstacle course, the In and Out Game breaks the flow of movement concept acquisition to work on relationship words. But we return to the group floor patterns created in lesson 10 to master them.
12	Bears in the night dance	This is a terrific companion to the In and Out Game. The children worked with relationship words in the game setting and now use many of the same words in a literature setting. It makes my pedagogical eyes gleam. They also get an introduction to ropes—they are allowed to play with the ropes here so that we can move into using them more academically next time.
12.5	Reflections and options	We have to consider now how we are going to end the classes. If you choose to consolidate and perfect the students' work into a show, I offer you a possible format. In this case you would not go on to the rest of the lessons because you would be practicing. If you choose to continue with more lessons, I offer you the following progression.
13	Ropes	Children explore rope skills and then use them to learn line shapes. They are introduced to the parachute.
14	Floor pattern using line shapes	The line shapes introduced earlier are transferred to a culminating floor pattern. This lesson also includes an introduction to the Grocery Store Dance and continued work (all our work should be this much fun!) with the parachute. Exciting props like the parachute must be offered two, and preferably three, consecutive times; not doing so would be torturous to the children.
15	Grocery store dance	This dance pulls together locomotor, nonlocomotor, levels, sequence, and fantasy play. We also perfect the floor pattern using different line shapes from last time and have a grand finale with the parachute.

LESSON 1

Rocking

Teacher to Teacher

Hats off to you. Early childhood teachers are the real superpowers; your influence on a child is deep and lasting. One reason your job is so difficult is that many early school-age children do not particularly want to please; their inner needs to explore and play are in the forefront. So, without coming down too hard, you need to entice and corral them into the discipline needed to teach. I have found the rocking lesson extremely successful because the increments of novelty are so small. At each point the children should feel confident and ready to move on. Your goal in this first lesson is to support their exuberance but only within firm controls; do not let them push you into relaxing that goal. They are young, but they are very smart and they can do it.

The rambunctious children will be testing you on one side but, perhaps more difficult, the timid children will be testing you too: "I don't wanna," tears, immobility. My first suggestion is to prepare them as much as possible before they come into the movement room: Teach them the Rocking Song and do a bit of rocking in the classroom, talk about taking off their socks and shoes and perhaps try it in the classroom, and tell them what they will be doing and have them peek at the room they will be in. Have the least amount of surprise possible. Once you are in the movement lesson you can pair up the reluctant child with an able student or encourage him yourself. Do not focus too much on the nonparticipating child. Do not allow his mother to stay. You do not want that negative behavior to get him a lot of attention. If worst comes to worst, move him to the side and go on, having as much fun as you can.

I congratulate you on starting. It is my unwavering belief that the effort you expend offering movement to your children will reap tremendous rewards.

Student Objectives

▸ Students will experience movement as a safe, enjoyable class.

▸ Students will demonstrate stopping on cue (Free Traveling Structure).

▸ Students will understand and demonstrate the concepts near and far.

▸ Students will gain strength and flexibility through conditioning exercises.

▸ Students will explore moving a ball in a variety of ways.

Materials Needed

▸ Tambourine.

▸ A sign with near on one side and far on the other.

▸ Balls, one per child (ideally 6-inch rubber balls, but virtually any bouncing ball will do).

Teaching Instructions

1. After their socks and shoes are put away, gather the children in the middle of the room. (Do not form a circle, just a loose gathering.) Teach the Rocking Song and do the rocking lesson (chapter 2).

   a. Sing and rock in various ways.

   b. Change the word *rocking* to words for various nonlocomotor movements: spinning, shaking, swinging. End with bouncing, heads, shoulders, knees, seat, whole body.

   c. Bouncing becomes jumping and is used as a transition to locomotor movements.

   d. Do jumping as a locomotor movement again; this time eliminate the words of the song but keep the rhythm.

e. Do several locomotor movements to the rhythm of the song: walking, skipping, crawling, jogging.

f. Finally, go back to skipping and change the rhythm to various rhythmic lengths—this is the Free Traveling Structure. Do many different locomotor movements in the Free Traveling Structure: gallop, baby crawl, crab crawl, roll, jazzy walk, run, run and leap.

2. Gather the children, show the *near* sign, and define *near* as close. Have them go near a door, their shoes, the walls, a black line on the floor, a red line on the floor, a person. Gather the children again, show the *far* sign, and define *far* as away. Have them go far from you, the piano, their shoes, the mats, all the walls, everybody.

3. Gather the children sitting near you: "We'll have to practice far next time. We are not quite ready for Perfect Spots today." Introduce Hello and Good-Bye and teach the concept *torso*; introduce Swordfish with each leg but not both. Have the children sit with crossed legs to listen.

4. Remind the children that when the sound stops they are to freeze. Show how to freeze with a ball or, if it gets away, freeze the body and let the ball go. Pass out the balls and allow about 10 minutes of free time. (Test the freezing once or twice.) Do guided movements with the ball: chase, bounce catch, roll with the feet, roll with no hands or feet, have the ball between the knees and jump, carry with no hands and jazzy walk, throw and catch, throw and catch and skip, spin the ball, drum, run and leap and throw and catch.

5. Put away the balls and gather the children sitting. Sing and rock to the Rocking Song, holding the ending still for several seconds. Rock sitting, kneeling, and standing; hold the standing balance for a few seconds and then ask the children to quietly go to their shoes.

≋ *Adaptations*

Easier

▸ You do not need to complete the entire progression to the Free Traveling Structure at one time. If you want, just stay with the song this first time and next time do the song rhythm and the Free Traveling Structure.

▸ Teach the Rocking Song in the classroom before coming to movement.

▸ Eliminate far; just practice near this first time and introduce far the next.

▸ Introduce Hello and Good-Bye and Swordfish; eliminate the introduction of *torso*.

▸ If the children do not seem ready to try the balls, eliminate that and end the class with a one-by-one roll down the incline mat (if you have one) or on a regular mat.

▸ If they seem ready for a short introduction to the balls, do free time and just two or three guided movements—chase, soccer kick, spin the ball.

Harder

▸ Keep the progression—teaching the Rocking Song, then using the rhythm of the song, and establishing the Free Traveling Structure—but pick up the pace and do more locomotor movements at the end, adding hop, hopscotch, and side-slide.

▸ Establish Perfect Spots: Introduce near and far, ending with far from everybody; ask for two fars, far from everybody and far from everything.

▸ Do Hello and Good-Bye, introduction to *torso*, and Swordfish in Perfect Spots.

▸ Do free time and guided movements with the balls, and end with a three- or four-part study with the balls. A study could entail, for example, (1) chase, (2) soccer, (3) ball between knees and jump, (4) run and leap with a little throw catch.

English Language Development

▸ The first step in English development is comprehension; the second step is speaking. In this lesson, there are several opportunities for the children to call out some words in English. When working with the Rocking Song, ask the children to begin naming body parts: "We have been doing our song on our seat [point]—say seat—good, now we will do it on our knees [point]—say knees—good . . ." Also when doing the various bounces, the children can call out head, shoulders, elbows, knees, all together.

▶ Another golden opportunity for naming English words comes when the children perform the locomotor movements in the Free Traveling Structure: Skipping, jumping, hopping, crawling, rolling, jazzy walking, and running are all great words to know.

▶ By the end of this lesson, *rocking, still, near, far, hello, good-bye, torso, swordfish, balls,* and *freeze* should be clear. These also can be called out.

▶ Be careful not to ask the class to call out too many words. I would not use any calling out when working with the balls. We want the children to focus on the movement activities and have an exuberant time. Calling out English words is terrific if it is used judiciously.

≈ Assessment

There are many assessment possibilities; it is a question of which to choose. Because this is your first lesson, concentrate your assessment on the class as a whole. Did they grasp the idea of moving to a sound and firmly stopping when the sound stops? If you had to remind or exhort several children, it is not a solid take. This honest assessment is crucial, and I implore you to be relentless in establishing the Free Traveling Structure. "I still see some of you moving when the sound stops. We will work on this next week."

Throughout the class you will naturally spot children who stand out in one way or another. Who were the children who could skip and jump evenly, crawl with oppositional hands and knees, and run leap? Who had great difficulty? Do you get the sense that the awkward children have coordination problems or, rather, that they have had no experience? Which children were able to focus their attention and exhibit control of their bodies, and which were all over the place? Do not jump to any conclusions yet. This first class brings out some strange behaviors that do not actually indicate serious problems. Just keep mental notes and see what happens.

LESSON **2**   PRESCHOOL – 1ST GRADE

Locomotor

≈ Teacher to Teacher

This lesson might be harder for you than the first. The rocking lesson is very controlled and soothing. Also, young children are often stunned during their first lesson, somewhat like deer frozen in headlights. Your biggest problem during the first lesson will probably be timidity. But this second lesson is something else. The shock is gone and they are getting a taste of exuberance doing locomotor movements freely about the room. It is imperative that you stick to your guns. Despite being young, I assure you that they are able to move freely and stop almost exactly when the sound does, they are able to get Perfect Spots, and they are able to freeze with a ball. Teachers of young children tend to be so nice and so helpful it can be hard for them to establish self-maintaining class structures. They either think young children should not be "regimented" or keep interfering to help. The class organizations are the outer fences that allow the children freedom and spontaneity—the opposite of regimentation; and the class needs to accept these structures within themselves, without your interference, in order for you to feel relaxed and happy. It is of paramount importance that movement class be enjoyable for you, and this can happen only if you trust that your children are in control. Ironically, a controlled class with a relaxed teacher is exactly what makes children happy.

Student Objectives

▶ Students will perfect stopping when the sound stops (Free Traveling Structure).

▶ Students will understand that some movements travel and will explore a variety of locomotor movements.

▶ Students will be able to find a place in the room that is far from everyone and far from everything (Perfect Spot). Students will gain strength and flexibility through conditioning exercises.

▶ Students will explore moving a ball and will sequence several movements into a remembered study.

▶ Students will gain eye-hand coordination by working with a ball.

▶ Students will demonstrate motor planning in "flying" off the incline mat.

Materials Needed

▶ Tambourine.

▶ A sign with *near* on one side and *far* on the other.

▶ Balls, one per child.

▶ Incline mat resting on a flat mat.

Teaching Instructions

1. Quickly review the rocking lesson, progressing through the song, the rhythm of the song, and the Free Traveling Structure. Do a few movements in the Free Traveling Structure, testing the children's ability to freeze by changing the duration of sound. Gather the children and teach the word *locomotor*. Use the term as you continue to warm up with locomotor movements in the Free Traveling Structure: skip, jump, hop, gallop, baby crawl, crab crawl, roll, spider crawl, jazzy walk, run, run leap.

2. Review near and far, practicing far more intensely: far from your shoes, the piano, the mats, all the doors, all the walls, and so on, ending with far from everybody. "Now we will do two fars to get our Perfect Spots: far from everybody—you already have that—and far from everything. Get your

Perfect Spot and sit down." Shake feet with the children who get their Perfect Spots, eventually shaking everyone's feet.

Review Hello and Good-Bye, including the torso. Do Swordfish again and add both legs. Teach a twist in the arms in preparation for a bridge and then attempt the whole bridge.

3. Review stopping with a ball and pass out the balls. Allow some free time and go on to guided movements: chase, bounce and catch, soccer, roll the ball with no hands or feet, spin the ball, drum on the ball, throw and catch, carry the ball with no hands and jazzy walk, place the ball between the knees and jump, dribble.

4. Gather the class and ask them to sit cross-legged with the ball in their laps, hands off the ball. (If they start playing with the ball, simply remove it and return the balls when performing the study. Congratulate the children who were able to follow instructions.) Collectively choose a four-part ball sequence, for example chase, spin, throw the ball against the wall, soccer. Have the children say it a few times and then perform without teacher help.

5. Introduce the incline mat. Have the children do a "fly" and then a side roll individually to their shoes.

Adaptations

Easier

▶ Take your time reviewing the rocking lesson so that it is virtually repeated.

▶ If the children did not understand far, do not attempt Perfect Spots now but keep working at it next time. Do Hello and Good-Bye and Swordfish with the children gathered near you.

▶ Eliminate the bridge.

▶ Eliminate dribbling the ball.

▶ Present a three-part study without the children's input; that is, you present it.

Harder

▶ When working with locomotor movements in the warm-up, introduce side-slide and hopscotch.

- After establishing the two fars for Perfect Spots, add facing front.
- In Perfect Spots, teach the bridge and shoulder stand, then introduce all of Blastoff.
- If most of the children can dribble a ball, add walk, then run and dribble.
- Create a five-part sequence together.
- Introduce a somersault down the incline mat.

English Language Development

- Have the children call out the locomotor movements before executing them. If they speak some English, consider gently, quickly, lightly correcting their pronunciation.
- When doing Hello and Good-Bye and Swordfish, the class should definitely shout out "hello," "good-bye," and "let me go."
- Do not have the children call out the moves in the ball sequence because this will interfere with their memory work.

- *Fly, roll,* and *flip,* when done down the incline mat, will become very real.

≈ *Assessment*

This lesson will allow you three major assessments: (1) You can readjust any first impressions about hyperactivity. Sometimes the first class is so exciting that the children are too stimulated to stop. Now it should be clear who truly cannot control her body enough to stop precisely. (2) Hello and Good-Bye with the torso, double-legged Swordfish, the bridge, and the incline mat work are activities that will point to any children who have gross motor problems. Do not do any major corrections now. Just note who might need further observation. (3) The ball study will allow you to identify any obvious eye-hand coordination difficulties. The study will also bring out major memory and concentration problems. Because children can follow each other, subtle problems might be hidden at this point.

2.5   PRESCHOOL – 1ST GRADE

Reflections and Options

I am assuming you will bite off as much as your class can chew and chomp as long as needed. That is why I am not deciding for you when and what to repeat. A perfect arrangement would be to have movement twice a week and simply repeat each lesson. Young children especially enjoy repetition because they love knowing what to do; they revel in anticipating what the teacher will say and in their own mastery. You might worry about finding the time, but I ask you to consider two factors.

First, movement is excellent preparation for schooling. Inherent within every movement class are activities that help children integrate their sensory processing systems. Vestibular and proprioceptive stimulation; work on midline, balance, and tracking; equalizing the two sides of the body while supporting dominance—all are underlying factors in helping the body process information efficiently. In addition, work on strength, flexibility, agility, endurance, and concentration helps children

grow and feel good about themselves. If a child has severe motor problems, a movement class once or even twice a week will not be enough to remediate. But for most children, even those with mild difficulties, movement will prove a great support in their acquisition of academic and social skills.

Secondly, having movement twice a week increases the teacher's ability to assess. During the early years, assessment is more important yet more difficult than later. We have an enormous responsibility because catching a potential problem in the first years of school will save a child untold hassles in the future. On the other hand, it is crucial not to draw conclusions without proper information. Young children are very individualistic; they do not have the social conformity of older children. A preschooler may pull up her skirt to show you her new underpants; another may shout for you to admire a bowel movement; still another may place her hands on your breasts and ask when she will get some. When preschoolers do things like this, we do not worry about personality disorders but smile at their innocence. It sometimes takes true wisdom to distinguish innocent uniqueness from budding disabilities. Discernment is also needed to distinguish learning problems from lack of experi-

ence: Without careful, and possibly professional, consideration we cannot tell if the child unable to catch a ball has eye-hand coordination difficulties or if he just has not caught enough balls. Movement classes provide a venue where we can observe children from many different angles, academically, socially, and physically. Having class twice a week allows us to balance active teaching with relaxed observation. Invaluable.

My most successful assessment took place 25 years ago and is still fresh in my memory. I was teaching a dance class for 4-year-olds at a studio; the room was full of chubby little legs in pink leotards and tutus. One of my students was a lovely, attentive little girl who seemed to be always a second behind the other children. The delay was barely perceptible but quite consistent. After several months of close observation, I mentioned the delay to her parents and suggested having her hearing checked. Lo and behold, she was severely hearing impaired! Her disability was greatly alleviated with a hearing aid, and we were all grateful that it was caught before she entered kindergarten. I am very proud of having helped that child; but sometimes, on grim nights, I stew about the possibilities of problems not seen.

LESSON 3   PRESCHOOL – 1ST GRADE
Mastering Two Class Organizations

〰️ *Teacher to Teacher*

I have often thought that teachers of young children should be paid in millions and given the respect accorded to brain surgeons. One of your many impossible jobs is gently, constructively, teaching moms how to parent. I would be willing to bet that the three children unable to perfect the Free Traveling Structure and Perfect Spots are out of control with their moms. I would be willing to bet that these moms chase down their children rather than expecting them to come

when called. I would be willing to bet that when the moms catch the children, they smile in that exasperated manner that says, "My kids are just like that. There is nothing I can do." Your mission, should you choose to accept it, is to teach moms (and dads) that young children can and must learn internal controls. The key is that parents must assume leadership and do whatever it takes to establish that authority. A book like Dobson's *The Strong-Willed Child* might prove useful.

≋ *Student Objectives*

▸ Students will demonstrate mastery of the Free Traveling Structure and will explore a variety of locomotor movements.

▸ Students will demonstrate self-discipline and motor control by stopping on cue.

▸ Students will be able to find Perfect Spots within 10 seconds.

▸ Students will gain strength and flexibility with conditioning exercises and learn the bridge position.

▸ Students will perform a ball study correctly without teacher help.

▸ Students will demonstrate correct behavior as an audience.

▸ Students will understand and attempt a rudimentary somersault.

≋ *Materials Needed*

▸ Tambourine.

▸ A sign with *near* on one side and *far* on the other.

▸ Balls, one per person.

▸ Ideally an incline mat resting on a flat mat, or two flat mats.

≋ *Teaching Instructions*

1. Children put away their socks and shoes and, without waiting for one another, start skipping. When the whole class is skipping, stop and verbally review what to do when the sound stops and what *locomotor* means. Continue with a warm-up of locomotor movements, using the word *locomotor* for each movement change: jump, hop, hopscotch (introduce), gallop, baby crawl, crab crawl, spider crawl, roll, jazzy walk, side-slide (introduce), run and leap. Occasionally test the children's ability to stop by playing with the length of sound.

2. Review near and far and get Perfect Spots. Add facing front. Play three rounds of Firecracker; practice getting Perfect Spots in fewer seconds.

3. In Perfect Spots, (1) do Hello and Good-Bye including the torso, (2) do Swordfish including both legs, (3) review the bridge and teach all of Blastoff.

4. Verbally review stopping with a ball, and then pass out the balls. Give the class about 5 minutes of free time and some guided movements: chase, dribble, soccer, jump with the ball between the knees, roll the ball without hands or feet, throw the ball up and catch, spin, drum, side-slide with the ball moving from hand to hand, run and leap with a small throw and catch. Review the four-part study from last time; practice and show. Have half of the class be the audience and half be the performers. "The audience has an important job. The audience needs to be silent, watch carefully, and clap at the end." "Performers, when you finish you will take gracious bows."

5. Line up on one side. Do a "fly" off the incline mat. For the second turn, introduce a somersault and do it twice. (This can be done on a flat mat.)

≋ *Adaptations*

Easier

▸ In the warm-up, eliminate hopscotch and side-slide. If you do introduce hopscotch, do not worry about the hop alternating legs.

▸ In Perfect Spots, teach only stage 1, or stage 1 and 2, of Blastoff.

▸ Make the ball study three parts.

▸ Save more time for the somersault. Young children can accomplish a somersault, but many will need individual help. If they are too timid, save the somersault for later and just log roll down the mat.

Harder

▸ If the class is completely at ease with the Free Traveling Structure and the concept locomotor, introduce nonlocomotor and warm up alternating locomotor and nonlocomotor movements.

▸ When introducing hopscotch, emphasize alternating legs for the hop.

▶ In Blastoff, concentrate on form as well as balance. That is, stage 1 should end in a high reach; the stage 2 bridge needs to be a high stretch with the head off the floor and dropped back; the stage 3 shoulder stand should have the seat raised, legs straight with toes pointed, and hands holding the waist.

▶ How about a five-part ball study?

English Language Development

▶ During the warm-up with locomotor movements, have the children call out the movement before executing it.

▶ When practicing near and far, have the children call out the object they are moving close to or away from.

▶ Do not have the class call out the ball activities when performing the study because this will negate the memory work.

≈ Assessment

This is the perfect juncture to evaluate the overall control of your class. Have they internalized the discipline necessary to stop on cue and to orient themselves in space? Can they execute these structures without your help? It is the inner discipline that is crucial here because if you have to constantly nudge and remind, you cannot rest on the structure and focus on the movement activity. My rule of thumb is if more than 3 children out of 20 need personal attention to execute the Free Traveling Structure and to get Perfect Spots, it is wise to reteach these structures to the whole class.

Although your focus is on the class as a whole, any diagnosis about individual behavior problems will be useful. The exercises in Perfect Spots and the somersault should reinforce previous assessments concerning children with motor problems. The ball study will point to eye-hand coordination difficulties.

LESSON 4   PRESCHOOL – 1ST GRADE
Teacher to Teacher

≈ Teacher to Teacher

Experienced teachers know this, but new teachers might need a reminder: Do not immerse yourself in helping one child so much that you lose your overview of the whole class. Specifically, when the class is doing Partner Shake, it would be great fun if you played too. You could quickly come in to shake hands while keeping an eye on all the other partner groups. If your class was an uneven number, your inclusion would be especially beneficial, smoothing out and simplifying the partner process. However, when the class is doing the partner ball activity, it is not a good idea to be someone's partner because (1) this activity is long and (2) the activity is complicated enough to require most of your attention. If you have an uneven number, it is better to form one group of three and teach

them how to roll and pass in sequence. Of course I am not advocating eliminating individual help, but that help needs to fit into your consistent control of the tone and rhythm of the class. For new teachers, do not forget that you can ask one child to help another, you can request a child to come to you, you can delegate, and you can ask for help.

≈ Student Objectives

▶ Students will understand the idea of stationary movements and explore a variety of nonlocomotor shakes.

▶ Students will gain a preliminary understanding of partner activities.

▶ Students will gain a preliminary understanding of directions.

- Students will practice ball skills and application of *near* and *far*.
- Students will understand and demonstrate the concept diagonal.

≋ *Materials Needed*

- Two items that make sounds, for example, a drum and a tambourine.
- Balls, one per child.
- A sign with *near* on one side and *far* on the other.
- A sign with a diagonal line drawn on it.
- The incline mat with a flat mat under it.

≋ *Teaching Instructions*

1. Gather the children and ask what it would mean to move and not go anywhere. Explore some of their suggestions for nonlocomotor movements. Alternate locomotor movements done individually with nonlocomotor Partner Shake:

   a. Skip—partners shake hands. After each partner shake, the children bow and say "thank you."

   b. Jump, hop, hopscotch—partners shake feet.

   c. Baby, crab, spider crawl, roll—partners shake elbows.

   d. Side-slide—partners shake knees.

   e. Jazzy walk—partners shake heads (if lice is not a problem).

   f. Run and leap.

2. Get Perfect Spots including facing front; play two rounds of Firecracker. Introduce Maybe I Don't; Maybe I Do to relax shoulders before reviewing Blastoff. Introduce Walk Down Your Front and Right and Left Bug.

3. The partner ball activity begins with the following directions: "Get a partner and sit, facing one another, with your legs wide." Loudly compliment any children who followed the instructions until all get the idea; give partner groups one ball and have them roll it back and forth. Partners are near one another as they roll the ball for a few min-

utes: "This is too easy. Go farther from each other [show the sign] . . . Go even farther . . ." (until the rolling balls are crisscrossing the entire room). Now go near [show the sign] your partner and, instead of rolling, gently bounce pass the ball." The children continue to bounce pass kneeling, standing, and while walking, jogging, and running. Partners bow and thank one another. Everyone who does not have a ball gets one; review and perform the ball study from last time. Then put the balls away.

4. Show a sign with a diagonal line; introduce the concept and find diagonals throughout the room. For a finale, set up the incline mat in the middle of the room on the diagonal. Children run the diagonal of the room shouting "Diagonal!" and somersault down the mat.

≋ *Adaptations*

Easier

- Eliminate the preliminary introduction to nonlocomotor movements; simply alternate locomotor movements with partner shakes.
- For this first time, have the children just shake hands each time rather than different body parts.
- When doing the partner ball activity, eliminate the bounce pass and have the children just roll the ball. Children practice going nearer and farther while rolling the ball but do not get too far.

Harder

- For Partner Shake, introduce the idea of a "brand-new" partner each time.
- You can make the Partner Shakes much more difficult by (1) using less common body parts, for example wrists, thighs, shoulders; (2) asking for two different body parts, for example knee to elbow, head to shoulder, hip to back.
- Do Walk Down Your Front keeping the legs straight.
- When doing the partner ball roll, encourage the children to get very far from each other. When they are running and passing the ball, have both children running continuously as they pass the ball.

English Language Development

- ▶ During the warm-up, have the children shout both the locomotor movement they are doing and the name of the body part they are shaking.

- ▶ It should be considered part of the exercise to call out "Maybe I don't . . ."; "Ten, nine . . . Blastoff!"; and "Hello, right ear . . ."

- ▶ Let partners shout "nearer" and "farther" as they demonstrate these with the partner ball roll.

- ▶ When finding diagonals, the children should call out the word "diagonal" as well as what object they are working with, for example, "The diagonal line goes from this corner to that one on the mat."

≋ Assessment

Because this lesson introduces several new concepts—nonlocomotor, partner work, diagonal—it is a good time to evaluate attention spans. For most of the children, these concepts will be brand-new, and grasping them will require a strong focus of attention. Notice the children who looked directly at you when you were presenting—those who were visually distracted will need specific instruction on visual focus. Notice the children who directly sought a partner during the Partner Shakes—those who went running randomly throughout the room will need specific instruction on kinetic focus. Notice the children who grasped the overall concept of diagonal and were able to apply it. Those who needed constant literal examples will need specific instruction on applying information.

I am hesitant to mention ADD (attention deficit disorder) or ADHD (attention deficit-hyperactivity disorder). These are current catchall diagnoses and possibly overused. Many children labeled with attention deficit would be greatly helped by (1) a more structured home environment and (2) a strenuous release of physical energy. However, there are children who are truly hampered by lack of attention. The type of assessment possible throughout this lesson will prove useful in starting a log of observations that concern attention and focus of mental energy. It is too early to judge here; this is the time just to notice.

4.5

PRESCHOOL – 1ST GRADE

Reflections and Options

Lesson 4, Approaching Partners, was an afterthought. I had written the sequence going directly from Mastering the Two Organizations to Partners and then realized it was not what I would do. It would be preferable not to move so quickly. All children, but especially young ones, like a small taste before being thrown into something. This "taste approach" is much like getting youngsters to try new foods: The chances of their accepting asparagus greatly increase if they are given a tiny taste along with what they are used to. So, in Approaching Partners, we give them a tiny taste of the idea of nonlocomotor and

diagonal. We encourage them to try different partners in the Partner Shake, but for only a few seconds. In the partner ball activity, they keep the same partner and focus their attention on the ball. Through limiting the amount of time with different partners and establishing a relationship that focuses on a prop, this preliminary partner work becomes nonthreatening. The tone of the class as a whole is light and just-for-fun.

There are two considerations concerning this taste approach. First, to introduce a tiny taste of something is not the same as formally teaching it. Do not assume that the class understands nonlocomotor or diagonal. Plan to present these two concepts again (lesson 6) and to talk more in depth about getting partners and being cooperative (lesson 5). Think of this as a foreshadowing of the upcoming lessons. Secondly, we do not always have the luxury of this kind of time. If you

are teaching movement for a specific number of sessions, for example a dance series at a studio or a specified time block at a school, you will probably feel the need to cover a lot of information very quickly. If you can implement the taste approach, though, you will find it very successful.

Lesson 5 works more intensely with partners, and lesson 6 formally presents nonlocomotor and diagonal, then establishes the Diagonal Structure. The ideas of locomotor, nonlocomotor, and partners are pulled together in the Eensy Weensy Spider Dance. Why, then, do we drop all these conceptual balls in lesson 7 and introduce an obstacle course? Because we need a break. Despite the light and fun tone, a lot of information has been presented, and it takes time to process it all. The obstacle course requires maximum physical exertion while allowing the academic focus to take a rest.

LESSON 5

PRESCHOOL – 1ST GRADE

Partners

Teacher to Teacher

The introduction of partner activities should clarify the distinction between a class organization, like the Free Traveling Structure, and a movement activity. You would not attempt partner activities before the class was trained to start and stop on cue. Once a class is trained in the Free Traveling Structure you do not teach it again; the behavioral control allows you to introduce activities like partner work. Once introduced, partner work is a delightful activity to revisit often. The class organizations are like a concrete foundation; movement activities rest on the foundation like an area rug.

How strictly you adhere to the class organization may vary a bit. The partner activities will not be quiet, and the stops will not be as precise as in other Free Traveling Structure work. Do not worry. There is no need to be a marshmallow, but relax your tough standard just a little. Do

not, however, relax any standards dealing with kindness, cooperation, or safety.

Student Objectives

► Students will gain understanding of social skills and will practice them.
► Students will experience a sense of class unity.
► Students will learn the movements to the Eensy Weensy Spider Dance.
► Students will practice a rudimentary somersault.

Materials Needed

► Tambourine.
► If you wish, a tape player and tape of "The Eensy Weensy Spider."
► Ideally an incline mat resting on a flat mat, or two flat mats.

≈ *Teaching Instructions*

1. Warm up with locomotor movements in the Free Traveling Structure: skip, jump, hop, hopscotch, baby, crab, and spider crawl, jazzy walk, side-slide, run and leap.

2. Gather and give the partner lecture (see p. 104), making clear that the children need to act cooperatively and never refuse a partner. Do a number of partner activities: hold both hands and spin (go the other way); hold both hands and side-slide front to front, then back-to-back; link elbows, sit and spin; "secret" roll, Wheelbarrow, Horsie, partner spider crawl, partner run and leap. "Remember who your running partner was."

3. Get Perfect Spots. Review all of Blastoff, Walk Down Your Front, and Right and Left Bug. Briefly review the idea of nonlocomotor. Teach two nonlocomotor moves: "Down came the rain" (shake the body while lowering from a standing reach to sitting) and "washed the spider out" (spin sitting, then get up quickly). "What dance do you think we are going to do?"

4. Teach the Eensy Weensy Spider Dance. (1) Gather and sing the song. (2) Teach the dance with the moves done individually rather than with a partner; stop at the end of each phrase. (3) Return to the "running partner" from the earlier activity and do the dance with partner moves, still stopping at the end of each phrase. (4) Do the dance with partners, eliminating the stop for phrase changes. At this point it would be possible to do the dance to taped music. (5) Have half the class perform, and switch.

5. Line up on one side, quickly review diagonal, and practice the somersault on the diagonal.

≈ *Adaptations*

Easier

▶ If it took more than 8 seconds to get Perfect Spots, or if too many spots were imperfect, do three rounds of Firecracker. If the whole idea of Perfect Spots does not seem solid, take the time now to reteach the structure.

▶ For the partner activities, have children keep the same partner for the whole time. Plan to do the same activities changing partners next time.

▶ When doing the Eensy Weensy Spider Dance, retain the stop between phrases. Attempt the continuous phrases next time.

▶ Add a helping hand to the somersaults.

Harder

▶ During the warm-up, start introducing harder locomotor movements, for example side-slide changing sides, hop holding the other leg, run leap turn.

▶ Have the children bow and change to a "brand-new partner" after each partner activity.

▶ Keep the same sequence to teach the Eensy Weensy Spider Dance, but pick up the pace. Do try the dance with taped music.

▶ Allow the children who want to take running steps before the somersault to do so.

English Language Development

▶ All partner conversations should be in English. When possible, pair your non-English speakers with those who do speak some English.

▶ The children should sing the song while dancing. Explain the meaning of "water spout" and "dried up all the rain."

▶ Have the children "fly" off the incline mat and shout a good-bye message in English.

≈ *Assessment*

There are two basic assessments here, one physical and one social. By this lesson the children have had enough exposure for us to evaluate their ability to stop on cue, their flexibility (stretching over their legs and in the bridge), their sense of balance, and their overall agility (as seen in the somersault). We certainly are not seeking perfection, but the children who are not close to these preliminary skills need to be evaluated further. The introduction to partner activities will also point to obvious social difficulties. Refusing to participate, refusing to switch partners, refusing to seek out a partner, being extremely rough, being extremely timid, getting frantically excited—all are red flags. In many cases, enlisting parental help (parents can have classmates over to their house) can promote social skills. Even if the child has siblings or family members to play with, forging a reciprocal friendship with one or two children from the class can speed up social development.

LESSON 6   PRESCHOOL – 1ST GRADE
Nonlocomotor Movements

〰 Teacher to Teacher

This is a grown-up lesson. The early school years span the widest range of ability levels: Some preschool classes could handle this lesson easily while some first grade classes might have enormous difficulties. Unfortunately, I have often found a three- to four-year difference among schools. Those children who are engaged in actual conversations at home and who are exposed to a wide variety of experiences will be able to grasp a conceptually chock-full lesson like this. Of course that is why the whole Head Start program was developed. But the difficulty for us is to discern whether the lesson is actually too hard or whether the class is not used to working at a given level and needs an intellectual boot-up. Early childhood teachers tend to be so kind and helpful that they rarely allow their children to struggle. Of course I am not advocating frustration and discouragement, but sometimes the greatest gift we can give our charges is the expectation of greatness.

〰 Student Objectives

- ▶ Students will understand the idea of stationary movements and explore a variety of nonlocomotor movements.
- ▶ Students will demonstrate an understanding of the words everybody and nobody.
- ▶ Students will perform a nonlocomotor movement study.
- ▶ Students will perform the Eensy Weensy Spider Dance without teacher help.
- ▶ Students will grasp the concept of diagonal and move in groups on the diagonal (Diagonal Structure).

〰 Materials Needed

- ▶ Two sounds, for example, drum and tambourine.
- ▶ A tape player and tape of "The Eensy Weensy Spider."
- ▶ A sign with a diagonal line drawn on it.

〰 Teaching Instructions

1. Gather and reintroduce the concept nonlocomotor: "If locomotor means going somewhere, what do you guess nonlocomotor [non means not] means? . . . That's right. You remembered we could move and stay in one place. Great." Explore some of the children's ideas for nonlocomotor movements. Alternate locomotor and nonlocomotor movements, using a different sound for each, for example the tambourine for locomotor movements and the drum for nonlocomotor movements.

   a. Skip—introduce swings.

   b. Jump, hop, hopscotch—introduce contract and stretch.

   c. Baby, crab, spider crawl, roll—introduce strike.

   d. Side-slide, jazzy walk—introduce spin.

   e. Run and leap.

2. Get Perfect Spots. Play with the words everybody and nobody using the nonlocomotor movements introduced in the warm-up: "Everybody do front and back swings . . . Nobody swing . . . Nobody contract and stretch . . . Now everybody contract

and stretch . . .". Then put the nonlocomotor movements into a study: front and back swings (four beats), standing contract and stretch (four beats), strike arms (four beats), spin one way and then the other (four beats).

3. Get partners and review the Eensy Weensy Spider Dance. Do the dance with taped music.

4. Review the concept diagonal. Ask for the partners from the dance to combine into groups of four and set up the Diagonal Structure. Do several movements on the diagonal: skip, run, run leap, run leap turn.

≈ Adaptations

Easier

▶ For the warm-up, it is perfectly fine to alternate locomotor movements with just one non-locomotor movement and explore that combination more fully. As an example, the following alternations would work: (1) skip—swing in various ways while standing; (2) jump, hop, hopscotch—swing sitting; (3) crawl—swing lying down; (4) jazzy walk—swing with a jump; (5) run and leap.

▶ The nonlocomotor movement pattern can be simplified in several ways: (1) Use fewer movements or even just one movement done in various ways; (2) give each movement a longer time, say, six or eight beats; (3) pause between movement changes.

▶ Do not use taped music for the dance; sing it instead.

▶ Setting up the Diagonal Structure would be easier if the group formations were eliminated; the class can return to their Spider Dance partners and not combine into groups of four. The problem is that moving on the diagonal will then take longer, and that might cause some restless inattention.

Harder

▶ Use more difficult locomotor movements in the warm-up, for example straddle roll, side-slide changing sides, run leap turn. Require alternate legs for the hops in hopscotch.

▶ You can make the nonlocomotor movement study harder by (1) using more moves;

(2) having less time for each move, say, two beats; (3) not pausing between moves.

▶ Doing a dance to taped music is harder than doing a dance while singing.

▶ After establishing the Diagonal Structure, ask for a study incorporating the nonlocomotor sequence from Perfect Spots. For example, the children can run to the middle of the room, do the nonlocomotor study in the middle, and jazzy walk to the end of the diagonal.

English Language Development

▶ Have the children call out just the nonlocomotor movements they are doing in the warm-up. If you have them call out both the locomotor and the nonlocomotor movements they might lose enthusiasm.

▶ Working with words like *everybody* and *nobody* is perfect English language development work. You might plan to include a couple of words each lesson. One area that seems to be especially hard for English learners is homonyms. Even if they are conversant in English, they have difficulty with homonyms, homophones, and multiple meanings; this shows up statistically on the standardized tests. Demonstrating homonyms and homophones through movement is the best and easiest way to enliven these words. Take ball and ball, for example. Pull out the balls; have the children bounce them for a minute, then set them down and pretend to be waltzing at a ball. Alternate these two types of "ball" several times as you hold up a sign with the word ball. Sometimes you can use simple pantomime. For eye, have the class circle their fingers around their eyes to make "glasses" and run around looking at things; for I they stand still pointing to themselves. Alternate several times while holding up a sign with the word. (For more ideas on working with words, see chapter 11, starting on p. 156.)

▶ At least once or twice, have the groups moving on the diagonal shout "Diagonal!" as they run across.

≈ Assessment

This is a good lesson in which to start assessing the rhythmic ability of the children. Rhythmic ability has been shown to have a strong correlation to math reasoning, and it is worth noting those who truly lack an innate beat. Who were the children that got the four-beat rhythm pattern of the nonlocomotor study, and who did not? Who inherently felt the phrase changes in the Spider Dance and who needed to be told when to change? It is too early to jump to any conclusions, but just as you are continuing to evaluate motor planning, focus of attention, and social skills, this is another area to keep in mind.

LESSON 7   PRESCHOOL – 1ST GRADE
Obstacle Course

Teacher to Teacher

You don't believe your squirmy kindergarteners can do an obstacle course like this, do you? They can. But the first course will be an enormous amount of work for you. Make sure that each activity follows in a visual sequence, and get ready to uphold your standards. This will be a confrontational crossroads. Do not lose sight of the ultimate lesson: If two or three children start acting wild, put them out (in separate corners); if the whole class feels out of control, stop the lesson. They must meet your standards of behavior or they do not participate. Start again with three or four children who are working correctly. Add the rest, a few at a time, as they appear ready. And don't lose heart. I assure you, the second lesson with this obstacle course will be startlingly better.

Student Objectives

▶ Students will gain strength and flexibility through conditioning exercises.

▶ Students will practice several gymnastics stunts and perform them in a remembered order.

▶ Students will explore numerous coordination activities in sequence.

▶ Students will demonstrate correct behavioral controls.

Materials Needed

Everything. It is ideal to have a stegel set up with a balance beam on the lowest notch (if there is a second beam, put it on the medium level), the ladder and slide set on the middle notch, tires in a row, jump ropes, hoppities, a scooter line, foot stompers, balance boards, beanbags, balls, balloons, scarves, two rows of mats, and the incline mat slanted down at the end of one of the mat rows (see figure 14.1).

Instructions for Children using the obstacle course:

1. Climb ladder, walk across the beam of own choice, and slide down.

2. Jump (not step) in the tires.

3. Jump rope 10 times.

4. Choose one vehicle to ride on the scooter line and return it; then choose the other vehicle, ride and return it.

5. Stomp on a foot stomper, catching the beanbag 10 times.

6. Throw and catch a beanbag while balancing on a balance board.

7. Bounce and catch a ball 10 times.

8. Bat a balloon up with different body parts 10 times.

9. Throw and catch scarves 10 times.

10. Somersault down the incline mat and continue rolling any way they want down the first row of mats.

11. Practice the short gymnastics routine learned in the warm-up (somersault jump, bridge, contract, shoulder stand) on the second mat. Start over.

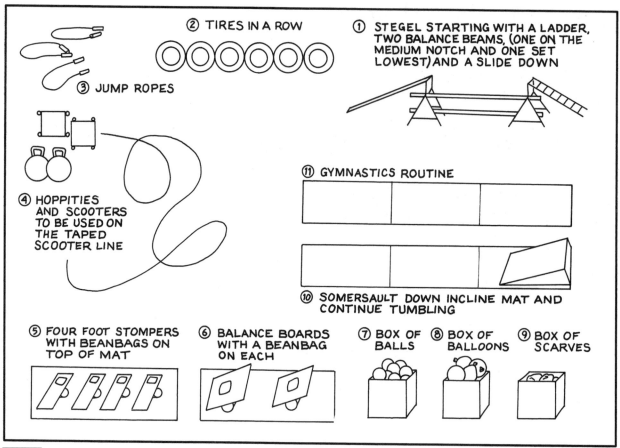

14.1

≋ *Teaching Instructions*

1. Children immediately sit on their own rectangular section of the mats. Do a quick but thorough warm-up: neck circling, torso wave, leg stretches, abdominal crunches, push-ups. Have the children rock back and forth, and then reteach the somersault. Practice continual somersaults, with the class all going the same direction. Reteach the bridge; do contract and shoulder stand. Put the sequence together: one somersault, jump, lie down and stretch into a bridge, contract, shoulder stand. Repeat several times.

2. Gather the class and explain the obstacle course. Emphasize keeping the order of the sequence.

3. Line up and indicate a starting signal, like "When the child ahead of you gets to the top of the ladder, then you go." Do the obstacle course continuously for the rest of the lesson.

≋ *Adaptations*

Easier

▶ Obviously you can shorten the course but, honestly, if the activities follow one another in a visual sequence, the children can do an amazingly long course.

▶ Get help. It would be wonderful to have someone at the jump ropes teaching those who are ready how to actually jump rope and at the scooter line directing traffic. Someone (probably you) definitely needs to be at the stegel/balance beam assisting with any balance problems. Mothers of children at this young age are still willing to help; if not, fifth and sixth graders work just fine.

Harder

▶ Teach the one-knee back roll and add it to the gymnastics routine: somersault, jump, bridge, contract, shoulder stand, one-knee back roll, stand ready to start again.

▶ Obstacle courses are best repeated two or three consecutive times. When you repeat this lesson next class time, introduce the idea of children starting at different points throughout the course to cut down on the initial wait time.

▶ Add a scooter to the stegel slide.

English Language Development

There are so many language possibilities in this lesson that your job will be choosing what to focus on. I recommend concentrating on some of the more abstract words or concepts inherent in an obstacle course. Getting on the balance beam in a stegel arrangement requires the children to go over the top of the stegel; have the children say the word as they execute the move. "No, Margarita, you are trying to go through; that is actually harder. I'll help you go over the top and you say the word over." Words like *loop*, *across*, *throw* and *catch*, *ride*, *kick*, and *stomp* are all excellent for language development.

≈ *Assessment*

The following is a grid of skills assessments drawn from the obstacle course. I think it is unrealistic to try to assess an entire class in all 12 areas during one lesson. If you presented this course two or three times and chose perhaps four or five skills, it would be possible to conduct the testing in a relaxed and lighthearted manner. (I have included the skills of the entire gymnastics sequence so you can continue to use this grid as you add the rest of the moves.) If a child cannot do the skill at all, draw a circle; if she can partially accomplish the skill, draw a slanted line; and if she has mastered the skill mark an "X." This way the symbols can be superimposed one on the other.

Skills Assessments Class Chart

Category													
1. Balance beam													
2. Motor planning (stegel climb)													
3. Legs together jump (tires)													
4. Jump rope													
5. Visual perception (scooter line)													
6. Eye-hand coordination (ball bounce)													
7. Somersault													
8. Bridge													
9. One-knee back roll													
10. Frog balance													
11. Memory of sequence													
12. Self-control													

LESSON 8

Levels

〜 Teacher to Teacher

This lesson brings up the issue of process and product. Teachers consistently, minute by minute, make decisions about what is important. When you gather the children to view the piece of paper for their first floor pattern, do you arrange the seating so everyone can see, or do you challenge them to organize themselves? Do you simply tell the floundering child where a certain line goes, or do you bring him back to the pattern and have him attempt self-correction? How long do you talk about the objects in the room? How perfect do you expect the corners to be? If you concentrate too long on the process, the class will get frustrated at not accomplishing a final product. If you take a tunnel vision approach to the end goal, you will miss many valuable teaching moments. As in most aspects of life, the key is balance. Choose what is most important. Take a few side trips but, on the whole, forge ahead to the goal. This balance of process and product will become easier as you become more experienced and know yourself as a teacher better.

Coming down from this philosophical realm, let me mention a very specific teaching technique. If you do not see imaginative, fanciful, creative play when the children first have free time with the scarves, go to guided movements and then return to free time either within that lesson or the next. If you still do not see fantasy work with the scarves that is not self-conscious, assess whether the tone of the class is safe and whether the children have known you long enough to trust you. Especially with young children, scarves normally bring out their unfettered imagination; and if this is not the case, it would be worthwhile finding out why.

〜 Student Objectives

▶ Students will understand the concept level and will explore levels using nonlocomotor movements.

▶ Students will improve their ability to move straight side with Cops and Robbers.

▶ Students will remember and perform a level study.

▶ Students will demonstrate motor control by stopping Temper Tantrum on cue.

▶ Students will understand the concept of maps and will perform a preliminary floor pattern.

▶ Students will recognize the geometric shape rectangle.

▶ Students will explore their own creativity with scarves.

〜 Materials Needed

▶ Items to make two different sounds, for example drum and tambourine.

▶ A piece of large white construction paper and a set of markers.

▶ Scarves, one per child.

〜 Teaching Instructions

1. Gather and talk about the different definitions of level. Say that in movement class, *level* means height and introduce the five levels: air, standing, knee, sitting, lowest. Briefly review the definitions of locomotor and nonlocomotor. Warm up alternating locomotor movements with nonlocomotor movements done on the five levels; use two different sounds, for example, the tambourine for the locomotor movements and the drum for the nonlocomotor movements.

   a. Skip—shake on all levels.

   b. Jump, hop, hopscotch—swing on all levels.

   c. Crawl, roll—contract and stretch on all levels.

d. Jazzy walk, side-slide—spin on all levels.

e. Run leap turn.

2. Get Perfect Spots. Introduce Cops and Robbers in order to perfect the side-slide; mention that the class will need side-slide a little later. Collectively create a level study. The class selects separate nonlocomotor movements for air, standing, knee, and sitting levels; each move gets four beats. For the lowest level, do an eight-beat Temper Tantrum. Possible outcome: air-level jump turn (four beats); standing-level shake (four beats); knee-level contract and stretch (four beats); sitting-level wide-stride position swing (four beats); lowest-level Temper Tantrum (eight beats).

3. Gather the class around a sheet of construction paper and introduce a room representation. Draw a four-line, rectangular floor pattern and incorporate the word rectangle; include side-slide for one of the lines (reminding class that the side-slide needs to be as clear as it was during Cops and Robbers). As each line is drawn, have one or a few children demonstrate; then divide the class in half and have the two halves take turns doing the whole floor pattern twice.

4. Children pick a scarf and have 5 to 10 minutes free time. Teach the children to fold the scarves when putting them away.

〰 *Adaptations*

Easier

▶ To simplify the level study, count the beats very slowly and call out the name of each level (the children remember the moves). Also, hesitate a second or two between levels.

▶ Take quite a bit of time in establishing the room representation and include many of the children's suggestions as long as the objects are on the edge of the room.

▶ Draw a three-line triangle for the first floor pattern; do use side-slide for one of the lines to tie in Cops and Robbers.

Harder

▶ Make the warm-up longer and include non-locomotor movements strike and twist on all levels.

▶ For the level study, count fairly quickly and do not hesitate between level changes. To make the study much harder, have half the class start on the sitting level and go up to air level while the other half starts on the air level and moves down to sitting; everyone concludes with the Temper Tantrum on the lowest level.

▶ It would be possible to introduce a five- or six-line floor pattern; I recommend a rectangle with a diagonal within it so that the words rectangle and diagonal can both be reinforced.

English Language Development

▶ The word *level* has so many meanings it is worth spending a little time considering multiple meanings. Have the children pretend to play video games and reach a higher level; have them pantomime driving on a level road and then show the antonym of level, a bumpy road; have them be elevators going to different levels of a department store, even extending the fantasy into what items they find in the store. Then introduce the five levels used in movement and, of course, have them call out the level names.

▶ When doing the level study, the class should call out the level and the movement, for example, "air-level shake."

▶ Floor patterns are a gold mine of English Language Development possibilities. When drawing the room representation, take some time identifying and talking about the objects you are drawing, for example, "Here is the desk in the corner of the room, next to the mats . . . What color are those mats? . . . Yes. Here is the piano with my coffee mug on it . . . What is a mug? . . . Good. These are the back doors leading to the playground. What are these? Where do they go? Great."

▶ In addition to the objects in the room representation, the floor pattern itself can be used to reinforce the names of the locomotor movements, the name of the pattern shape (e.g., rectangle), and the word *diagonal*.

▶ Scarves are another English Language Development gold mine. Have the children tell you, in English, what they are pretending. Words like *bride* and *groom*, *matador* and *bull*, *grandma*, *Ninja*, and *ballet dancer* will definitely come up.

Assessment

The main assessment in this lesson is visual perceptual work. In lesson 7, the obstacle course, you observed children following the scooter line and noted who could not track the loops correctly. In this lesson the visual perceptual work is broadened to include the child's overall spatial awareness. Were there children who could not use the room representation to orient themselves in the room? Was any child totally confused as to the direction of the drawn lines? That is, did she start going opposite everyone else? As I say so often,

do not jump to any conclusions, but this is a good opportunity to further observe those children who you already suspect might have visual perceptual problems. Subtle visual or spatial problems will probably not show up here—since the floor pattern is done in groups, someone having difficulty can rely on following everyone else. But often you can just tell who does not really get it by the hesitancy of her movement.

It might be time now to identify who does not land a jump equally on both feet and who cannot skip. Why not use jump and skip in the floor pattern so you can see the children clearly? If a child has enormous difficulties, that information will reinforce other observations and can be used to write up a referral. For children whose troubles with jumping and skipping do not fit an overall pattern of motor problems, it is time to take them aside and give them a few minutes of individual tutoring.

LESSON 9   PRESCHOOL – 1ST GRADE

Star Floor Pattern

Teacher to Teacher

One of the hardest things for a teacher to do is nothing. Most teachers, myself included, are so helpful as to verge on controlling. When you give your class free time with the scarf, let them be. Do not give them ideas and, unless what they want to do is dangerous or destructive, let them try out their wildest fantasies. Sit back and really observe: Enjoy them, laugh with them, note what they are drawn to. It is hard for us to let our students alone because we are driven to impart more and more information, but sometimes, especially with the scarves, that is what they need. One time a state team was evaluating our school. They came into my movement class as the children were exploring free time with balls. They stayed only a minute and left before they could see me "teach"; in fact

I had not said a word while they were there. Later their report described movement as "children just running around." Ah, the tortures of being misunderstood. Despite that, I encourage you to sometimes teach by doing nothing.

Student Objectives

▶ Students will gain an understanding of the four directions and will explore them with locomotor movements.

▶ Students will perform the level study correctly without teacher help.

▶ Students will grasp the concept of middle and be able to apply it in a variety of ways.

▶ Students will perform the star floor pattern.

▶ Students will explore moving with scarves and learn a scarf study.

≋ *Materials Needed*

▸ Tambourine.

▸ For a class of 20, 10 pieces of rope or yarn approximately 1 yard long.

▸ A piece of white construction paper and a set of markers.

▸ Scarves, one per child.

≋ *Teaching Instructions*

1. Gather and introduce the four directions. Warm up alternating locomotor movements done in all four directions with the moves chosen last time for the level study:

   a. Skip forward, backward, sideways, turning—whatever nonlocomotor movement was chosen for air level.

   b. Jump all four directions—whatever movement was chosen for standing level.

   c. Crab crawl all four directions (if the children cannot figure out front, have them sit down, register where front is, and then resume the crawl)—whatever movement was chosen for knee level.

   d. Jazzy walk all four directions—whatever movement was chosen for sitting level.

   e. Run all four directions—Temper Tantrum on lowest level.

2. Get Perfect Spots. Revisit Hello and Good-Bye and Swordfish. Review the level study from last time and perform.

3. Gather and introduce *middle*. Hold a piece of yarn approximately one yard long. Have a student grasp where she thinks the middle is and test her guess by folding the yarn in half to see if the two sides are the same. Have two or three children try to guess. Divide the class into partners and give each partner group a piece of yarn; have the partners practice guessing the middle. Put away the yarn and gather again. Find the middle of objects in the room; end by finding the middles of all four walls and marking each middle.

4. Draw a star floor pattern (see figure 14.2). Using the marked middle of walls, draw and

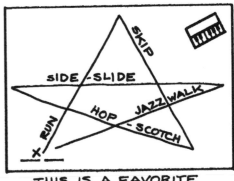

14.2   THIS IS A FAVORITE

demonstrate each line of the star. Divide the class in half and have each group perform the floor pattern two or three times.

5. Have the children pick out their scarves. Extend free time as long as they are truly playing. Go on to guided movements. Have children throw and catch the scarf with different body parts; twirl; pick the scarf up with the toes and hop, then switch feet; roll with the scarf; jazzy walk; side-slide holding the scarf straight; and do sword fight, bull and matador, bride and groom, ballet dancer, Magic Scarf. Children sit cross-legged with the scarf in the lap and choose four scarf activities for a scarf dance, and perform it once.

≋ Adaptations

Easier

▸ Simplify the movements chosen for direction work. The easiest locomotor movements to do in all four directions are walk, jump, baby crawl, and run with high knees.

▸ For finding the middle of a piece of yarn, have the children work together as a class. Ask individual children to guess the middle as you hold the yarn; have approximately four demonstrations and tell the rest of the class they will have a chance next time. (Make sure to do the partner yarn guess next time.)

▸ Have the middle of the walls clearly marked before attempting the star floor pattern.

▸ Eliminate the scarf study and incorporate it next time.

Harder

▶ Be persnickety that the locomotor movements stay the same in all four directions. Watch especially that the skip does not turn into a side-slide sideways, and that the crab crawl stays a crawl and does not become a seat-scoot.

▶ Make sure that each level change takes no extra time and that the movement starts exactly on count 1.

▶ Establish the middle of the walls but do not have the markers there when you teach the star floor pattern.

▶ Choose six scarf moves for a scarf dance sequence.

English Language Development

▶ The way we worked with *middle* is a good example of how movement can be used to make abstract words concrete. The initial presentation can be conducted in English; and when the children are working with partners and guessing the middle of the yarn length, encourage them to converse in English.

▶ One of my favorite English Language Development lessons is using scarves. Have the children call out the body part names as they throw and catch their scarves. For example, you can direct them, "Catch your scarf with your shoulders," and have them shout "shoulder" as their scarf lands on their shoulder. When they are ready, use less standard body parts, such as wrist, calf, hip, bottom, abdomen, neck, thigh.

≋ Assessment

This is another juncture at which to assess your class as a whole in order to decide whether they have the concept of floor pattern and are ready to build on it, or instead need to stay here a while and practice. Did they get middle, and could they find the middle of various objects? Do they need a specific lesson on corner? Could they remember the five lines of the star pattern without your help? Are they itching to go on, or would they like to repeat the star pattern and then work on a few more four- to six-line patterns? Floor patterns can encompass an enormously complex curriculum, but it is of no use if the initial concepts of orientation to the room and line design are shaky.

LESSON 10   PRESCHOOL – 1ST GRADE
Creating Their Own Floor Patterns

≋ Teacher to Teacher

Be brave. Honestly, young children can do a cooperative lesson. It will not be wild and crazy. They will love it and rise to the challenge. I have two suggestions. First, cover as many bases as you can; details can make or break a lesson. Make sure you have enough room representations drawn so that when a group destroys one or several, you do not need to make more. Make sure you have enough sets of crayons so groups do not have to share, and if you are using markers, check that they work. Make sure the room is set up the way you

have drawn it. Second, at each step assess whether you can go on or whether you need to stop and consolidate the information. For example, if most of the children were not at ease putting the room representation straight, do not go on to the cooperative lesson; do a helping floor pattern and perform it, then approach the cooperative study another day. If the class had difficulty creating the helping floor pattern, practice this one and plan to do several more before assigning the study. This is just the way you work in reading and math, but sometimes teachers forget that movement is a subject like any other.

≋ *Student Objectives*

▶ Students will gain an awareness of how to find the spelling of various locomotor movement words.

▶ Students will grasp the procedure for creating a floor pattern (helping floor pattern).

▶ Students will work cooperatively to create a floor pattern.

▶ Students will correctly perform the scarf study without teacher help.

≋ *Materials Needed*

▶ A chart with the basic locomotor movements printed on it.

▶ Tambourine.

▶ Approximately 10 sheets of large white construction paper with room representations drawn on them, five sets of markers or crayons.

▶ Scarves, one per child.

≋ *Teaching Instructions*

1. Warm up with locomotor movements in the Free Traveling Structure, but instead of saying the movement word, spell it out and point to the chart. The children call out the word before demonstrating it. Do skip, jump, hop, hopscotch, side-slide, crawl, roll, jazzy walk, and run and leap with a partner.

2. Gather the children around one of the already drawn room representations and talk about placing the diagram straight the way things are in the room (see figure 14.3). Have a few children practice putting the room representation straight. Draw a four-line helping floor pattern; emphasize the connection between lines.

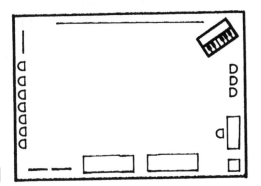

14.3

3. Children return to their "running partner" from the warm-up and combine into groups of four, sitting in a circle on the floor. As soon as one group completes these instructions, give them a room representation and a set of crayons; continue until all the groups are organized. Assign a four-line floor pattern; point to the chart used in the warm up or help write the locomotor movement words. Check each pattern before the group is allowed to practice. Save the performance for next time.

4. Children pick their scarves and review the scarf study from last time. Practice and perform.

≋ *Adaptations*

Easier

▶ Divide this lesson in half. Do the spelling warm-up and introduce the helping floor pattern; perform this pattern and go on to the scarf study. The next time do another helping floor pattern and then ask the class to attempt their own.

▶ It seems obvious that an assignment of a three-line floor pattern would be easier, but if the groups consist of four children this causes extensive social negotiations. It is fine to form groups of three; however, keep in mind that you will need more room representations and crayons, and that performance will take longer. If you decide to form groups of three, do not ask for "running partners" in the warm-up.

▶ Can you get some help for this lesson? Consider asking a couple of moms or two or three sixth graders to assist with this first cooperative study.

Harder

▶ Include more locomotor movement words in the spelling warm-up: gallop, jog, slide on the floor, kick, run and click heels, run and turn around.

▶ No matter how mature your class, I recommend still assigning a four-line floor pattern to groups of four. If they say, "This is a cinch," tell them to just wait.

▶ Review the room representation as you did the last two times, but go faster.

▶ The scarf study could easily be extended to five or six parts.

English Language Development

▶ The spelling warm-up is excellent English Language Development work. If you want to extend the activity, ask the class to spell the names with you and then call out the word; be careful that Spanish-speaking children say the letters "i" and "e" correctly.

▶ If you have mostly Asian children, consider putting endings onto the locomotor movement words—for *skip*, for example, *skips, skipped, skipping*—because this is an area of difficulty for them.

▶ Emphasize the word *connect* by having children touch their two index fingers together while calling out "connect".

▶ Require the groups to call out the locomotor movement before demonstrating each line of their floor pattern. This should be a consistent part of floor pattern activities with English learners.

▶ When reviewing the scarf sequence, ask the children to verbally name the moves but do not have them call the names out when they are performing.

≈ Assessment

The two observations that will stand out in bold relief are spatial awareness and social skills. Note the children who had great difficulty in aligning the room representation; this is a more significant evaluation than the actual floor pattern. Does the lack of orientation fit into other spatial concerns? For example, does the child have trouble tracking, especially backtracking? Does the child move awkwardly in general, especially bumping into furniture and people? These concerns can branch into more specific evaluations of midline difficulties, vision problems, or sensory integration needs. Working in groups will quickly bring out any social dysfunction. Who was not able to join a group? Who immediately found a reason to sulk away? Who was calling you to help him because the others did not want his ideas? Who was trying to run the entire group? Who did not feel able to offer any ideas? This first cooperative study is a great time to evaluate social skills and at the same time a golden opportunity to specifically instruct children in working together.

LESSON 11   PRESCHOOL – 1ST GRADE

The In and Out Game

≈ Teacher to Teacher

This is the most competitive we get. Even so, many young children do not like competition and do not deal well with it. Notice in the "Assessment" section at the end of this lesson that I veer away from the term *winner*. I avoid the words *winner* and *loser*, preferring "those that were able to stay in the game" and "those that were not." Also, any bad behavior like sulking, arguing, kicking, cheating, or throwing equipment gets a warning and then, if continued, the child is out for that day. Better to play a good game with half the class than tolerate petty tyrants. But the most important factor in instilling good sportspersonship is your attitude. If the game is kept lighthearted, fast paced, and playful, that joyful spirit will overcome any rough edges coming from competitiveness.

≈ Student Objectives

▶ Students will understand and be able to demonstrate a myriad of words through the In and Out Game.

▸ Students will exhibit good sportspersonship.

▸ Students will correctly perform their group floor patterns without teacher help.

▸ Students will gain a concrete sense of number and computation.

▸ Students will practice motor planning through the Foam Jump.

≋ *Materials Needed*

▸ Scatter virtually any equipment available throughout the room: three mats lying flat, two mats standing like little houses, all the foam squares from the Foam Jump, tires, plastic hoops, a stegel end, a few tables, several chairs (preferably the nonfolding kind), beanbags, foam shapes, cones, the incline mat.

▸ The children's group floor patterns from last time.

▸ Tambourine.

▸ The foam squares and mat necessary for the Foam Jump (used in the In and Out Game as well).

≋ *Teaching Instructions*

1. Have all the equipment scattered before the children come in. As soon as they have their socks and shoes put away, ask them to skip over objects in the room, not touching anything but the floor. Warm up with different locomotor movements going over things: jump, hop, crawl, jazzy walk, leap.

2. The children sit on one side of the room; individual children demonstrate each of the following words:

   a. On top
   b. Under
   c. Above (same as on top)
   d. Below (same as under)
   e. Beneath (same as under)
   f. Around
   g. In
   h. Beside a chair
   i. Behind a chair
   j. In front of a chair
   k. Between . . . (specify two objects)
   l. Through

3. Play the In and Out Game. Call out a word and count to 10. Those children not there on time or not demonstrating the word correctly have to sit out; on the way they say "Oh well, it's only a game." When a few children are left, make them all finalists if they do the last word correctly.

4. After the children clean up the equipment, return their floor patterns. Check that the groups put their maps down on the floor and that the room representations are aligned the way things are in the room. Give them time to practice, then have each group perform.

5. End with the Foam Jump.

≋ *Adaptations*

Easier

▸ You could divide this lesson in half. Review the children's floor patterns and introduce the Foam Jump. Then, in a separate lesson, play the In and Out Game and do the Foam Jump again.

▸ Use fewer words: on top, under, around, in, beside a chair, behind a chair, in front of a chair, and possibly between.

▸ Count slowly.

▸ After returning the floor patterns, help every group read what they have written.

▸ Use only five or six pieces of foam for the Foam Jump.

Harder

▸ Use all the words listed previously plus geometry vocabulary.

▸ Require precision from the group floor patterns: Check that the corners are fairly sharp and that the lines go exactly where they are drawn.

▸ Use 10 pieces of foam for the Foam Jump.

English Language Development

▸ This is English language development heaven. The In and Out Game is designed specifically to teach relationship words and geometry vocabulary. Of course the game should be conducted strictly in English; non-English speakers need to have a partner for help. For classes that are mostly non-English speaking, use fewer words and go a bit slower; as soon as they catch on, add the rest of the words and pick up the pace.

▶ The group floor patterns are an excellent English language tool especially if all negotiations are conducted in English. Groups should call out the locomotor movement before executing a line.

▶ The Foam Jump is excellent for working with the names of the numbers as well as computation of numbers: "I want to jump six; add two more on."

≋ Assessment

It is very curious that the children who do extremely well with the In and Out Game are not necessarily those with a command of the language or those that are especially athletic. The children who remain until the end of the round are the problem solvers. They understand that by manipulating one or a few pieces of equipment, they can execute most of the words. This activity is an excellent evaluation of their overall problem-solving skills. In addition, the way they handle "losing" speaks volumes about their social skills and sportspersonship. Did they argue with you? Were they able to say, "Oh well, it's only a game" even through clenched teeth? Did they try to cheat? In addition to enabling you to assess the skill levels of the children, this is a golden opportunity to teach directly to their problem areas. In this case the most effective teaching is positive reinforcement and modeling: "Wow, Karla stayed in the game until the end again. Do you notice how she focuses hard on what I am saying and then finds ways of showing the words by moving equipment or going to nearby equipment? She does not go racing across the room to be with her friends. She also knows that there are many ways of showing a word. That really helps her stay in the game." "Rodney, you have a class warning for cheating. One more warning and you're out. This is not how to play a game."

LESSON 12   PRESCHOOL – 1ST GRADE
The Bears in the Night Dance

≋ Teacher to Teacher

This lesson can be memorable or ordinary, depending on how much you ham it up. The children's enthusiasm will mirror your own. This applies to all lessons but especially to literature dances and silly guided movements. "Out-of-bed-to-the-window" is very different from "Out of bed! To the window!" And "The-rope-is-a-snake" will not generate the same excitement as "Eek! A snake is following me! Help!" Of course you must be who you are, but I encourage you to let loose and enjoy playing with the children. I remember as a new mother being scared to death of doing something wrong; I took meticulous care of my firstborn but I was a little grim. After a few weeks an experienced mother showed me how to have fun with my baby. It was one of the most important lessons I ever learned.

The Bears in the Night Dance is repeatedly requested. The children would probably enjoy doing it again next time, and then you could revisit it every once in a while. The whole idea of revisiting past dances or studies is actually an important issue. We want to charge ahead and present more and more material, but sometimes the best idea is to go back to a dance that we know and love. Like a well-worn book, dances revisited are comforting but also take us to deeper levels of understanding.

≈ Student Objectives:

▶ Students will gain a greater understanding of relationship words.

▶ Students will experience the story and sequence of *Bears in the Night*.

▶ Students will explore a variety of ways of moving with a rope.

▶ Students will begin to acquire the skill of jumping rope.

▶ Students will practice the computational and motor planning skills of the Foam Jump.

≈ Materials Needed

▶ The book *Bears in the Night* by Stan and Jan Berenstain.

▶ Setup for the story: one stegel end with the slide attached, foam pieces at one end of a mat, a table, the parachute, four folded mats forming an arrangement of two sets of two mats with a small space between them, tires, the incline mat.

▶ Ropes, one per child.

Description of diagram (see figure 14.4):

1. Two mats on top of each other make a bed with a cover.
2. One stegel end with paper "curtain" for a window and a slide for "down the slide."
3. Foam pillows make a "wall" adjacent to a mat.
4. A table is a bridge.
5. The parachute is the "lake."
6. Two sets of two mats stacked on top of one another with a small space between allow students to squeeze "between the rocks."
7. Tires randomly placed make the "woods."
8. The incline mat rests on a flat mat for "Spook Mountain."

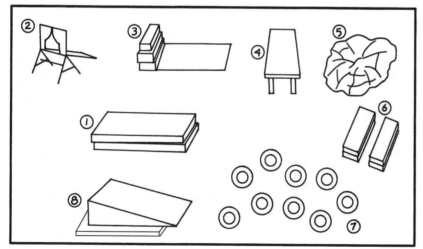

① "IN BED"
② "THROUGH THE WINDOW" AND "DOWN THE TREE"
③ "OVER THE WALL"
④ "UNDER THE BRIDGE"
⑤ "AROUND THE LAKE"
⑥ "BETWEEN THE ROCKS"
⑦ "THROUGH THE WOODS"
⑧ "UP SPOOK MOUNTAIN"

14.4

≋ *Teaching Instructions*

1. Read *Bears in the Night* and do the dance with half the class performing at a time; the audience half does the sound effects. The children help with cleanup of the equipment.

2. Children get a rope and have some free time; during their free time, sit them down and demonstrate how to jump rope, then allow additional free time so they can practice. Go on to guided movements:

    a. Lay the rope straight on the floor and jump side to side; walk on it as on a tightrope; do a football run; do a crazy walk.

    b. Make a circle out of the rope and jump in and out, run around it, leap over it.

    c. Act silly by making the rope into a snake, playing Broken Leg, swinging jazzy circles, using the rope as a microphone.

    d. Get partners and play telephone; end with Horsie.

3. Do the Foam Jump again, this time asking for a math statement, for example, "I want to jump over six, add two more".

≋ *Adaptations*

Easier

▸ Read *Bears in the Night* in class once or twice before movement class. Consider having a third of the class, rather than half, perform at a time; leave the squirmiest ones for the last group. Go slower.

▸ Eliminate teaching regular jump rope for this time.

▸ For the Foam Jump, the children just ask for the number they want, not making the math statement—for example, "I want to jump five."

Harder

▸ Quicken the pace of the Bears in the Night Dance.

▸ When working with ropes, definitely spend some time practicing regular rope jumping.

▸ When the rope is in a circle, introduce a cartwheel—hands in and legs over; also when the rope is in a circle, introduce the pattern jump in and out, side to side, front and back, open and closed.

▸ For the Foam Jump, ask for a complete equation; for example, "I want to jump six, add two more; four plus two equals six."

English Language Development

▸ Doing the Bears in the Night Dance, especially after the In and Out Game last time, is excellent English Language Development work. Remember to keep everything, even the initial instructions, the behavior reprimands, the cleanup work, in English.

▸ All the guided movement ideas with the rope should be done with verbalization, for example, "Help! There's a snake following me" and "Oh, no, I broke my leg! Now I broke my other leg."

▸ The "microphone" activity with the rope is wonderful for English learners; take extra time and encourage them to make a speech or sing a song in English.

▸ Make sure that the partners in the rope "telephone" converse in English.

▸ When doing the Foam Jump, have the children say the number equation in English even if it means repeating you.

≋ *Assessment*

This lesson provides a generalized evaluation of maturity levels and specific assessments of coordination skills. If I were considering retaining a child, his execution of the Bears in the Night Dance would be strong corroborative information. Perhaps this is too much emphasis to place on one activity but its format does make it an encompassing assessment tool. Maturity is the balance of self-interest with the needs of others and the goal as a whole. A child who acts so goofy that she destroys the flow of the dance is exhibiting immature behavior. A child who enjoys himself yet stays within the boundaries of the story sequence is showing a lot of maturity. We can encourage and help children grow into more mature beings, but sometimes we need to simply give them another year to grow up. Of course I am not saying that their performance of The Bears in the Night Dance should be the crux of retention, but their ability to delay immediate gratification is an important consideration.

Working with ropes allows many opportunities to observe the children jumping. I do not expect many of the children at this young age to be able to actually jump rope; but I would be concerned about any child who could not, for the most part, jump with a two-foot landing. (It might not be a perfectly equal landing, but it is visibly a two-foot rather than a "gallop" landing.) Check to see if one leg is much weaker than the other by observing the child hop on either foot. If hopping on one foot (usually the left) is a great deal more difficult than on the other, does that fit into a pattern of lack of balance or general awkwardness?

Is the child's muscular development weak on the whole? Does she have other noticeable coordination problems? Does she have difficulty with small-muscle control? Nothing is set in stone, but a child who has enormous, consistent trouble jumping should be evaluated further.

The Foam Jump can be used for further evaluation of motor coordination ability. What I find especially interesting about the Foam Jump is noting which children are more internally focused and which are more externally focused. The internally focused children will pick a number of foam pieces that they think they can succeed with; the externally focused children pick a number that they think will impress the other children, and they often end up sprawled on the mat. Unless I think it too dangerous, I let them choose.

12.5

Reflections and Options

Are you proud of what your students have accomplished? I hope you are proud of what you have accomplished—this has been a huge and scary undertaking. You are to be congratulated. Now you need to decide how you will end the movement classes this year. You have three main options: Keep teaching, plan a just-for-fun class, or present a show. (I say main because you can modify or combine these options, for example a just-for-fun class with the parents invited or a show that is actually a demonstration class.)

The advantages of simply continuing to teach are that the students need all the information they can get, it is the easiest plan for you, and young

children get hyperexcited very easily. If you choose this route I urge you to tell the children a few weeks ahead and remind them several times so that the ending will not come as a shock. Do a brief good-bye activity like "flying" off the incline mat with a good-bye message, or do Mushroom (p. 141) and tell them good-bye while they are under the parachute. The following lessons continue to present new material.

A just-for-fun ending is also easy and you can continue teaching almost to the last class. Ask the children what they would like for their last class, but do not wed yourself to their suggestions. They will probably say an obstacle course, the In and Out Game, the parachute, and balls. Impossible. You could combine an obstacle course or the In and Out Game with a little parachute time at the end; or you could warm up with balls and have the children play with the parachute and incline mat for a good last class. Do not try to cram too much in. It will not be fun.

You might notice that I have not included the Opposite Game in the lesson plans for this age group. Older children love it and would definitely request it for the last class. Very young children sometimes do not like this game because they are uneasy with my pretending to be mad at them—they are so literal. (Did I ever tell you about the time I told a first grade class to head back in the Grocery Store Dance—meaning to return to their spots—and they all tilted their heads back?) But some mature young children get the game and love it; those classes will definitely want the Opposite Game for their last lesson. Try the game before the last session and plan to do it at least twice to see if the children are mature enough to enjoy it.

I personally lean toward a showy ending. A show is terrific experience in mastery, poise under pressure, and self-responsibility; it also provides a complete sense of closure. Shows are crucial for private schools and studios in order to build up goodwill and financial support—parents want to see what their tuition checks are accomplishing. In the lower-socioeconomic-level schools, children have very few performance opportunities and truly need the experience.

But shows are a lot of work, and in some ways, shows with very young children are the hardest. (1) Young children will do the unexpected. You can almost count on one child peeing on the floor and one getting a bloody nose; your most reliable student will get the heebie-jeebies and refuse to participate—meanwhile both his parents, his grandparents from Florida, and several other relatives will have come to watch him. The child you least expected to do brilliantly will do brilliantly and have no one to witness it. (2) The younger the class, the more guests (and video cameras). It will be hard to balance the children's acting "cute" for the cameras (being too performance oriented) with just wanting to play (not being performance oriented enough). Given all these dire warnings, young children can pull together fabulous shows; we need to expect it and work for it.

1. Considering the foregoing curriculum, the following is a possible show. The Bears in the Night Dance makes a spectacular opening. Half the class performs at a time. Have the room already set up and have five older helpers ready to clean it up. (Do not clean up yourself; rather while the Bears in the Night Dance setup is being put away, ask the class to get Perfect Spots. You want as little transition wait time as possible.)

2. Have the children get Perfect Spots and calm down with Hello and Good-Bye and Blastoff. Mention to the visitors that getting Perfect Spots is difficult for young children and that this is an important part of the performance. Sometimes audiences need to be told what treasures they are seeing.

3. Still in Perfect Spots, do the nonlocomotor study (lesson 6) and the level study (lesson 8).

4. Get partners and present the Eensy Weensy Spider Dance. The partners should be arranged beforehand and be taken from the cooperative groups that created their own floor patterns.

5. Show the created group floor patterns (lesson 10).

6. Get scarves and show the scarf sequence (lesson 9).

7. End with the whole class performing the line shape floor pattern combined with scarves (lesson 15). If you do not get this far

in the lesson plans, go from the group floor patterns to a whole-class star floor pattern; then end with the scarf sequence.

Phew! Just a few thoughts:

▶ Plan for at least four full practice sessions. This is not wasted time.

▶ Practice the transitions as much as the dances themselves. Even at this age, transitions should

be quiet and smooth. "Show me where you are at the end of the Bears in the Night Dance; now get your Perfect Spots. No, too slow. Again. No, too noisy. Again. Again."

▶ Expect that the show will go much faster than planned. If it looks like an hour show to you, it will probably be over in 40 minutes. The show just described is under an hour.

▶ Take your vitamins.

LESSON **13**   PRESCHOOL – 1ST GRADE

Ropes

≋ Teacher to Teacher

A continual high point of my teaching career has been introducing the parachute to young children as I do later in this lesson. That introduction creates such a sense of glee and pure enjoyment. However, it creates a tension for us teachers: We want to play and let loose but we want the class orderly. There is no formula for that balance, but I offer a few suggestions. (1) Always start with Ocean, in which the children vigorously shake the parachute. This will tire them out and allow them to release all that excited energy. (2) Do not allow any children to wreck or slow down the activity for the rest. If some children will not come out of the parachute before it lands on them, warn them and then put them out. This is not pleasant but is only fair to the rest; moreover, if some children get away with wild behavior, the rest will be tempted to follow. (3) If you are up for it, consider going on the Ocean and under the Whoosh with them. The class will love it, and it will greatly heighten the sense of play. Who knows, you might love it too.

≋ Student Objectives

▶ Students will gain experience and coordination skills working with ropes.

▶ Students will understand the difference between several line shapes.

▶ Students will experience a sense of exuberance and class unity with the parachute.

≋ Materials Needed

▶ Ropes, one per child.

▶ Chart of the various line shapes.

▶ Three cones or other markers.

▶ One 24-foot parachute and one ball.

≋ Teaching Instructions

1. Children immediately get a rope and have some free time.

   a. Review how to jump rope and take time to practice.

   b. Try other activities with the rope that were introduced last time: Lay it straight on the floor and jump side to side; walk as if it were a tightrope; football run; make a circle with it and jump in and out, run around it, leap over it; pretend it is a snake following behind; make jazzy circles; play Broken Leg; use it as a microphone and a telephone; play Horsie using one rope for each partner group.

2. Have the children stay with the partners from Horsie and, together, make the line shapes shown on the chart: straight, curved, wiggly, zigzag, and spiral.

3. Have them stay with that partner and combine into groups of four, ready to move on the diagonal.

   a. Do a couple of locomotor movements going straight on the diagonal: skip, run, run and leap.

   b. Run a curved line on the diagonal.

   c. Run a shallow wiggly line on the diagonal.

   d. Walk a zigzag line on the diagonal.

   e. Teach a huge wiggly line with markers; take one marker away at a time until the children can do the line on their own.

4. Introduce the parachute. "Last week we used the parachute as our lake in the Bears in the Night Dance; this week we'll see what else we can do. Open the parachute up and hold the edge. Start shaking!" Do: Ocean, Whoosh with Hamburgers and French Fries, and Shark.

≋ Adaptations

Easier

▶ When working with line shapes, use only straight, curved, wiggly, and spiral lines. Save zigzag and looped for next year.

▶ If the class is not ready, do not push taking the markers away for the huge wiggly line; save that for next time.

▶ It would be wonderful to have at least two other bigger people when working with the parachute—form a triangular arrangement among the children.

▶ Do Whoosh using a girl-boy division instead of Hamburgers and French Fries.

Harder

▶ Introduce the looped line in the rope warm-up and try it in groups when working in the Diagonal Structure.

▶ Be more persnickety about how the line shapes are done in movement, especially how close to or far from the edges of the room the lines come.

▶ In addition to the parachute activities listed in the lesson, introduce Trap.

English Language Development

▶ Review all the verbalization accompanying the work with ropes.

▶ Have the children call out the line shapes they make with the ropes.

▶ I would not recommend having the children call out the line shape when working on the diagonal. It will take all their concentration to execute the movement correctly, and the verbalization might hinder them.

▶ Parachute activities incorporate many language possibilities: Edge, shake, on top, under, hamburgers, French fries, taut, float down, and shark will become embedded in their vocabularies if you are scrupulous in speaking only in English. Choose a few of the words you feel are most important for the children to shout out.

≋ Assessment

This lesson delves more deeply into the area of spatial awareness. Note any children who could not make their rope into the various line shapes, although this will not be a totally accurate assessment because they are in partners. The one activity to watch carefully is the huge wiggly line. Children with midline and tracking problems will have enormous difficulty reversing their line from one side of the room to the other and tend to go directly from cone 1 to cone 3. Note whether this fits in with other visual perceptual problems, like any seen in the scooter line from lesson 7. What is so beneficial about this backtracking activity is that it points to visual perceptual difficulties and at the same time helps remedy them.

LESSON **14**　　　　P R E S C H O O L – 1ST G R A D E

A Floor Pattern Using Different Line Shapes

≋ Teacher to Teacher

This lesson has several difficult transitions: going from the partner rope activity to the whole-class demonstration of the floor pattern, dividing into groups to perform the floor pattern, and then returning to whole class for the parachute and dance introduction. That brings me to the general topic of transitions. The three class management organizations (Free Traveling Structure, Perfect Spots, Diagonal Structure) provide control during the movement activities. Where the class is most likely to get out of control, or at least waste time, is going from one activity to the next. To minimize this possibility, work to smooth the transitions by planning ahead. For example, at the end of the warm-up with ropes, the children do Horsie with partners. If they remember this partner, they can easily combine partners into groups of four to perform the floor pattern. Combining partners is significantly easier than forming groups from scratch. It is also easier because the children did this same procedure in the last lesson: After working with a partner using ropes, they combined partners to move on the diagonal. If you want to perform the floor pattern with larger groups, again return to the Horsie partners and count them off by twos into groups of six or eight.

Do not worry about this. If you are a beginning teacher you might not be ready to think about subtle transition strategies. That is fine. If the students lose a little time going from one thing to the next it is OK; they are still getting the benefits of a movement program. If you are more experienced, give a thought to easing the transition of activities by preparing the social arrangements.

≋ Student Objectives

▶ Students will practice coordination activities with the rope, especially two-foot landings.

▶ Students will demonstrate their understanding of different line shapes by performing a floor pattern utilizing these shapes.

▶ Students will continue to experience the exuberance and class unity of parachute work.

▶ Students will demonstrate motor planning and self-discipline with parachute activities.

▶ Students will exhibit a freedom of expression with the introduction of the Grocery Store Dance.

≋ Materials Needed

▶ A chart of line shapes.

▶ White construction paper and a set of markers.

▶ One 24-foot parachute and one ball.

▶ If possible, a piece of Swiss cheese, one plum, one ear of corn on the cob, and a couple of string beans.

≋ Teaching Instructions

1. Immediately get ropes and take a few minutes for free time. Review many of the rope activities from last time. End with Horsie using one rope for each partner group. Have the children stay with that partner, and review forming various line shapes with

the rope. The children put the rope away by hanging it up from the middle.

2. Gather around one piece of construction paper and draw a floor pattern using various line shapes (see p. 91). Have one or a few children demonstrate each line as it is drawn. Groups take turns performing the pattern two or three times.

3. Review the parachute activities from last time: Ocean, Whoosh with Hamburgers and French Fries, Shark. Add Mushroom.

4. Introduce the Grocery Store Dance. Show a slice of cheese and ask how the children would move like "cheese walking on its knees"; take a few ideas and then have the whole class try the pantomime. Show a plum and teach the class how to twiddle their thumbs; have them walk turning in a rounded position twiddling their thumbs—"There were plums, plums, twiddling their thumbs." Show corn on the cob and ask the children to pretend to silently blow horns—"There was corn, corn, blowing on their horns." Finally, show a string bean and ask the children to act like beans trying on a pair of jeans that are too tight—"There were beans, beans, trying on some jeans." Ask the class to remember these pantomimes for next time.

≈ *Adaptations*

Easier

► The floor pattern can be reduced to three lines; use a straight, a wiggly, and a spiral line.

► Have half the class perform the floor pattern at a time. If possible, go with the groups the first time they perform and then have them try it on their own.

► Get two helpers for the parachute.

► Divide this lesson in half: End with the parachute this time; next time review the floor pattern and introduce the Grocery Store Dance.

Harder

► Introduce zigzag and looped lines when working with the ropes, and then include these lines in the floor pattern.

► The floor pattern can be extended to six or seven lines.

► Be strict about how the lines are executed.

► Introduce harder parachute activities like Merry-Go-Round or Rock and Wave.

English Language Development

► When working with the ropes, ask the children to call out many of the words they are demonstrating, for example in and out, around, snake, help, broken leg, microphone, telephone, Horsie, middle.

► Do not have the children call out movement vocabulary while doing the floor pattern; they need to concentrate on the spatial challenge.

► The introduction to the Grocery Store Dance is a perfect English Language Development lesson combining realia, verbalization, and movement. Spend extra time here: Talk (in English) about different foods that use cheese, what people's favorites are, if they like the smell, and so on. It would be fine to bring in more foods to pantomime and then mention that we will be using only cheese, plums, corn, and beans for the dance.

≈ *Assessment*

There are three main assessment areas in this lesson: motor coordination, spatial awareness, and personal development. When working with the ropes, continue to check the children's jumps, especially when the rope is on the floor and they are jumping side to side over it. Notice if they take off and land on both feet equally; anyone with a clearly lopsided jump needs to be evaluated more thoroughly. When they are performing the floor pattern, notice any children who are completely lost in the room, especially if the rest of their group is doing OK. These children need more visual perception evaluation. And notice the attitude of the children while doing the pantomime of cheese and the other foods. Usually children enjoy this enormously. Is there a child who is too shy to try it? Is she standing stiff and simply looking around at what the others are doing? Does this timidity fit into a pattern of extreme reserve? We do not want to jump to conclusions, but these observations are useful when compiled with many others.

LESSON 15   PRESCHOOL – 1ST GRADE

The Grocery Store Dance

≋ Teacher to Teacher

Please do not give up. If the year did not go as well as you would have liked, I implore you to try again. The second time will be 100% better. And even if it was not perfect, the children gained a great deal. If you were pleased with the results, I encourage you not to forget. The thought of undertaking another year of movement classes might feel exhausting and overwhelming. You will be under enormous pressure to use that time for "academic" endeavors. But look at the smiles and sweat on the children and remember.

≋ Student Objectives

- Students will remember the entire Grocery Store Dance.
- Students will exhibit self-expression in performance.
- Students will demonstrate spatial awareness by mastering the floor pattern using different line shapes.
- Students will integrate scarf work with the spatial design.
- Students will continue to experience the exuberance and class unity of parachute activities.
- Students will exhibit motor planning and self-discipline through parachute work.

≋ Materials Needed

- Stereo and audio recording of Raffi's "The Corner Grocery Store."
- The floor pattern you created last time.
- Scarves, one per child.
- One 24-foot parachute and one ball.

≋ Teaching Instructions

1. Warm up to the steps of the Grocery Store Dance:
   a. Skip freely. Then ask for just four skips and stop, repeating this several times—do the four skips while singing or saying, "My eyes are dim, I cannot see."
   b. Side-slide freely. Then ask for just four side-slides and stop, repeating this several times—do the four side-slides while singing or saying, "I have not brought my specs with me (define specs.)."
   c. Children run and leap freely. Then ask them to run and leap, stretch up pretending to crash into something, then fall down and immediately get up; repeat a few times. Combine the three parts into a sequence: four skips; four side-slides; four beats of run leap, stretch up, fall down, and quickly get up. Repeat a few times and ask the children to put the sequence in the back of their heads for a while.
   d. Review "cheese walking on knees," "plums twiddling thumbs," "corn blowing horns," and "beans trying on jeans."
   e. Sit the boys on one side of the room and teach the refrain to just the girls; then

teach the boys their part. Put the entire refrain together and practice twice. Select half the girls and half the boys to go to the other side of the room for the verses. Do the entire Grocery Store Dance to music. Switch places and do it again.

2. Review the floor pattern using different line shapes from last time. Keep the class division from the dance and perform the floor pattern, half the class at a time, twice.

3. Choose scarves and have a few minutes of free time. Repeat the floor pattern with the scarves kept high in the air.

4. Review the parachute activities already covered and end with Mushroom, telling the children good-bye under the parachute.

Adaptations

Easier

► Plan for three lessons to put together the Grocery Store Dance: (1) Introduce the verses, "cheese," and so on; (2) teach the refrain; (3) put it together.

► Eliminate the scarves from the line shape floor pattern.

► Get help for the parachute.

Harder

► Have the children perform the Grocery Store Dance without your help.

► Have groups of children continually feeding in to the line shape floor pattern.

► Be strict about form.

► Do Trap and Rock and Wave with the parachute.

English Language Development

► Singing is always an excellent English language development tool. Teach the children all of "The Corner Grocery Store" and have them sing while they dance.

► Take the time to explain dim and specs.

► Explore the idea food movements in rhymes, for example, figs trying on wigs (you will have to explain, preferably show examples of, figs and wigs), grapes climbing the drapes (drapes will need explanation), meat taking a seat, French fries putting on their neckties, and so on. This is extremely valuable both for vocabulary work and for practice in rhyming.

Assessment

If this is your last class, sit back and take a broad look at how much your children have grown. Truly this is the most important evaluation. Do they love to move? Are they comfortable in their own bodies? Do they push themselves to exert? Have they internalized the management techniques and exhibit self-control? Are they enjoying themselves? Classroom teachers need to follow up any concerns with either a formal request for evaluation or a note in the child's folder so that the teacher next year can watch his development. I understand I am advocating more paperwork when you are already drowning in it; but your assessment of motor, social, and developmental skills as seen in movement class is invaluable. Specialists might consider tactfully mentioning concerns to the parents or keeping track of them if the child will be seen again.

This is also the time to take a look at your growth. Did you ever get over your fear of teaching movement? Did you firmly establish the class management techniques so that future activities rest on a base of control? Would you approach things differently next year? Did you have fun? Was it worth it?

Chapter 15

Lesson Plans for Second and Third Grades

The curriculum for this age grouping is the most basic presentation of the material in this book. It is a straightforward, one-step-at-a-time approach—no half-steps like the primary lessons and not too many leaps as in the forthcoming ones. We work methodically but hopefully not laboriously. For teachers and elementary school children who have had zero movement, this is the best place to start. The following table is an overview of the second and third grade curriculum:

Second and Third Grades Curriculum

Lesson plan number	Lesson plan name	Purpose/Notes
1	Foundations	We jump right in and establish the first two class management organizations—Free Traveling Structure and Perfect Spots. Relying on these structures we introduce exercises and balls. This first class is geared to convey the attitude that "Movement is fun and challenging; it is a subject, and you need to behave with self-discipline." All in one 45-minute lesson.
2	Locomotor	The children understand that some movements travel, and they explore a wide range of locomotor movements. The students get a tiny, preliminary taste of the gymnastics moves we will need in lesson 4. Most importantly, we set forth the standard of mastery by requiring solid, self-directed class management organizations and a perfected ball study.
3	Nonlocomotor	Children now understand that while some movements travel, others are stationary; and they expand their nonlocomotor vocabulary. They experience their first nonlocomotor dance and continue to prepare for the forthcoming gymnastics work. The third class organization, Diagonal Structure, is established.
3.5	Reflections and options	I point out that in three lessons, we have covered all the basics: the three class organizations, the concepts locomotor and nonlocomotor, a study, a dance, and a bit of gymnastics. We need a breather—like an obstacle course—to process all this information.

(continued)

Second and Third Grades Curriculum (continued)

Lesson plan number	Lesson plan name	Purpose/Notes
4	Obstacle course	Although strenuous and very valuable in itself, the obstacle course gives our conceptual brains a rest. It is the perfect place to assess children individually. This lesson needs to be repeated consecutively two or three more times.
5	Levels	We continue with movement concepts—here, vertical space. A second nonlocomotor dance is created, foreshadowing group creative efforts. Students open up to fantasy play with the scarves.
5.5	Reflections and options	I alert you to some considerations about partner activities, which follow.
6	Partners	We delve into the area of social skills with partner activities and the Jig Along Dance. This dance pulls together concepts of locomotor, nonlocomotor, and level as well as partner skills. We return to the scarves and create a study.
7	First floor pattern	We progress on the social skills strand with partner activities, the Jig Along Dance, and Spaghetti. We also begin work on spatial awareness with a room representation and floor pattern.
7.5	Reflections and options	I talk about the strand approach—developing several themes simultaneously. So far we have presented six strands: class management organizations (these should be so ingrained that they are invisible), movement concepts, dances and studies, social skills, props and creative expression, and spatial designs.
8	In and out game	Like the obstacle course, this game is a break from the conceptual work. Yet it is extremely valuable in its academic applications. We also show the process of creating a floor pattern to ready the class for their first group study.
9	Group floor patterns	Here is the children's first cooperative creative effort. Floor patterns are the best form of initial collaboration because they are the easiest to organize and control.
9.5	Reflections and options	I bemoan not being able to teach everything all at once and remind both of us that we sometimes need to stop and consolidate information.
10	Ropes	Ropes provide outstanding conditioning and coordination work; they also prepare the class for their more academic application next time. Groups master their created floor patterns. This completed group pattern integrates all the strands presented so far. Students also get a glimpse of the reality of math.
11	Line shapes	Line shapes provide more intense work in spatial awareness. We return to the ropes, revisit the exploration and conditioning activities, and then use the ropes to introduce line shapes. Then the lines are applied and abstracted into a floor pattern. We continue to add dances with the Grocery Store Dance, which is excellent for freedom of expression.
11.5	Reflections and options	I break down some of the elements in an artful lesson plan. We also need to stop here and decide how to end the classes. If you choose to tackle a show, I present a possible format. In that case the rest of the lessons will be practice. If you choose to continue with lessons, the following lessons offer a good sequence.
12	Partner obstacle course	This is a marvelous integration of obstacle course coordination activities and intense socialization.
13	Directions	We introduce another basic movement concept—directions; we explore the four directions and apply them to the Row, Row, Row Your Boat Dance. This dance integrates directions, problem solving, locomotor movements, floor patterns, and partner work. We also introduce the parachute because the children will need several consecutive lessons with this exciting prop.

Lesson plan number	Lesson plan name	Purpose/Notes
14	Wild things	We exercise brain and body with a concept warm-up in preparation for a terrific culminating activity—the Wild Things Dance. This dance requires enormous displays of self-discipline as well as memory, sequencing, freedom of expression, and language work. We continue with the exuberance and the class cohesion fostered by the parachute.
15	Balloons	We continue the hoopla. Balloon work offers a spectacular integration of coordination and sport activities, language, partner skills, self-discipline, and pure fun. The Opposite Game is mischievously fun as well as good language work. And a mastered Wild Things Dance results in a terrific show even if it is just for ourselves.

LESSON 1

2ND AND 3RD GRADES

Foundations

≋ Teacher to Teacher

This first class establishes your tone: Be friendly but tough, do not "close an eye" to anything, and keep the pace fast. It is important that you respect your needs for order and not go beyond your comfort level.

Since we introduce balls in this class, a few tips will be useful. (1) Make sure all the balls are equally blown up so there are no "better" balls. (2) Prepare for the distribution. I pass balls out by dumping the box out so the balls (and children) scatter, but you can ask groups of children to come up ("Everyone wearing green pick out a ball"). (3) Introduce self-discipline. When presenting the ball study, ask the children to sit near you with their legs crossed, balls in their laps, hands off their ball. Tell them you are looking for those who have good self-discipline; without using too many words, simply take away the ball of those playing and return it for the study.

≋ Student Objectives

▶ Students will experience movement as fun, challenging, and orderly.

▶ Children will stop moving when the sound stops (Free Traveling Structure).

▶ Children will find a spot in the room that is far from everybody and everything (Perfect Spots).

▶ Students will explore moving a ball and execute a ball study.

≋ Materials Needed

▶ Tambourine.

▶ One large card with near on one side and far on the other.

▶ Balls, one per child.

≋ Teaching Instructions

1. Teach the Free Traveling Structure: Go from isolated, to nonlocomotor, and finally to locomotor movements.

2. Warm up with locomotor movements in the Free Traveling Structure: skip, jump, hop, hopscotch, baby and crab crawl, roll, jazzy walk, gallop, side-slide, run and leap. Insist on precise stops.

3. Teach Perfect Spots through near and far.

4. Do exercises in Perfect Spots: Hello and Good-Bye and Swordfish.

5. Introduce balls. Talk about freezing with the ball or letting the ball go and freezing one's body. Allow about 10 minutes of free time and 10 minutes of guided movements. Then have the children sit with the ball in their lap, hands off the ball. Collectively choose six moves for a beginning study, for example (1) dribble the ball, (2) throw it up and catch, (3) spin it on the floor or on a finger, (4) run as if it were a football, (5) roll it without using hands or feet, (6) run and leap throwing and catching.

≈ Adaptations

Easier

▶ Take longer and use more movements at each step of establishing the Free Traveling Structure.

▶ Take the hopscotch and the side-slide out of the warm-up. Take time to demonstrate each move.

▶ Do not plan to reach Perfect Spots. Practice many nears and fars, but save the two fars (which establish Perfect Spots) for another time. Simply gather the children to do the exercises.

▶ Do a four-part study with the balls, or save the study for next time.

Harder

▶ Do not skip steps, but pick up the pace when introducing the two structures.

▶ Make the locomotor movements in the warm-up more difficult, for example hopscotch backward, waltz walk, one-legged skip, leap turn.

▶ Use more difficult exercises in Perfect Spots, include a nonlocomotor pattern like the jump pattern, or do both.

▶ Do an eight-part ball study, and think about reversing it.

English Language Development

▶ Your best English language development tool is conducting movement class completely in English. It is important to establish that in the very first lesson. You will be tempted to speak the children's primary language for speed of comprehension, but once they know you will translate, they will not focus on internalizing the new English vocabulary.

▶ When establishing the Free Traveling Structure, spend more time with the isolated body parts and have the children call out the body part names as they move.

▶ Have the children call out the locomotor movements before moving. For more intense English Language Development work, go back and forth between movements, for example skip, jump, back to skip ("What do we call this?"), side-slide, skip ("What was this move again?"). Have the class answer as a whole so that one child is not put on the spot.

▶ Take some time with words that have double meanings. After working with *skip* as a locomotor movement, have the children line up on one side: One child shakes hands with the first person, then *skips* three children and shakes the next person's hand, *skips* two more and shakes, and so on.

▶ Have individual children yell "Good-bye" (or any other word you want to reinforce) in the air as they leap to their shoes.

≈ Assessment

The most important assessment is the overall attitude of the class. Were they with you? Did the Free Traveling and Perfect Spots Structures get established, or are the children playing with the idea? Note any children not stopping on cue. Do you have a sense that the problem is motor development or self-discipline? Note any children who did not get Perfect Spots. Again, was it lack of spatial awareness or lack of control? Be on the lookout for children who could not hop on either foot equally well; in addition to strengthening their weaker side, these children should be checked for midline problems. But, during this first class, do not jump to any conclusions—keep mental notes, but wait to see what happens.

LESSON **2**
Locomotor

≋ *Teacher to Teacher*

The best advice I have is never ask a class to go near a piano unless it is firmly shut. This locomotor lesson brings with it a delicate balance. On one hand, you want to teach correctly executed locomotor movements; on the other hand, especially at the beginning of a movement program, you want children to feel free, safe, and exuberant. There is no formula to follow, but at this point I would suggest leaning on the side of free-flowing movements. Mentally note the children who need individual help and perhaps take a moment while the rest of the children are putting on their shoes to show a quick correction. But, on the whole, if they are trying their best, let them go. Of course this free flow does not apply to being lax on the structures. Children might have been on best behavior for the first class and attempt to test you during the second. Hang tough.

≋ *Student Objectives*

- ▶ Students will understand the concept locomotor and experience varied locomotor movements.
- ▶ Students will perfect the Free Traveling and Perfect Spots Structures.
- ▶ The class will perform the ball study correctly without teacher help.

≋ *Materials Needed*

- ▶ Tambourine.
- ▶ Three cards with printed words: near, far, locomotor.
- ▶ Balls, one per child.

≋ *Teaching Instructions*

1. Teach the term locomotor by having the class guess what the word means; then have them do locomotor movements while saying the word.
2. Review the Free Traveling Structure and practice locomotor movements in this structure. (Use the term locomotor for each movement, for example, "Now let's do the locomotor movement gallop.") Do skip; jump; hop; hopscotch; gallop; baby, crab, and spider crawl; roll; jazzy walk; side-slide; run and leap.
3. Practice the Perfect Spots Structure with Firecracker, gathering the class and seeing how fast they can get Perfect Spots.
4. In Perfect Spots, review Hello and Good-Bye and Swordfish. Teach Blastoff.
5. Pass out balls; do a few minutes of free time and guided movements. Review the ball study introduced last time; practice it and show.

≋ *Adaptations*

Easier

- ▶ Take your time and play with the introduction to locomotor: "What locomotor movement would a baby do?" "How would a ball move downhill?" "What movement does a horse do?"
- ▶ During the warm-up, formally teach hopscotch and eliminate the side-slide.
- ▶ Review several nears and a lot of fars. If the class is ready, establish Perfect Spots, but do not rush this concept.
- ▶ Do only the first position of Blastoff.
- ▶ Teach a short ball study, perhaps three or four parts long.

Harder

▶ Pick up the pace when introducing locomotor and use difficult movements in the warm-up: side-slide changing sides, waltz walk and waltz-walk turns, one-legged skip with different leg positions, straddle roll.

▶ If Blastoff feels too babyish for your class, directly teach the bridge and shoulder stand. Teach the one-knee back roll. Put these moves into a pattern: bridge, contract, shoulder stand, one-knee back roll, stand. (This pattern can be done without mats.)

▶ If you taught a pattern like the jump pattern last time, review it and ask to see it while you just watch and count out the beats.

▶ After reviewing the ball study from last time, consider doing it in the original order and immediately repeating it in the reverse order; or perform the sequence as a canon, that is, with one group starting and the second group starting the same sequence one phrase later.

English Language Development

▶ Continue movement class as an English-only zone, even with initial instructions on where to put shoes, rules about drinking water, and so on.

▶ Even though the word *locomotor* is the formal lesson, put more emphasis on recognizing and saying the names of numerous locomotor movements. In addition, start to slip in descriptive words: walk *high* and *low*; skip *fast* and *slow*; jump *little* and *big*; walk *jazzy*, *crazy*, *tired*, *strong*, like a *robot*.

▶ When working with *near* and *far*, emphasize the object word: near the mats, or possibly near the red mats, near your shoes, near my shoes, far from the piano, far from all the walls.

▶ During Blastoff, emphasize the numbers said backward. Often children learn the names of numbers as a unit, "onetwothree . . ." Saying the numbers backward helps to distinguish the words.

▶ The ball study can include body parts—for example, roll the ball with your elbow, try bouncing the ball off your knee, and so on. Use the locomotor movements you worked on at the beginning of class. Also the study is a good place for work on ordinal numbers—*first*, *second*, and so on. During work on the study, words like *practice*, *again*, *perfect*, and *fabulous* should become clear.

≈ *Assessment*

Locomotor movements are a gold mine of assessment possibilities. The inability to land a jump on both feet, skipping and hopping only on one side, and most significantly crawling without hand-knee opposition (right hand moving with left knee) are all red flags requiring further, possibly professional, testing. More generalized assessments include overall endurance levels and the ability to remember a sequence. The balance positions in Blastoff will point to agility and flexibility levels. Remember, if you are assessing, not to help. Teachers have a hard time seeing their class flounder, but it is important to find out what they know. Also remember that we do not know yet if the difficulties we see are a result of physical disabilities or lack of experience.

LESSON **3**

Nonlocomotor

≋ Teacher to Teacher

About now you are going to want to loosen your precision standards because they require so much work. Exact starts and stops, perfect Perfect Spots, mastered studies, groups meticulously traveling on the diagonal—that is an enormous amount of mastery work. Congratulations for coming this far. Do not give up. We will take a sort of break in the next lesson.

Teaching the first somersault presents a dilemma. When teaching a new move, like the somersault, it is theoretically not a good idea to use the Diagonal Structure because children are watching each other. On the other hand the somersault needs to be done correctly, with the head tucked sharply under, or it can be dangerous. My thinking is that—in preparing for the gymnastics routine in lesson 4—I need to check every child; so I "err" on the side of safety and use the Diagonal Structure. But when checking the somersaults, do whatever it takes to stop any embarrassing laughter. (Your instincts tell you the difference between mocking and genuine joyous laughter.) "We are here to help one another; your laughter is making it harder. Everybody needs help sometimes; if you don't need help with this somersault , maybe you will need help with a headstand or with math or something else. Our job is to help one another. Got it?" If a child continues to mock, I suggest not letting him do the somersault—that will give him pause.

≋ Student Objectives

▶ Students will understand the concept of stationary movement and experience varied nonlocomotor movements.

▶ Students will understand the concept of diagonal line and experience moving on the diagonal.

▶ Students will accomplish a correct somersault.

≋ Materials Needed

▶ Two sounds, for example, tambourine and drum.

▶ A large card with a diagonal line drawn on it.

▶ Ideally an incline mat resting on a flat mat, or two flat mats.

≋ Teaching Instructions

1. Teach the term *nonlocomotor* by having children guess what the word means: "If non means not, what would you guess nonlocomotor means?" Explore some of their suggestions.

2. Warm up in the Free Traveling Structure by alternating locomotor and nonlocomotor movements, using a different sound for each, for example the tambourine for the locomotor movements and the drum for the nonlocomotor movements. Use this time to introduce some nonlocomotor movements, and include the moves that are in the Eight Plus Eight Dance. Do:

   a. Skip—swing, especially front swings.

   b. Hopscotch—shake, especially shaking while lowering the body.

   c. Baby, crab, and spider crawl—spin, especially spinning on the seat.

   d. Jazzy walk—teach contract and stretch, making sure to include contract on the lowest level on the side, as well as stretch on the knee level.

   e. Run and leap.

3. In Perfect Spots review Blastoff and teach the Eight Plus Eight Dance.

4. Teach the concept *diagonal* by finding many diagonal lines in the room. Have the class get into groups of four and establish the Diagonal Structure. Do several locomotor movements in this structure: skip, run and leap, kicks.

5. Place the incline mat (or two flat mats) on the diagonal and teach a somersault. Have each child try one. End with a fly off the incline mat to the children's shoes.

≋ Adaptations

Easier

► Keeping nonlocomotor movements stationary is difficult for many children. Go slowly and praise those children who stay in place; stop and correct those who travel.

► For the warm-up, consider working on just one nonlocomotor movement in between the locomotor movements. A possible sequence is skip; swing just the arms in various ways; hop, then jump, then hopscotch; swing just the legs in different ways; baby crawl, then crab crawl; swing the torso and head while sitting; jazzy walk; swing the whole body on different levels; run and leap.

► Since only the first position of Blastoff was taught last time, review it and finish the whole sequence.

► Teach only the first eight beats of the Eight Plus Eight Dance.

► Resist the urge to help with the groupings for the Diagonal Structure. Use only run to establish the structure.

Harder

► Pick up the pace when introducing nonlocomotor and use more difficult movements

such as twist, especially spiral twist sit. Use different levels as well as different body parts when exploring swings, contract and stretch, and spin.

► In Perfect Spots, review any patterns previously taught. Do the Eight Plus Eight Dance as a canon, with one group starting with the locomotor part while another group begins with the nonlocomotor section. (A girl-boy division works easily.)

► After establishing the Diagonal Structure, do many locomotor movements on the diagonal and include physical challenges, for example, run and click heels in the air, run leap turn in the air. Possibly include some short sequences like one-legged skips with the leg front, side, and back on consecutive skips; kicks done front, back, and side.

► Have each group create a short study on the diagonal: "In your groups choose one locomotor movement to do to the middle of the diagonal, three nonlocomotor movements in the middle, and a different locomotor movement to finish the diagonal."

► If most of the children are at ease with the somersault, have them do it again with a running start.

English Language Development

► As with the lesson on locomotor movements, emphasize the names of nonlocomotor movements and body parts. Repeat many of the same descriptive words used last time—*high, low, fast, slow, crazy, jazzy*—so they are used in different contexts.

► If most of your class is non-English speaking, teach the initial concept for diagonal in their primary language but quickly switch to English to emphasize objects in the room and to establish the term *diagonal*.

≋ Assessment

The major area to watch is the motor control needed to (1) stop a locomotor movement immediately on an aural cue and (2) keep the nonlocomotor movements in place. You must decide whether any difficulty comes from an inability to control the body or a lack of self-discipline. Your intuition is usually right.

When introducing the concept *diagonal*, ask as many individual children as possible to demon-strate a diagonal line—make sure to check your more "spaced-out" students. Note any who were not able to apply the concept and consider if they might need more visual perceptual assessment. Finally, in establishing the Diagonal Structure, make sure that the children do not lose the idea of diagonal lines by rounding the corners.

3.5

Reflections and Options

The previous three lessons have been very intense. We have firmly established the three class organizations—Free Traveling Structure, Perfect Spots, and Diagonal Structure—and have distinguished the first two concepts of movement education, locomotor and nonlocomotor movements. We have introduced patterns, the first prop, and mastery of a study. More importantly, the children have been exposed to movement as a subject and to control of their bodies. This is a tremendous amount of information.

About this time, and it does not have to be exactly lesson 4, I like to give all of us a break by presenting an obstacle course or stations. This type of lesson requires strenuous physical activity and self-discipline, but it is of a different form—not so academic and definitely flashier. If you have enough equipment, set up an obstacle course; if you have very limited equipment, set up four or five stations. It will take you about half an hour to set up an obstacle course the first time; after the children have done it once, they will be able to help you set it up.

Plan on doing the obstacle course lesson (lesson 4) at least two times and preferably three. I mean doing the whole lesson all over again; within each lesson, children should do the course many times. It is always more fun repeating an

obstacle course. In the future, plan on presenting different obstacle courses approximately every six weeks. Six weeks or not, an excellent time to do an obstacle course lesson is during standardized testing. This type of lesson relaxes the children while expending all their nervous energy.

LESSON 4

Obstacle Course

≋ Teacher to Teacher

This obstacle course is a time to enjoy the children and perhaps have a moment of individual time. "Nathalie, you made it across the beam! I am so proud of you! Give me a hug/high five." "Wow, Muong, you went across the beam so easily. Do you want to try it backward?" "Alex, is that you in that perfect frog balance? Terrific! Do you want to try lifting your legs up into a headstand?"

However, you must be strict about doing the activities correctly, which means keeping the order and not racing. You also need to be strict about stops. Control of the obstacle course is the opposite side of the Free Traveling Structure; here the children move without an aural cue and stop to a sound (a loud drum strike, piano chord, etc.). It is imperative that they freeze exactly where they are. Test them sometime during the course and put out (for a minute or two) the children who did not stop. If more than three children had trouble stopping, stop the whole course and do not go on until the class is under control.

At the end of class, ask the children to freeze and tell them four things: (1) You did a great job (if it is true). (2) I promise you this exact course next time (if it is true). (3) Everybody wants one more turn; we need to be fair and stop right now with no extra turns. (4) You must have your shoes on and tied before helping with the cleanup.

≋ Student Objectives

▶ Students will experience myriad physical activities.

▶ Students will demonstrate their ability level in several activities (for assessment purposes).

▶ Students will have fun and expend a lot of energy.

≋ Materials Needed

▶ All the movement equipment you have available: mats and incline mat, balance beam or stegel (preferably with an attached slide and ladder), tires, pogo balls, jump ropes, scooters, hoppities, balls, scarves, balloons, scoopers and soft balls, foot stompers, balance boards and beanbags, geometric foam shapes, plastic hoops.

▶ Masking tape for a scooter line.

≋ Teaching Instructions

1. Set up an obstacle course, ideally before your class time.

2. Children sit on their own rectangular section of the mats. Do a very strenuous warm-up emphasizing neck and back stretches: back wave and rocking back and forth, leg stretches in straight and straddle positions, abdominal crunches, push-ups. Practice bridge, contract, shoulder stand several times.

3. Reteach the somersault. Have the children practice repeated somersaults by rolling only in one direction. (Children who are obese should roll over their shoulders rather than their neck.) Teach the one-knee back roll and the frog balance. Put together a gymnastics routine: one somersault, jump, lie down and go into a bridge, contract, shoulder stand, one-knee back roll, frog balance. Repeat several times.

4. Gather the class and explain the obstacle course; emphasize keeping the order and not skipping anything. Designate a starting signal—for example, "When the person ahead of you reaches the top of the ladder, you go." Assign two or three different starting points for approximately half the class so

there is not a long wait time; children starting at various places throughout the course still keep the established sequence. Children do the obstacle course continuously for the rest of the lesson.

≋ *Adaptations*

Easier

▶ Save the frog balance for another time. Substitute balancing on one foot in the gymnastics routine.

▶ The most obvious way to simplify the obstacle course would be to eliminate activities, but I encourage you not to. The wonder of an obstacle course is having all those different tasks to taste. If the activities follow in a consecutive pattern around the room, the children will not have difficulty following the sequence.

▶ Eliminate sliding down the slide on a scooter for the first lesson (have them just slide on their bottoms) and introduce the scooter slide the second time the course is presented.

▶ Even though the wait time will be long, do not start children at different starting points. The children actually enjoy watching each other, and the sequence will be clearer. Consider staggered starts the second time the course is presented.

Harder

▶ The gymnastics routine can increase in difficulty: diving forward roll, jump turn in the air, bridge with one leg lifted, a headstand instead of the frog balance. Cartwheels, round-offs, and ending splits can lengthen the routine.

▶ The obstacle course can be more challenging: Put the balance beam on the top notch (if there is a second beam, keep it in the middle so there is a choice). Ask for challenge combinations, for example, "If you can do the pogo ball easily, try jumping rope while you are on the pogo ball."

▶ For the scarf activity, teach the class to juggle scarves.

▶ After the first lesson, have the class start anywhere they want as long as they keep the order.

English Language Development

▶ There are so many language possibilities that it is important to choose three or four and not overwhelm the students. Possible choices: Have them say "over" while climbing over the top of the stegel onto the beam; count to 20 while jumping rope; shout "basketball" while shooting baskets. Also, ask if they need a helping hand across the beam and correct any grammar mistakes: "I don't need no hand" to "Thanks, I don't need any help."

▶ When they are keeping the balloon up using various body parts, have them call out the body part as it hits the balloon. This is a good review of the words used in the previous lesson.

≋ *Assessment*

As with the language possibilities, the great number of potential assessments could feel overwhelming. I suggest you look at two or three specific tasks for each child; the second lesson with this course could focus on other skills. At this point several skills are the most significant to assess. Are the children's motor planning skills developed enough for them to easily climb over the top of the stegel and back down onto the beam? Can they walk fairly easily on the beam or are they a nervous wreck? Did the children follow the scooter line correctly or did they skip or reverse any of the loops? Could they land their jumps on both feet, and could they hop equally well on either foot? Can they jump rope? Throw and catch a ball? Dribble a ball? How much of the gymnastics routine could they do?

The following page offers an assessment grid that will help you chart the progress of your students. Use a circle to indicate lack of the skill, a slanted line to indicate partial mastery, and an "X" for accomplishment. This way the symbols can be superimposed one on the other as the children grow. However, as valuable as this assessment can be, do not let it destroy the exuberant fun inherent in an obstacle course. Keep the assessment casual and secondary to the joy of the lesson.

Skill Assessments Class Chart

Category															
1. Climb over top of stegel															
2. Walk on balance beam															
3. Jumping rope															
4. Jump in tires															
5. Hop right															
6. Hop left															
7. Scooter line															
8. Throw and catch ball															
9. Dribble a ball															
10. Somersault															
11. Bridge															
12. Shoulder stand															
13. One-knee back roll															
14. Frog balance															
15. Headstand															
16. Remembers gymnastics routine															
17. Follows order of obstacle course															

From *Step by step: A Complete Movement Education Curriculum*, by Sheila Kogan, 2003, Champaign, IL: Human Kinetics.

LESSON 5

2ND AND 3RD GRADES

Levels

Teacher to Teacher

Scarves are pure magic. They open up children's imagination and fantasy world. By this time in the movement program the children should be feeling safe and accepted by you and each other. If you think they are still hesitant, use another prop for now—perhaps beanbags or plastic hoops—and save the scarves for later. When you do introduce scarves, if free time feels awkward rather than wonderfully creative, go to guided movements and then return to free time.

Student Objectives

▶ Students will exhibit clear behavioral constraints: stopping on cue, finding their own space, moving on the diagonal.

▶ Students will demonstrate an understanding of locomotor and nonlocomotor movements.

▶ Students will gain an understanding of vertical space through the concept level.

▶ Students will exhibit behavioral and motor control with Temper Tantrum.

▶ Students will explore their creative imaginations with scarves.

▶ Students will experience a sense of exhilaration as well as motor planning with Freeway.

≋ *Materials Needed*

▶ Items that make two different sounds, for example a tambourine and a drum.

▶ Scarves, one per child.

≋ *Teaching Instructions*

1. Verbally review the Free Traveling Structure and the meaning of locomotor and nonlocomotor movements. Teach the concept of levels by exploring different meanings of the term and then having the children guess how it is used in movement. Practice the five levels: air, standing, knee, sitting, lowest.

2. Warm up in the Free Traveling Structure alternating locomotor and nonlocomotor movements—use a different sound for each. Explore each nonlocomotor movement on all five levels. A possible sequence is skip—shake on all levels; hopscotch—swing on all levels; baby and crab crawl, roll—contract and stretch on all levels; jazzy walk, side-slide—spin on all levels; run and leap.

3. Get Perfect Spots (review if necessary). Do Hello and Good-Bye and review the Eight Plus Eight Dance. Briefly identify the levels used in the Eight Plus Eight Dance.

4. In Perfect Spots create a level pattern by collectively choosing different nonlocomotor movements for each level: air, standing, knee, sitting (each of these levels gets four beats). For lowest level do a Temper Tantrum for eight beats. Practice so the class can do the pattern while you only count the beats.

5. Pass out scarves and allow free time. Do guided movements: throw and catch the scarf with different body parts, skip and swing, twirl on different levels, side-slide holding the scarf straight across the body,

roll and circle the scarf, jazzy walk, leap. Continue with silly scarf activities like sword fight, bull and matador, bride and groom, ballet dancer, and Magic Scarf. Have children fold and put away scarves.

6. Have children get into groups of five and line up for the Diagonal Structure. Do several locomotor movements on the diagonal and end with Freeway.

≋ *Adaptations*

Easier

▶ Do two separate warm-ups. First review the Free Traveling Structure, and alternate several locomotor and nonlocomotor movements. Gather the class again and teach level; do another, longer warm-up alternating locomotor movements and nonlocomotor movements using levels.

▶ Skip the Eight Plus Eight Dance review and go directly to creating a level pattern in Perfect Spots. Count the four beats slowly and pause between levels. If necessary, call out the levels so the children need to remember only the movements.

Harder

▶ Three ways to make the level pattern harder: (1) After choosing the movements, mix up the order of the levels, but keep the Temper Tantrum for last. (2) Count fairly quickly and allow no extra time for level changes. (3) Much more difficult—have each child or pair of children create their own level pattern, all ending with the Tamper Tantrum on lowest level.

▶ After free time and guided movements with the scarf, introduce a scarf study.

▶ Two possibilities for making the movements in the Diagonal Structure more challenging: (1) Keep the scarves from the previous activity and do the locomotor movements with scarves held high in the air. (2) Groups can create a study on the diagonal using two different locomotor movements—one to the middle and the other from the middle to the end of the diagonal—and three different nonlocomotor movements done on three levels in the middle of the diagonal.

English Language Development

▶ The names of the levels are excellent words to learn, especially in combination with the movement; for example, "Let me see spinning on the knee level . . . Why do you think it is called the knee level?"

▶ The words *temper* and *tantrum* will be quickly assimilated.

▶ Throwing and catching the scarf can be used to reinforce the names of body parts, especially less common terms that even English speakers need; "Catch your scarf with your thigh . . . your calf . . . your forearm."

▶ During Freeway, phrases like *close call* and *no disasters* should become clear.

≈ Assessment

The overall assessment here is whether the class understands the movement concepts locomotor, nonlocomotor, and levels and is able to combine them. Are the movements clear and fairly precise? If not, reintroduce nonlocomotor movements more formally. Are the class management structures embedded within the class, or do you have to work to maintain control? If control is not there backtrack until the structures are solid, and be more demanding. How precise were the four-beat phrases in the level pattern? Rhythmic patterns are good math work in themselves. This assessment also tells us whether we can go on to more difficult rhythmic sequences or if we need to stay with sets of fours.

5.5
Reflections and Options

2ND AND 3RD GRADES

How did it get to be lesson 6 already? The following lesson on partner work could have come earlier in the curriculum, perhaps even by the third lesson, but I held off until now for several reasons: Partner work is crucial for building friendships, learning to choose when to act on feelings, and fostering overall respect. For these reasons I want to introduce it early in the program; on the other hand, partner work can backfire. If children are made to feel excluded or unwanted, the tone of the class will deteriorate. Partner activities can start with one partner who is kept throughout the activities; this is in many ways easier but loses the principle of getting along with everyone. However, to have children constantly get new partners, as suggested in lesson 6, requires enormous authority on

your part. By the third partner switch, children will be with someone they are not fond of; by the fifth switch they will be in extremely uncomfortable combinations that entail some girl-boy issues. You must have the power to demand respect whether it is felt or not. If it is too early in the year, your authority might not be fully established. You know the saying, "Assume a virtue if you do not have one." In this case, your class must assume an attitude and appearance of cooperation even if they do not feel it. Prepare them, but be prepared to demand this of them.

LESSON 6

Partners

Teacher to Teacher

Partner work has the potential to tax the outer limits of your diplomacy and authority. My professional advice is to go with your gut. You will instinctively know whom to scold ("You absolutely cannot say 'no' to a partner. Sit out with one warning!") and whom to coax ("Next time, sweetheart, you go and find a partner yourself. Don't always wait for friends to come to you."). This is an intensive course in socialization, and the best help we can give is to be honest.

Student Objectives

▶ Students will demonstrate behaviors of cooperation, respect, and politeness.

▶ Students will learn the Jig Along Dance.

▶ Students will remember and execute a scarf study.

Materials Needed

▶ Tambourine.

▶ Stereo and audio recording of Raffi's "The Corner Grocery Store."

▶ Scarves, one per child.

Teaching Instructions

1. Warm up briefly with a strenuous series of locomotor movements in the Free Traveling Structure. Do skip, hopscotch, side-slide, crawl, roll, jazzy walk, gallop, run and leap. Gather the class and talk about (1) getting partners, (2) exhibiting cooperation whether it is felt or not, (3) never rejecting a partner.

2. Do a fairly long warm-up, alternating locomotor movements done individually with partner activities. Do:

   a. Skip alone—elbow position skip with a partner.

   b. Hopscotch alone—side-slide holding both hands, then Wring Out the Dishrag.

   c. Crawl alone—sit facing partner, hold both ankles, and travel.

   d. Roll alone—roll, holding a partner with two hands.

   e. Gallop alone—Wheelbarrow.

   f. Jog alone—Horsie.

   g. Run and leap alone—synchronized run and leap with a partner. Keep the last partner for the "Jig Along" refrain.

3. Teach the refrain of the Jig Along Dance: elbow position skip (four beats), switch elbows and skip (four beats), hold both hands and swing arms (four beats), Wring Out the Dishrag (four beats). If possible, have the children do this refrain to the music, just standing still for the verses. Partners conclude by bowing and saying, "Thank you very much."

4. In Perfect Spots review the level pattern created last time; change the movements to include a partner. For example, if the air-level movement was jump spin, do the jump spin with a partner holding both hands. Standing-level forward and backward swings could be done with partners holding one hand; knee-level contract and stretch could be done with the contract curled together and the stretch holding one hand and pulling apart; sitting-level rocking could be done back-to-back with a partner. Keep the lowest-level Temper Tantrum individual.

5. Pass out scarves and allow several minutes of free time. Review many of the guided movements from last time: throw and catch with various body parts, twirl, side-slide, jazzy walk, leap, sword fight, bull and matador, ballet, Magic Scarf. Children sit with their scarves in their laps, hands off the scarf. Collectively decide on five movements for a scarf dance. Practice and show half the class at a time.

≋ *Adaptations*

Easier

▸ Have students keep one partner the whole time, or have fewer partner switches.

▸ Do the level pattern without partners.

▸ Shorten the scarf sequence to three or four parts.

Harder

▸ If your class is not too rambunctious, eliminate the initial warm-up and spend more time with the partner warm-up.

▸ Switch to a brand-new partner for each partner activity.

▸ Do the partner moves of the level pattern in opposites. For example, if the air-level movement was jump turn, one person jumps and her partner jumps immediately as first

jumper lands; for standing-level swing, one child swings forward while her partner swings back. Knee-level contract and stretch can be done with one person contracting while her partner stretches. Rocking on the sitting level can be done with the partners facing one another, in straddle position, one person stretching forward while the other rocks back. The lowest-level Temper Tantrum is done individually with partners facing one another.

▸ The scarf sequence can be seven or eight parts long, or groups of children can make up their own sequences. (Since so much of the class has been in partners, combining partners into groups of four or six will work better than groups of three or five.)

English Language Development

▸ Learning each other's names, short phrases ("How do you do?" "Thank you very much"), and short conversations can be added to the partner activities. Brand-new English learners need specific dialogue to say.

▸ Partner activities in themselves stimulate a great deal of language: "Who will do this first?" "Not so hard!" "My turn." All dialogue needs to be in English.

▸ Learn some of the Jig Along song, or all of it; nothing teaches language as quickly as singing.

≋ *Assessment*

Assessment of partner work is a cursory view of the children's social skills. Take note of those children who wanted to rebuff others and the ones who were rebuffed, those who seemed desperate, and those who never chose a partner but only waited to be picked. These are all possible topics for discussion and instruction.

During the refrain of the Jig Along Dance, notice who felt the rhythmic changes and who did not. It is generally thought that rhythmic ability heightens mathematical ability.

LESSON **7**
2ND AND 3RD GRADES
Floor Pattern

≋ *Teacher to Teacher*

This is probably more than teaching advice, but here goes: Know when to let go. Teachers tend to want to help all the time, and sometimes the best help is to see if your students can do something by themselves. When doing a dance, it is fine to call out the moves at first and then say, "Now let's see if you can do it on your own." With the floor pattern, let the individual or small group that is showing the line go ahead and make a mistake. Ask the other children not to help for a moment, and bring the errant children to the drawn pattern: "Here is the line we drew. You went over here. Can you see the difference? Can you do it like the drawing?" I see many children not taking responsibility for themselves and just following the crowd. Each time we push them into thinking for themselves (without undue pressure) we achieve the highest level of teaching.

≋ *Student Objectives*

▶ Students will practice and display partner manners.

▶ Students will complete the Jig Along Dance.

▶ Students will be able to orient themselves to a drawn representation of the room.

▶ Students will understand and demonstrate a spatial design.

▶ Students will gain a sense of class unity and bonding with Spaghetti.

≋ *Materials Needed*

▶ Stereo and audio recording of Raffi's "The Corner Grocery Store."

▶ Large white construction paper and a set of markers.

≋ *Teaching Instructions*

1. Review partner manners: acting friendly whether one feels friendly or not, bowing and saying "thank you" when leaving. Warm up with a review of partner activities. Do:

   a. Skip, holding a partner with one hand—elbow skip, switching elbows several times.

   b. Side-slide holding partner with both hands—Wring Out the Dishrag.

   c. Partners hold each other by one foot and hop.

   d. Wheelbarrow and Horsie.

   e. Spin holding partner with both hands; spin the other way.

   f. Synchronized run and leap.

   g. Practice the refrain from the Jig Along Dance.

2. Gather the children near you with their last partner. Decide together what partner activities they want for the five verses of the Jig Along Dance. If they choose an activity that requires a switch of positions (like Wheelbarrow or Horsie), that activity has to encompass two verses because there is not enough time to switch within one verse. For example: verse 1—Horsie; refrain; verse 2—Horsie with partners in switched positions; refrain; verse 3—partner spin; refrain; verse 4—Wheelbarrow; refrain; verse 5—Wheelbarrow with partners in switched positions; refrain plus ending bow. Do with music twice.

3. Introduce floor patterns. Gather the children around a large piece of construction paper (ask the children in front to sit while those in back kneel or stand). Draw a room representation such as the one in figure 15.1.

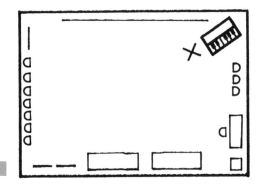

15.1

4. Draw a floor pattern with four to seven straight lines (see figure 15.2). As you add each line, have one to three children demonstrate the pattern so far. When the pattern is complete, half the class performs while the other half watches; switch and repeat.

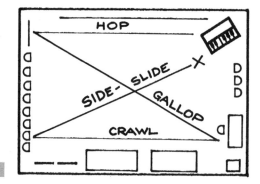

15.2

5. End with Spaghetti. Children get Perfect Spots standing stiff like uncooked spaghetti. Slowly they soften like cooked noodles. Drag the noodles into the middle of the room, piling up a plate full of spaghetti.

≋ Adaptations

Easier

▶ For the Jig Along Dance, stick to partner activities that require a switch of positions—

like Horsie and Wheelbarrow—so that they encompass two verses and therefore there are fewer movements to remember.

▶ The most obvious way to make the initial floor pattern easier is to shorten it; it can be as simple as a three-line design. Also make sure that each line goes to a definite spot—a corner, a specific table, chair, or marker—so the children do not have to approximate their destination.

Harder

▶ The Jig Along Dance is much harder if the partner groups choose their own activities for the five verses. Allow each partner group to jot down their own sequence; this will help them remember what they have chosen and allow you to repeat the dance in the future.

▶ For a fancier and even more difficult dance, each partner group chooses their own verse activities and adds props, like scarves or jump ropes. Props should be carried (for example, a scarf in a pocket) or placed on the edge of the room so they are easily accessible.

▶ Do not skip steps in introducing floor patterns but add more lines.

English Language Development

▶ As mentioned before, songs are one of the best ways to learn a new language. Since the Jig Along Dance is about animals, you can ask partners to move like animals for the verses and call out each animal's name.

▶ Floor patterns are a gold mine of English language development activities. Of course locomotor movements, both ordinary and sophisticated, are chosen, written, and called out. In addition, objects in the room will need to be identified and remembered. In future patterns you can easily include adverbs and adjectives—fast, slow, high, low, jazzy, and so on.

▶ The activity Spaghetti entails many good vocabulary words: stiff, boiling, melt, limp, drag, and, of course, spaghetti and stop giggling.

≋ *Assessment*

As with lesson 6, this lesson is a good opportunity to note who was able to feel the rhythmic changes and who was not. Floor patterns are an excellent resource for assessing spatial awareness and visual perception. Notice in particular—and try to distinguish—children who were not clear where the lines went in the room as well as those who could not remember the sequence. These are different brain functions: spatial orientation and memory.

7.5
Reflections and Options

2ND AND 3RD GRADES

We are now knee-deep in the curriculum aspect of this movement program. Most physical education programs cover one sport for, say, a six-week unit; they introduce the skills needed for that particular sport and then progress into full-fledged games. There is a logic and order to the curriculum. Movement has simultaneous strands of curriculum that all need to be developed. Ideally they work contrapuntally, like a Bach fugue, one theme fitting with another and then reappearing again combined with another theme.

We started with the three class organizations, Free Traveling Structure, Perfect Spots, and Diagonal Structure; these are not themes but the foundation on which the program rests. Once these class organizations are understood, they are not taught again unless the class needs a review after a long break such as winter vacation. All subsequent movement activities use one of these organizations for class management; for example, the partner activities introduced in lesson 6 would be totally chaotic if the children were not well trained in the Free Traveling Structure. As it is, partner activities will be quite noisy, but they will be basically orderly.

In addition to the three class organizations, we have introduced movement vocabulary: locomotor and nonlocomotor movements, levels, floor patterns (we are still missing directions). We also have introduced an obstacle course, the rudiments of gymnastics, and first steps in a dance repertoire. We have many options for lesson 8. I chose to start lesson 8 with the In and Out Game and then to continue developing floor patterns by introducing a helping floor pattern. Logically, it would have made sense to start lesson 8 with a helping floor pattern and then go on to have children make their own patterns, but I felt the children needed a break from the intense social control that partner work and group floor patterns require. The In and Out Game, although an extremely valuable language tool, feels simply like exuberant good fun. We will venture into group floor patterns in the lesson following.

LESSON 8

In and Out Game

≋ Teacher to Teacher

I know I have said it now several times but I simply must repeat: Keep the pace fast. The In and Out Game has the potential of becoming one of the children's favorite activities (the one they choose for the last "fun day") only if the pace is fast and the tone light. I have seen teachers kill this game with a ponderous tone and too much wait time. Do not belabor points: If you made a questionable call and a child starts arguing, simply say you are the referee and are doing your best. This is a good time to practice good sportspersonship. Use your gut judgment about whether to overlook a very close call, but I recommend putting children out honestly (even brand-new, fragile, non-English-speaking students). "You got out early this round, but watch carefully and see if you can stay in longer next time."

Safety note on Tackle: Have two lengths of mats under the incline mat. Tell the taller children to scrunch down a little so that they do not overshoot the incline mat.

≋ Student Objectives

▶ Students will understand and physically demonstrate relationship words such as: over, on top, under, above, below, beneath, in, around, in front of, behind, beside, between, and through.

▶ Students will understand and physically demonstrate geometry vocabulary terms such as: horizontal; vertical; diagonal; perpendicular lines; right, obtuse, and acute angles; symmetry and asymmetry; and parallel lines.

▶ Students will comprehend what steps are used to draw a group floor pattern.

▶ Students will practice motor planning and experience a sense of exhilaration with Tackle.

≋ Materials Needed

▶ One or two tables, five or six chairs, foam pillows, cones, three mats lying flat, two mats standing like houses, tires, plastic hoops, boxes or crates, foam shapes, beanbags, and anything else you can think of, scattered throughout the room.

▶ One large piece of white construction paper and a set of markers.

▶ An incline mat resting on two flat mats.

≋ Teaching Instructions

1. If at all possible, set up for the In and Out Game before class. Warm up using the relationship word "over" with the children moving over the equipment: "As soon as your socks and shoes are neatly put away, start skipping over things. Don't touch anything but the floor." Have the class go vaguely in the tracklike circle they use for ordinary warm-ups. Continue with "jump over things" (make sure the jumpers clear the entire tire or plastic hoop rather than land in them)—"Is there anything you can hop over?" Conclude with crawl, jazzy walk, and run and leap over things. This is a nice way to ease a class into representing relationship words with movement.

2. The class then sits down on one side of the room. Quickly demonstrate each of a series of words with an individual child.

   a. On top. Stop and talk about safety here: Pillows can be slippery and therefore the children need to step directly on them rather than slide into them; folding chairs can fold and therefore children need to kneel rather than stand on them.

b. Under

c. Above and below. I indicate above and below in the same way I do on top and under.

d. Beneath

e. In

f. Around

g. In front of, behind, and beside a chair. These three words use an object like a chair that has a clear front, back, and side.

h. Between. Specify the objects the children are to go between, e.g., two tires; two chairs; two mats; or, harder, a mat and a hoop, a table and a tire.

i. Through. Take a moment to teach through: "I got so strong from my karate lessons that I could take a brick [I hold an O-shaped foam piece or a plastic hoop] and smash my fist through it." (I forcefully strike my fisted hand through the circle and hold it there.) "What else could you go through?" Help the children see other possibilities, like tires standing vertically, the backs of chairs, the open section of a stegel, and so on to demonstrate through.

j. Finally, remind the class that they started with over and that this word will be used in the game.

This whole introduction should take 10 to 15 minutes. End with the rule that when people get out they are to shrug their shoulders, open their hands and say, "Oh, well, it's only a game."

3. Play three rounds of the In and Out Game. At the end of each round, if you want to eliminate children quickly, do double (or triple) commands, for example, "At the same time, show me on top and under . . . Show me in, under, and around." Also, you can cut the time for each command to 5 seconds. Keep the pace fast!

4. After playing the game, clean up in the same mode; that is, "You have 10 seconds to clean all this up perfectly." (Count slowly.) If the next class is going to play this game, clean up by pushing all the equipment to the sides of the room so it is easy to put back. When the room is clear, do a few locomotor movements just to "break loose": skip, side-slide, hopscotch, run leap.

5. Gather the class around a large piece of construction paper on the floor and, together, draw a helping floor pattern. (Do not consider putting the paper up on a board. It would require enormous visual manipulation to transfer the room representation from a vertical position to a horizontal one—the way things are in the room.) Emphasize the connection of lines: "Where does line 2 have to start? . . . Yes, line 2 has to start right where line 1 stopped." Show an example of each line with one or a few students and then perform the entire pattern with half the class at a time.

6. End with Tackle using the incline mat as each child goes to his shoes.

≋ *Adaptations*

Easier

▸ Most second and third grade classes can handle all of these relationship words, but you certainly can eliminate some the first time. The children should have a clear understanding of the relationship words *on top* and *under* before you add the *above*, *below*, and *beneath* concepts. *Between* and *through* are the most difficult relationship concepts to grasp.

▸ Keep the pace fast but count to 10 a little more slowly.

▸ When introducing the helping floor pattern, take a little longer establishing the room representation—this is the key to future success. Ask questions like "Where would I draw my desk?" even if you do not actually draw it.

▸ Use fewer lines in the helping floor pattern and make sure the lines go to specific destinations.

Harder

▸ Add more words to the In and Out Game: horizontal; vertical; diagonal; perpendicular lines; right, obtuse, and acute angles; symmetry and asymmetry; parallel lines, and so on (see p. 162). It is possible to start with the 13 relationship words and play one round, then sit the class down again, introduce the other words, and include them in the next rounds. If your class is very sharp, introduce all the words right away.

▶ When playing the game, count to 10 fairly quickly; and when about half the class is out, cut the counts to 5.

▶ Include several dual or triple commands.

▶ When introducing the helping floor pattern, make the room representation quite abstract, drawing only two or three objects, and make the floor pattern longer.

English Language Development

▶ To point out that the In and Out Game is a superb English Language Development lesson is to invite a "No duh" response. Demonstrating a word or concept physically is the most powerful reinforcement available. It is always a good idea to have the students call out the word as they perform it. But there is another powerful learning factor in this game: getting out. It takes tremendous inner effort to learn another language, and it is easy to slip into two unproductive frames of mind: I'll-never-get-it-anyways or I-don't-really-need-it. If very few children in your class are learning English, you have to be extra gentle and give the non-English speaking students a classmate to follow. If, as is the case in my present school, almost everyone is limited-English speaking, I sug-

gest being a little tougher and not giving any leeway in putting errant children out. When the environment is bilingual, children often need a competitive push to make learning English worth their while.

▶ When establishing the helping floor pattern, emphasize both the objects in the room and the movements to them.

▶ Even Tackle can be useful for words: Children can call out their favorite football team or player, even the city and the team.

≋ Assessment

Most obviously, the In and Out Game will point out what relationship words the children actually know and which they are still confused about (check especially the differentiation between *in*, *under*, and *through*). It is a good idea to extend the activity into paper and pencil tasks, for example putting an "X" above, below, and in a box or making a circle around a shape or letter. But on a higher level, you will have a good observation of the problem-solving techniques of your students. I have seen many examples of limited-English-speaking children beating English-only children because they were more flexible in their thinking; instead of trying to go under the table when there clearly was no room, they switched gears and went under a mat. They put together vertical and horizontal lines to create perpendicular lines. They saw how moving equipment would allow them to demonstrate two words more easily. These are good thinking strategies, and to a certain extent they can be taught.

LESSON 9

2ND AND 3RD GRADES

Group Floor Patterns

≋ Teacher to Teacher

The following lesson will integrate most of the behavioral and conceptual skills we have worked on so far. You will be delighted with how far the children have come. With good preparation—a clear understanding of room representation and a solid helping floor pattern—this lesson will be a snap. There are two potentially tricky areas: (1) The children might draw the room representation vertically instead of horizontally. There is no way to correct this; just start over. (2) The children, even prepared, might draw lines without connecting them: "How are you going to get from here to there, fly? Let me help you by drawing a connecting line". Do not worry about mistakes; they are our best teachers.

Student Objectives

- ▸ Students will practice spelling movement words or students will practice memory retention with Brain Catcher (depending on the warm-up option you choose).
- ▸ Students will demonstrate cooperation in working with a group.
- ▸ Students will create a group floor pattern.
- ▸ Students will experience the exhilaration and exhibit the motor planning learned in Tackle.

Materials Needed

- ▸ A chart of basic locomotor movements.
- ▸ Ten to 20 sheets of white construction paper.
- ▸ At least five containers of markers or crayons.
- ▸ One incline mat resting on flat mats.
- ▸ Tambourine.

Teaching Instructions

1. Warm up with one of the following options. If your class is primarily limited-English speaking or you think they will have trouble spelling basic locomotor words, like *skip*, do the spelling warm-up in which you spell out a movement from a chart and they call it out while performing it. If you think your class will have little trouble writing the movement words, do a warm-up of Brain Catcher in which you combine concepts learned so far. As an example of a Brain Catcher, you might say, "Do the locomotor movement skip once around the room, then stop and do the nonlocomotor movement swing on the knee level."

2. Gather the class around one piece of construction paper and draw a simple room representation. Talk about how the representation has to stay straight; if it were turned upside down,

the room would be all wrong. Practice putting the room representation straight a few times. Do a helping floor pattern emphasizing the connection between lines. You do not need to demonstrate this helping floor pattern; say that instead of doing this pattern they will be creating their own.

3. Children form groups of four sitting in a small circle on the floor. As the groups get organized, give each a piece of paper and a container of markers. This distribution method will give you a chance to check for unworkable combinations and to include the remainders: "I'm putting you with this group and they will welcome you."

4. Each group draws a room representation. (You dash about checking that the representations remain straight, "the way things are in the room," not turned upside down.) If the room representations are correct, the groups proceed to draw a four- to seven-line floor pattern.

5. Once the floor patterns have been checked (watch particularly that the lines connect), the groups practice their patterns—yes, everyone practicing at one time. Then each group performs, without their paper, for the rest of the class.

6. End with another Tackle on the incline mat.

Adaptations

Easier

- ▸ Definitely choose the spelling warm-up and offer to help write any movement words as needed.

- ▸ Make the room representations yourself. (It takes only a few minutes to draw these; make double what you think you will need.) The room representation is the pivotal point of success for this first cooperative effort and for all future floor patterns. Spend a longer time during the introduction turning the representation around and asking individual children to put it straight.

- ▸ Specifically assign a four-line floor pattern. If a group has five children, they are to draw five lines. This will greatly reduce all the social arrangements.

Harder

- ▶ Definitely choose a strenuous Brain Catcher warm-up. Keep the pace fast, say the instructions only once, and include some partner work. As an example, "Do the locomotor movement run and leap once around the room; grab a partner and do contract and stretch on two different levels; then, by yourself, gallop around the room." If they do not get it right, repeat it.

- ▶ Do not skip over the review of making a room representation and helping floor pattern; just move quickly.

- ▶ If the children are in groups of four, assign a floor pattern that has "no less than five lines and no more than seven." (You will probably have to explain *no less* and *no more*.)

English Language Development

- ▶ The spelling warm-up is an activity straight out of a class in English as a second language.

- ▶ The cooperative floor pattern lesson includes an enormous amount of language work. Request all dialogue in the groups to be in English.

- ▶ The concepts *no less than* and *no more than* are excellent language work.

≋ Assessment

During the Brain Catcher, check that the class is so at ease with the concepts that they actually enjoy mentally manipulating them. If they seem hesitant, they need a thorough review of each concept.

Floor patterns are one of the best ways to assess visual perceptual problems. What is tricky is that the student having difficulty can just follow along without really understanding. This is actually all right because she will learn by following; but if you want a true assessment, you will have to ask the child to do it alone (maybe in private) or to lead. However, it will be noticeable if the child is not oriented in the room and is just following blindly.

9.5
Reflections and Options

2ND AND 3RD GRADES

Heavens! What happened to directions, and another dance, and middle, and a hundred other concepts? I am tempted to start lesson 10 with an introduction to directions, cleverly add changes in direction to the already created floor patterns, and show them again. For a mature, accelerated class, that would be a good progression. Truthfully, I would probably not go that way. Concepts often need longer developmental time—of course with the pace of individual classes kept fast and fun. I believe it is better to teach fewer concepts thoroughly while not underestimating the potential of a class. Correct developmental pacing is one of the most delicate facets of education. I vehemently disagree with the trend to set curriculum

so as not to lose the lower-achieving, high-risk, students; but I do not think that blindly imposing standards-based curriculum makes sense either. I believe in stretching every child (and consequently I spend almost every lunch period helping children). Observers are sometimes shocked by the level of difficulty I ask of my students, especially in movement class, but adequate preparation and logical sequencing of concepts will yield amazing results.

To get back to lesson 10, rather than diving ahead and introducing the concept directions, I have the children solidify and master their group floor patterns. I then introduce ropes so we can develop floor patterns by including different line shapes in lesson 11. This is what I mean by mastery and preparation work. If I were adamant about using directions now, I would have planned to introduce them a few lessons back and then include them with the floor patterns.

LESSON **10**

Ropes

2ND AND 3RD GRADES

≋ *Teacher to Teacher*

It is our acceptance of the crazy/weird/far-out side of children that allows them to feel loved as they are—and I can think of no better gift we can give them. Sometimes it is hard to find the balance between acceptance and maintaining control, but that thin line is worth seeking. So, when doing Microphone in this lesson, I encourage you to let the children climb on the mats or chairs and pretend to be rock stars. Do I see you blanching?

When completing their group floor patterns, some groups will finish quickly and others will need a lot more time. Tell the groups that are done to have each person look at the map and watch the other three in their group demonstrate the pattern. By the time each group member has had a turn, the other groups should be ready.

The Foam Jump, especially with mathematical terms, takes longer than you would think. If a child is a fantastic jumper, challenge him by putting the tenth pillow up vertically. It is good for the whole class to see the top students being challenged.

≋ *Student Objectives*

▸ Students will experience using ropes in a variety of ways.

▸ Students will perfect their group floor patterns and be able to perform them without teacher help.

▸ Students will demonstrate being a considerate audience.

▸ Students will have concrete experience with mathematical computations and practice motor planning.

≋ *Materials Needed*

▸ Jump ropes of any kind, one per child.

▸ The children's floor patterns from last time.

▸ Ten foam pillows and a mat.

≋ *Teaching Instructions*

1. As soon as the children have their socks and shoes put away, they choose a rope, get Perfect Spots, and start jumping "as many different ways as you can think of." (Jump ropes are one of the two props—plastic hoops being the other—that require Perfect Spots for safety. Ask for Perfect Spots, but do not be too strict if someone wants to try a running jump rope step.) After a short time, stop the class and have them sit

in their spots, ropes in their laps, hands off the rope. Teach the whole class how to jump rope (see p. 132), "just to make sure you all know." (Many third graders, especially boys, do not know how to jump rope and are embarrassed to ask.) Then give the class at least 5 minutes more of free time so they can try out their new skills.

2. Do guided movements with the rope: with the rope in a line on the floor, the children jump side to side, tightrope walk, crazy walk, and football run. With the rope in a circle on the floor, the children jump in and out, over, and around. End with silly rope activities like Snake, Jazzy Rope, Broken Leg, Microphone, and Telephone and partner Horsie. Tell the class they will use the rope next time, and have them put the ropes away.

3. Before returning the group floor patterns, explain that it is harder to read a pattern than to make one. The crucial part is putting the room representation straight. Ask each group to study their map, memorize it, and practice. Walk around and make sure the patterns are straight.

4. Groups sit on one side of the room and watch each other perform their patterns.

5. End the class with Foam Jump. The children are already on one side of the room; start with only four or five foam pillows and a mat. Ask all the students to leap over the foam to warm up their ankles. The second time they can ask for the foam tower to be as high as they want. If you want, ask the children to request a preferred height using mathematical terms: "There are six foam pieces; I want nine; add three more."

≈ Adaptations

Easier

▶ Initially, when the groups are performing their floor patterns, help each group by calling out any movements or destinations they do not know.

▶ Afterward, have the group do the pattern by themselves.

Harder

▶ When doing guided movements with the ropes, include the in and out jump pattern and an introduction to cartwheels.

▶ You might want to end the rope section with a short, remembered study—for example, (1) regular jump rope, (2) football run over a straight rope, (3) in and out pattern, (4) Jazzy Rope, (5) Broken Leg, (6) Microphone.

English Language Development

▶ There is so much language in the rope activities that it is wise to choose a few words to concentrate on. I suggest focusing on (1) *in, out, over,* and *around,* used when the rope is in a circle because this repeats what the students worked on in the In and Out Game, lesson 8; (2) the word *microphone* and the ensuing speeches and songs they broadcast; and (3) the word *telephone* and their English phone conversations.

▶ When they are performing their group floor patterns, ask the children to call out the locomotor movement before doing it.

≈ Assessment

It is worth quickly and informally testing each child to see if she can jump rope, but only if you can do this surreptitiously and not break the fun-paced rhythm of the class. Jumping on both feet equally and being able to jump rope are, in my experience, strong indicators of the general coordination level of a child.

The approach a child has to mastery and performance is also an important indicator of future success. I have worked at several elite, expensive, private schools as well as many low-socioeconomic-level public schools; the most consistent difference I see between these two classes of schools is the students' approach to performance. Privileged kids assume that a show rests entirely on them and take on the ensuing pressure. Disadvantaged kids act as though they are not responsible for the outcome. Of course these are broad generalizations but it is worth remembering that we might need to lighten the performance stress of some students while raising the bar for others.

LESSON **11**

2ND AND 3RD GRADES

Line Shapes

≋ *Teacher to Teacher*

These "Teacher to Teacher" sections seem to verge on the therapeutic, but this lesson is one that can help you decide how much of a perfectionist you want to be. It is valuable to know your own inclinations and to pre-plan the level of polish you wish to achieve. Obviously I tend toward mastery and repetition-until-right. With line shapes you need to consciously choose what is "correct enough" for your class. For example, if they do a spiral line with three circles rather than four, is that OK? (I say yes.) If they spiral without the circles getting smaller or bigger, is that OK? (No.) If they do a zigzag with more zigs and zags than have been drawn? (Yes.) If they do a zigzag line without sharp corners? (No.) A looped line with more loops? (Yes.) A looped line without backtracking? (No.) My concern is that the lines be clearly distinguished one from the other, that the class gain heightened visual perception and spatial awareness, that they are concentrating and having fun. Get too picky and the whole program bogs down; too permissive and the class will fly off into a free-for-all.

≋ *Student Objectives*

▶ Students will practice jump rope activities.
▶ Students will understand and be able to execute various line shapes.
▶ Students will be able to combine line shapes into a remembered floor pattern.
▶ Students will learn a new dance.

≋ *Materials Needed*

▶ Chart of different line shapes.
▶ Jump ropes of any kind, one per child.

▶ One sheet of white construction paper and a set of markers.
▶ Stereo and audio recording of Raffi's "The Corner Grocery Store."

≋ *Teaching Instructions*

1. Children immediately get ropes and start jumping more or less in Perfect Spots; that is, they are far from each other for safety but can try some locomotor jumps. Repeat the warm-up from the previous class with less time for each activity and an even quicker pace.

2. Since the children end the warm-up with Horsie, ask them to remain with their partner and put one rope away. Show the picture of each line shape—straight, curved, wiggly, zigzag, looped, spiral—and ask the partners to replicate that shape with their rope. Walk around checking, complimenting, and helping. Tell the class they will now use these shapes in a floor pattern, and have them put the ropes away.

3. Ask the children to remember their partners as they gather around a sheet of construction paper on the floor. Draw a floor pattern using different line shapes (see p. 91). Divide the class in half by asking partners to decide who will watch first and who will perform. (Check that they are evenly divided by asking them to point to their partner.) Do the floor pattern two or three times with each half.

4. Since the class is already divided into two groups, ask them to form one line on the side of the room with the groups separate (see figure 15.3 a and b).

a ✗ ✗ ✗ ✗ ✗ ✗   ○ ○ ○ ○ ○

b ✗ ✗ ✗ ✗ ✗ ✗ ✗ ✗ ✗ ✗   ○ ○ ○ ○ ○ ○ ○ ○ ○ ○ ○ ○

↓ **THESE CHILDREN GO TO THE** ↓
15.3   **OTHER SIDE FOR THE VERSES** ↓

Work with one group at a time teaching the refrain of the Grocery Store Dance: skip forward (four beats), side-slide to one side (four beats); run and leap to the middle, pretend to crash, fall, and run back to the starting place (four beats). Practice with each group two or three times and then together twice more.

5. Ask all the children how they would enact "cheese walking on knees," "plums twiddling their thumbs" (you will have to teach them how to twiddle their thumbs), "corn blowing on horns" (silently), and "beans trying on jeans." Help them to ham up the pantomime, especially the beans trying on jeans—ones that are too tight.

6. Ask the class to line up as they were when practicing the refrain. Take half of each of the two groups to the other side of the room for the verses (see figure 15.3, a and b).

    Do the entire Grocery Store Dance and then switch sides and repeat.

7. If you have time, have the children go back to their original partners, and review the Jig Along Dance.

≋ *Adaptations*

Easier

▶ The most difficult line is the looped line; second most difficult is the zigzag. You can eliminate these or plan to specifically teach them later.

▶ Encourage the partner groups to help each other when replicating the line shapes.

▶ If the class as a whole is having a lot of trouble with the huge wiggly line, stop and do the complete backtracking lesson with this line.

▶ To simplify the Grocery Store Dance, have the two groups divided into girls and boys—this clarifies who goes where. Have the boys sit on one side of the room and watch as you teach the girls the refrain; tell the boys that their part is very similar. Then have the girls sit and watch the boys. Finally put everyone together and continue with the rest of the dance.

Harder

▶ Do not skip any lines in preparing or in creating the floor pattern, but use all the line shapes and consider adding an element like symmetry. Adding symmetry is especially neat here since the children are already in partners.

▶ It is possible to jump ahead and do this line shape floor pattern as a helping floor pattern, with children helping create the design in preparation for their own patterns.

▶ During the last verse of the Grocery Store Dance ("There was more, more, just inside the store . . ."), have the children think of rhymes to portray food in motion, for example, "figs trying on wigs," "grapes climbing up drapes," "pears sitting on chairs." Ask the children to call their rhymes out as they enact them.

▶ Review the Jig Along Dance and have the class do both dances, one after the other, as a suite.

English Language Development

▶ Line shapes are good language work in themselves if you include calling out the words.

▶ Pantomime is a terrific language teacher. Use the verses in the Grocery Store Dance to explore the foods mentioned. If possible, bring in tastes of cheese, plums, corn, and beans, or at least bring in a sample. This should lead to a great deal of oral language concerning different or favorite foods, as well as descriptive words like *juicy*, *spicy*, *yummy*, and *nasty*.

≋ Assessment

The key assessment in this lesson is the ability to backtrack. Doing a huge wiggly line requires the same backtracking skill that reading does.

You will see children who have difficulty in this area almost forcibly shift their own bodies one way and then the other. Children with more severe backtracking disabilities will not be able to switch at all. Luckily, physically working on backtracking activities (even with a partner helping) will facilitate the skill. But children with severe backtracking difficulties need to be evaluated further.

11.5
Reflections and Options

2ND AND 3RD GRADES

Let us look at some aspects of planning a smoothly functioning lesson that are possibly not obvious. In lesson 11, the preceding one, I wanted to use ropes for an introduction to line shapes so I managed to introduce ropes the lesson before. Children will not want to do what you want to do until they have had time to explore on their own. With the ropes already tried out in lesson 10 and this exploration repeated as the warm-up in lesson 11, most of the children will be eager to move on to a new direction using ropes, in this case line shapes. Floor patterns have already been introduced and developed with group studies. The class is confident and ready to move on in this area. With this preparation, the floor pattern and line shapes should merge smoothly and easily.

In the social sphere, we eased the transition to partners working with line shapes by keeping the partners formed in the last warm-up activity, Horsie. Then we utilized these same partners by asking them to divide themselves into two groups (a good lesson in itself). It is not the end of the world to have children in partners and then ask for groups of three, or to have children in partners and then ask later for different partner forma-tions—but these procedures do not make smooth, elegant transitions. And it is the transitions that have the greatest potential for chaos. Do not get me wrong; the children do not care if the transitions are elegant or not. They will do anything, even behave, in order to have movement. These are just subtle refinements to consider.

On to a totally different matter. Now is the time to plan for the last class. There are three possibilities: (1) Keep teaching; (2) have a "fun day"; (3) present a show. The first option simply means continuing to introduce and combine concepts, concluding with something like the parachute. A "fun day" (as differentiated from all the rest?) means planning an entire day of the children's favorite activities. Among typical possibilities to choose from are (1) In and Out Game, parachute, and one flip down the incline mat; (2) obstacle course for the whole time; (3) ball play, parachute, Opposite Game, and Freeway. Having a "fun day" or continuing to teach allows you to offer new information until almost the very end. A show will require a lot of practice, and you need to devote the rest of the lessons to this. What is better for your class is your call. New information is always beneficial, but so are polishing material and conquering stage fright. You need to look at your children and see what would help them grow the most.

On the whole, I favor shows: Children love them, parents love them, the administration loves them, and most importantly, the skills needed to put on an excellent show are for life—perseverance, self-discipline, delayed gratification, dealing with fear. Giving a show is also a lot more work for you, and that certainly needs to be factored in. If you decide to show, here is a workable presentation gathered from the previous lessons:

1. A sequence using scarves or balls. (I prefer scarves because balls have a tendency to get out of control during shows.)
2. Small-group floor patterns.
3. Whole-class floor pattern using line shapes.
4. Grocery Store Dance and Jig Along Dance.
5. Where the Wild Things Are Dance.

This is about a 30-minute show—shows always go faster than planned. My estimate is that it will take three or four full class times of practice to be ready to perform. Because it does not make sense for me to write a lesson plan saying "Practice," I direct you to the section on shows (see p. 148) and continue to describe lessons introducing new information.

LESSON 12   2ND AND 3RD GRADES
Partner Obstacle Course

≋ Teacher to Teacher

I hope you have as much fun with the partner obstacle course as I do. The two tricky parts of this lesson (other than setting it up) are (1) what to do with the unpartnered child and (2) how to keep the partner groups together. There is no option for the remaining child but to form one group of three. A group of three is not great, but I absolutely do not recommend that you be the remainder's partner because you need to keep an eye on the whole scene. Encourage the group of three by saying, "I don't know how you are going to manage these activities in three, but I know you will figure it out." Allow all safe and happy solutions. Most of your class will be delighted to stay with their partners, but one or two pairs will not want to stay together. Usually I will sit both children out with a warning. The only exception is the situation in which one child is really trying and the other clearly not cooperating; after sufficient warning, the uncooperative child will have to watch this time. Do plan on doing this lesson at least one more time; in subsequent classes encourage different partner groups.

≋ Student Objectives

▶ Students will show greater capabilities in working with a partner.
▶ Students will understand and be able to differentiate the concepts cooperation and compromise.

- Students will demonstrate cooperation and compromise when working with a partner.
- Students will practice a variety of coordination skills.

≋ *Materials Needed*

- Following is a list of the equipment I use, of course adaptable to what you have available: stegel with two beams at the same height; two rows of mats; the 10 Foam Jump pillows with a mat behind them; the incline mat with a mat behind it; tires in two rows; jump ropes; scooters in an open space; balance boards with beanbags; balls; balloons; plastic hoops; scarves; paired hoppities; and scoopers and soft balls.
- Tambourine.
- A sign with *compromise* on one side and *cooperation* on the other.

≋ *Teaching Instructions*

1. Set up the partner obstacle course, ideally ahead of time.
2. Children begin sitting on the mats. Do a strenuous warm-up: Include stretches (especially for the back), abdominal exercises, push-ups, and the gymnastics routine learned in lesson 4 (somersault, jump, bridge, contract, shoulder stand, one-knee back roll, frog balance).
3. Get partners and stand one in front of the other ready to work on the mats, so the class is divided into group 1 and group 2. Do the gymnastics routine once or twice, one group at a time. Demonstrate how to help lift the legs from a frog balance to a headstand. Partners talk to one another indicating whether they want help. Repeat the gymnastics routine and add the headstand (with or without help); each group performs twice.
4. Partners stay together as the class gathers, sitting on the floor. Show the word *cooperation* and ask for ideas. Generally children know this word and quickly conclude that it means being nice or respectful. Show the word *compromise* and, after hearing ideas, demonstrate its meaning. Ask one set of partners to stand and separate (about 10 feet apart); ask them to shake hands. "How are you going to do that?" Usually they will solve the problem with one person walking to the other. "That's right, one of you walking to the other would work, but it isn't compromise. Compromise means that both sides have to give in a little. [The two children move toward each other.] Now, in the obstacle course, you are going to have to walk on the balance beam holding your partner's hand. What if one of you wants to walk fast and the other wants to walk slow? How could you compromise? . . . Yes, they could do half the beam slow and half fast . . . Great, one person could speed up and the other slow down. I think you have it." Quickly explain the rest of the course.
5. Do the obstacle course for the rest of the lesson. Plan to repeat this lesson at least one more time.

≋ *Adaptations*

Easier

- Obviously you can shorten the course by eliminating some of the activities, but if the course follows a circular pattern, it can be quite long and still be easy to follow.
- Have some kind of bar, a ruler or a drumstick perhaps, for the partners to hold rather than hands.
- Change the partner scooter ride to a partner scooter train in which children sit on their own scooter, hold on to each other, and travel.
- For the section in which partners create a gymnastics routine, assign a three-movement pattern.

Harder

- Include Massage and Trust Walk in the obstacle course.
- Definitely include a partner scooter ride.
- Assign a seven-part gymnastics sequence done in synchronized moves.

English Language Development

- This is another lesson that is so rich in language possibilities that you will have to limit the focus. In addition to cooperation and compromise, I would emphasize words like *higher* and *lower, faster* and *slower, throw* and *catch, flip* and *tackle,* and *scooter ride.*

▶ When the partners create their gymnastics routine, have them call out the names of the moves immediately before executing them. Insist that both children call out the names.

≈ Assessment

Unless you need to check a specific motor task, concentrate less on evaluating the children's coordination and more on assessing their social skills. Who had great difficulty staying with a partner? Who abandoned his partner? Who kept getting left? These are strong indicators of larger social problems, and I encourage you to take them as seriously as a physical or academic problem. Many mental health services have social skills groups for youngsters, or perhaps these social difficulties indicate the need for individual counseling. The partner obstacle course will provide concrete examples with which to approach the school psychologist or parents. Of course I am not advocating hysteria. This is one situation; it is serious only if it fits into a continuing pattern of social problems that are causing difficulties for the child or for you. If it is an isolated incident, we can chalk it up to a bad day.

LESSON **13**

Directions

2ND AND 3RD GRADES

≈ Teacher to Teacher

In all teaching we need to balance taking the subject seriously while keeping the tone light. In movement it is easy to err on either side. Many teachers see movement as a nice form of recess, and it is not. There is much to be learned here. A study like the following direction pattern includes spatial and midline skills, creative problem solving, motor planning and coordination skills, and listening and concentration activities. This type of movement lesson needs to be approached like any other academic subject: errors corrected, the children focused on task, and the goals clear to you and the class. Yet this approach does not need to be ponderous. We all learn so much better in an environment of good humor and support. Movement especially, since it touches a very vulnerable part of us, needs to be taught with warmth and fun.

≈ Student Objectives

▶ Students will gain knowledge of and experience in the four directions.

▶ Students will apply the concept of directions to the Row, Row, Row Your Boat Dance.

▶ Working with the parachute, students will experience tactile-sensory stimulation, group unity, and a sense of exuberance.

≈ Materials Needed

▶ One piece of white construction paper and a set of markers.

▶ A 24-foot parachute.

▶ One ball.

▶ Tambourine.

≈ Teaching Instructions

1. Start in Perfect Spots. Do Walk Down Your Front and Right and Left Bug to introduce directions.

2. Identify the four directions—forward, backward, sideways, turning. Do the following movements in all four directions: jumping, walking, side-sliding (since side-slide moves

inherently sideways, gallop for the forward and backward directions).

3. Teach this sequence: three jumps forward, five steps backward, four side-slides to the right, three side-slides to the left, and end with a turn. The sequence makes an L-shaped design. Repeat the sequence and sing "Row, Row, Row Your Boat." Tell the class to remember this pattern for later (figure 15.4).

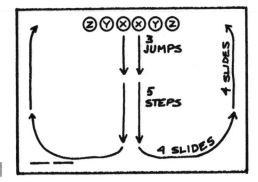

15.4

4. Have children get into groups of five ready to move on the diagonal. Run on each diagonal to reestablish this structure. Ask: "Do you remember the 'Row, Row . . .' pattern we learned in Perfect Spots? That's right; it went three jumps forward, five steps backward, four side-slides right, and four side-slides left ending with a turn. Now here is the million-dollar question: How can you make this sequence go on the diagonal to the other side of the room?" This will be fun to watch. Most groups will do the jumps forward very big and then walk backward with tiny steps; the side-slides usually remain perpendicular to the diagonal and therefore do not get them any farther across the room. Wait them out. It will take a while and then hit like a thunderbolt: They can turn their bodies on the diagonal (see figure 6.3 on p. 84). Once the students understand, have them do the direction pattern while singing "Row, Row . . ."; groups start eight beats apart.

5. Do the same sequence in a floor pattern (figure 15.4). "You did such a good job—let's make it even harder and add a floor pattern. Get a partner." This is the type of floor pattern that you have to set up with the first partner group in the center, the second partner group on either side, and so forth (see figure 15.5).

15.5

QZOXXOZQ

6. "You did a lot of thinking work today. I have something special for you." Pull out the parachute and immediately throw a ball in the center. Play Ocean, with the children vigorously shaking the ball out for a few minutes; then take turns putting children on top of the parachute and shake them up. Play Whoosh, in which the parachute is lifted and children take turns going under; Shark, in which children get pulled under the chute; and end with Mushroom, in which the parachute is lifted and the class captures the air by sitting on the edge.

≋Adaptations

Easier

▶ You can prepare the class for the question of how to transform the L-shaped pattern into a diagonal line. Before presenting the question, do several locomotor movements using directions on the diagonal; for example, skip forward for one diagonal, run backward for one diagonal, side-slide changing sides for one, run and leap turn for one. This almost gives away the solution, but you might be surprised to find your students still puzzled.

Harder

▶ After the children solve the problem of putting the "Row, Row . . ." pattern on the diagonal, have them try several directional switches across the diagonal—for example, skip forward to the middle and then waltz walk turning from the middle to the end. See chapter 6 for more direction studies in various degrees of difficulty.

▶ Ask groups of children to create a direction study either going across the diagonal (e.g., "Pick four locomotor movements in four different directions and fit them on the diagonal line") or as a floor pattern (e.g., "Create a floor pattern of six lines, using six different locomotor movements; include all four directions and at least three levels").

English Language Development

▶ When working on Walk Down Your Front and Right and Left Bug, make sure to reinforce the names of body parts and include more, for example, hips, thighs, calves, torso.

▶ Take a few minutes to examine what "rowing a boat," "gently," "down the stream," "merrily," and "life is but a dream" mean.

▶ Do all the parachute activities in English. When dividing into groups to go in or under the parachute, use names you would like to reinforce. I use "Hamburgers and French Fries," but different animals, colors, or even professions will work: "OK, it's the doctors' turn to go under the parachute . . . OK, now the architects."

≋ Assessment

There are three major assessments here. First, identify whether any of the children had trouble with the actual moves in the sequence three

jumps forward, five steps back, four slides one side and four slides the other, ending with a turn. Most of the dances and studies done in the program work on the phrase level; this study uses exact steps, and some children will not have the motor command needed to move this precisely. Second, the problem of how to fit the study on the diagonal will give you some insights into the students' problem-solving techniques. These are more important than the actual solution, so notice who grappled with the problem and who left it for someone else. Third, the parachute activities will tell you a lot about how your students deal with excitement: Did they go crazy and have a difficult time listening to instructions? Were they timid about the parachute and reluctant to go inside? Do they have so much nervous energy that all they wanted to do was shake it? These kinds of observations tell a great deal about individual children and about a class as a whole.

LESSON 14   2ND AND 3RD GRADES
The Where the Wild Things Are Dance

≋ Teacher to Teacher

Isn't teaching hard work? This lesson especially requires "active teaching" for almost the whole time. The concept of movement combinations and the story dance will involve almost constant corrections. You do not have to be harsh, but you do have to be unrelenting in expecting correct solutions to problems and solid boundaries of behaviors.

I allow my class incredible freedom in the mischief part of the Where the Wild Things Are Dance. They tickle people in the audience, climb on the mats, pound on the piano (each child can pound only a few times, though), and even hang off the bleachers. But I am a fanatic that when the tambourine stops they are absolutely frozen—wherever they are. I say "1, 2, 3" and

they all scurry into the middle of the room, and we proceed with the dance. This type of abandon within strict boundaries is very important. It tells the children that I want them to have a lot of fun but that they must have control; I am unwavering in demanding this. The balance of abandon and control is a fabulous life skill and, in addition, makes for a wonderful dance.

≋ Student Objectives

▶ Students will explore the story *Where the Wild Things Are* and demonstrate it through movement.

▶ Students will expand their experience with the parachute.

▸ Students will demonstrate motor planning and control in close calls during Freeway.

≋ *Materials Needed*

▸ *Where the Wild Things Are* by Maurice Sendak.

▸ A 24-foot parachute.

▸ One ball.

▸ Tambourine.

▸ Equipment for a rumpus: in addition to the parachute, a few hoppities, scooters, scarves, foam pieces, a few balls, jump ropes, and plastic hoops.

≋ *Teaching Instructions*

1. Do a strenuous Free Traveling Structure warm-up alternating locomotor movements with concept combinations:

   a. Skip, side-slide, gallop individually—get a partner and travel with each person on a different level but still touching.

   b. Jump, hop, hopscotch individually—get a different partner and travel with each person moving in a different direction but still touching.

   c. Crab crawl, baby crawl, roll individually—get a different partner and travel with each person on a different level, moving in different directions, and still touching.

   d. Jazzy walk, jog, run and leap—introduce the difficult step that will be done later on the diagonal (see step 4).

2. Teach the Where the Wild Things Are Dance. If possible, read the story to the class before this lesson; if not, read the book now. Talk about the word *mischief*, and plan some possibilities. Practice up to mischief, making sure that when the tambourine stops the class is perfectly still—you will probably need to repeat this first part several times. Continue teaching the dance up to the rumpus. Talk about the idea of a wild scene and plan some movement possibilities, for example "flying" the parachute, riding hoppities and throwing foam pieces around the room, making

a scooter train, flinging scarves throughout the room, bouncing balls, jumping ropes, spinning plastic hoops. As with mischief, make sure that the rumpus ends the instant the tambourine stops. Complete the whole dance. If they are dying to repeat it, why not? Clean up except for the parachute.

3. Bring the parachute to the middle of the room and repeat the activities done last time: Ocean, Whoosh. Introduce Trap, in which half or a third of the children go under the chute and the rest hold the sides down. Introduce Shark, in which the class is seated around the parachute and one person starts pulling the others under until all the children end up as sharks under the parachute. End with Mushroom, in which the parachute is whooshed up, the children sit inside on the edge, and the chute stays up for a while.

4. Get into groups of four ready to move in the Diagonal Structure. Practice several locomotor movements going across the floor, for example run leap, kicks, side-slide changing sides, run and clip heels. Do the Row, Row, Row Your Boat Dance from last time on the diagonal: Practice it once and then have the children repeat it, coming in eight beats apart, while singing the song. Present a short diagonal study, for example the kick pattern, the step-hop pattern (see p. 43), or the waltz-walk pattern. If you choose one of these more difficult locomotor movement patterns, teach the step in the warm-up at the beginning of class.

5. End with Freeway, groups crossing the diagonals very fast but with no disasters.

≋ *Adaptations*

Easier

▸ The primary difficulty in the Where the Wild Things Are Dance is freezing the movement after the mischief and the rumpus. There is nothing to do except practice. If most of the class is able to stop promptly, definitely consider putting the others out. You can simplify the rumpus by having fewer props. Divide the class into thirds: One group flies the parachute, one group bounces balls or hits balloons, and one group plays with plastic hoops.

▸ There is no reason to introduce new parachute activities if the class is just beginning to understand and relax with the activities started last time.

▸ Do not introduce a difficult locomotor movement or pattern this lesson. Just do ordinary movements on the diagonal and then go to Freeway.

Harder

▸ The warm-up can be made harder through the use of more difficult steps throughout. For example, instead of plain skips, do one-legged skips with changing leg positions; instead of just a jazzy walk, include waltz walks and waltz-walk turns; instead of just run and leap, include a turn in the middle of the leap and leap patterns.

▸ The Where the Wild Things Are Dance has degrees of polish: Have the unison sections very synchronized; have many different props in the rumpus section; and have perfect starts and stops.

▸ Work on the Diagonal Structure can put together many difficult locomotor movement patterns; the study the children are assigned can include all concepts covered so far.

English Language Development

▸ The idea of asking children to combine concepts and demonstrate them is possibly the best form of English Language Development work because they are forced to start thinking in English. If they are not ready for abstract combinations, ask for specific problems: Partners have one person skipping and one leaping while holding on to one another; partners move slow and fast while holding on; partners move forward and backward while holding on.

▸ Doing story dances like the Where the Wild Things Are Dance and the Bears in the Night Dance is perfect for language development. Consider adapting some of the class reading selections or possibly Aesop's Fables as future story dances.

▸ The parachute will elicit an enormous amount of excited chatter. Just ask for all of it to be in English.

≈ *Assessment*

This lesson will give you an excellent view of the mental development of your class. The concept combination warm-up will immediately point to any concepts that are unclear or those that are not solid enough to be adapted. Watch especially for children who do not risk grappling with the problems at all and who wait for someone else to do so. A story dance like the Where the Wild Things Are Dance will certainly point out language, memory, and sequencing problems, but even more, you will see which children want to take advantage of an opportunity to act wild. This is an excellent test for their level of self-discipline.

LESSON **15**
Balloons

≋ Teacher to Teacher

Congratulations! For you to have completed this curriculum of movement education is a real accomplishment. I know it was not easy. Movement requires so much preparation—getting the room, equipment, and lesson ready. Balancing the children's enthusiasm with class management requires so much energy. No one but another teacher can know how hard you work. I commend you; you have given your students an immeasurable gift. Their growth is your greatest reward.

≋ Student Objectives

▶ Students will experience a sense of exuberance and closure.

▶ Students will explore moving a balloon in a variety of ways.

▶ Students will perfect the Where the Wild Things Are Dance and perform it correctly.

▶ Students will gain concrete experience with antonyms and will increase their sense of class unity.

≋ Materials Needed

▶ Thirty sturdy round blown-up balloons (for a class of 20).

▶ Containers to hold the balloons: two stiff mats standing, large garbage bags or large boxes.

▶ Equipment for the rumpus: the parachute, hoppities, scooters, scarves, foam pieces, balls, jump ropes, plastic hoops.

▶ Tambourine

≋ Teaching Instructions

1. Children choose a balloon as soon as their shoes are put away. Give them a lengthy free time (10 to 15 minutes) with the balloon.

2. Do guided movements with the balloons: Hit the balloon with hands and then add a jump; hit it with the head, elbows, knees, toes, bottom, abdomen; move the balloon without touching it (blow on it); bounce the balloon; balance it on one finger; punch it (be careful not to hold the tied end while punching). Try some sport activities with the balloon: volleyball setup and spike; baseball bat and catch; tennis forehand and backhand; football throw, catch, run, spike; basketball dribble and shoot.

3. Get a partner and put one balloon away so that partner groups have only one balloon. Play sports with the partner and then put all balloons away.

4. Quickly set up for the Where the Wild Things Are Dance and run through it once or twice.

5. Play the Opposite Game. Introduce the game by talking about opposites and telling the students that this will be their golden opportunity to do the opposite of what you say; emphasize that when you say the game is over, it is definitely over. Ask the children to stand/sit; stand straight/crooked; start on one side/the other; move fast/slow; high/low; forward/backward; light/heavy; happy/sad; together/apart. End by saying, "This class is just terrible. I don't know what I'm going to do. Just move silently. Game over!"

≋ *Adaptations*

Easier

▶ Simplify this lesson by going slower and eliminating a few of the activities.

▶ Keep in mind that if you remove the partner ending to the balloon section, some classes will have a hard time parting with their balloons.

Harder

▶ Work with balloons can be made harder in two ways. (1) Use the sport activities to actually teach sport skills. The children can learn the names and hand positions for tennis forehand and backhand, volleyball setup and spike, and so forth. (2) It is possible to insert a quick balloon study: "In groups of four, come up with six different ways to move the balloon in a remembered sequence."

▶ The Where the Wild Things Are Dance can be made more exciting by the presence of an audience. Either divide the class in half or informally invite someone, like your principal or another class.

English Language Development

▶ Hitting the balloon with various body parts is a perfect activity for reviewing body part names.

▶ When trying out sport moves, make sure the children understand what sport they are working on and that they call out the name.

▶ As mentioned before, danced literature provides one of the best ways of building up vocabulary.

▶ The Opposite Game looks like the perfect activity for English learners, but it is not. It works only if the class as a whole is past the "preproduction" stage. If most of the class speaks very little or no English, they will not enjoy the word play.

≋ *Assessment*

This is an excellent time to evaluate how much your class has grown. Watch their ease with large-motor skills like jumping and hitting the balloon, bouncing the balloon, and hitting the balloon with their head. Check their eye-hand coordination as they try out various sport skills and as they balance the balloon on one finger. Assess their memory, concentration, and sequencing during the Where the Wild Things Are Dance. On a higher level, look at how much fun they are having, how comfortable the children are with their own bodies, and how at ease they are with you. Notice how carefully and easily they work with a partner. Most important of all, check how much they have grown in self-discipline and control. When I see a class set up for the Where the Wild Things Are Dance quickly and efficiently, when I see them act out mischief and then instantly freeze, when I see them delight in their "misbehavior" during the Opposite Game and then stop when the game is over, I know they have gained the greatest skill, enjoyment with control.

Chapter 16

Lesson Plans for Fourth Through Sixth Grades

Hold on to your hat. Although this curriculum also presents the three class management organizations and the basic movement concepts, it is oriented toward integrating ideas into complex wholes. Completing a group-created symmetrical floor pattern using sophisticated locomotor movements, nonlocomotor movements, levels, and directions requires an armload of concept strands. Mastering a dance like the Pachelbel Canon Dance requires advanced physical skills along with self-discipline and control. The results move beyond pedagogical studies into art. This is step by leaping step. The following table is an overview of the curriculum for fourth through sixth grades.

Fourth Through Sixth Grades Curriculum

Lesson plan number	Lesson plan name	Purpose/Notes
1	Obstacle course	There is one overriding reason to start the intermediate-level curriculum with an obstacle course—it will win the children over. It is also an extremely useful assessment tool to evaluate individual coordination levels, social skills, motor and behavioral controls, and focus of attention. Plan to repeat this lesson consecutively one or two more times.
2	Locomotor movements	This is the real conceptual start. First we establish the first two class management organizations—Free Traveling Structure and Perfect Spots. Then we rely on these organizations to introduce and explore locomotor movements, work on conditioning and gymnastics, broaden the range of ball-moving possibilities, and create a study. Not bad for one lesson.
3	Nonlocomotor movements	With the addition of the Diagonal Structure we have all three of the class management organizations as well as a foundation of locomotor and nonlocomotor movements. We also have a ball study and a nonlocomotor movement dance to show.

(continued)

Fourth Through Sixth Grades Curriculum *(continued)*

Lesson plan number	Lesson plan name	Purpose/Notes
4	Levels and floor patterns	This lesson presents two concepts and integrates them. Levels are introduced and then explored in the warm-up and in creating a partner level sequence. (This partner collaboration is preparation for the partner work in the next lesson.) When the floor pattern is introduced, levels are incorporated into design.
4.5	Reflections and options	We discuss the question of imposing our taste on youngsters. Is it our duty, or are we overstepping educational bounds?
5	Partners	We jump into the deep water of social skills. Students try out many partner activities, getting new partners each time, and they learn the fairly complicated Partner Dance. We also prepare them for creating their own floor dance patterns by introducing a helping floor pattern.
6	Lines	We continue work with partners while reinforcing geometry concepts and mastering the Partner Dance. Partner skills expand into a group cooperative floor pattern integrating parallel and perpendicular lines introduced at the beginning of class.
7	In and out game	It looks as though we are taking a break with this game, but that is an illusion. We are still reinforcing the geometry introduced last time, the concept of symmetry (which will be used next time), and relationship words that are used all the time. We also introduce directions and scarves with an eye on the culminating assignment in lesson 10.
8	Symmetry	This is an in-depth look at symmetry, which is important both academically and artistically. We use scarves to expand into line shapes and integrate everything into a group symmetrical floor pattern using scarves.
9	A sophisticated dance and sophisticated locomotor movements	We expand gymnastics and nonlocomotor movement vocabulary into a lyrical dance. In approaching the Pachelbel Canon Dance, I offer a teaching technique in which the dance steps are taught in the warm-up and then taught again as a completed dance. In addition, students learn sophisticated locomotor movements in preparation for the culminating study next time.
9.5	Reflections and options	This is an X-ray into my decision-making process in choosing this sequence of movement activities.
10	A culminating study	We have been building up to this for a long while. Students are assigned a group study that integrates symmetry, floor patterns, sophisticated locomotor movements, line shapes, levels, and directions. We incorporate downtime with the parachute.
11	Mastering the culminating study	Brain Catcher warms up the children's brains as well as bodies. We then set about polishing the study created last time.
11.5	Reflections and options	It is time to plan for the end of movement classes. If you choose a performance, I offer a format; the rest of the classes will be practice. If you choose to continue lessons, I offer the progression that follows.
12	Partner obstacle course	In addition to being great fun, this course presents some intense partner skill work—that is why it is offered after the class has had many cooperative experiences. We also slip in an introduction to balance in preparation for the in-depth work next week.

Lesson plan number	Lesson plan name	Purpose/Notes
13	Balance	This lesson is a model of how to take any concept or movement—fall, turn, contract and stretch, focus—and use it as a base for cooperative studies. Lessons 12 to 14 outline a very functional progression: Introduce a concept one week (lesson 12); integrate it with other concepts and create a study the following week (lesson 13); expand the concept and perfect the study the week after (lesson 14). We use Freeway as an exciting release of energy.
14	Beanbag balance	We expand the idea of balancing on various body parts to balance a prop. The group studies are developed, perfected, and performed. We relax with the Opposite Game (requested daily once introduced).
15	Yankee doodle dance finale	We kick up our heels with the In and Out and the Opposite Games. (It has always been astounding to me how much children delight in these two academically valuable games.) And we conclude with the rousing Yankee Doddle Dance.

LESSON 1

4TH – 6TH GRADES

Obstacle Course

≋ Teacher to Teacher

So much rests on this class. Younger children want to please and will do almost anything in order to move. Intermediate children also want to please, but peer and internal pressures are much stronger; few will take the chance of looking foolish. Everything will work better if this first class is well organized: (1) Prepare the students. Tell them at least a week in advance that they will be barefoot and why. Talk about what clothes would be appropriate to wear and describe some of the activities they will be doing. (Keep a few pairs of old shorts for boys and leggings for girls just in case.) (2) Prepare yourself. Set up the course beforehand, know exactly what exercises you plan to do, decide if you will demonstrate the gymnastics routine yourself or if you will select a volunteer, and plan how you will start the course (i.e., will the class wait to start at the beginning or will they start at various points along the course?).

Also prepare yourself mentally. You must be in charge. If one or even a few students will not take off their shoes, do not let them join. You can try enticing them or ordering them, but do not bend your rules. The same is true for children who are acting wild, racing through the course, being too loud, not keeping the sequence, or not replacing equipment after using it. Even if they are "not too bad," I recommend warning them and then putting them out. Your ace here is the natural fun of movement; and, in the long run, your students will appreciate the physical and emotional safety that a controlled class provides. What I am saying is, act confident even if you don't feel confident.

The issue of control came up in my class last year. I had a very difficult student with an unfortunate home life. This child was an enormous problem for me because he relentlessly caused minor disturbances (pushed a desk, burped in someone's face, jabbed someone in line, etc.).

Because these were minor offenses I did not feel justified in putting him out. I bent over backward trying every management technique I knew to win him over. By spring I had to acknowledge failure. At that point I sighed in resignation and instituted a three-strike system—three annoyances and he was out of my class. I do not know if my more stringent attitude helped him or not (it certainly did not appear to hurt), but it definitely helped the rest of the class and me. A great tension was lifted when it was clear that we were not going to tolerate his petty behavior. How does this story tie in to the first class? Do not let one or a few students erode your self-confidence. You are a good and brave teacher or you would not be trying this program. Set up an exciting course, include physical challenges, tire the students out, and do not accept any of their garbage. You have done enough.

Student Objectives

▶ Students will fully grasp that movement class is controlled fun.

▶ Students will feel physically and emotionally safe yet challenged.

▶ Students will gain strength and flexibility through conditioning activities.

▶ Students will learn and demonstrate several gymnastics stunts.

▶ Students will experience a myriad of coordination and visual perceptual activities.

▶ Students will correctly follow the course sequence.

Materials Needed

▶ Everything available. Ideally, a stegel with the balance beam set on the medium and high notches, mats, jump ropes, tires, pogo balls and pogo sticks, scooters, hoppities, foot stompers, balance boards, beanbags, foam shapes, balls, balloons, an incline mat, scarves, scoopers and foam balls.

▶ Masking tape for the scooter line.

Teaching Instructions

1. If at all possible, have the obstacle course set up before class. Children put away their socks and shoes and get places on the mats. Do not wait. When a third of the class is ready, begin with a thorough warm-up. Do stretches for the neck, back, and legs, abdominal exercises, and push-ups. Review bridge-contract-shoulder stand several times and teach a one-knee back roll. Have children rock back and forth, then teach a somersault and practice continuous somersaults in one direction. Teach a frog balance and have children practice frog balances on their own.

2. Put together the entire gymnastics routine: somersault, jump, bridge, contract, shoulder stand, one-knee back roll, frog balance. Do the whole routine three times.

3. Gather the class and teach the obstacle course. Children go through the course continuously for the rest of the lesson.

Adaptations

Easier

▶ The most difficult move in the gymnastics routine is the frog balance. Eliminate it for now and teach it either next time or in a few months when you present a different obstacle course.

▶ For very heavy or very timid children, change the somersault to an over-the-shoulder roll.

▶ You can simplify the obstacle course itself by lowering the balance beam and by reducing the number of activities.

Harder

▶ Make the warm-up exercises and the gymnastics routine more difficult by polishing the form of each position, for example tummies tucked, legs stretched fully and toes pointed, the bridge done with fully extended arms and head dropped back.

▶ The somersault can be upgraded to a diving somersault or one that uses specific leg positions like pike or straddle.

▶ The frog balance can move up to a headstand.

▶ The whole routine can flow like a dance with each move transitioning smoothly to the next.

▶ The obstacle course becomes more difficult if you (1) have one beam on the highest notch; (2) have a second beam at a low height and challenge the students who are extremely at ease on the beam to try jumping rope, but only on the lowest beam; (3) offer other equipment combinations, for example bounce a ball and balance a balloon, jump on a pogo ball and include a jump rope, circle a plastic hoop and hit a balloon.

English Language Development

▶ I encourage you to establish movement class as English only. Do not translate. Use gestures, demonstrations, and physical manipulations to get your point across. However, if safety is at issue, do what you need to.

▶ Choose a few words on which to concentrate, for example *somersault*, *bridge*, *balance beam*, *precarious*, and *help*. Ask the children to call the word out while performing the movement.

≋ *Assessment*

Where shall we start? This lesson is a treasure trove of assessment possibilities; the trouble will be choosing what to concentrate on. I recommend selecting a few skills and jotting down quick evaluations. The following grid will help you keep track of children's initial performance and subsequent improvement (see p. 288). I use the following grade indicators: a circle for great difficulty, a slanted line for halfway, and an "X" for an accomplished skill. I like this sequence of marks because they can be superimposed one on the other as the child improves. But please, do these evaluations lightly, almost surreptitiously. The children should absolutely not feel the pressure of being tested. If they ask you what you are doing with the chart, just say you are seeing who needs help in the future.

A crucial assessment during this first class is that of attitude. Who is reluctant? Who is going to need extra challenges? Who is going to use movement class to test your authority and who is attention starved? How does the class as a whole feel about movement and about their bodies? For this first class, an assessment of attitude is actually more relevant than an evaluation of physical skills.

Skills Assessments Class Chart

Category																				
1. Agility (climbing on ladder and over stegel)																				
2. Dynamic balance (walking on beam)																				
3. Dynamic balance (riding a hoppity)																				
4. Static balance (frog balance)																				
5. Static balance (headstand)																				
6. Eye-hand coordination (dribbling a ball)																				
7. Eye-hand coordination (shooting a basket)																				
8. Eye-hand coordination (catching a ball with a scooper)																				
9. Visual perceptual (scooter line)																				
10. Large-muscle coordination (jumping rope)																				
11. Large-muscle coordination (hopping right)																				
12. Large-muscle coordination (hopping left)																				
13. Large-muscle coordination (jumping in tires)																				
14. Flexibility (bridge)																				
15. Flexibility (somersault)																				
16. Flexibility (leg stretches)																				
17. Following sequence																				
18. Overall behavior																				

From *Step by step: A Complete Movement Education Curriculum*, by Sheila Kogan, 2003, Champaign, IL: Human Kinetics.

LESSON 2

4TH – 6TH GRADES

Locomotor Movements

≈ Teacher to Teacher

Be tough. If you demand precision in the class management structures, Free Traveling Structure and Perfect Spots, all future movement activities will flow more easily. You might feel it is petty to correct a child for taking three steps after the tambourine has stopped, but it is important. An approximate movement is like an almost correct math answer—it won't work. You do not need to be harsh; you can work primarily by positive reinforcement, but your standards need to be spectacularly high. A teacher once said, with reference to me, "Oh, she's the one that gets her kids to stop on a dime"—one of the greatest compliments I ever got.

≈ Student Objectives

- Students will stop exactly on cue (Free Traveling Structure).
- Students will understand that some movements travel and will explore a variety of locomotor movements.
- Students will demonstrate finding a place far from everyone and far from everything, facing front (Perfect Spots).
- Students will gain strength and flexibility with conditioning exercises and practice of gymnastics moves.
- Students will explore many ways to move a ball.
- Students will create and perform a sequence of ball activities.

≈ Materials Needed

- Tambourine.

- A sign with near on one side and far on the other.
- Balls, enough for one per child.

≈ Teaching Instructions

1. After putting away their socks and shoes, children sit in the middle of the room; when about half are ready, begin the lesson. Establish the Free Traveling Structure. Do isolated movements (fingers, hands, toes) starting and stopping with the tambourine; then do nonlocomotor movements (spin, shake, bounce) to the tambourine. Use jump as a transition to locomotor movements.

2. Before changing the jump from a nonlocomotor to a locomotor movement, sit the class down and teach the term locomotor. Go on to do many locomotor movements in the Free Traveling Structure; each time use the entire phrase "Now we will do the locomotor movement . . ." Do jump, skip, gallop, side-slide, hop, hopscotch, baby crawl, crab crawl, roll, jazzy walk, run, run and leap.

3. Establish Perfect Spots. Show the sign with *near* and have the children go near several items in the room. Show the sign with *far* and have them go far from various objects. End with "far from everybody"; then say, "Now we are going to go far from two things: far from everybody and far from everything. That is your Perfect Spot. Find your Perfect Spot and sit down." When the children have their spots, add "facing front" to complete Perfect Spots.

4. Do exercises in Perfect Spots. Review the abdominal exercises and push-ups done in

the previous lesson and do more repetitions. Review bridge, contract, shoulder stand, and possibly the one-knee back roll. (If done correctly, the one-knee back roll does not require mats. Include it if your class is ready.) Do some leg stretches and rocking back and forth. End with 100 jumping jacks, distinguishing odd and even numbers (you call out the odd numbers and the class shouts the even ones).

5. Introduce balls. Talk about freezing when the sound stops even if the ball gets away. Pass out the balls and allow a lengthy free time (perhaps 10 minutes); during the free time, test the children's ability to freeze. Do guided movements with the balls: Have the students dribble with one hand, with the other hand, alternating hands, through the legs. Do soccer dribbling; roll the ball without hands or feet; throw the ball high and catch it, then add a spin before the catch; spin the ball on the ground and then try spinning it on one finger; put the ball between the ankles, jump it up and catch it; carry the ball without hands and jazzy walk; run and leap while throwing and catching.

6. Create a ball study. Gather the class near you: legs crossed, the balls in their laps, hands off the ball. Collectively choose six ball activities and put them into a sequence. Practice and perform the study.

≋ Adaptations

Easier

▶ Go a little slower in the progression to establish the Free Traveling Structure and hold the freezes just a bit longer.

▶ Eliminate the one-knee back roll from the exercises in Perfect Spots.

▶ Save the ball study for next time.

Harder

▶ Do not eliminate any steps in establishing the Free Traveling Structure and Perfect Spots, but pick up the pace and keep the class constantly moving.

▶ When introducing locomotor movements, include some difficult steps such as one-legged skip, waltz walk, straddle roll, and run leap turn.

▶ Do more repetitions with polished form during the exercises in Perfect Spots.

▶ Extend the ball study to a sequence of eight.

English Language Development

▶ If you establish movement class as English only, the children will build up their listening vocabulary. Be careful: It is easy for them to slip into their primary language just for ease and speed. "Take off your jacket" takes a few seconds to gesture for comprehension, but it is important that the children get used to the process of thinking in English.

▶ It is a good idea to choose a few words for the children to say as they do the movements. During the locomotor movement practice the class can call out the names of movements as they perform them.

▶ Do not have children call out movements while working with the balls because they will want to concentrate totally on the ball.

▶ When working with near and far, emphasize the object names in English.

≋ Assessment

The obstacle course, in the previous lesson, was the perfect venue for evaluating individual skills. This lesson will give you an overall assessment of the control level of your class. How well and how easily did they freeze during the Free Traveling Structure? When establishing Perfect Spots, how thoroughly did they comprehend the concepts and how willing were they to internalize the control of space around them? How easily did they come up with a ball sequence, and did they have any trouble memorizing it? During the ball study did they sneak in shooting baskets, or did they want to perform the study correctly? What you really need to know is if the children in this class have any background in disciplining themselves or if they are just depending on you to make them behave. If it is the latter, you have your work cut out for you.

LESSON 3

Nonlocomotor Movements

≋ Teacher to Teacher

About this time you might reach a plateau. We began with such a bang! We were excited and they were exuberant; we didn't seem to mind the preparation and expended energy that movement class requires. Now you might feel a letdown. "Oh, maybe we should skip movement this week because we have all that work to finish." "I am feeling pulled in so many directions. Do I really want to continue with this program?" "The multipurpose room is dirty and I am sick of sweeping it myself; maybe I'll just skip it." I have two things to tell you: (1) I understand completely and (2) I implore, recommend, and plead that you keep going. We teachers are under so much pressure to show academic results that it seems almost a frivolity to skip, swing, and leap. It isn't. Remember how much benefit your children are getting from movement: They are learning an untold number of skills, both immediate and life forming. They are releasing their own stress and bottled-up emotions. They are having fun and associating enjoyment with school. Movement is worth the effort.

With motivation rebooted, let's check if movement class is harder on you than it need be. The three class management organizations, Free Traveling Structure, Perfect Spots, and (after this lesson) Diagonal Structure, should be on automatic pilot and not require much energy to maintain. In your classroom I am sure you have established systems like quiet hands and single-file lines; you are not hushing students all the time and reviewing how to make a row. The class management organizations in movement parallel these systems and allow you to teach with a minimum of fretful energy. If these organizations are not firmly in place, now is the time to virtually start over and get them solid.

Once you can relax (almost) about class management, you can start having fun with the students. Perhaps you will start associating enjoyment with school. Another thought is that it will be mentally easier if you make a firm commitment to movement class at a specific time every week and then put that decision on automatic. Your students will definitely help you by clamoring for it, and you will not have to re-decide the issue every week.

≋ Student Objectives

▶ Students will understand stationary movement and explore a wide variety of nonlocomotor movements.

▶ Students will experience a nonlocomotor movement dance.

▶ Students will demonstrate a command of the Free Traveling Structure and Perfect Spots.

▶ Students will understand the concept diagonal and competently move in groups across the diagonal (Diagonal Structure).

▶ Students will correctly perform the ball study.

▶ Students will exhibit courteous audience behavior.

▶ Students will accelerate the somersault into a flip.

≋ Materials Needed

▶ Two items that make different sounds, for example tambourine and drum, or piano and tambourine.

▶ A sign with a diagonal line drawn on it.

▶ Balls, one per child.

▶ An incline mat resting on two flat mats.

〰 *Teaching Instructions*

1. Children sit in the middle of the room. Verbally review the Free Traveling Structure and the term *locomotor*. Introduce *nonlocomotor*: "If locomotor means traveling, what do you guess nonlocomotor means?" Try out several of the students' ideas. Proceed to a warm-up alternating locomotor and nonlocomotor movements using the two different sounds. Do:

   a. Skip—various shakes, especially shaking while lowering.

   b. Jump, hop, hopscotch—various swings, especially front and back.

   c. Baby crawl, crab crawl—teach contract and stretch, specifically lowest-level contract and knee-level stretch.

   d. Jazzy walk—various spins, specifically spinning on the seat.

   e. Side-slide, jog, run and leap.

2. Get Perfect Spots. Do a brief run-through of the stretches, abdominal exercises, and push-ups from last time. Teach the Eight Plus Eight Dance, pointing out that it is a sequence of nonlocomotor movements: swing jump front and back (beats 1 and 2), shake down (3 and 4), spin on the seat (beat 5), contract lying on side (beat 6), stretch up on knee level (7 and 8). Introduce the 8 beats of locomotor movements and put the 16 beats together. Have half of the class start the dance with the nonlocomotor section while the other half begins with the locomotor section.

3. Work with balls. Review freezing with a ball; then dump the box of balls out. Give the class a fairly lengthy free time and then do some guided movements. Have the children do dribbling and then running and soccer dribbling, put the ball between the ankles and jump catch it, throw the ball high and see how many claps they can do before catching it, spin the ball on a finger, drum on the ball, throw the ball hand to hand and skip, run and leap with the ball. Practice the ball study from last time and show it with half the class as the audience; then switch.

4. Establish the Diagonal Structure. Show a picture of a diagonal line; find various diagonals throughout the room; find the two diagonal lines on the floor of the room. Have the class get into groups of four and practice moving on the diagonal. Make sure the groups get ready by moving into the corner and start on their own. Do skip, run leap, run leap turn, run and click heels in the Diagonal Structure. Do a short study: one locomotor movement to the middle of the room, three nonlocomotor movements (four beats for each) in the middle, and then a different locomotor movement from the middle to the end of the diagonal.

5. End with a flip down the incline mat (this is a running somersault).

〰 *Adaptations*

Easier

▶ Do the Eight Plus Eight Dance with the class as a whole rather than dividing in half.

▶ Practice the ball study with the class as a whole rather than dividing the class into audience and performers.

▶ Eliminate the study on the diagonal; simply establish the structure and practice several locomotor movements on the diagonal.

Harder

▶ When alternating locomotor and nonlocomotor movements in the warm-up, include more difficult moves such as one-legged skips, waltz walk, run leap turns.

▶ Do a very strenuous exercise session in Perfect Spots.

▶ After establishing the Diagonal Structure, have the groups create their own study on the diagonal using locomotor and nonlocomotor movements.

English Language Development

▶ It is known that anyone learning a new language will be able to comprehend well before they are able to speak. Movement is perfect for English language development work because it provides (1) opportunities for the kinesthetic recognition of a word and (2) the opportunity to shout out words in a group. Combining a word with its action is a superb reinforcement. When we ask children to shout out the word as well as perform it, we are incorporating a full sensory approach. Because the children call out the English word in unison, no one is on the spot and all are able to practice in safety. There are opportunities all through this lesson for the class to call out the names of movements. In the warm-up the children can say the names of the locomotor movements, the nonlocomotor movements, or (if they are more advanced) both types of movements.

▶ When introducing the Diagonal Structure, have individual children (if they are ready) say where the diagonal would go and put the location into a sentence. They might say, for example, "The diagonal line would go to this [pointing] corner of the mat . . . The diagonal line would go to that corner of the floor."

≋ Assessment

The focus of assessment for this lesson is accuracy. How well does the class as a whole stop when the sound stops? How well does the class keep the nonlocomotor movements in place? How clear are the diagonal lines? Are there children who blur the distinction between locomotor and nonlocomotor? What is preventing precision in their movements? Are they not concentrating? Are they testing you? Are they physically unable? A majority of the time, lack of precision stems from lack of focus; but some children might be testing your authority, and one or two might actually be unable. It is important to distinguish the cause because our response will differ accordingly. If the class in general is getting sloppy, it is time for the movement-is-a-subject lecture and a tightening of your expectations. Authority testing needs to be eliminated; and if there is a child at this grade level without the motor control to make accurate moves and precise stops, this should be a red flag that the child might need further testing by a professional.

LESSON 4

4TH – 6TH GRADES

Levels and Floor Patterns

≋ Teacher to Teacher

I hope you will love floor patterns as much as I do. It is amazing to me how one sheet of paper and a set of markers provide a lesson that will intrigue virtually every child, teach a great deal of information, and be easy to control. As usual I recommend that this introduction be quite formal and precise so that future lessons using floor patterns will go smoothly. There is not much to do about the groups racing through the pattern except to tell them not to and praise those who are in control. In a real pinch, put the most flagrant racers at the end of their group.

≋ Student Objectives

▶ Students will understand the concept of vertical space (levels) and apply it to locomotor and nonlocomotor movements.

▶ Students will demonstrate a remembered sequence of nonlocomotor movements using levels.

▶ Students will collaborate with a partner.

▶ Students will be able to orient themselves to a room representation and perform a spatial design (floor pattern) incorporating levels.

≋ *Materials Needed*

▸ Tambourine.

▸ Large white construction paper and set of markers.

▸ An incline mat resting on two flat mats.

≋ *Teaching Instructions*

1. Children sit in the middle of the room. Review locomotor and nonlocomotor movements. Ask what they think *levels* means and explore the multiple meanings for a short while. Say, "In movement class level means height and we use five basic levels. Let's try them." Practice moving through lowest, sitting, knee, standing, and air level. Proceed to do a warm-up alternating locomotor movements with nonlocomotor movements changing levels. Do:

   a. Skip—shake going through all the levels.

   b. Hopscotch—swing on all levels.

   c. Side-slide changing sides—contract and stretch on all levels.

   d. Crawl—spin on all levels.

   e. Jazzy walk—strike on all levels.

   f. Run and leap.

2. Get Perfect Spots. Review the Eight Plus Eight Dance and identify the levels; divide the class into two groups by having students get partners and asking them to split; do the dance as a canon. Go back to the partners and create a level pattern; partners choose moves to do on each level, four beats for each move, with no extra time to change levels. Ask for all partner studies to end with Temper Tantrum for eight beats on the lowest level. Watch half the partner groups at a time perform their level studies.

3. Gather the class around a sheet of construction paper (make sure everyone can see) and introduce floor patterns. Start with a room representation; then create a five-line pattern using only straight lines. Include a diagonal line in the pattern to review that concept. Make each line a locomotor movement on a different level, for example run leap, roll, crawl, jazzy walk, seat-scoot.

(Choose higher-level movements for the longer lines, and use the lower-level movements for the shorter lines.) Go back to the previously formed partners and combine into groups of four or six to perform the floor pattern. Each group performs at least twice, the first time with you calling out the movements and the second time completely on their own.

4. Set up the incline mat and review the flip (running somersault) from last time. End with Tackle using the incline mat.

≋ *Adaptations*

Easier

▸ Do the Eight Plus Eight Dance in unison with no division into audience and performers.

▸ Create the level study with the class as a whole collectively choosing the movements.

▸ Make the floor pattern shorter and make sure to draw each line to a specifically marked destination.

Harder

▸ In the warm-up, identify the levels of locomotor movements and include level changes with locomotor movements as well as with nonlocomotor movements.

▸ Make the partner level studies harder by asking for each move to include an opposite. For example, air-level jumps can be done with one person doing a leapfrog over the other; standing-level swings can be done with one person swinging forward as the other swings back; knee-level contract and stretch can be done with one person contracting while the other is stretching; sitting-level spin can be done with the spins going in opposite directions. (Keep the Temper Tantrum for the lowest level.)

▸ A different way to make the level patterns harder is to forget the Temper Tantrum and have the partner groups create a separate move for each level, four beats for each move. Some groups start on the lowest level while some start on the highest, and they do their patterns simultaneously. Since each movement gets four beats, it all fits together nicely, "connecting" on the knee level.

▶ The floor pattern can be extended to as long as 10 lines, with 2 lines for each level.

English Language Development

▶ *Level* is one of those great multiple-meaning words that so often stump children on the standardized tests. You could make up a test question using level:

She is on the knee *level*.

   In which sentence is the word *level* used in the same way:

Please level with me.

Is this table level?

Joe is on the standing level.

I'm on level 3 of this video game.

▶ When creating the floor pattern, ask individual children questions appropriate to their level. For a beginning English speaker, the question can call for a one-word answer: "What shall we do from the piano to the doors?" For a more advanced speaker, ask for a complete sentence in English. The question could be,

for example, "Where should we draw this line and what movement shall we do?" Possible answer: "Draw the line from the mats to the tables and let's do run and leap."

≋ Assessment

Again we are looking at precision. During the level patterns, could the children move for exactly four beats and immediately change levels? Could they control the Temper Tantrum so that it lasted precisely eight beats? Did any children use the tantrum as an opportunity to get out of control? When performing the floor pattern, could the children remember the movements and the line destinations? Did the children blur the line destinations? Did they start the movement at the beginning of a line or did they take a running start? Did the groups stay more or less together or were they racing? It is important to have this first floor pattern solid both intellectually and behaviorally because so much future curriculum rests on it. If your assessment is that the class is not ready to move on to more difficult floor patterns, it is fine to reintroduce the concept as many times as necessary.

4.5
Reflections and Options

4TH – 6TH GRADES

Let's glance back to lesson 4 and forward to lesson 5 for a moment. Lesson 4 included a partner-created sequence on different levels. Be forewarned; you will need to tread a thin line. If the children choose movements that are their own, for example current dance moves, break dancing, acting silly, that is fabulous. I allow anything that stays within the assigned parameters, but I do not allow what I consider sexually explicit moves current in the hip-hop dance style. I am not a prude. I think hip-hop dance is fun, but the hip gyrations are not appropriate for elementary age children. As I said, there is a delicate line between wanting them to be free and imposing your taste. Your gut feeling

needs to be respected. You do have the authority and the right to say, "This is not appropriate." C.S. Lewis remarks that the purpose of education is to train children to love what is lovable and hate the hateful. Sensuality is wonderful; but allowing, even encouraging, young girls to imitate adult sexuality is vulgar and possibly dangerous. I believe we adults have been remiss in not teaching what is tasteful. As a wonderful music professor once said about an unappealing composition, "It comes down to taste and mine is better."

I rewrote lesson 5 four times. I kept trying to make it chock-full, combining the introduction to parallel and perpendicular lines, now in lesson 6, with the introduction to partners and throwing in a few of the Partner Dance steps as well. It was not total lunacy: If an intermediate class has had movement for several years and knows how to work with partners and how to combine movements into dance sequences, it is possible to combine those concepts into a fairly complicated but workable whole. However, even an experienced class prefers a more focused approach; for a novice class, more focus is crucial. The most effective lessons clearly state the desired educational outcome, for example, "I want you to be able to work cooperatively with anyone in this room" or "You need to be clear on the difference between parallel and perpendicular lines." Then there is a pattern of activities that supports the goal.

In lesson 5 we move from partner activities to individual practice of dance moves. The pattern is consistent; I did not mix partner activities in the dance practice or individual skills with the partner activities. Even if the dance steps and the partner challenges get extremely difficult, the pattern of what is going to come next is stable and therefore comforting. Lesson 6 also involves a distinct pattern: The children do a locomotor movement on their own; they get a partner and do that same movement in parallel and then perpendicular lines; they thank that partner and separate to start again. Once they have done this progression twice, they know the sequence and enjoy that consistency. Children thrive on a routine in the classroom; knowing what comes next gives them a sense of security. These small patterns of events are a microcosm of larger class routines. Knowing the pattern allows the students to concentrate more fully on the particular concept that is being taught.

LESSON 5
Partners

4TH – 6TH GRADES

〰 Teacher to Teacher

Lesson 5 has a number of technical moves that compel me to share some very specific considerations. This is probably just an old dance teacher's moment of triumph; but after many years of having trouble teaching the move from a lying-down position into the sitting triangle position, I found that if you start sitting and go down from there you can teach it quite easily. This must sound utterly absurd to classroom teachers, but dance and movement specialists will understand. Also, if the Partner Dance introduced in this lesson is not working, I would be willing to bet that the person doing part two is coming down from the bridge too quickly. It is necessary to take all four beats to come down in order to give part 1 the time to get into the high bridge position.

The Foam Jump might raise two areas of concern. One is the whole issue of danger. If the child asks for the foam to be stacked too high for her ability, is it dangerous? It can be, but my experience is that children normally self-regulate. Also, if you have plenty of mats underneath, all that will happen is that a child will knock over the stack and fall on the mats. However, if you get a scared feeling about a child's choice I recommend respecting that and simply saying that you think the stack is too high for now and want to see a lower jump first. Second is the issue of children laughing at one another. There is no way to stop this completely, because some of the jumps will be funny. However, your inner sense will tell you when laughter is actually mocking. Again I recommend respecting that inner voice; warn the offending children and/or do not let them jump. Not letting a child do the Foam Jump is an extreme punishment and should be used very judiciously. We teachers are trained in all sorts of curriculum advances and pedagogical techniques, but the bottom line is that we must include our gut level instincts—sometimes they are the most important tool we have.

Student Objectives

▶ Students will demonstrate cooperation and consideration with a partner.

▶ Students will experience a variety of partner activities.

▶ Students will learn and execute the Partner Dance.

▶ Students will understand the process of creating a floor pattern (helping floor pattern).

▶ Students will perform the created floor pattern correctly.

▶ Students will gain experience with math computation.

▶ Students will practice motor planning with the Foam Jump.

Materials Needed

▶ Tambourine.

▶ A few sheets of large white construction paper and a set of markers.

▶ One mat and, ideally, 10 pieces of foam.

Teaching Instructions

1. Children sit in the middle of the room. Give the "partner lecture" informing them that whoever chooses them is their partner and that, no matter what they feel, they will act cooperatively (see p. 104). Also, every time they complete work with a partner, they will bow and thank each other. Do a warm-up alternating partner activities with the steps to the Partner Dance (see p. 193); switch partners for the partner activities, but work on the dance steps individually. Note that in the sample progression that follows, italic type (partner activities) is alternated with regular type (individual dance steps) to highlight the alternating required in the warm-up.

   a. *Partners hold both hands and side-slide front-to-front and then back-to-back with elbows linked. They continue with Wring Out the Dishrag, in which partners hold hands, lift one arm, and then both go under.*

   b. Teach the triangle position, that is, sitting with the right leg tucked and the left leg bent in front. Have the children, from this sitting position, practice lying down and, starting with the right leg, sitting up into the triangle position.

   c. *Partners hold both hands and spin, then go in the other direction. Same partners find a different way to hold on to each other and spin.*

   d. Teach the first eight beats of part 1 of the Partner Dance. Children begin on their abdomens and sit up into the triangle position (beats 1 and 2), push up onto the feet (beats 3 and 4), sit back into the triangle position (beats 5 and 6), and lie back down (7 and 8). Emphasize that each move is assigned a specific beat.

   e. *Partner hop—each person holds his partner's leg and hops; switch legs.*

   f. Teach the second eight beats of part 1 of the Partner Dance. Children lift into a high push-up position (beats 9 and 10), remain in that position and cross the left leg over (11 and 12), come back to the original push-up position (13 and 14), and sit facing the right side of the room (15 and 16).

   g. *Partner Wheelbarrow and Horsie.*

   h. Teach all 16 beats of part 2 of the Partner Dance. Children start sitting; they lie back (beats 1 and 2), push up into a bridge (beats 3 and 4), come down from the bridge (beats 5-8); they slide on their back while tickling hands (beats 9-12), then sit, spin, and lie down on their abdomens (beats 13-16).

   i. *Partner-synchronized run and leap. Tell the class to remember these last partners because we will return to them.*

2. Get Perfect Spots and reteach the entire Partner Dance. Emphasize that the moves must occur exactly on their specified counts. Have the class return to their partners from the last warm-up activity (Horsie) and try the sequences together, that is, part 1 and part 2 at the same time. It probably will not work correctly this first time. Pick a partner group that got it to demonstrate so the class can model the interrelationship of parts. Have the class try the dance with their partners again.

3. Keep the partners from the Partner Dance and gather the class around one piece of construction paper. Introduce a helping floor pattern, with individual children helping to create the design. Do a seven-line pattern and include levels. Combine partners into groups of six and perform the pattern.

4. Do the Foam Jump first with just five pieces of foam to warm up the ankles, and then with the number of pieces chosen by each child.

≋ *Adaptations*

Easier

▶ During the warm-up, teach smaller sections of the Partner Dance. For example, after the first partner activity, teach only the triangle position; after the second partner activity, introduce only the move from sitting in the triangle position to lying down and back up again; after the third partner activity, introduce the push onto the feet from the triangle position, and so forth.

▶ Teach only part 1 of the Partner Dance and save part 2 for next time, or teach both parts but save the combination until next time.

▶ Create a shorter helping floor pattern.

Harder

▶ In the warm-up, do some simple partner activities and then move on to partner challenges; for example, contract together like one big rock and then pull apart, while holding on, for the stretch; contract and stretch in opposites; choose two different levels, hold on to one another and move; do a locomotor and a nonlocomotor movement, touching each other and staying together.

▶ Complete the Partner Dance and emphasize not only the exact counts of each move but also a smooth transition between moves so that all the parts flow like a lyrical whole.

▶ Do the helping floor pattern in the original order and then in the reverse order. If you have time, have one group start in the original order while another group performs the pattern in reverse.

English Language Development

▶ Have you made movement class an English-only area? Research now says that it is best to have a clear demarcation between where children speak their native language and where they speak English. Ideally, we are told, they should speak their native language at home so as to build up a rich vocabulary and complex thinking skills and should speak only English at school. Of course this is not always possible or even always desirable; bilingual classes in which teachers work to transition the children's language can work well. However, we can encourage even early English learners to practice when they feel safe and supported. Situations like the warm-up partner activities are perfect for practicing conversational English. I am completely opposed to the current political strain that harshly prohibits children from speaking their native language in school. Our job is to gently and rationally explain why practice is important and to set the tone of our class so that the risk is not too high.

▶ Before working on the helping floor pattern, have the children bring two fingers together and say the word *connect*. As they are creating the pattern, ask individual children not only to draw the line but also to formulate a complete sentence about where the line came from and where it is going.

▶ During the Foam Jump, requests for the number of foam pieces should be in a complete English sentence—for example, "I want to jump nine and there are six so add three more."

〰 *Assessment*

Three comprehensive areas of assessment are possible in this lesson: (1) social skills, (2) motor planning, and (3) visual perception. Watch carefully during the partner activities for timid as well as aggressive behavior. No single assessment should label a child; but extreme difficulty in choosing a partner, cooperating with classmates, or enjoying tactile and social stimulation should be a red flag for general problems in social skills. Our task is somewhat like triage; we must determine whether the social difficulties stem from lack of experience, which we can provide, or from internal emotional problems, which are beyond our scope.

We teachers need to look seriously at social skills because they affect every aspect of a child's life; there is no way we can limit our focus to simply academics. Not only are more jobs requiring teamwork, but the ability to get along is an important part of becoming a full human being.

Motor planning is seen in the Partner Dance and in the Foam Jump. Children who have enormous trouble putting their body parts in shown positions might have a more generalized problem with their proprioceptive sense. This can manifest in awkward movements, difficulty with sports, and trouble with fine motor work. If a child does show great difficulty in this area, a consultation with a specialist (an occupational therapist or sensory integration therapist) would be warranted.

Floor patterns in general will signal any visual perceptual problems, most especially if a child has no clue where a line goes in the room. Keep note of this and again see if it seems to result from lack of experience or seems to be more pervasive.

LESSON 6

Lines

4TH — 6TH GRADES

〰 *Teacher to Teacher*

Choices, choices, choices. We teachers are constantly choosing whether to lean a little here or there. The Foam Jump is a perfect example: On one hand the jump itself is great fun, especially for the athletic boys, and everyone gets very excited. On the other hand, the Foam Jump is a spectacular reinforcement of math computations. If we concentrate on the math, the rhythm of the activity will slow down so much that it will lose its excitement; if we use the jump purely as a physical activity, we lose a golden academic opportunity. I cannot give you a formula here. You are used to making these types of choices throughout your teaching day. I personally recommend erring on the side of more excitement. If children feel a heavy

pedagogical weight, especially if that weight is keeping them from something they are dying to do, they will turn off. Sometimes we can teach with less repetition if the reception is perfectly tuned.

〰 *Student Objectives*

▶ Students will understand, differentiate, and apply the concepts perpendicular and parallel.

▶ Students will demonstrate cooperation and consideration with a partner and with a group.

▶ Students will perform the Partner Dance correctly without teacher help.

▶ Students will collaborate in creating a floor pattern.

▶ Students will experience the reality of math computations.

▶ Students will practice motor planning with the Foam Jump.

≋ *Materials Needed*

▶ Two signs, one with the word parallel and a picture of parallel lines; one with the word perpendicular and a picture of perpendicular lines.

▶ Tambourine.

▶ Ten to 20 sheets of white construction paper and seven containers of markers.

▶ Two mats and, ideally, 10 pieces of foam.

≋ *Teaching Instructions*

1. Review the rules of cooperation with a partner; that is, "Whoever chooses you is your partner and you need to look and act friendly." Show the sign with the word and picture for parallel lines, and ask the children to find examples of parallel lines in the room. Each time they point to a set of parallel lines, show how the lines are the same and equidistant. Ask two children to side-slide in parallel lines, concentrating on staying relatively equidistant. Repeat the procedure for perpendicular lines: Show the picture and word and ask for examples of perpendicular lines in the room. Point out that these lines connect a horizontal and vertical line. Have two children demonstrate perpendicular lines. Proceed to do a warm-up in the pattern presented next. Note that in the sample progression shown, regular type (individual movements) is alternated with italic type (partner activities) to highlight the alternating required. Make sure students bow and thank each partner.

   a. Skip individually.

   b. *Get a partner and skip in parallel lines; skip in perpendicular lines.*

   c. Side-slide individually.

   d. *Get a different partner and side-slide in parallel lines; side-slide in perpendicular lines.*

   e. Hopscotch individually.

   f. *Get a different partner and hopscotch in parallel lines; hopscotch in perpendicular lines.*

   g. Do any type of crawl individually.

   h. *Get a different partner and do parallel push-ups, then perpendicular push-ups. Stay with that partner and do parallel abdominal crunches, then perpendicular abdominal crunches.*

   i. Roll individually.

   j. *Get a different partner and attempt parallel and perpendicular rolls. Then simply lie down in parallel and perpendicular lines.*

   k. Jazzy walk individually.

   l. *Get a different partner and jazzy walk in parallel and then perpendicular lines.*

   m. Run and leap individually.

   n. *Get a last partner and run and leap in parallel and then perpendicular lines.*

2. Have children remember the last partner. Children get in Perfect Spots and review parts 1 and 2 of the Partner Dance in unison. They return to the last partner and try the dance combining the two parts. Have half the class watch each other.

3. Ask partners to combine into groups of six. Review the elements of creating a floor pattern: (1) drawing the room representation and keeping it straight, (2) putting an "X" where the pattern starts, (3) connecting all lines. Give this assignment: Create a floor pattern that has no less than five but no more than seven lines. Each line has to be a different locomotor movement. Within your pattern you must include at least one set of parallel lines and one set of perpendicular lines. (Have the assignment written out.) Show an example and then pass out one piece of construction paper and a set of markers to each group.

4. Have groups practice and show their patterns.

5. End with the Foam Jump.

≋ *Adaptations*

Easier

▶ At first glance it would seem logical to simplify the warm-up by introducing either parallel or perpendicular lines. You certainly can do that. I have found that teaching both concepts does not make the introduction significantly harder and, in fact, clarifies the difference between the two line relationships.

▶ What would simplify the warm-up a little is to stay completely consistent with the established pattern: After the children move in a crawl, have them do the crawl in parallel and perpendicular lines; eliminate the roll altogether. The more consistent the pattern, the easier the lesson.

▶ Floor patterns are more easily created in groups of four. The trouble with groups of four is that, in a class of 32, there are so many patterns to watch at the end—it takes forever. If your class is smaller or if you think groups of six would be too difficult socially, definitely combine into fours.

▶ Again it would seem logical to simplify the floor pattern by not assigning both parallel and perpendicular lines; but since we introduced these lines in the warm-up, it makes no sense not to apply them. Go a little slower and do one pattern all together, modeling the assignment. You could point out that a simple rectangle fulfills the entire assignment.

▶ If you want a much simpler first floor pattern, do not start with this warm-up but go to a spelling warm-up, spelling locomotor movements from a chart while the children perform them. Then assign a floor pattern of five to seven lines using different locomotor movements.

Harder

▶ Keep the pattern of the warm-up, but make it more challenging by asking for more difficult locomotor movements or possibly combinations of steps. For example, use a sequence like skip-skip-run-run-run-leap, and ask for that movement to be done in parallel lines and then in perpendicular lines.

▶ When doing perpendicular lines, talk about "close calls" and ask for the children to come very close to bumping into one another with no disasters.

▶ It would be possible to complicate matters delightfully by introducing directions in the beginning along with the two line relationships. The children work individually in all four directions. Then with a partner, they demonstrate parallel and perpendicular lines with two different directions. Examples are skipping individually in all four directions, parallel lines done with one person skipping forward and the other skipping backward, perpendicular lines done with one person skipping sideways and the other skipping turning.

▶ The floor pattern assignment (1) can be longer, (2) can include level changes, (3) can include directions.

English Language Development

▶ At the end of this lesson your English learners might not know the word *house* but will know *parallel* and *perpendicular*. When introducing a new word, especially a long word, it is best to break it up and play with the syllables: "per . . . per . . . per . . . pen . . . pen . . . perpen . . . di . . . di . . . cular . . . cular . . . dicular . . . pendicu lar . . . per pen di cu lar . . ." and so on. If at all possible, teach the whole lesson in English, including words like *horizontal* and *vertical, same* and *equidistant;* there are enough visual cues for the class to get it without translating.

▶ It is very important to have a chart of locomotor movement words up when you are asking English learners to create their own floor patterns. The words will provide movement ideas and correct spelling.

▶ It is always possible to ask the groups to shout out the movement immediately before performing it. I normally do this when working with sophisticated locomotor movements, but it can be done at any time.

▶ Take the time to ask for an equation sentence in English before children jump the foam—for example, "I want to jump nine; there are six, add three more" or "I want to jump nine, three times three equals nine." Once the first few children say their sentences, the rest will essentially use the same words—although the numbers will vary.

≈ Assessment

It is important to do a formal paper and pencil assessment of parallel and perpendicular soon after this lesson. An easy test would show examples of the two line relationships, give the words, and ask the students to match the pictures correctly. A more challenging test would be to ask them to draw parallel and perpendicular lines. In both cases, ask the children to write the definition of the line sets. It is only in writing that you can check for concepts such as equidistant, matching, horizontal, and vertical.

When executing these concepts in their floor patterns, watch that the parallel lines are not reduced to backtracking the same line but remain distinct and equidistant. Watch that the right angle created by perpendicular lines has a sharp corner.

The Partner Dance is the perfect venue for assessing how much responsibility a child is willing to shoulder. So many children (does it seem like more these days?) wait for the teacher or another child to tell them what to do. In the Partner Dance this simply will not work. This is one of those wonderful self-corrective moments; each person must do the specified moves right on the beat or the "tickling under" part (beats 9-12) will not happen.

The Foam Jump is an excellent assessment tool for both motor planning and for how easily students formulate math equations.

LESSON **7**

The In and Out Game

4TH – 6TH GRADES

≈ Teacher to Teacher

As with past lesson plans, I ask you to prepare the room before the children come in. This is important first of all because of the time. If five children help you set up the In and Out Game during recess, the setup will take 10 minutes. If the whole class "helps" set it up at the beginning of the lesson, it will take 20 minutes. Further, having the equipment set up tells the class that movement is a subject and that it is important to you. With the equipment ready, the lesson proceeds in a quicker and more organized manner—there is no hint of recess. And you are more focused, relaxed, and on top of things. But it can't always happen. Sometimes the room is being used before your class; sometimes an emergency takes all your recess time; sometimes you are simply overextended. Don't fret about it

and do not act apologetic. Just do your best and it will be fine.

Now a few notes about scarves. Scarves are a fabulous prop because they tap children's fantasy. But the children must feel extremely safe with you and each other for this imaginative world to come out. If you have had a rocky start or if you feel that the class has not unified into a supportive whole, hold off on the scarves. Introduce another prop, like ropes or balloons, and bring in the scarves later. Sometimes the children feel safe enough but, because they are "older," have gotten out of touch with their fantasy world. If they look interested but hesitant during free time, go on to guided movements with the scarf and then give them free time later. Smile and enjoy their flights of fancy. Your facial expression and attitude will have a lot of influence here.

≋ Student Objectives

▶ Students will understand and demonstrate specified relationship words and geometric terms.

▶ Students will understand and clearly execute the four directions.

▶ Students will experience freedom of expression with the scarves.

≋ Materials Needed

▶ A lot of "stuff" scattered throughout the room: three mats lying flat, two mats standing like little houses, all the foam squares from the Foam Jump, tires, plastic hoops, a stegel end, two tables, 10 chairs, beanbags, foam shapes, cones, incline mat.

▶ Tambourine.

▶ Scarves, one per person.

≋ Teaching Instructions

1. If possible, have all the "stuff" scattered about before the children come in. As soon as the children get their socks and shoes put away, ask them to skip over things, not touching anything but the floor. If someone does touch a mat or hoop, tell her that if you were playing the game she would be out. Go on to jump, hop, hopscotch, crawl, jazzy walk, and run and leap over things.

2. The class sits on one side of the room. Use individual children to demonstrate each of the words you will be using in the In and Out Game. I suggest the following:

   a. On top
   b. Under
   c. Above (same as on top)
   d. Below (same as under)
   e. Beneath (same as under)
   f. Around (Use around to introduce the four directions, forward, backward, sideways, turning, e.g., "Go around something in the backward direction.")
   g. In

   h. Beside a chair
   i. Behind a chair
   j. In front of a chair
   k. Between two specified objects (e.g., between two tires)
   l. Through
   m. On something and showing vertical lines
   n. On something and showing horizontal lines
   o. On something and showing diagonal lines
   p. On something and showing perpendicular lines
   q. Parallel lines
   r. Right angle, obtuse and acute angles
   s. On something and showing a shape that has symmetry

3. Play three rounds of the In and Out Game. End with everyone "winning" by demonstrating five words at the same time: on top, vertical, horizontal, diagonal, and perpendicular lines. Clean up as if this were part of the game: "You have 10 seconds to put everything away. No throwing!"

4. Do several locomotor movements in all directions: skip, hopscotch, crawl, jazzy walk, and run leap.

5. Children choose a scarf and have free time. Do guided movements with the scarf: throw and catch with a jump; throw and catch with different body parts; twirl; side-slide; roll and circle; jazzy walk; leap; then creative activities like sword fight, matador and bull, ballet, bride and groom, magic scarf, magician scarf. Fold the scarves and put them away.

≋ Adaptations

Easier

▶ The In and Out Game is loved by children in kindergarten through the sixth grade; it has an enormous range of difficulty. Start with some of the words, and add more in subsequent rounds or wait and add more in future games. Begin with over, on top of, under, around (using directions), in, beside, behind, in front of, through, between, horizontal, vertical, perpendicular, and parallel.

▶ Count to 10 more slowly.

▶ At the end of rounds, combine only two words—"Everybody is going to win if you can show me, at the same time, on top and under."

Harder

▶ There are three ways to make the In and Out Game harder: (1) Use all the words and any more that need reinforcement from the classroom. (2) Count to 10 fairly quickly, and midway through a round cut it to five counts. (3) Do more combinations, for example, "At the same time show me under, around in the forward direction, and in."

▶ Pick up the pace.

▶ After free time and guided movements with the scarf, ask for a seven-part study; include locomotor and nonlocomotor movements, level and direction changes.

English Language Development

▶ There is no better English language development lesson than the In and Out Game. One of the best techniques for teaching any language is "total physical response," in which a word is matched kinesthetically with its meaning. Here, not only is the word immediately demonstrated, but there is added excitement because of the time limit, which heightens focus.

▶ If you have a few English learners in your class, see if each needs a partner to follow through-

out the In and Out Game. I always encourage, praise, and applaud cooperative help.

▶ When they are throwing and catching the scarf with different body parts, have the children call out the name in English. *Sword fight, bull* and *matador,* and *bride* and *groom* are all fun words to shout out.

≈ Assessment

Unfortunately, even if the children appear to understand all the relationship and geometric terms in the game, they might not be able to apply this knowledge immediately to paper and pencil tasks. When possible, I like to give a short test before and after playing the In and Out Game. Here are some of the test items:

1. Draw a circle in the triangle.
2. Put an "X" below the rectangle, a "Y" above the rectangle, and an "O" beside the rectangle.
3. In this series of letters, A-B-C-D-E, put an "X" between the "D" and "E."
4. Draw perpendicular lines. Where is the right angle?
5. Draw a horizontal line in red and a vertical line in blue, and a diagonal line in yellow.
6. Draw a shape that has symmetry.
7. Draw diagonal parallel lines.

Most children love this kind of test. I tell them not to worry: They will take it before the game and then take the exact same test after the game and see how much they learned. I find that this approach activates both sides of the brain during the In and Out Game so that the children are more open to a larger application.

LESSON 8
Symmetry

4TH – 6TH GRADES

≈ Teacher to Teacher

Here are a few persnickety notes on symmetrical shapes. When the children are demonstrating

individual shapes, check that their hips and heads are center; they cannot lean or look to one side. When the children are creating partner shapes, tell them not to be symmetrical by themselves;

in fact, I ask them to take the weirdest position they can and then see if the partner can match it. Also see if they can match their partner's facial expression; a wink, a raised eyebrow, a half-smile, require detailed attention to the midline. For these partner shapes it is fun to play the old-fashioned game of Statue: One person is the clay and the other the sculptor; the sculptor puts the clay in any position he chooses and then has to match the design himself; of course they switch.

A difficult symmetrical floor pattern entails quite a bit of time and energy to master; lines like crossing figure "S" or matching loops will require many practices and a lot of corrections on your part. But there are so many levels of accomplishment here. The visual perceptual work is solid and valuable; the conceptual work will transfer to other academic areas; and, perhaps most importantly, the team cooperative effort and sense of class unity will make you glow for the rest of the day.

≋ *Student Objectives*

▶ Students will expand their understanding of symmetry and be able to demonstrate this concept in a variety of ways.

▶ Students will practice moving clearly in the four directions.

▶ Students will practice cooperating with a partner.

▶ Students will understand and execute various line shapes.

▶ Students will continue to explore their creativity with scarves.

≋ *Materials Needed*

▶ A few sheets of white construction paper and a set of markers.

▶ Scarves, one per person.

▶ Tambourine.

≋ *Teaching Instructions*

1. Quickly review the concept of *symmetry* and mention the idea of *midline*. Start a warm-up in which children alternate performing locomotor movements in different directions and making symmetrical shapes individually. Do:
   a. One-legged skip forward direction—symmetrical shape standing.
   b. Hopscotch backward—symmetrical shape kneeling.
   c. Crawl sideways—symmetrical shape lying down.
   d. Run leap turn.

2. Interrupt the warm-up to show how a symmetrical shape could be made with partners. Take time to identify the line of symmetry and point out whether a limb is moving toward or away from the midline. Continue the warm-up alternating partner locomotor movements and partner symmetrical shapes. Do:
   a. Side-slide changing sides, partners holding both hands (this will require a Wring Out the Dishrag move)—partner symmetrical shape sitting.
   b. Straddle roll, partners holding both hands—partner symmetrical shape lying down.
   c. Jazzy walk backward, linked elbows with partner—partner symmetrical shape standing.
   d. Synchronized run and leap holding on to one hand. (Children need to remember this partner.)

3. Distribute scarves and allow a long free time. "Today we are going to use the scarves to work on line shapes." Show each line shape—straight, curved, wiggly, zigzag, looped, and spiral—and have the children "paint" the shape with their scarf. "In a few minutes we are going to use these line shapes in a symmetrical floor pattern" (see figure 16.1). Go on to guided movements with the scarf, especially the silly activities.

4. Go back to the last partner from the warm-up as the class gathers around a piece of paper. Draw a symmetrical floor pattern. Set up the organization of partners and do the pattern first with every partner group moving separately and then with partners starting in a canon. If the class had no difficulty, add scarves to the floor pattern.

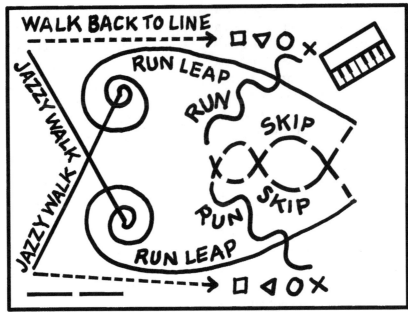

WALK BACK TO LINE

JAZZY WALK

JAZZY WALK

RUN LEAP

RUN

SKIP

RUN

SKIP

RUN LEAP

□ ▽ O ✕

□ ◁ O ✕

16.1

PARTNERS ON OPPOSITE SIDES OF THE ROOM

≋ *Adaptations*

Easier

▶ The warm-up can be simplified in several ways: (1) Use more basic locomotor movements, for example skip instead of one-legged skip. (2) When you get to the partner symmetrical shapes, eliminate the locomotor movements and just concentrate on the partner shapes. (3) Have children keep the same partner for the whole time.

▶ The symmetrical floor pattern can be as simple or as difficult as you wish.

Harder

▶ You could really go to extremes with this warm-up: (1) Instead of even a challenging locomotor movement, use short locomotor patterns, for example one-legged skip done with the leg changing positions. (2) Have some mats scattered about and expand the symmetrical shapes into gymnastics—for example, "Do a symmetrical shape while in a frog balance or, if possible, a headstand." (3) It is not a bad idea to review parallel and perpendicular lines during the partner locomotor movements. (4) Change partners after every set of locomotor movements and shapes.

▶ The line shapes, introduced with the scarves, can include symmetry: "With a partner, each of you do a wiggly line, but make the combined shape symmetrical."

▶ The floor pattern can be very difficult. Do watch each partner group separately before putting the pattern into a canon. When the children perform the canon, have them totally responsible for starting at the right time.

▶ Consider going on to pyramids. Pyramids are group symmetrical shapes that involve children balancing on one another. Clump double-thick mats into separate areas, and form groups of no less than six children. Groups design and execute three-tiered pyramids.

▶ Work on symmetry can also extend into the wonderful activity called Mirror and Shadow.

English Language Development

▶ As complicated as this warm-up might seem, it can be executed completely in English because it is full of visual cues. Simplify the locomotor movements and ask for several individual symmetrical shapes on different levels: "Show me a shape that has symmetry on the knee level

. . . Show me a shape that has symmetry on the sitting level . . ."

▶ You might notice that I keep the word *symmetry* rather than using the form *symmetrical*, because for English learners the two might sound like different words.

▶ Recognition of synonyms is a big component in standardized tests. If your kids are up for it, this might be a good time to offer a few: *same, identical, alike, twin, match, imitate, copy.*

▶ When working on the symmetrical floor pattern, call out in English the locomotor movement and the line shape. As an example, say "Run the wiggly line to the middle of the room . . . Skip the curved line to the middle of the bleachers . . ." and so on. Briefly quiz the children on the difference between locomotor and line shape: "What is the locomotor movement of the wiggly line? . . . What is the line shape of the run line? . . . Where does the wiggly line go?

. . ." This is in fact good language work for all children.

≋ Assessment

It is important to assess the children's understanding of midline. Most of the test questions on symmetry deal with the line of symmetry, or midline. I have had the disconcerting experience of seeing my students, who are symmetry whizzes, miss many of the questions because they were not trained in working with the midline. Notice who is unclear when asked, "Which arm is closest to the line of symmetry? . . . Is your right foot pointing toward or away from the midline?" Transfer this to paper and pencil by drawing shapes and asking for a midline and a matching drawing.

The symmetrical floor pattern will clearly point to those children who have visual perceptual problems. If extreme difficulty learning this spatial design fits into a pattern of perceptual problems, it is definitely time to write a referral or call in a specialist.

LESSON 9

4TH – 6TH GRADES

A Sophisticated Dance and Sophisticated Locomotor Movements

≋ Teacher to Teacher

I hope not, but the Pachelbel Canon Dance might bring up some bad feelings in you. "I'm not a dancer. What am I doing here?" "I'm too fat [thin, tall, short, awkward, stiff, old]." "I remember when I was six and fell down during a ballet performance and was totally embarrassed." Dance is very close to the bone; it opens us up and makes us vulnerable. I just want to take a minute to applaud you. Whatever you look like, you are bringing something very

special and valuable to your children—and that makes you beautiful.

≋ Student Objectives

▶ Students will learn the Pachelbel Canon Dance.

▶ Students will gain experience with sophisticated locomotor movements.

▶ Students will demonstrate sophisticated locomotor movements and apply them to a symmetrical floor pattern.

≋ Materials Needed

▶ Recording of Pachelbel's "Canon," any rendition.

▶ Chart with a list of sophisticated locomotor movements.

▶ Tambourine.

▶ White construction paper and markers.

≋ Teaching Instructions

1. Warm up by alternating locomotor movements in different directions and the steps to the Pachelbel Canon Dance. Note in that the following progression, regular type (locomotor movements) alternates with italic type (dance steps) to make the changes more obvious.

   a. Skip in all directions.

   b. *Introduce the concept of fan, and have children fan one and then both arms, one and then both legs. Teach the specific move of fanning the right leg, then crossing that leg behind, and pivoting to face the back of the room (beats 1 and 2).*

   c. Hopscotch in all directions.

   d. *Introduce the spiral sit. Teach the specific spiral sit continuing to a spin on the seat as in the Pachelbel Canon Dance. Have the children practice the entire first four beats of the dance.*

   e. Crawl in all directions.

   f. *Stay on the ground and do some conditioning exercises: rock back and forth with legs going overhead and then stretching forward; 10 back waves; 50 abdominal crunches; 20 push-ups. Reintroduce the one-knee back roll counting beats 6-8. Do the entire first eight beats of the Pachelbel Canon Dance.*

   g. Jazzy walk in all directions.

   h. *Introduce the fish turn. Review the first eight beats of the dance; add beats 1 to 4 from the second phrase.*

   i. Run and leap forward; do plain run for backward and sideways; run and leap turn in the air for turning direction.

   j. *Introduce the entire dance: fan, pivot, spiral sit, spin, one-knee back roll and stretch (beats 1-8); lower to abdomen, fish turn, straddle roll, triangle sit, and get up (beats 1-8).*

   k. Any locomotor movement they choose done in all directions.

2. In Perfect Spots, reteach the Pachelbel Canon Dance to music. Ask the children to be exactly on the beat and yet to melt one move into the next so the movement becomes fluid. Attempt the dance as a canon: The class divides in half, the two halves coming in eight beats apart.

3. Gather the class in front of the chart of sophisticated locomotor movements and go through them, grouping the ones that are similar (see table 16.1). Refer to the Vocabulary Words section in chapter 11 for an explanation.

4. Review the symmetrical floor pattern from last time and change the locomotor move-

Table 16.1 Chart of Sophisticated Locomotor Movements

Sophisticated locomotor movements	Movement description
Amble, stroll, meander	Slow walk
Creep, slink, stalk	Sneaky walk
Strut, saunter	Walk with attitude
Scurry, bustle	Fast walk or run
Stride	Fast walk with attitude
March, tramp, trudge, plod, stagger	Rhythmic walk that gets more and more tired
Limp, hobble	Restricted walk
Race, sprint, scamper, scramble, frisked, dodge	Run
Prance, trot	Jog

ments to sophisticated locomotor movements, for example sprint instead of run, meander instead of skip, scurry instead of run leap. Have children get partners, set up the organization for the floor pattern, and perform it as a canon—that is, each partner group starting one line after the group ahead.

≈ *Adaptations*

Easier

▶ Do not attempt the Pachelbel Canon Dance as a canon. Keep the class working in unison and call out the moves. If they are having a lot of trouble, just teach the first eight beats and save the second phrase for next time.

▶ Do only half the sophisticated locomotor movements from the chart; have the class choose which ones to do.

Harder

▶ A canon is easier if the room is divided in half so that part 1 and part 2 are physically separated. It would be much harder if the children paired up and did the Pachelbel Canon Dance with one person starting and her partner coming in eight beats later.

▶ Work on the style of the Pachelbel Canon Dance: legs straight and toes pointed for the fan, legs together and toes pointed for the fish turn, stretched legs for the straddle roll, and so on. Also emphasize the elegance and fluidity of the movements.

▶ The class can create a more difficult symmetrical floor pattern using only sophisticated locomotor movements.

▶ The idea of a canon can be explored with the children creating their own canons.

English Language Development

▶ It might surprise you to hear that working on the sophisticated locomotor movements is not good for beginning English learners. It is simply too much language. It is excellent for all children who have some command of English (intermediate English proficiency level and higher) because it truly broadens their vocabulary. But brand-new English learners will get overwhelmed. If you have just a few beginning English learners in your class, introduce sophisticated locomotor movements but reassure the non-English speakers that you do not expect them to remember so many new words.

▶ Definitely have children call out any movement before performing it in a floor pattern.

▶ Work on sophisticated locomotor movements can transfer into class writing time. The children need to be encouraged to use variations in their word choice in order to say exactly what they mean. This can extend to nonmovement words. For example, a list of verbs more specific than *said— whispered, yelled, muttered, replied, screamed, murmured*—provides interesting distinctions.

≈ *Assessment*

On the most basic level, this lesson will point out any problems in sequencing, memorization, and moving on the correct beat. But the Pachelbel Canon Dance is the first true lyrical dance presented; it will point to those children who have the impulse to dance from their heart. It is my experience that the best dancers are not always the most proficient. The most beautiful dancers are those who lose themselves in the emotion of the moment and allow their bodies to speak for themselves. You certainly will not be writing up referrals for children who are clumsy, self-conscious, stiff, or inelegant; but if you find a real dancer in your class, wipe the tear from your eye and tell the child's parents.

This lesson is a good time to assess yourself. Where do you want to set your standards? Unless you are in a dance studio environment, you probably do not want to focus on the dance too much, but how smooth do you expect the sequence to be? How clear a distinction should there be between meander and amble? How accurate do you expect the symmetrical floor pattern to be? Whatever standards you consider appropriate are probably correct, but it is important to consider your standards before the class chooses them for you. If you need to readjust, that is fine; but I encourage you to walk in with a goal in mind rather than a let's-see-how-they-do attitude.

9.5
Reflections and Options

Lesson 9 was another case of agonizing decision making. I always have to balance my desire to smother you with everything I know against the intention to make these lessons as realistic as possible. Matters get more complicated working with an abstract class. If I knew you were teaching experienced dance studio students, I would lean toward developing polished dances; for novice public school classes, I would lean toward academic applications.

I decided to introduce the Pachelbel Canon Dance in lesson 9 for several reasons. The first is that particular dance is loved by boys and girls because it is beautiful. Many teachers feel impelled to use only current music and in-style moves in order to win the children's attention. This is excellent up to a point. Children love and respond to beauty. I believe we unnecessarily limit them when we do not expose them to grandeur. I have a story that is almost relevant. A few years ago I took my third grade class on a field trip to Muir Woods, an exquisite area of stately trees, lush ferns, and dappled light. One little girl came from an extremely protective home; before she was allowed to go, I had to promise her mother I would personally hold her hand throughout the trip. When we stepped into the forest, Lusia looked up in awe, touched in the deepest core of her being. "Oh," she gasped, "I feel I am coming home." Truthfully I wanted to share the story because it is lovely, but my point is that we all have a thirst for beauty and that even young children appreciate the opportunity to tap into that side of themselves.

The second reason for including the Pachelbel Canon Dance in this lesson has to do with the music. My original impulse was to teach a concept like falls and then ask the class to create studies by sequencing their own falls. Teaching concepts and then creating group studies work very well with this age group. I describe that progression in lesson 13 working with balance. However, I decided to go with the Pachelbel Canon Dance here because of the music. Both the Eight Plus Eight Dance and the Partner Dance are done to counts; I wanted to bring in a new element, introducing the children to a very accessible piece of classical music.

Finally, I chose the Pachelbel Canon Dance because I wanted to show you a neat pedagogical trick: Introduce difficult dance steps in a warm-up and then reintroduce the dance later as a musical whole. Everyone learns best the second time around. If students master the steps—even one or two of the steps—beforehand, they feel confident and will look forward to putting them together. For a very inexperienced class, it is a good idea to warm up with just one move from the forthcoming dance, in this case alternating locomotor movements with just the spiral sit, done on both sides for equal strength work.

The second part of lesson 9 moves on to sophisticated locomotor movements. My intent was to show how to weave a number of concepts together with an eye on a culminating study. Our goal is the amazing assignment in lesson 10:

Create your own symmetrical floor pattern using only sophisticated locomotor movements in different line shapes and including at least three level and directional changes. How many concepts are included here! First, there is an underlying expectation of cooperative partner and group work. Second, the children must have a firm grasp of symmetry and floor pattern design. Third, they need to know the difference between ordinary locomotor movements and "sophisticated" ones, remembering what these grown-up words mean. They also need to apply the correct line shape to a given movement; for example, meander would not be an appropriate movement for a straight line but would fit well with a wiggly line. Fourth, the children need to understand the concepts level and direction and remember the five levels and the four directions. Finally, this study requires the ability to juggle concepts, checking and rechecking that they fulfill the assignment. The culminating assignment in lesson 10 was actually in mind from lesson 2; it took at least eight lessons to build up to it. It is worth telling the children that you have an amazing goal in mind and that they are progressing toward it. Even if you do not specifically tell them, they will know from your attitude that you have an end in sight and that you know what you are doing.

LESSON 10   4TH – 6TH GRADES
A Culminating Study

Teacher to Teacher

I hope you take a few minutes to sit and enjoy your very deserved laurels. Just a few further notes: Floor patterns are symmetrical with respect to design, not necessarily because the number of students on each side is the same. If the pattern is drawn with two matching sides, any number of children can execute it. So, when you end up with a remaining child forming a group of five, that is OK; the symmetry can be fulfilled with two children on one side and three on the other. It is important to not have fewer than four in a group (two on one side and two on the other) so that if someone is absent when the children are performing these studies, the show can go on. Some groups will attempt a four-part symmetrical pattern, like a four-leaf clover. I think this is terrific, but be ready to help with the initial execution.

Student Objectives

▶ Students will integrate sophisticated locomotor movements with line shapes and directions.

▶ Students will collaborate in groups to create a symmetrical floor pattern assignment.

▶ Students will experience the exuberance and class unity of parachute activities.

▶ Students will practice motor planning with parachute activities.

Materials Needed

▶ Four charts: sophisticated locomotor movements, line shapes, levels, directions.

▶ White construction paper and sets of markers.

▶ A 24-foot parachute and one ball.

▶ White construction paper and sets of markers.

▶ Tambourine

Teaching Instructions

1. Warm up by reviewing sophisticated locomotor movements. Conclude by asking questions that refer to combining these movements with directions and line shapes: "What movement would work well in the backward direction? Yes, a creep would be perfect. Could you do sprint backward? . . .

I agree it would be very hard and might be dangerous. What movement lends itself to the turning direction? . . . You're right, strut works well turning. What movement do you think would fit a zigzag line? . . . Of course, dodge is already like a zigzag. Good thinking. You will need to think like this when I give you this impossible assignment."

2. Children form groups of four and are given the assignment: Create a symmetrical floor pattern using only sophisticated locomotor movements in different line shapes; include at least three level and direction changes. When the patterns are finished and checked, the groups practice. The studies are performed without the map, and children shout the movement names before each line.

3. Introduce the parachute. Do Ocean, Whoosh, Hamburger and French Fries, and Mushroom.

≈ Adaptations

Easier

▶ Eliminate the level and direction changes. To make the activity even easier, eliminate the requirement that each line be a different line shape. Just doing a symmetrical floor pattern using sophisticated locomotor movements is a difficult and worthwhile lesson.

▶ Do a helping floor pattern modeling the assignment immediately before setting the groups out on their own.

▶ Make sure that the assignment is written out and that charts of the sophisticated locomotor movements, line shapes, and levels and directions, if being used, are accessible.

Harder

▶ If you want to get crazy, add nonlocomotor movements: "Include at least three different nonlocomotor movements. These could be added to the intersection of two locomotor movements or included with the locomotor movements." Let the children figure it out!

▶ The degree of perfection demanded is up to you. You can get very picky with lines going exactly where they are drawn, the specific number of loops facing the way indicated, and so forth. Also the pattern as a whole can be polished as a dance with fluid transitions and strong dramatizations of the movements.

English Language Development

▶ If a majority of your class is non-English speaking, the whole sophisticated locomotor movement chart is probably too much. Offer five or six very clear movements, possibly creep, strut, meander, dodge, and scurry, from which to choose. If your non-English speakers are the minority, the whole list of sophisticated locomotor movements will work as long as the groups are heterogeneous.

▶ It is important for all children to shout out the name of the movement before each line; for English learners, this is imperative.

≈ Assessment

Floor patterns always provide a good venue for assessing visual perception abilities. This lesson allows an overall assessment of how children work with the challenge of juggling concepts. To fulfill the assignment, children must hold several thoughts in mind at the same time. The process is much like solving a two-clue puzzle—for example, if you were asked to think of a word that is a color and has a short "i" sound. It takes mental acuity to figure out that pink fulfills both conditions. This floor pattern assignment requires the same kind of mental gymnastics, and it is worth observing how your students deal with it. Who are the racers, putting anything down and then needing to redo? Who are the meticulous ones, weighing all options and having trouble committing themselves? In addition to observing, you can use this lesson to encourage extension into behaviors that are not natural inclinations, pushing risk taking or restraint as needed.

The complicated group work in lesson 10 is an excellent time for social assessment. Who are the leaders? The followers? The ones "out to lunch?" Who is able to put aside personal issues for a group result, and who simply cannot see the bigger picture? Social interaction is as crucial an assessment as more academic parameters; those children who are truly deficient in social skills need to be referred to a social skills group or possibly a counselor. This type of deficiency rarely gets better when left alone.

LESSON 11
Mastering the Culminating Study

4TH – 6TH GRADES

≋ Teacher to Teacher

I want to make the case for stringent mastery work. Sometimes we just get too tired to force the issue: The study has most of the elements and they do it pretty well, so let's call it done. But I think it is very important to push the children beyond their comfort level. Kids are so used to instant results, microwave dinners, channel surfing, fast food, 10-second sound bites, no rewrites, no rereads. There is no way around it; we cannot buck MTV, but here and there we can ask for real mastery. The group study should be completely memorized, with no help from you. The group should be able to do it even if the leader is not there: "That was great, but could you guys do it even if Chris wasn't there? Let's see." The lines need to go exactly where they were drawn or the drawing needs to be revised. The sophisticated locomotor movements need to be hammed up and clearly differentiated; the whole group is to shout the name of the movement so that the audience understands the movement. Level and direction changes need to be sharp and executed without hesitation. And the pattern as a whole needs to be infused with power and energy so that it is exciting to watch. This is not asking too much. It will not happen quickly or easily; it will not happen without consistent demands from you; it will not happen in one lesson. But the results, both internal and external, will definitely be worth the effort.

≋ Student Objectives

▶ Students will activate memory, concept understanding, and motor control with the Brain Catcher.

▶ Students will master and perform the culminating study.

▶ Students will demonstrate social skills and self-discipline working with a group.

▶ Students will demonstrate understanding and wide application of the concept symmetry.

▶ Students will demonstrate a thorough understanding of specified sophisticated locomotor movement words.

▶ Students will continue to experience exuberance, class unity, and motor planning with the parachute.

≋ Materials Needed

▶ The students' group studies.

▶ A 24-foot parachute and a ball.

▶ Tambourine.

≋ Teaching Instructions

1. Warm up with Brain Catcher alternated with simple calisthenics. Brain Catcher can combine all concepts learned so far. For example, first do the locomotor movement

trudge in the backward direction in a wiggly line; second, do the nonlocomotor movement spin on the knee level; third, do scurry in the forward direction in a looped line. Brain Catcher can also combine locomotor and nonlocomotor movements; for example, do the locomotor movement stalk while doing the nonlocomotor movement contract and stretch in the sideways direction while moving in a spiral line. Take mental breathers between Brain Catchers with simple calisthenics: abdominal crunches, push-ups, jumping jacks.

2. Return the group floor patterns from last time; groups memorize their patterns and practice. Each group performs their study.

3. Relax with parachute activities: Ocean, Whoosh, Shark, Trap, Mushroom. Introduce Merry-Go-Round.

≋ Adaptations

Easier

▶ Brain Catchers can be much easier if you eliminate concepts and shorten the sequence—for example, do the locomotor movement march in a zigzag line and then the nonlocomotor movement contract and stretch on the sitting level.

▶ The first time a group performs their floor pattern, help them by calling out what to do and then immediately have them repeat the pattern by themselves.

Harder

▶ Brain Catchers can become so hard that you have to jot the sequence down for yourself. However, do not make them longer than a sequence of four.

▶ Have the children do their floor pattern as a canon; that is, part of the group starts one line after the other.

▶ Polish the floor patterns so that the lines transition smoothly and quickly, and emphasize clear dramatization of the locomotor movements.

▶ Floor patterns can extend into more fluid assignments in the future. You might give the following assignment: "Write your name [or any word if you want group patterns] in cursive as a floor pattern. Make sure to include at least five locomotor and five nonlocomotor movements, two level and direction changes, and scarves if you wish." Or this assignment: "Divide 32 beats into a floor pattern that uses at least six locomotor movements and leaves no extra time to change." Generally the less structured the assignment, the harder it is.

English Language Development

▶ Do Brain Catchers in English, but reduce the number of concepts involved. For example, first do skip turning direction in a spiral line, then do swings on the standing level.

▶ Use the calisthenics to do rote memorization work; for example, do jumping jacks shouting the even numbers to 100; do push-ups shouting the names of the continents three times over.

▶ During Whoosh with the parachute, work with words that describe shapes; for example, "When you go under the parachute this time, stay under and take a strange shape and freeze; we'll whoosh it up to see you." Other shapes could be weird, rounded, straight, connected, one-legged, high, low, vertical, horizontal.

▶ Use the parachute for work on circumference, radius, and diameter.

≋ Assessment

The major assessment here is the degree of mastery in the group study. The thrust to complete and polish a project is an important life skill. Because the children are working in groups, it will be difficult to evaluate those who fall in the middle, but the leaders and distracters will be obvious. Again, social skills, the ability to compromise, and self-discipline will become clear. It would be very valuable, after this lesson, to test the concept of symmetry with paper and pencil work: Create a work sheet with several line shapes and have the students draw the midlines and matching shapes.

11.5
Reflections and Options

Phew! We certainly need a break from this intense mental activity. The following partner obstacle course is the answer because it is fun and strenuous but not particularly academic. However, as in the other grade level curriculums, we need to stop here and decide what we are going to do for the last class. A show is always a great idea, most especially if your class put a lot of effort into the culminating floor pattern. In fact, the prospect of a show is an enormous incentive to mastery. The following is a good progression for a 40-minute demonstration:

1. The ball study from lesson 2.

2. The students' level studies from lesson 4.

3. The Eight Plus Eight Dance, followed immediately by the Partner Dance, and then the Pachelbel Canon Dance.

4. The students' culminating floor pattern studies.

5. A whole-class symmetrical floor pattern done with scarves.

To have a great show you will need to devote a minimum of three full classes to practice. This is not wasted time. The self-discipline and delay of gratification, the pursuit of mastery and required perseverance, the sense of accomplishment and pride—all are well worth the time and effort. I must warn you that it does take an enormous effort, especially from you. Without becoming mean, you must be relentless. "No, that transition was too sloppy and I heard someone talk. Do it again . . . Uh oh, did you bounce that ball getting into place? Out. Come back when you are ready to do it right. No, again . . . No, again . . . Yes." Do not let them get away with inappropriate behavior because "they're only kids." They should move from one study to the next silently, smoothly, and quickly; the transitions are as important as the dances. Each dance needs to have their full cooperation and concentration. A mistake will not wreck the show, but half-heartedness will. Show business is a tough road.

If you are planning a show, do the partner obstacle course in the next lesson, but eliminate the work on balance and just do a strenuous gymnastics warm-up, like the one included in lesson 1. Save 15 minutes at the end of class to plan the show: Decide what you will perform, who will be invited, what to wear (ordinary play clothes), and so on. All your subsequent lessons will be devoted to intense practice. If one of these practice sessions is especially efficient, think about ending with the parachute, Foam Jump, Tackle, Opposite Game, or a few minutes of free time with a prop.

If you decide against a show (and who can blame you?), definitely plan to repeat the partner obstacle course two or three times. You might also consider inviting just the principal or a neighboring class to see an informal presentation of the students' culminating floor patterns, the perfected Pachelbel Canon Dance, or both. Not having a full-fledged show has the benefit of allowing you to teach until the very last. Since it would be absurd for me to write "practice" for lessons 13 to 15, I will complete the curriculum without a performance.

LESSON **12**

4TH – 6TH GRADES

Partner Obstacle Course

≈ Teacher to Teacher

This course is so much fun. All your work on partner activities, group cooperation, and tone of the class will come to fruition here as you watch your students helping and enjoying each other. It will (almost) make setting up worth the effort. The biggest problem will be what to do with the remaining child—and there never fails to be a remaining child. I do not recommend becoming a partner yourself; you need to oversee the whole room. Your options are (1) forming a group of three, (2) letting one child move by himself, and (3) recruiting an extra child from another class. There are pros and cons for all three. Having groups of three is very difficult for some of the activities, especially the partner scooter ride and Trust Walk; there is nothing for it except to have one person go twice. If a child goes by himself, make sure he is OK, and do not allow the loner of the class to be the one in this position. Borrowing a child is great if the other teacher does not mind. Normally I go with a group of three; I pick the most cooperative kids and tell them that I am sure they will figure it out. Any of these options should be fine if you plan ahead.

The other problem is the girl-boy combinations: What do you do if the class is even but the last two are a boy and a girl? My best solution is to ask if any boy and girl would be willing to work together, maybe a set of cousins or long-time friends. If I do get volunteers, I praise them extravagantly; if I don't, I do not push girl-boy combinations at this age for this course, and might just end up with two groups of three.

≈ Student Objectives

► Students will demonstrate advanced skills of cooperation and consideration with a partner.

► Students will understand the concept balance and apply it in a variety of ways.

► Students will gain strength, flexibility, and coordination through conditioning and gymnastics work.

► Students will remember and perform a gymnastics routine.

► Students will understand and demonstrate the terms precarious, cooperation, and compromise.

≈ Materials Needed

► Everything you can dig up for an obstacle course, set up in twos: the stegel with two balance beams placed on the middle notches, a pillow on the slide, two rows of tires, jump ropes, the incline mat set up for Tackle, the pillows set up for Foam Jump, four scooters in a fairly large designated area, four hoppities, four soft balls, four balloons, four plastic hoops, four scoopers and balls, four foam footballs, four chairs, four scarves.

► Two rows of mats, ideally enough for each student to have her own space.

≋ *Teaching Instructions*

1. With everyone sitting on the mats, immediately do a very strenuous gymnastics warm-up: (1) neck and back stretches; (2) rocking back and forth; (3) leg stretches; (4) 100 abdominal crunches; (5) 20 push-ups; (6) bridge, contract, shoulder stand, one-knee back roll, three times; (7) continuous somersaults; (8) frog balance.

2. Demonstrate how to help lift someone's legs from the frog balance into a headstand. Divide into partners with one person sitting on the mat and a partner standing behind her. All the children sitting are designated group 1; all those standing are group 2. Children tell their partners whether they want help lifting up into a headstand. The groups take turns doing the gymnastics routine two or three times.

3. Introduce the idea of combining balance (not falling) with precarious (dangerous or difficult). Try out several balances; use your ideas and theirs: "We did a precarious balance in the headstand. Can you think of another way to balance?" Put four or five of these balances into a sequence, moving smoothly from one to the next. If you have enough mat space, groups 1 and 2 explore the balances simultaneously. If it is crowded, keep the groups divided and switch back and forth quickly.

4. Talk about the difference between cooperation and compromise (see p. 119).

5. Show the partner obstacle course. Within the course, partners create a gymnastics routine of five different moves, two of them precarious balances. Also include within the course the following: Trust Walk, Massage, partner scooter ride, and sliding together on the pillow. Run through the obstacle course continuously for the rest of the lesson time.

≋ *Adaptations*

Easier

▶ The warm-up does not need to be quite so strenuous or fast paced.

▶ Introduce and explore the idea of balance, but save the sequence of balances for next time.

▶ Save distinguishing between cooperation and compromise for next time.

▶ Put the balance beams on the lowest notch.

▶ Replace the foam footballs with regular balls. (There is something about footballs that seems to bring out aggression even off the football field.)

▶ A full partner obstacle course includes Trust Walk and Massage. These activities, although not difficult, work best with mature classes. The Trust Walk necessitates your trust that children will handle their partners carefully and competently; if you have any reservations, skip it. Massage is not dangerous; but if the class is immature, it can dissolve into silliness. The partner work can be accomplished just fine without these two activities.

▶ The intended course also includes a gymnastics routine to be created by each partner group. You can simplify this activity by presenting a routine or by allowing the mats to be used for exploration work without a remembered routine.

Harder

▶ Do not put the balance beams on the highest notch; I believe that is too dangerous with partners.

▶ If you want to make the balance beam a bit more challenging, have the partners stop in the middle and balance on one foot for 10 seconds.

▶ The hardest part of this course is the created gymnastics routine. You can make it still harder by (1) making it longer, (2) asking that the moves be executed in perfect form with smooth transitions, (3) requiring the partners to be synchronized.

English Language Development

▶ *Balance*, *precarious*, *cooperation*, and *compromise* are not a bad haul of English words for one day.

▶ Have the children call out the body parts they are balancing on (e.g., "Balance on one knee!"

"Balance on half-toe!" "Balance on one foot and one elbow!") while executing the moves.

▶ Require all conversations between partners to be in English. It might be worthwhile to pair up your non-English-speaking students with those who have more command of the language. It is important not to be judgmental about conversations in the children's native language; you simply want to explain that it is better to speak that language at home and work on English in school: "It is important that you speak Mien or Spanish at home so that you keep up your own language, but in school you need to practice English."

≋ Assessment

As usual, an obstacle course will provide innumerable assessment opportunities. This partner course is the perfect matrix for observing social skills. There will most likely be one or two children who simply do not want to stay with their partners. (I start with a warning, saying that if they cannot stay together they will not be able to do the course; if they still refuse to cooperate, I will—reluctantly—put them out.) But it is worth watching the difficulties for a while before interfering. Is the trouble fairly equally distributed between the two children? Would they do better with different partners? Or is one child making life difficult for the other? Is he rushing? Throwing the ball too hard? Being generally too rough? Is this typical behavior for that child? This type of specific documentation is very valuable to share with the school counselor or to use in any referrals. Social skills are essential, especially at this age, because a child who is not liked will cause trouble. If the social problems continue into junior high school, the troubles escalate.

The work on balance in this lesson—both dynamic balance on the balance beam and static balance in the gymnastics routines—will point to those children having centering difficulties. You probably already know who they are, but this will be a clear indication. If a child has enormous difficulties with balance and seems awkward in general, I would recommend a full medical exam, especially of the ears, and possibly an evaluation of the vestibular system.

LESSON 13

Balance

4TH – 6TH GRADES

≋ Teacher to Teacher

It is so exciting to see groups of children bursting with imaginative ideas. You have a very delicate role here. You set the stage with a thorough introduction of the concept and an appropriately challenging assignment. You watch out for impossible pairings but otherwise let the partners sort themselves. You provide opportunities for individual creativity by suggesting props and equipment. Now what do you do? Walk around, encourage, watch, and occasionally intervene. This is the chance to be a teacher on the highest level. We need to cultivate an open, sure-let's- try-it attitude yet know when to give honest criticism. Support the children by getting what they need and giving them space. Encourage them by matching their enthusiasm and telling them they're great (if it's true). Stretch them by requiring their very highest level of work.

≋ Student Objectives

▶ Students will understand the terms balance and precarious.

▶ Students will demonstrate a wide variety of balances.

▶ Students will collaborate to create a study.

▶ Students will practice locomotor movements on the diagonal.

▶ Students will demonstrate motor planning with Freeway.

≋ *Materials Needed*

▶ Five to 10 mats.

▶ Tambourine.

≋ *Teaching Instructions*

1. Scatter the mats randomly throughout the room, leaving space between them. Gather the class and review the concept balance and the term precarious. Alternate locomotor movements done on the floor with precarious balances done on the mats. Note that in the following sample progression, regular type (locomotor movements) alternates with italic type (balances) to highlight the alternating required.

   a. Locomotor movement skip; locomotor movement gallop; then four skips, four gallops repeated.

   b. *Do 100 abdominal crunches. Balance on the seat, on half a seat, on the abdomen; try a no-hand shoulder stand.*

   c. Locomotor movement kick to the front, back, and side; then four kicks front, four kicks back, eight kicks side, repeated.

   d. *Do 20 push-ups. Balance on one hand and one foot, one knee only, one foot only.*

   e. Locomotor movement waltz walk and waltz-walk turns; then two straight waltz walks and two waltz-walk turns repeated.

   f. *Bridge, contract, shoulder stand, three times. Balance in a bridge with one leg off the ground, a frog balance, a headstand.*

   g. Locomotor movement run and leap turn; run and click heels; then one run leap turn, one run and click heels repeated.

   h. *Get a partner and balance by holding one hand and pulling away from each other, then pushing back-to-back and "sitting". Stay with this partner.*

2. Form groups of six by combining three partner groups. Give the assignment: Create a study of at least five precarious balances. Make the transitions between balances interesting; include at least two locomotor movements during the transitions. You may use mats, chairs, or any props you need.

3. Keep the same groups and line up ready for the Diagonal Structure. Do several locomotor movements or short locomotor patterns and then end with Freeway.

≋ *Adaptations*

Easier

▶ The warm-up can be greatly simplified. One way is to have each child find a place on the mats scattered about the room and do a strenuous gymnastics workout individually. Another way to simplify is to have the children alternate one locomotor movement with just one or two balances. For example, have the children do locomotor skip on the floor and then go to their original place on the mats to balance on one knee and one foot.

▶ What makes the assignment so hard is that it is open-ended. The tighter the structure, the easier it is to accomplish. An easier study would be to create a sequence of four balances, each one on a different level (air level is not possible), moving smoothly from one to the next. Another fairly easy assignment would be to create a sequence of four precarious balances with locomotor movements in between; the locomotor movements have to use different directions and the balances have to be on different levels. These easier assignments do not suggest using props or other equipment.

▶ Since I am assuming you will not include pyramids, the groups can be downsized to four; this size is easier to manage.

Harder

▶ The whole lesson will jump in difficulty if you allow pyramids. Pyramids can be included toward the end of the warm-up as one of the possible balances. The assignment might include a pyramid as an open-ended suggestion (e.g., to create a sequence of five precarious balances one of which is a pyramid).

▶ Putting the finished study to music will help mold it into a polished dance. I recommend having one piece of music for all the studies; otherwise there will be logistical problems in rehearsing. I also recommend a good beat without lyrics—Scott Joplin rags or upbeat jazz works well.

▶ When working on the diagonal, explore some short locomotor sequences, possibly referring back to the short patterns from the warm-up.

English Language Development

▶ The words *balance* and *precarious* should be well ingrained by the end of this lesson.

▶ Have the children call out the body part they are balancing on, for example, "Balance on the seat!"

≋ *Assessment*

The physical skill apparent in this lesson is, of course, balance. Note those children who have difficulty with virtually all the balances. If their lack of center fits in with other movement problems, I would recommend a referral, ideally to a movement therapist, occupational, or physical therapist. Balance has a huge impact on the ability to focus and therefore is crucial for academic success.

The broader assessment for this lesson is the ability to work cooperatively and accomplish a project within the assigned guidelines. Corporate America has shifted from an individual work mode to the team model. Companies want their employees to be able to work together, and children must start to learn these skills in elementary school. We have approached teamwork with partner activities and the partner obstacle course; we required a group effort in the culminating floor pattern study. This assignment, because it is looser and more creative, will be more difficult to manage. Your assessment will be to discern which children are so behind in their social skills that they need outside help to catch up, as well as those children who need a coach to guide them through the group process. If a child is willing to be coached, stay close by and actually whisper in his ear the kinds of teamwork dialogue he is lacking—for example, "Now, instead of going off in a sulk, say it is your turn to pick and offer your idea . . . OK, they didn't want to do it, hang in there and give another suggestion . . . Don't do it halfway, give it your all, even if you don't agree."

LESSON 14
Beanbag Balance

4TH – 6TH GRADES

≋ *Teacher to Teacher*

Let's think a bit more about your job as choreographic coach. If you have never created movement studies yourself, you might feel hesitant to offer suggestions to the groups as they create theirs. But your intuitive perceptions are valid. Trust yourself. If a study is boring to you, then it probably is boring. I would not tell the group exactly that, but I would say that their study could be more exciting if they used more level and directional changes. Another way to enliven a movement sequence is to include rhythmic differentiations, for example, have some movements very slow and some fast. You can tell if the group intends to be synchronized but looks completely ragged. Suggest that the children practice their unison sections more and take turns watching each other. If a study grabs your attention, makes you laugh, or warms your heart, they have done a good job. Tell them.

∼ Student Objectives

- ▶ Students will expand their application of balance.
- ▶ Students will practice eye-hand coordination with beanbags.
- ▶ Students will increase conditioning through held balances.
- ▶ Students will perfect their cooperative study.
- ▶ Students will deepen their understanding of antonyms.
- ▶ Students will experience class bonding through the Opposite Game.

∼ Materials Needed

- ▶ Beanbags, one per child.
- ▶ Mats.
- ▶ Any props, equipment, or music needed for the balance studies.
- ▶ Tambourine.

∼ Teaching Instructions

1. Begin the warm-up with a few minutes of free time with the beanbag. Then alternate locomotor movements tossing the beanbags with an exploration of balance. Table 16.2 shows a locomotor movement paired with a beanbag balance exercise.
2. Go back to the balance studies from last time. Suggest the possibility of including beanbags in the studies if the children wish. Students perfect, practice, and show their studies.
3. Introduce and play the Opposite Game.

∼ Adaptations

Easier

- ▶ You can simplify the warm-up by limiting the difficulty of the balance explorations (see table 16.3).
- ▶ There is a wide range of mastery for the study. On the simplest level, you call out balance 1,

Table 16.2 Locomotor/Beanbag Warm-Up Suggestions

Locomotor movement and balance		Beanbag exercise
Skip	while …	tossing the beanbag from hand to hand.
Balance on one foot	while …	balancing the beanbag on various body parts, for example, head, shoulder, forearm. Use the students' ideas as well as yours. Make sure children stand on both the left and right foot.
Hopscotch	while …	tossing and catching the beanbag.
Balance on one knee and one hand	while …	balancing the beanbag on the back, hip, elbow, and so on.
Jazzy walk	while …	throwing the beanbag very high and catching it with one hand, alternating hands.
Using mats, warm up with 50 abdominal crunches and 20 push-ups. Do a frog balance	while …	holding the beanbag between the feet. Then …
…try a headstand	while …	holding the beanbag between the feet (someone else can place the beanbag). Take the students' ideas for balancing the beanbag while on their heads.
Baby crawl	while …	balancing the beanbag on the back. Then …
…crab crawl	while …	balancing the beanbag on the abdomen.
Using mats, warm up with bridge, contract, shoulder stand, one-knee back roll done three times.	then …	balance in a bridge with the beanbag on the abdomen; attempt to lift one leg up. Take their ideas for balancing the beanbag while in a bridge.
Run and leap	while …	tossing the beanbag and catching it.
Ask the children to think of their own combinations of body and beanbag balances.		
Ask the children to do their own locomotor movements while tossing the beanbag.		

Table 16.3 Simple Locomotor/Beanbag Warm-Up Suggestions

Do locomotor movement		Beanbag balance exercise
Skip and toss	then ...	balancing on one foot, beanbag on the head.
Hopscotch and toss	then ...	balancing on one knee and one hand, beanbag on the hip.
Crab and baby crawl with the bag on the torso	then ..	balance on the seat, beanbag on one shoulder.
Jazzy walk, then run and leap and toss	then ...	balance on half-toe, beanbag on the back of the hand.

balance 2, and so on as the groups perform. Ultimately, the children follow the guidelines but go beyond the assignment into creating a full-fledged dance.

Harder

▶ The warm-up can become more complicated in several ways: (1) if the children do more difficult locomotor steps or a more difficult combination of steps while tossing the beanbag, (2) if they try stunts with the beanbag such as keeping it in the air by bouncing it off different body parts, (3) if they do more difficult gymnastics moves like cartwheels, round-off, handstands, splits.

▶ As already mentioned, the balance study can have a wide range of mastery. Demand that any unison sections be done truly in unison. If the study is too predictable, suggest that, once or twice, the whole group not be in the same balance but instead make an arrangement of various balances. Consider a pyramid for a grand finale, maybe including beanbags. Demand that props be included with no break in the flow of the study; for example, if scarves will be used for one of the balances, they can be hidden in pockets and pulled out as a surprise. Be picky about the transitions between balances—they should be smooth and well choreographed.

English Language Development

▶ The balance work is excellent for reviewing body part names. Whenever possible, have the children call out the name as they balance the beanbag—shoulder, elbow, forearm, thigh, and torso are good vocabulary extenders.

▶ Encourage, perhaps require, that all conversations needed for creating studies be in English. However, if you have a truly non-English speaker, it is much more important that the child participate and give his ideas than worry about which language to speak or how correct his English sounds.

▶ The Opposite Game is great English language development work for English learners who have some command of the language. Those who speak no English will feel overwhelmed. It is important that you use both opposites when you play the game; for example, "Let me see you move as light as a feather . . . Oh, no, you look as heavy as elephants. OK, move as heavy as an elephant . . . Oh, no, you look light. What a terrible class!"

≋ Assessment

The work with beanbags will reinforce the assessment of balance problems from last time. It is very important to have several assessments, on different days, in different contexts, before referring a child for testing. We know from our own physical development that some days are simply difficult. Beanbags are also an excellent prop for evaluating eye-hand coordination. At this grade level, the children should have no trouble tossing and catching a beanbag with one hand. If students are having consistent difficulty catching the beanbag, it is worth considering other eye-hand and midline tests or possibly a vision screening.

LESSON 15

Yankee Doodle Finale

Teacher to Teacher

It makes sense to end with two favorite games, the In and Out Game and the Opposite Game, but why introduce a new dance? Why not? Children love the Yankee Doodle Dance, and it is easy enough to master in one lesson. I see nothing wrong with teaching something new on the very last day of school. (However, that is my personality, and I have been called a bit compulsive.) If you want a completely flashy last class, substitute parachute activities for the dance and throw in Tackle.

One of the scariest and greatest teaching experiences I ever had happened about 10 years ago. I was asked to do a workshop at the University of Iowa for 200 physical education teachers. I asked for a fourth grade class for my demonstration; but when I appeared at the gym, nervously scanning the show-me-what-you've-got-faces in the audience, I found I had been given a reluctant, show-me-what-you've-got sixth grade. I considered doing a simple, flashy, fun and games class but decided to go ahead with my more serious, academic lesson on symmetry, including a creative group study. I was taking a big chance because I wasn't sure I could even get the children to take off their socks and shoes. But they did, and they really enjoyed the mental as well as the physical challenge. The greatest moment came when the observing teachers questioned the students after the class and the students said, "We'd like to have this all the time." Children love to learn. If they feel that you have new and important ideas to teach them and that you will help them succeed, they will be very grateful. They will want to do it all the time.

Student Objectives

▶ Students will practice the language skills in the In and Out Game and the Opposite Game.

▶ Students will experience a sense of exuberant fun with these games.

▶ Students will learn and perform the Yankee Doodle Dance.

Materials Needed

▶ A lot of "stuff" scattered throughout the room: three mats lying down, two mats standing like little houses, all the foam squares from the Foam Jump, tires, plastic hoops, a stegel end, two tables, 10 chairs, beanbags, foam shapes, cones, the incline mat.

▶ Tambourine.

▶ Stereo and audio recording of "Yankee Doodle" (any version).

Teaching Instructions

1. Quickly review the In and Out Game and add any words that were not included last time. (See p. 161 for the list of words.) Play three fast rounds and clean up.

2. In the Free Traveling Structure, practice skipping and galloping. Do four skips and four gallops repeated. Add four jumps backward. Practice twist down for two beats and up for two beats. Practice side-slides on both sides and then run and leap. Put these steps into a sequence: four skips, four gallops (beats 1-8), four jumps backward, twist down and up for four beats (beats 1-8), side-slide

for four, side-slide the other side for four (beats 1-8), side-slide the original way for four, and run and leap for four (beats 1-8).

3. Teach the Yankee Doodle Dance. Divide the class in two, each half lined up on either side of the room. The sides alternate verses of the dance and then walk to meet each other at the end for a bow. Try it without music once and then with the tape.

4. Play the Opposite Game.

≈ Adaptations

Easier

▸ The In and Out Game and the Opposite Game can range from kindergarten to sixth grade depending on the complexity of the words used.

▸ The only tricky part of the Yankee Doodle Dance is changing from a skip to a gallop. If you need to simplify the dance, it is possible to gallop for eight beats at the beginning.

Harder

▸ The In and Out Game can be much harder if you (1) combine concepts, for example, show a diagonal parallel line, or do in, under, and around at the same time; (2) shorten the time allotted from 10 seconds to 5; (3) quicken the pace in general.

▸ The Yankee Doodle Dance can be more challenging if you ask for exact steps on the counts. The music is quite fast and each move gets one beat. Also the form can be polished. For example, the twist down should spiral all the way to the back and the hands should slap the floor; the side-slides need to be very straight and always facing front; the run and leap should be high off the ground with straight legs.

▸ Even the Opposite Game can be upgraded with the use of more difficult opposites, for example, crooked/straight, contract/stretch, bold/timid.

English Language Development

▸ The In and Out Game and Opposite Game are excellent English language development activities because they combine a physical response with English comprehension. Greater reinforcement is possible when the children also call out the word while they do the movements. If your class is mostly non-English speakers, go slower, use fewer words, and repeat more. If your class has a mixture of language abilities, pair up your non-English speakers with those who have more command.

▸ It is possible to use language with the Yankee Doodle Dance—have the class call out the moves (skip, gallop, and so on), the counts, or teach them the words and have them sing.

≈ Assessment

This lesson can help you note those children who still are weak in the vocabulary that has been presented and those who cannot move rhythmically to exact counts. These are good observations for their final report cards and for any last-minute referrals.

This last lesson is a wonderful time to look over your class as a whole and see what progress they have made. Can you remember how they started, how timid and awkward they were? Do you see most of them blossoming out, enjoying their bodies in motion and willing to take physical and imaginative risks? Can you remember when they were hesitant to work hard, when 50 abdominal crunches seemed like a feat and 12 minutes of aerobic warm-up felt excessive? Are they proud of their newfound strength, and do they look forward to a challenge? Do you remember starting from scratch with vocabulary like *locomotor, nonlocomotor, level, direction,* and *floor pattern*—and do these words now seem like old hat? And for yourself, do you remember how scared you were trying something new like this program? Now you can run through a lesson with barely a peek in the book. Do you now take side trips of your own creation within the lesson? You have come a long way; it is time for applause all around.

About the Author

Sheila Kogan has taught movement education and dance in every possible environment: public schools, private schools, dance studios, recreational settings, preschools, and college courses. She has been in charge of teacher preparation for movement education on the college level and has given workshops for teachers nationwide. She also choreographed the dances and organized and led the dance group for the millennium celebration of 18,000 people at the Oakland Arena.

Kogan holds a BA in music theory and composition from the University of California at Berkeley and an MS in education, with a concentration in movement education, from Dominican College at San Rafael, California. She is also a certi-fied teacher and language development specialist. Kogan has been teaching for 37 years, including 8 years as a classroom teacher in inner-city schools. She currently teaches third grade at an elementary school in San Pablo, California, where she includes movement within the curriculum, supervises student teachers, and oversees other ongoing movement programs.

A member of Dance Educators of California, Kogan loves dance in any form, especially modern dance. She enjoys taking classes as well as attending performances. Her other favorite activities include reading, gardening, and walking her dog, Jack. She has three grown sons and lives in the San Francisco Bay area with her husband.

*You'll find
other outstanding movement
education resources at*

www.HumanKinetics.com

In the U.S. call

1-800-747-4457

Australia... 08 8277 1555
Canada..1-800-465-7301
Europe... +44 (0) 113 255 5665
New Zealand....................................... 0064 9 448 1207

 HUMAN KINETICS
The Information Leader in Physical Activity
P.O. Box 5076 • Champaign, IL 61825-5076 USA